The Emperor's New Clothes

The Emperor's New Clothes

EXPOSING THE TRUTH
FROM WATERGATE
TO 9/11

Richard Ben-Veniste

Thomas Dunne Books St. Martin's Press
New York

THOMAS DUNNE BOOKS.
An imprint of St. Martin's Press.

THE EMPEROR'S NEW CLOTHES. Copyright © 2009 by Richard Ben-Veniste.
All rights reserved. Printed in the United States of America. For information,
address St. Martin's Press, 175 Fifth Avenue, New York, N.Y. 10010.

www.thomasdunnebooks.com
www.stmartins.com

Design by Level C

LIBRARY OF CONGRESS CATALOGING-IN-PUBLICATION DATA

Ben-Veniste, Richard.
    The emperor's new clothes : exposing the truth from Watergate to 9/11 /
Richard Ben-Veniste. — 1st ed.
        p. cm.
    Includes index.
    ISBN-13: 978-0-312-35796-2 (alk. paper)
    ISBN-10: 0-312-35796-6 (alk. paper)
    1. Special prosecutors—United States—Biography.   2. Lawyers—United
States—Biography.   3. Watergate Affair, 1972–1974.   4. National Commission
on Terrorist Attacks upon the United States.   I. Title.
    KF373.B46A3 2009
    973.92092—dc22
    [B]   2008044617

First Edition: June 2009

10   9   8   7   6   5   4   3   2   1

*For Donna Marie, Danielle, and
Lulu—with all my love*

Contents

CONTENTS

A nation of sheep will beget a government of wolves.

—EDWARD R. MURROW

The Emperor's New Clothes

Introduction

In the midst of the 9/11 investigation, I opened the *New York Times* to find that veteran conservative pundit William Safire had again mentioned me in his column. "Ben-Veniste, a likely candidate for Attorney General in a future Kerry administration, is too partisan for the job." I shook my head in silent appreciation of the economy of Safire's effort. In one brief sentence he had implied that I might be seeking high office in a Democratic administration if George W. Bush were defeated in the upcoming 2004 election, while at the same time branding me as "too partisan" to properly serve in such an important post. Particularly after my questioning of National Security Adviser Condoleezza Rice in April 2004, a chorus of right-wing radio, television, and newspaper commentators attacked me as being politically motivated. Lacking Safire's finesse, Robert Novak called me an "attack dog" for the Democrats, while the editorial pages of the *Wall Street Journal* and *New York Post* chimed in with the "highly partisan" tagline, which they invariably used whenever referring to something I said or did as a member of the 9/11 Commission.

Why the special attention? It had become clear that when facts were brought out inconveniently inconsistent with their political agenda, the knee-jerk reaction of the right-wing media machine was to question the motives of the interlocutor.

On the other hand, hundreds of individuals went out of their way—most of them complete strangers—in letters and e-mails, at airports and restaurants to express their thanks for "asking the hard questions," "not letting them dodge the facts," and the like. For me, service on the 9/11 Commission was a very simple proposition. I saw my responsibility as finding the answer to one overarching question: How was a group of nineteen fanatics able to defeat the defenses of the world's most powerful nation and wreak unbelievable death and destruction upon us on a single morning in September 2001? I believed then, as I do now, that our nation is strong enough to deal with the unvarnished facts and, indeed, must know the facts in order to learn the lessons of our mistakes so we can take steps to avoid repetition.

I don't like being lied to. Never have. Over a long career as a lawyer, I have sometimes had the opportunity to do something about it. Exposing the hypocrisy and mendacity of officials in positions of power has held a special appeal for me. Hans Christian Andersen's iconic tale of hubris, hypocrisy, and chicanery, "The Emperor's New Clothes," must have made an indelible impression on me as a child.

As a young federal prosecutor in New York City I cut my teeth on organized crime and labor-racketeering cases. Usually, the major villains were "honest" about their crimes. If caught and convicted, they did their time as the cost of doing business. I soon gravitated to the investigation and prosecution of corrupt officials. In the late 1960s, a crooked lawyer named Nathan Voloshen was found to be operating an influence-peddling ring out of the office of Democratic Speaker of the House John W. McCormack. We soon linked Voloshen to McCormack's longtime administrative assistant, Martin Sweig, whom the aging Speaker had increasingly relied upon to run his office. Regularly, Voloshen would fly the shuttle from New York to Washington, where he would be installed behind McCormack's district office desk, with full access to staff, phones, and stationery. His requests for special consideration for his well-heeled clients at various federal agencies were accompanied by calls from Sweig, who could mimic the Speaker's voice perfectly, expressing the Speaker's personal support for whatever favor Voloshen sought. My boss, U.S. Attorney Robert Morgenthau, a prominent Democrat himself, was entirely supportive of the investigation. The mantra of the office was simple: Do the right thing. Nothing could provide greater luxury to a young, idealistic lawyer.

What particularly got my attention were the cases in which the Speaker's office interceded on behalf of young men drafted into military service. McCormack was a voluble and consistent hawk on the Vietnam War. But having the office of the second most powerful elected official in government win discharge and other favorable treatment for the rich and well connected, while tens of thousands of others were being killed and maimed, was a truly reprehensible piece of hypocrisy. I prosecuted Sweig in two separate cases involving young men discharged from the military. Sweig was convicted of bribery and perjury, notwithstanding McCormack's testimony on his behalf. Voloshen pleaded guilty and died shortly thereafter. While no evidence surfaced implicating Speaker McCormack in the scheme, he recognized it was time to hang up his spikes and decided not to run for reelection.

Given my role in investigating the office of a powerful Democrat, it was mildly surprising that Richard Nixon's political spin machine branded me (along with Archibald Cox and the rest of the Watergate special prosecutor's staff) as a political partisan out to get Nixon. As the thirty-year-old chief of the task force investigating and prosecuting the criminal obstruction of justice conspiracy that involved the president of the United States, I had a front-row seat for the most extraordinary political scandal of our times. In the end, it was Nixon's own hubris and hypocrisy—expressed in a smorgasbord of criminal and constitutional violations—that brought him down. Had he accepted responsibility early on for his underlings' criminality instead of launching a massive cover-up, Nixon's presidency might well have survived. In the end, Nixon's outright lies to the American people about his role in the conspiracy to obstruct justice—proved irrefutably by his own secretly tape-recorded conversations—made for a choice between certain impeachment or resignation.

The FBI's Abscam investigation exposed greed and stupidity by an alarming number of sitting members of Congress. But by the same token, the methods relied upon by the FBI and the Carter Justice Department to lure elected officials into a honey trap were dangerous and ill advised. Inadequate standards and the absence of prudent safeguards allowed a convicted swindler to skew the investigation far afield from what was being reported to officials in Washington in a process that more closely resembled *Candid Camera* than due process of law. In defending a Philadelphia lawyer who found himself cast in the role of a central middleman between the FBI's agent provocateur and members of Congress—despite the fact that he didn't know a single congressman before the bizarre undercover operation began—I was determined to show the machinations and misconduct that accompanied this unprecedented "honesty test," where criminality was manufactured in the absence of provable real-life criminal activity.

As chief counsel to the Democratic minority during the Senate Whitewater Committee's investigation of Bill and Hillary Clinton's involvement in an ever-expanding litany of alleged improprieties, I faced a Republican chairman determined to use the committee to "take down" the president of the United States. Inconveniently for Senator Alfonse D'Amato and his most partisan colleagues on the committee, evidence to support the hyperventilated charges was woefully lacking. It was one thing to find a ready megaphone in an uncritical news/entertainment establishment to amplify the pseudoscandals churned out by the right-wing anti-Clinton apparatus, but quite another thing to prove them in the bright light of open hearings where witnesses could be cross-examined. Allegations about the Clintons' improprieties regarding a failed investment in a land development deal called Whitewater, and a baker's dozen of other charges, proved to be unsupportable. In the end, with no credible claims of Whitewater impropriety remaining, it was left for Bill Clinton to hand his enemies the Monica Lewinsky affair that nearly ended his presidency.

An independent, bipartisan commission to investigate the 9/11 attacks was created over President George W. Bush's early opposition. As one of the ten commissioners, I was committed to avoiding the mistakes of the Warren Commission's investigation of the Kennedy assassination and determined to make the facts revealed by our investigation available to the public. The commission surprised skeptics with a collegial approach to our task in which partisan impulses were more often than not put aside. Despite individual differences in emphasis, we were able to agree to a unanimous report that was enthusiastically received by the American public. But fulfilling our mandate to investigate and report the facts was often at odds with the Bush administration's penchant for secrecy and its unwillingness to admit mistakes. On occasion, it would take a blowtorch and pliers to extract critical evidence from the White House. Political embarrassment rather than legitimate concern over national security motivated the effort to keep secret the August 6, 2001, presidential briefing, "Bin Laden Determined to Strike in U.S." The public testimony of National Security Adviser Condoleezza Rice in which the classified title of this document was revealed became the commission's most dramatic moment. Administration statements professing that "no one could have anticipated commercial planes being used as weapons" and claims that Saddam Hussein had aided and abetted the 9/11 attack were shown to be disingenuous, at best. Our opportunity—after a long battle—to question George W. Bush provided a revealing window into how the president operated, what he knew, and what he didn't know.

The revelations that have emerged detailing deception, misdirection, disingenuousness, propaganda, and outright mendacity in selling the Iraq war to the American people only emphasize my belief that our democracy is dependent on hearing the truth from our elected leaders. Nothing less is acceptable. Policies built on a foundation of lies will in the end crumble. And where untruthfulness has fouled the halls of our American institutions, I believe that sunlight is the best disinfectant. As patriots who believe in our system of government, we should all be partisans . . . for the truth.

IN THIS BOOK I provide highlights and personal impressions of five important matters—one from each decade from the 1960s to 2000—in which I played a role. As each could be (and one already has been) a book in its own right, I have extracted those elements that were the most memorable and interesting to me.

CHAPTER ONE

Watergate

I watched John Dean drone through his fantastic testimony about the Watergate cover-up on television in the living room of my Manhattan apartment. Dean's monotone belied the explosive content of his allegations, detailing a ten-month cover-up orchestrated by the most powerful men in government, including President Richard M. Nixon himself. How could anyone believe that Nixon, wizard of the dark arts, had entrusted this young, blond, bespectacled twerp with the authority to run an insanely stupid and dangerous obstruction of justice right out of the White House counsel's office? My instincts as a prosecutor with all of five years of experience, albeit in the most highly regarded U.S. attorney's office in the nation, told me that Dean was exaggerating the role of higher-ups in an effort to escape punishment for his own misdeeds. Indeed, the Senate Watergate Committee, led by Sam Ervin of North Carolina, had already granted Dean immunity as a condition of his willingness to testify. I had seen many targets of criminal investigations try to plea-bargain their way out of serious prison time by turning state's evidence against their former friends and accomplices. The criminal justice system is dependent on this process. One of the most difficult tests of a prosecutor's judgment and integrity is the ability to separate the wheat from the chaff in such situations—to make a determination about the credibility of accusations from the mouths of people under tremendous pressure to save themselves by implicating others.

I shook my head in disbelief. Despite the details, Dean's story just didn't add up. One hell of a fight would be shaping up in Washington.

My thoughts about the implications of Dean's testimony were interrupted by a telephone call that would change my life. Jim Vorenberg, a Harvard law professor and friend of the newly appointed Watergate special prosecutor, Archibald Cox, called to ask if I would be interested in interviewing for a job on Cox's staff. Vorenberg told me that Cox would be interviewing federal prosecutors who could jump in to conduct grand jury investigations and then try cases in the event indictments were returned. I was high on Vorenberg's list of possible candidates. Time was of the essence for assembling a staff. I told Vorenberg I would be on a plane to Washington the next day. If offered the job, I suspected I would be moving to Washington and would play a role in unwinding the greatest political scandal in American history.

Watergate had entered my life at a crossroads in my fledgling career. I had become restless at the U.S. attorney's office, even after my promotion to head the special prosecutions/anti-corruption unit. My relationship with the woman I was living with wasn't working out, and I was thinking seriously about leaving New York. A few months earlier, I had given a lot of thought to accepting an offer by the Department of Justice to head the Organized Crime Strike Force for Northern California, Oregon, and Washington. I would be based in San Francisco and would also have jurisdiction over Hawaii. But there was one major hitch—there was hardly any organized crime there. The Mafia in California was, at best, a joke. Would I be willing to accept a professional diet of chasing small-time gamblers in return for the benefits of the natural beauty and relaxed lifestyle that came with the territory? I agonized over my decision for weeks before turning down the offer.

The next morning, I stepped off the Eastern Airlines Shuttle, oblivious to Washington's famous humidity. Watergate promised to be the most compelling drama to be played out on America's stage. It seemed as though providence had guided my hand in turning down the strike force job when Watergate was just around the corner.

I met Jim Vorenberg in the special prosecutor's suite of offices—two floors at 1425 K Street N.W. in the heart of Washington's business corridor. I liked Jim immediately and found his lack of pretension and ready sense of humor a welcome change from the stereotypical law professor. Jim had done some background research on me and said that my experience in prosecuting corrupt public officials made me an attractive candidate for a senior position, despite my youth. If Archie—as everyone on staff called the reserved Yankee law professor—agreed, Vorenberg would recommend me to lead one of the task forces that had been created to address the broad categories of investigation that lay ahead. Vorenberg ticked off campaign finance, dirty tricks, the plumbers, and ITT as possibilities. The only task force leader's position that was taken was the one dealing with the Watergate cover-up. James Neal, an experienced former prosecutor who had established a highly successful criminal defense practice in Nashville, had already been selected for that position and had been on the job for a month. Cox and Neal had known each other from the Kennedy administration, for which Cox had been solicitor general and Neal had prosecuted Attorney General Robert F. Kennedy's number-one target—Teamster president Jimmy Hoffa. At forty-five, Vorenberg was a couple of years older than Neal. In the Kennedy administration, he had served under Bobby Kennedy as chief of a newly created Office of Criminal Justice. Immediately after Cox was sworn in, Cox and Vorenberg's first call was to Neal to see if their former colleague would join them in Washington.

I told Vorenberg that titles were not important to me; the only part of the investigation that truly appealed to me was the cover-up. I would gladly pick up and move to Washington for the opportunity to be Jim Neal's number two on the cover-up investigation—if Cox and Neal were to offer me that position. Jim sat back in his chair and thought for a moment. "Let's see how it goes with Archie. Then you can meet with Neal and see whether the two of you could work together."

Archibald Cox had a reputation as a stern and forbidding legal scholar, self-righteous and unyielding. His roots and background were about as different from mine as anything I could imagine. My interview lasted fifteen minutes. Professor Cox's appearance—tall, ramrod straight, with close-cropped steel-gray hair and clear blue eyes—did nothing to suggest the slightest connection between us. The starkness of his office, freshly painted white and unadorned with anything on the walls to personalize it, was of a piece with his unfashionable gray suit and drab narrow necktie. By contrast, I wore my hair in the longish contemporary style of the early 1970s, particularly unflattering in my case, given its tendency to frizz up at the slightest mention of humidity. Summer in the reclaimed swamp that is our nation's capital is synonymous with humidity. I was wearing a wide paisley tie—equally contemporary and an equally unfortunate fashion statement, given the benefit of hindsight. Photographs of me from this period evoke spontaneous gales of derisive laughter from my daughters. If my appearance was disconcerting to Cox, he gave no indication of it. He was all about substance, a trait I could be thankful for as I look back on our first encounter.

Archie spoke slowly, carefully choosing his words, as they flowed into full sentences, the sentences into perfect paragraphs. He gestured for emphasis with the stub of a missing finger, the casualty I surmised of a long-ago accident chopping wood, one of his favorite activities for exercise and relaxation (with the added Yankee virtue of usefulness). After going over some of the cases I had prosecuted, Archie quizzed me on my reaction to a series of hypothetical situations involving bribery or conflict of interest, referring to himself as the perpetrator. What would I do as the prosecutor in each of the hypotheticals? What process would I use in reaching my decision? As our brief meeting ended, Cox gave me no indication of whether I had passed or failed.

After ducking his head in for a brief chat with Archie, Vorenberg cheerfully led me down the hallway to meet with Jim Neal. Apparently, I had survived Cox's scrutiny. As different as Archie Cox was from me in one direction, Jim Neal was in the other. A dyed-in-the-wool Southerner, Neal had gone to the University of Wyoming on a football scholarship before attending law school at Vanderbilt. Barrel-chested and bandy-legged, Neal's booming Nashville twang could be heard throughout the office as he greeted me. Neal's ruggedly handsome face broke into a big smile as he removed a large unlit cigar from his teeth and shook my hand. Introductions over, Vorenberg excused himself and left us to feel each other out.

Neal and I hit it off from the start. He was an accomplished trial lawyer, the real McCoy. While he had won a conviction against Jimmy Hoffa, I had prosecuted Hoffa's de facto successor as head of the free-spending Teamsters pension fund, Allen Dorfman. We compared notes on our experience with the cast of characters surrounding Hoffa and soon were regaling each other with anecdotes that had us laughing until tears were rolling down my cheeks. We discussed the Watergate cover-up allegations and the best way to proceed with an investigation. John Dean of course would be central to our focus. Neal knew Dean's canny lawyer, Charles Shaffer, as a former colleague in the Kennedy Justice Department. He believed Charlie to be both highly skilled and completely trustworthy, an assessment that proved entirely accurate. Jim confided that his obligations to clients and his partner would require his return to his two-man law practice in Nashville in the near term. He would turn over the day-to-day running of the cover-up investigation to his next in command with the hope that he would be able to return to participate in any major

Watergate trial. If that happened, he would share the trial responsibilities with me. Our conversation had morphed from the theoretical to the practical. This was an offer I couldn't refuse. We sealed our understanding with a handshake. "How soon can you get down here?" Neal asked, lighting his cigar. I thought I could convince my boss, the U.S. attorney, to allow me a week to transition and reassign ongoing matters to my deputy, a very capable and ambitious young lawyer named Rudolph Giuliani.

I circled back to Jim Vorenberg with news of my agreement with Neal. We stopped for a perfunctory good-bye handshake with Archie, and I was on my way back to New York. As sophisticated and worldly as I supposed myself to be, I began to realize that New Yorkers could be just as parochial and limited as anyone from Hicktown, USA. I was in for a real educational experience.

A week later, July 4, 1973, I moved into the Hilton Hotel at 16th and K, which was to be my home for two months until I could find an apartment. I immediately dove into the mountain of memos and transcripts that were required for me to get up to speed. On my first day on the job, I glanced into the office of another of my new colleagues, a Harvard law professor who was in earnest conversation with Tony Ulasewicz, the Runyonesque former New York City cop-cum–private investigator, who had been enlisted by Nixon's personal lawyer, Herbert Kalmbach, to secretly deliver cash to the five Watergate burglars and their supervisors, E. Howard Hunt and G. Gordon Liddy. To my astonishment, the professor was discussing giving Ulasewicz "informal" immunity in return for his version of events. In what was a total departure from cordial manners, I asked the professor if he might step into the hallway for a moment, introduced myself, and told him not to interview any other cover-up witnesses, much less make any promises to them in connection with their cooperation. The contingent of law professors was soon relieved of any responsibility for gathering facts and making deals that could bind the Watergate special prosecutor in any later proceeding.

The Watergate Task Force, as the group assigned to investigate the cover-up/obstruction of justice case was known, grew to seven in number. Jill Wine, a Chicago native who had been a year behind me at Columbia Law, had already distinguished herself as a tough Department of Justice lawyer specializing in labor racketeering—the first woman organized crime prosecutor in the department's history. George Frampton and Gerry Goldman had been top students at Harvard Law and each had been rewarded with a prestigious clerkship with a Supreme Court justice. Peter

Rient, who had overlapped with me in the U.S. attorney's office, became the "law man" on our team, assigned legal research and brief-writing responsibilities. Larry Iason and Judy Denny, both promising young legal scholars, rounded out our team—average age, thirty-one, even with "old man" Neal at the helm.

The months from July to October were grueling fourteen-hour daily marathons, as we began to assimilate the prior investigative work of the original prosecutors from the DC U.S. attorney's office and the Senate Watergate investigators (two of whom, Terry Lenzner and David Dorsen, had also been colleagues of mine in the Southern District of New York) and build upon that foundation. Our priorities were set by Archie Cox. Even though John Dean had been granted immunity by the Senate Watergate Committee in return for his extensive testimony, Cox was determined not to let Dean off the hook. We would make every effort to find a way to prosecute the young White House lawyer for his central role in the cover-up, even though following the Senate's lead would have given us cover and greatly expedited our effort to investigate the involvement of the most senior White House officials.

The revelation by Nixon aide Alexander Butterfield of a surreptitious White House taping system crashed upon Watergate's shores. Cox publicly pledged to seek access to the tapes for evidence they might yield about the alleged cover-up. The stakes regarding Dean's cooperation as a witness for the prosecution grew dramatically.

Archie came under tremendous pressure from the White House to back off and agree to a "compromise" that would deny us a firsthand review of the taped conversations among Nixon and his top lieutenants, H. R. Haldeman, John Ehrlichman, John Mitchell, and Chuck Colson, that we had identified, using a combination of White House logs and insider testimony. Yet Archie remained firm about Dean. "If everything else goes down the drain, the one thing I can cling to is Dean's venality," he explained.

Nixon, of course, pegged Cox as a part of the Eastern elite establishment, a Kennedy man at that, who was "out to get" Nixon. The reality was much different. Cox was bent on providing a scrupulously fair investigation that would withstand scrutiny by any objective observer. On several occasions when we updated Archie on the progress of our investigation, our boss questioned us closely on the appropriateness of various investigative tradecraft. It was not enough to point out "this is what prosecutors do." "But is it fair?" was the bottom-line question to which Archie always returned. So to some extent we were obliged to reinvent the wheel and think through issues I had never questioned. I developed a tremendous admiration for Archibald Cox and what he stood for. Nixon, on the other hand, was playing by a different set of rules.

John Dean found himself between a rock and a hard place. The White House mounted a furious attack on Dean, focusing on his alleged motive of trying to besmirch others in an attempt to save himself from a jail term. Yet Cox rejected anything less than a plea to a felony count of obstruction of justice, which carried a maximum five-year penalty. Charlie Shaffer felt he was holding good cards and refused to budge: We needed Dean; moreover, everything he had testified to before the Senate was protected by the "use immunity" the Senate had conferred upon his client. Eventually we would have to back down and give immunity to Dean also.

But what if we could find an area of possible prosecution that had not been the subject of Dean's extensive Senate testimony? Combing carefully through the record, the team found just such an omission. It involved Dean's attempt to induce James McCord, one of the Watergate burglars, to plead guilty rather than go to trial by making him a veiled offer of presidential clemency if he did so. We knew about this episode through witnesses who had testified *before* Dean's Senate appearance. We drafted an indictment outlining such a charge to show Dean that Archie meant what he said. Neal told Shaffer that we had Dean boxed. It was time for his client to plead guilty and throw in with the good guys.

Meanwhile, the drama over the White House tapes had moved from hot to white hot. Cox's appointment as Watergate special prosecutor had been the result of Nixon's attempt to shore up his administration's eroding credibility by appointing Elliot Richardson, his Boston Brahmin secretary of defense, to be attorney general. Coinciding with his announcement of the resignations of Haldeman and Ehrlichman, his two closest aides tarnished by Watergate revelations and dumped overboard by the chief, the Richardson appointment was the type of bold move Nixon reveled in. Richardson's spotless reputation for integrity would surely head off the growing political sentiment for an independent inquiry into Watergate. But the Democrat-controlled Senate wanted more—a guaranty that Richardson would appoint an independent special prosecutor who would investigate allegations of a Watergate cover-up and other abuses of executive power free from White House control. It was more than a suggestion. The Senate Judiciary Committee made it clear that Richardson's confirmation as attorney general would depend on his selection of a special prosecutor with guarantees of independence. Richardson signaled his acceptance of such a condition and his willingness to name an individual who would pass muster. Richardson picked his former Harvard

Law professor, Archibald Cox, who appeared with the nominee before the Judiciary Committee and testified to Richardson's promise of independence, further guaranteed in a written charter. Cox could be removed only for "extraordinary improprieties." Richardson was confirmed two days later.

By mid-October, the behind-the-scenes maneuvering shadowing our attempt to have the courts enforce our subpoena for Nixon's tape recordings of seven specified conversations had reached its zenith. On October 12, the Court of Appeals for the District of Columbia Circuit affirmed the decision of District Court Chief Judge John Sirica ordering Nixon to turn the tapes over to the grand jury. The appellate court gave the president one week to comply.

During one of our task force meetings with Archie, I suggested that it might be a good idea to ask Judge Sirica for an order sequestering the tapes while the president appealed Sirica's ruling. Archie brushed aside my suggestion. "The president of the United States is not going to tamper with evidence under subpoena. To seek such an order would look like overreaching." While he was mistaken on the first count, Archie was right about the second. And he was under enough pressure to back off his demand to get the tapes that he didn't need to open a second front by suggesting that Nixon couldn't be trusted to safeguard the tapes in his custody during the legal battle.

Meanwhile, Nixon had cooked up a fiendishly disingenuous "compromise" to avoid turning over the original tapes to us. Styled the "Stennis compromise," Nixon proposed that he would submit *summaries* of the subpoenaed conversations to Senator John Stennis of Mississippi, who would verify that the summaries accurately portrayed what was on tape. Cox would then give up any attempt to get the actual recordings.

There were two reasons why the proposal was a nonstarter. Summaries, or even verbatim transcripts, would be inadmissible as evidence in any case we might wish to bring. If that were not enough, there was good reason to suspect that Stennis would be suboptimal as an authenticator. Although a Democrat, the ultraconservative Stennis saw eye to eye with Nixon on the conduct of the Vietnam War and supported strong measures to curb dissent. Moreover, there were serious questions about whether the seventy-two-year-old senator had the endurance or hearing acuity to verify what was on the tapes with any degree of reliability. Beyond age alone, Stennis was recovering from gunshot wounds to his head from a recent mugging in his Capitol Hill neighborhood. To top it off, Nixon's new White House counsel, Fred Buzhardt, formerly counsel to the Defense Department, had worked closely in the past with Stennis, who as the powerful chairman of the Senate Armed Services Committee had earned the nickname "the Undertaker" for the Pentagon secrets that stayed buried under his leadership. Buzhardt would be "helping" Stennis with the verification process. Archie didn't need to get into the second reason for concern—a political trap were he to question the senior Democrat's bona fides. The inadmissibility of summaries as evidence would suffice as a cogent reason not to accept Nixon's offer.

What was unknown publicly was how strongly Elliot Richardson pushed Archie to agree to the Stennis compromise. Archie tried to reason with his former student, to no avail. Then a new demand was added: Not only would he have to content himself with summaries, Cox would have to promise not to seek judicial enforcement of any additional subpoenas for White House tapes. How could a prosecutor voluntarily abandon a demand for specific evidence that two courts had ordered be turned over, not to mention forswear seeking what promised to be the most reliable evidence of what was said behind closed doors between and among those being investigated?

Richardson's strong desire to continue on as attorney general provided Nixon and Haig with the leverage to put crushing pressure on him to get Cox to agree to their terms. Richardson knew that unless Cox either acceded or resigned under pressure to do so, he would be forced into the position of firing the man he had promised would not be discharged "except for extraordinary improprieties" or tendering his own resignation.

As October 19, 1973, the date the Court of Appeals had set for Nixon to turn over the subpoenaed tapes, approached, the efforts to persuade Dean to plead guilty accelerated. The draft indictment had convinced Dean of the seriousness of our intention that he would not get off scot-free. Shaffer told us his client was ready to plead guilty. Led by Jim Neal, we engaged in a marathon session with Dean and Shaffer that went on into the early morning hours of Thursday, October 18. We insisted on a provision in the plea agreement that would leave Dean vulnerable to an additional prosecution for perjury if the tapes proved him to be a liar. Dean readily consented.

It was agreed that Dean would enter his plea on Friday, the same day as the deadline for Nixon to comply with the order to turn over the tapes. Dean's guilty plea was a dramatic step forward in the effort to build a case against the higher-ups Dean claimed had ordered the cover-up. I had worked intensely with Jim Neal for more than four months since our first meeting. With Dean's plea of guilty to conspiracy to obstruct justice, Jim would return to his law practice in Nashville. Friday would be his last day.

We returned to the office from Judge Sirica's courtroom to say our good-byes to Jim. Despite the important milestone of securing John Dean's guilty plea, the mood in the office was somber. Nixon had handed off "negotiations" from Attorney General Richardson to Charles Alan Wright, a prominent constitutional law professor from Texas. No longer was there any pretense of give-and-take. Wright's message was take it or leave it. Unless Cox accepted the Stennis compromise, the president would "follow the course of action in the best interests of the country." What the hell did that mean? Cox wrote back that he could not accept a proposal totally at odds with his guarantee of independence. Wright responded that further communications would be futile: The president would do what he had to do. The constitutional law professor pen pals ceased postal artillery between K Street and Pennsylvania Avenue. The clock ticked down as the time for filing court papers expired. Archie looked totally forlorn. His belief that at the end of the day, the president of the United States would act honorably and in conformity with the pledges so publicly made to him was eroding by the minute. At 6:30, Elliot Richardson called to read Cox a letter from Nixon to Richardson, in which the president had instructed his attorney general to tell Cox to make no further attempts to compel production of presidential tapes, notes, or other memoranda.

At 9 P.M., the White House went public. Nixon would not pursue an appeal to the Supreme Court. Nor would he turn over the subpoenaed tapes. Rather, he had made a very generous and reasonable offer to Cox in order to avoid the continued "strain" the Watergate investigation had imposed on the American people. In order to avoid a constitutional confrontation, Nixon offered a summary of the tapes, which would be verified by Senator John Stennis, a distinguished and respected American patriot. In return, Cox had been ordered not to subpoena any more tapes. Breathtaking in the president's disregard for the rulings of the two courts and the attorney general's earlier assurances of Cox's independence, the White House sprang a final surprise. Senators Sam Ervin and Howard Baker, the leaders of the Senate Watergate Committee, had endorsed the Stennis compromise as a resolution of the committee's parallel demand for the tapes. This was a shocking stab in the back. Judge Sirica had ruled *against* the Senate, distinguishing between a grand jury's preeminent right to gather evidence in a criminal investigation and Congress's desire to compel a co-equal branch of government to disgorge its confidential communications. The Watergate Committee, which had moved the investigation along so importantly, was selling us out and giving Nixon cover for flouting the legal process. I was stunned and disillusioned; I could hardly imagine Archie Cox's distress.

In fact, Archie was busily at work, scratching out on a yellow legal pad an outline of his reasons for rejecting Nixon's offer. He intended to explain his position directly to the American people in a press conference the next day. Meanwhile, at the White House, General Alexander Haig, who had replaced H. R. Haldeman as Nixon's chief of staff, was war-gaming the possible outcomes. The smart money was on Richardson staying on message; the hope was that Cox would resign.

Saturday morning was my first day as leader of the Watergate cover-up team. As events unfolded at warp speed, it could easily have been my last. The entire staff assembled in our office library at 11 A.M. so that Archie could explain what was going on. The mood in the room reflected both anger and despair. We were being outflanked by Nixon and abandoned by our natural allies, the Senate Watergate Committee leaders. Archie had traded his signature bow tie for a standard maroon striped four-in-hand. With a blue button-down oxford shirt and a gray tweed suit, he still appeared far more professor than Washington lawyer. His unkempt, bushy eyebrows with wiry hairs going every which way contrasted with his salt-and-pepper buzz cut. He gave a brief summary of the past week's events and told us he would try to explain at the press conference why he could not accept the president's demands. For the first time I saw Archie's natural reserve break down as he told us how proud he was of his staff and how much he appreciated the hard work we had put in since he was appointed. It was possible the president would fire him; if that happened, he hoped we would stay on as long as possible, for our effort was important to the country.

The possibility that Nixon would lash out and fire Cox for disobedience had been the subject of discussion among us for weeks. In fact, we had assembled copies of important memos summarizing evidence and transcripts of key testimony, which George Frampton had then squirreled away in his grandmother's attic in Virginia. But such precautions seemed a stretch. After all, we were lawyers, working as part of the Department of Justice, not rebel bomb throwers. What could the president do?

At 12:30, we walked to the main hall of the National Press Club, a few blocks south down 14th Street from our office, to take seats for the one o'clock press conference. The room was rapidly filling and seats were becoming scarce. The television networks were covering it live. Could the Harvard law professor and former solicitor general, so comfortable with abstract legal principles, hold the attention of a lay audience, much less battle the entire White House spin apparatus?

Archie spoke in the slow, measured cadence that I had grown to know so well in our staff meetings. He started off by referring to the morning's news reports.

"I read a headline in one of the newspapers this morning that said, 'Cox Defiant,'" he began. "But I don't feel defiant." He didn't want a fight, least of all with the president. He did not want to provoke a constitutional confrontation, nor was he "out to get" the president. Indeed, he was brought up to have the highest regard for the presidency. He worried about the possibility that he had grown "too big for my britches." He wanted to assure the public that his was not some manifestation of his own vanity but an expression of the principle of law to which he was dedicated. In the vernacular of *The Godfather,* which was still some years off, Cox made clear this was not personal; it was a matter of business. He looked the American public in the eye and told them how he had decided that following a path that would lead to evidence admissible in a court of law was the only "responsible" course of action he could follow. The message came through clearly that Cox took his responsibility seriously. By his words and demeanor, Archie communicated that there was not a whit of vanity about him. The rejection of the president's offer did not imply any doubt about Senator Stennis's integrity, Archie continued, but rather a commitment to adhere to established principles rather than some one-off recipe for avoiding confrontation. He detailed the communications with Nixon's representatives over the past weeks and ended with an apology for being "professorially" long-winded. As he opened the floor to questions from the press, I reflected that Archie had humanized himself not only as a man of integrity and dedication to principle, but also as a man who could be introspective and worried about taking himself too seriously. It was a bravura performance of courage and principle. How could America not get it?

The questions from the floor gave Archie the opportunity to expand upon his theme and deal with the critical question of how Elliot Richardson would behave. Given the defections of Ervin and Baker, if Richardson found some way to justify abandoning his pledge to Cox that he could conduct an independent investigation, as Nixon and Haig were hoping, all might be lost. Archie had clung to the belief that in the end, Elliot would act honorably. There was some reason to hope for such an outcome.

When Richardson had read Nixon's letter to him, he made clear to Archie that he was *informing* Cox of the president's demand, not *ordering* him to abandon his quest for the tapes. Now Cox sought to stitch Richardson into the fabric of his defense of principle. What if he were fired after this news conference? asked one of the journalists. Only the attorney general could legally fire him, Cox replied. What if Elliot Richardson fired him on the president's order? was the follow-up question. Archie launched into a bit of constitutional history, asking the reporter to "remember" that when Andrew Jackson's secretary of the treasury refused the president's order to transfer money from the central bank, he fired him and appointed a new treasury secretary. When the new secretary also refused the order, Jackson fired him too and appointed a third, who finally agreed to do the president's bidding. Cox was trying to escalate the political cost to Nixon of pursuing a strategy of firing him. If Richardson would not execute an order to fire Cox, despite the efforts he had made along the way to convince Archie to accept a compromise, would Nixon be willing to sacrifice Richardson in the bargain? We would not have to wait long to find out.

We milled around after the press conference, talking in hushed tones about Archie's performance. For me, it was then and remains today the single most inspiring act of personal courage and commitment to the core principles of the rule of law that I have ever witnessed. I was enormously proud to be associated with Archibald Cox.

The ball was now squarely in Nixon's court. The president had ordered Cox to drop his pursuit of the tapes, and Cox responded that he would neither resign nor obey Nixon's demand. There was nothing we could do but wait. Judge Sirica had set a court hearing for Tuesday, where he would hear the formal White House response to the appellate court's order. I was accustomed to waiting for juries to finish their deliberations in cases I had tried. Nothing productive could be accomplished during deliberations—you had already done everything you could do to affect the outcome. So we all went home to wait. There was no point hanging around the office. After all, nothing official ever happens in Washington on a Saturday night.

I had arranged for a quiet dinner at my apartment with a woman I was dating. The television was on in the other room, just in case there was some news of Nixon's response. NBC broke into its regularly scheduled programming to report alarming developments in the battle over Nixon's secret tapes. Legal correspondent Carl Stern reported breathlessly from the White House lawn that President Nixon had fired Watergate Special

Prosecutor Archibald Cox and had abolished the special prosecutor's office. FBI agents had been dispatched to Cox's office to seize his files. Attorney General Elliot Richardson had resigned his office after refusing Nixon's order to fire Cox. Deputy Attorney General William Ruckelshaus, also refusing Nixon's orders, had been fired.

As I rushed to leave for our office to see firsthand what was going on, the phone rang. It was John Dean, who had entered his guilty plea before Judge Sirica only the day before. With Jim Neal gone, Dean was looking to me as responsible for his care and feeding. Dean's monotone betrayed no emotion, but he wanted to know how we would respond to the decapitation of our leader. He added, unnecessarily, that he had a lot invested in the outcome. "No shit, take a number," I thought to myself. I assured Dean that I was on my way to the office and would call him the next morning.

The scene at 1425 K Street was bedlam. Television crews had illuminated the entrance to the building, which was crowded with reporters and curious passersby. Upstairs, the situation was more grim. Our suite of offices had been taken over by the FBI. No papers could be removed, although the agents made exceptions for photographs and personal items. Particularly shocking was the fact that the same FBI agents who were detailed to us earlier to assist in our investigation were now enforcing a presidential fiat to close us down. Law enforcement had been turned on its head. Emotions ran high. If this was not a coup, it was the closest thing to one I had ever seen in my country. A few weeks before, as the tapes controversy heated up, I joked that we would know we were in trouble if General Haig began wearing his uniform to the office. This was no joke. Naked force had replaced the rule of law.

We had demonstrated some forward-looking situational awareness in moving copies of important documents out of the building. Archie also had been prescient in predicting the cost to Nixon in finding someone to execute the order to fire him. The person who did the deed that Richardson and Ruckelshaus refused was Solicitor General Robert Bork, third in line at the Justice Department. Bork's firing of Cox would later become a factor in the Senate's decision not to confirm him for the Supreme Court seat he coveted. Richardson, on the other hand, left Washington with his reputation for moral rectitude burnished by standing up to Nixon. So far as I know, Cox never publicly commented on the pressure Richardson had put on him to accept a compromise. It was enough for Archie that Elliot had acted honorably when the final showdown came.

As the dust began to settle in the aftermath of the Saturday Night Massacre, it turned out that in the confusion over the firing of Cox, nobody had actually fired the staff. In the following days we met in small groups in private homes and borrowed offices and then together as a whole, as if we were small drops of mercury coalescing to become the larger original ball. Except our leader was missing. At one meeting at a rather grand Georgetown home on R Street, where California staffer Chuck Breyer was housesitting, about a dozen of us sat cross-legged on the back lawn, thinking our conversations were less likely to be bugged electronically if we were outdoors. What more was Nixon capable of? Was our personal security in jeopardy?

I had always thought of myself as a streetwise kid from New York, not easily intimidated. I had prosecuted Mafia tough guys who were capable of brutal vengeance. But then, I had gun-toting federal agents from the IRS, FBI, and DEA, not to mention U.S. Marshals, looking out for my safety. This was a different kind of deal. Who would be watching my back here?

The answer was quick in coming.

The firestorm of negative public reaction to the events of Saturday night was unprecedented in Washington's history; Western Union was unable to handle the flood of telegrams, while telephone switchboards at the White House and Congress lit up for days on end. In the midst of the hubbub, Senators Ervin and Baker "clarified" their prior endorsement of the Stennis compromise. They had no idea Nixon would use such a proposal to prevent Cox getting the evidence he needed, they explained. Much later, Stennis himself repudiated the plan, claiming that the White House had misrepresented the role he was to play.

Although intellectually we had accepted the possibility that Archie might be fired, the reality was quite another matter. Still shocked and dazed by the lesson in executive power Nixon had delivered, we discussed our options. I had already met with John Dean and told him I was personally committed to continuing the fight to the end, whatever that might be. As we sat in Breyer's borrowed backyard, I learned that most of my colleagues shared my view—including all the members of the cover-up task force. But there were a few (not Chuck) who thought they ought to resign "in protest" of Nixon's actions.

My mother had taught me long before that the best way to deal with a bully was to give him a swift kick in the shins. I told my colleagues in this and other meetings in the immediate aftermath of the Saturday Night Massacre that resignation would be absurd. "First of all, no one is thinking of Cox's staff, and if they were, they would assume we had also been fired. Let's continue to do our jobs until we get axed, or whatever. There must be some really incriminating shit on those tapes if Nixon would risk so much to keep them from us." The same thoughts were expressed in different words by Henry Ruth, Cox's deputy, who became the temporary head of the office. Meanwhile, we were cheered by the thousands of telegrams and letters from citizens all across the country urging continuation of our mission.

Nixon's oversight in not firing the rest of the staff was one in a continuum of miscalculations that cost him the presidency. The firestorm of protest over Nixon's firing of Cox, exacerbated by the dramatic resignation of Richardson and firing of Ruckelshaus, forced Nixon to stay his hand in any further action he might have contemplated against us.

By the following Tuesday, unsure of our legal authority, the task force showed up in Judge Sirica's courtroom to hear the president's formal response to the Court of Appeals' order to turn over the tapes. The FBI had withdrawn from the occupation of our offices, and we had returned that morning to receive Archie Cox's emotional farewell address, in which he urged us to continue what we had banded together to do. He explained that he would be returning to his country home in Maine for the winter and then would resume teaching at Harvard. The finality of Cox's decision to accept his firing was one more blow to be absorbed.

Now, sitting together in Sirica's courtroom, we were Archie's orphans. Judge Sirica had ordered the two grand juries before which we had been presenting evidence to appear in court. As chief judge of the district court, he was officially in charge of supervising the grand juries. Sirica assured the jurors that their tenure would be unaffected by the "recent events" and that they would not be dismissed until they had concluded their work. This Republican judge of modest background, whose steely determination to protect the legitimacy of our criminal justice system rightly made him the central hero of the Watergate affair, assured the grand jurors, "In due course the questions which now plague us will be answered, and you may rely on the court to safeguard your rights and protect the integrity of your proceedings."

Judge Sirica turned his gaze to Charles Alan Wright, the Texas law professor representing the White House who had so brusquely informed Cox the week before that his objections to being steamrolled were pointless. In stern tones, Sirica read selected passages from the Court of Appeals decision upholding his own prior decision ordering the president to turn over the tapes called for in the grand jury subpoena. Sirica asked Wright to provide the president's response. Wright, unaccountably got up in a lime green shirt with a brown suit, announced, "I am authorized to say that the President will comply in all respects" with the court order. As though not believing his own ears, Sirica asked whether the tapes would be delivered as ordered. Wright reconfirmed, adding, "This President does not defy the law, and has authorized me to say that he will comply in full with the orders of the court."

Another "holy shit!" moment. This was a complete turnabout from yesterday's intransigent Nixon. We had won! Nixon had capitulated. But we had lost our leader in the process. A horrifying thought crossed my mind. What if there really was nothing on the tapes after all, and the whole episode had simply been a plot to get rid of Archie?

As it turned out, there was plenty of evidence on the tapes to demonstrate Nixon's central complicity in the obstruction of justice that followed immediately on the heels of the Watergate break-in. Everything that John Dean had testified to under oath before the Senate Watergate Committee, and more, was irrefutably corroborated by the tape-recorded words of the conspirators themselves.

The break-in and burglary of the Democratic National Committee's headquarters at the Watergate office building on June 17, 1972, was not the isolated and loopy "third-rate burglary" portrayed by the Nixon administration's spin control managers. It was a significant violation of law authorized by Nixon insiders at the highest level—if not the president himself—to *continue* illegal electronic eavesdropping and photographing of confidential records. For the same team had previously broken into the same DNC office; the June 17 break-in was supposed to replace a malfunctioning bug from the earlier intrusion.

Indeed, it is a tribute to the skill of the Nixon spinmeisters that their "third-rate burglary" tag—coined to deflect attention from the higher-ups involved—endures. The Watergate break-in was just one link in a chain of abuses that Nixon Attorney General John Mitchell aptly dubbed the "White House horrors." These included the break-in at a psychiatrist's office looking for information that could be used to smear Daniel Ellsberg, who had exposed the secret government history of the Vietnam War known as the Pentagon Papers; the misuse of the Internal Revenue Service and other federal agencies to punish those on the president's "enemies list"; the illegal wiretapping of journalists and members of Nixon's own administration; the deliberate falsification of government documents to enhance Nixon's political agenda; the proposed fire-bombing of the Brookings Institution as a diversion for the theft of documents; the surreptitious surveillance of political opponents; and the hiring of thugs to brutalize political protesters.

The subsequent cover-up was not an irrational reaction to an insignificant, stupid break-in. Rather, it was a reflexive attempt to counter the threat that the administration's widespread abuses of governmental authority would be exposed once investigators began asking questions. Nixon's imperial view of the presidency had encouraged a competition among his lieutenants. They catered to his dark side, disregarding legal boundaries to strike at and punish his adversaries and critics. As the cover-up unraveled, facts emerged about the extent of Nixon's willingness to misuse his power to prevent the truth from coming out. Nixon directed the deputy director of the CIA to tell the FBI, falsely, that the country's national security would be jeopardized by a full investigation of the money trail left by the Watergate burglars. Several of Nixon's top advisers committed perjury, including John Mitchell, who had been the nation's chief legal officer, as well as Nixon's chief of staff, H. R. Haldeman. There was more. Offers of presidential clemency were dangled before certain members of the burglary team, and all were paid significant sums of hush money from a secret slush fund—financed by campaign contributions controlled by the president and Haldeman and delivered by the president's personal attorney.

Transcripts and summaries of illegally tape-recorded conversations at the Democratic National Committee headquarters, as well as other incriminating evidence, were burned and shredded. E. Howard Hunt, a former CIA officer, was a stalwart member of the burglary team. Incredible as it may seem, certain contents of Hunt's White House safe were destroyed by Nixon's appointee to head the FBI, L. Patrick Gray, acting on John Ehrlichman's suggestion that they "not see the light of day."

But as we trooped back from the courthouse to K Street on October 23, 1973, all of that was still in front of us. We needed to regroup and absorb the shocks the Watergate roller coaster had delivered. The next loop-the-loop presented itself only a week later when White House counsel J. Fred Buzhardt (what was with these guys and their disdain for their own first names? G. Gordon Liddy, E. Howard Hunt, L. Patrick Gray, H. R. Haldeman . . . ?) asked Judge Sirica if he could meet with us and Judge Sirica privately. Buzhardt, a short, slight man with the pallor of a lifelong chain-smoker, explained that two of the conversations we had subpoenaed simply had never been tape-recorded. According to the White House counsel, a June 20, 1972, call between Nixon and Mitchell, three days after the break-in, was made by Nixon from an upstairs phone in the White House residence that was not a part of the extensive wiretapping and bugging system Nixon had installed. A second conversation between Nixon and Dean on April 15, 1973, the day Nixon learned that Dean might be turning state's evidence, had not been recorded because the timing system had malfunctioned and a new reel-to-reel tape had not been installed before the existing tape ran out.

By this point, I was not willing to trust anything the White House had to say. If Buzhardt told me it was raining out I would look for myself before bothering with an umbrella. I told Judge Sirica we ought to hold a hearing to explore the issue of the supposedly unrecorded conversations. Perhaps a hearing could be avoided if the technicians who ran the taping system were made available to us for interview, Buzhardt suggested. We agreed to table our hearing request while we talked to the technicians.

The next morning a young lawyer on Buzhardt's staff arrived at our office with secret service technician Raymond C. Zumwalt in tow. Despite the lawyer's demand to be present for the interview, I sent him to the reception area, telling him the days of White House lawyers monitoring interviews were over. This was an unsubtle reference to John Dean's access during the original Watergate investigation. He could tell Buzhardt he could take it or leave it. The alternative would be to see us in open court. Wishing to avoid a public hearing, Buzhardt accepted our ground rules. Zumwalt was a portly, talkative fellow who explained the details of the taping system. Despite Buzhardt's explanation, Zumwalt had never heard of any malfunction in the timers for the taping system.

The time had come to kick the bully in the shins. I telephoned Buzhardt to say that Zumwalt had been helpful in his explanation, but just the same I thought we should get it on the record before Judge Sirica. "Why don't we just get it done this afternoon, Fred?" Judge Sirica was amenable. It was Halloween day. For the last five months we had been conducting interviews and calling witnesses before the grand jury, slowly putting together the pieces of the jigsaw puzzle that would prove a conspiracy to obstruct the FBI investigation of Watergate. The outstanding group of lawyers, led by Philip Lacovara and Peter Kreindler, who researched and drafted the briefs supporting the legal basis underpinning our claim for the tapes, had also labored in anonymity. For the first time the public would see the staff that Cox had assembled.

Before a courtroom crowded with press, Buzhardt revealed that two subpoenaed conversations could not be produced because they didn't exist. As Judge Sirica gaveled the courtroom to order from the commotion this news caused in the gallery, Buzhardt provided the same explanation he had offered us in Judge Sirica's chambers the day before. The timer had malfunctioned. He then called Zumwalt to the witness stand as his expert on the taping system. Under Buzhardt's questioning, Zumwalt testified that the system had not captured the April 15 Dean-Nixon conversation because the seven-day timer had failed to switch on that evening.

On cross-examination, I asked Zumwalt to explain how he was now able to remember that the system malfunctioned on April 15, when only that morning he told us he had never heard of a malfunction. The answer: Mr. Buzhardt told him that was what happened! Amid laughter and other signs of disbelief emanating from the spectators, I then suggested that other witnesses might be better suited to provide useful testimony. Judge Sirica adjourned the hearing to the next day.

From that point and for the next few weeks, we beat the crap out of the White House in court. As the hapless Buzhardt went from one unsatisfactory explanation to the next, I ran the table on calling live and usually ill-prepared witnesses from the bowels of the White House technical staff all the way up to chief of staff Alexander Haig himself. At the close of each day's hearing, I would announce demands for the production of new White House witnesses and relevant documents. Buzhardt proved incapable of stanching the bleeding or publicly objecting to each day's new demands. New questions outnumbered incomplete or misleading answers by a substantial margin. For example, despite assurances the tapes were securely locked away, it turned out that a quantity of original tapes had been loaned out to Nixon's former chief of staff, H. R. Haldeman, a target of the criminal investigation, for his personal review. Keeping track of the items in the lending library was, if one were inclined to be charitable (and I was not), suboptimal. Records relating to the custody of the tapes were produced on scraps of brown paper bags.

The vaunted well-oiled machinery of the White House run by Nixon's two "German shepherds," Haldeman and Ehrlichman, was shown to have rusted out. Indeed, faced with a choice between incompetence and venality to explain their constantly changing stories, the White House chose the former. Others were no longer willing to give the president the benefit of the doubt. Calls for Nixon's impeachment or resignation that began after the Saturday Night Massacre increased in volume and stridency. The *New York Times* called for Nixon to resign; *Time* magazine proclaimed that Nixon had "irredeemably lost his moral authority"—this coming from an influential newsmagazine that had endorsed Nixon's presidential candidacy in 1960, 1968, and 1972. Indeed, by the anniversary of his election victory, Nixon's public support had plummeted from 68 percent to 27 percent.

And this was before the next seismic event in Nixon's downfall—the revelation that one of the seven subpoenaed tapes, a recording of a critical conversation between Nixon and Haldeman on June 20, 1972, had a gap of 18½ minutes where no conversation could be heard. June 20 was three days after the Watergate burglars were arrested and the first day Nixon, who had been in California, was reunited with his chief of staff. Haldeman's notes of that meeting indicated that the Watergate break-in had been discussed. Coincidentally, that was the same portion obliterated by 18½ minutes of electronic humming and buzzing.

Meanwhile, in the surrealistic aftermath of the Saturday Night Massacre, Nixon set out to demonstrate his willingness to have his administration independently investigated by a *new* Watergate special prosecutor whom his chief of staff, General Alexander Haig, had vetted: Leon Jaworski, the sixty-eight-year-old senior partner of the prominent Houston-based law firm of Fulbright & Jaworski. In addition to having been president of the American Bar Association, Jaworski was identified in news reports as a prominent Democrat and confidant of President Lyndon Johnson. Nixon's claim to finding an independent-minded Democrat to finish the Watergate investigation was somewhat tempered, in my view, by Jaworski's outspoken support for Nixon in the 1968 and 1972 elections, and his close friendship with Nixon's ally, John Connolly.

What had motivated Jaworski to accept the president's offer to take over the reins at 1425 K Street? Certainly, he had a bona fide record of public service. Justifiably alarmed by the Saturday Night Massacre, following on the revelations of the Senate hearings and the reporting of Bob Woodward and Carl Bernstein at the *Washington Post,* the American public was becoming increasingly less inclined to give their twice-elected president the benefit of the doubt when it came to issues of credibility. Did "public service" favor putting an end to the "distraction" of the Watergate investigation, as Nixon had repeatedly urged his "fellow Americans" to do? Or did it mean following the evidence wherever it might lead, as Cox and his idealistic young staff had pledged to do?

I first met Leon Jaworski when he addressed the full staff in Archie's former office. His white-on-white shirt with French cuffs, black suit, and formal manner reinforced his image as an emissary of the Texas big oil legal business establishment. We had learned that everyone at Fulbright & Jaworski addressed him as "Colonel," a reference to his World War II service as a military prosecutor. That would be a little hard for us to swallow, so we made a point of addressing him as "Leon" from day one. He voiced no objection. Also to his credit, he did not bring a single staffer with him, although he could have taken his pick among scores of willing lawyers at his firm.

He told us of the assurances he had obtained in order to guarantee his independence. He pointed to his unwillingness to meet with Nixon during his White House interview with Alexander Haig as an indication of his determination to avoid any perception that he might favor the man who had fired his predecessor and appointed him to the job. We later learned that as part of the effort to get him to say yes, Haig had informed Jaworski that Nixon was considering him for appointment to the Supreme Court! At that point, nothing Nixon might be considering to save his skin would have surprised me. My anger over Cox's firing would translate, fairly or unfairly, into a wary, wait-and-see approach toward our newly installed leader. As far as I was concerned, I would operate under the assumption that Jaworski had been hired to perpetrate the biggest fix of all time.

My relationship with Jaworski developed over time, but it never became anything close to warm and fuzzy. In our first private meeting, Leon recounted that he had been told by "people" at the White House that there were a group of young prosecutors on Cox's staff who were out to get the president, and that they should be fired. There was no doubt that my name was at the top of the list. I didn't cross-examine Leon about who these unnamed people were or why they felt they could have such a discussion with him. Rather, I told him I was doing my job to the best of my ability and hoped that he would reserve judgment until he became more familiar with the facts.

Our task force had become even more cohesive after the Saturday Night Massacre. During the tapes hearings, we began to operate more like a trial team, with me and Jill cross-examining the White House witnesses every day in court and the rest of the team doing the essential digging and research that made us look good. Jill's cross-examination of Rosemary Woods, Nixon's loyal personal secretary and designated scapegoat for the 18½-minute gap, was brilliant. She had Woods reenact how she supposedly mistakenly erased the tape while transcribing it. Because of the configuration of the equipment on Woods's desk and her use of a foot pedal to run the tape during the transcription process while at the same time answering phone calls, her explanation would require a contortion that would be difficult to sustain for more than a few seconds, let alone 18½ minutes. Incredibly, the White House defense team obligingly photographed Woods at her desk outside the oval office performing what became derisively known as the "Rosemary stretch"—demonstrating the implausibility of the White House explanation. We received a lot of

favorable attention in the press for being unafraid to demand information from the White House and being unwilling to accept at face value
the half-truths and misrepresentations the White House was serving up
in court. Our team held varying degrees of skepticism about Jaworski's
commitment to the same principles that were motivating us; we learned
that Hank Ruth, Carl Feldbaum, and others in the "front office" held
similar concerns. They had become alarmed at Jaworski's unexplained
absences from the office, suspecting that he was secretly meeting with
Alexander Haig.

But at the same time, Jaworski was not interfering with the conduct of
the tapes hearings and was supportive of the other task forces' requests to
the White House for additional information. After the bombshell of the
18½-minute gap and the constantly changing stories by White House
witnesses, a jointly selected expert panel of scientists concluded that the
gap was the result of at least five separate manual erasures. Jaworski began to gain his sea legs. When I pressed General Haig on the witness stand
to reconcile the different explanations of how the tape of a key conversation could have been obliterated, Haig replied that perhaps a "sinister
force" was responsible. Haig's attempt at humor proved closer to the truth
than other White House theories. Jaworski could only shake his head in
wonder.

Nixon's credibility nose-dived among members of his own party in
the two and a half months between Buzhardt's claim that Zumwalt would
clear up the missing tapes issue and the expert panel's report. John Anderson of Illinois, House Republican conference leader, saw the report as
a further link in the chain of evidence suggesting a deliberate effort to
obstruct justice by the White House. Conservative columnist George
Will saw the expert panel's conclusion as moving Watergate to the "impeachment stage"—because now "we *know* there is corruption in the
precincts of the Oval Office." And this was before we heard word one of
what was on the tapes.

On December 12, 1973, seven weeks after Charles Wright's announcement that his client would turn over the subpoenaed tapes, we received
copies of seven tape-recorded conversations. Carl Feldbaum, a former assistant district attorney from Philadelphia who served as our primary
interface with the expert panel, set up a reel-to-reel tape recorder (with
the Record button disabled) on the desk in my office. The task force members huddled around the desk, some of us wearing large earphones plugged
directly into the recorder to better hear what was on the tapes. I had a
fair amount of experience listening to surreptitious tape recordings of

face-to-face conversations made by undercover operatives and infor-
mants. Depending on the quality of the equipment and the extent of
background noise, they could pose a real challenge to the listener. I chose
to begin with the March 21, 1973, conversation among Nixon, Dean, and
Haldeman, in which Dean had testified, he told Nixon that the cover-up
was a "cancer on the presidency." If Dean had exaggerated or embellished
upon the critical conversation in which he said he laid out for Nixon the
various steps that had been taken to obstruct and contain the FBI investigation following the arrest of the Watergate burglars, he would be DOA
as a witness for us. The stakes could not have been higher.

What we heard on that day was to change the course of American history. As we listened in shocked disbelief, not only did Dean's account
prove to be unembellished, it was considerably more favorable than Nixon
deserved.

Dean laid out for the president in chapter and verse the origins of the
Watergate break-in and the follow-on obstruction of justice through the
payment of hush money to the burglary team right up to that moment,
prefacing his summary with the warning that the situation was "a cancer—
within—close to the presidency that is growing. It's growing daily. It's
compounding, it grows geometrically now, because it compounds itself." Dean explained how the same team that had broken into Daniel
Ellsberg's psychiatrist's office in California had become a part of an
"intelligence-gathering operation" approved by John Mitchell, pushed by
Chuck Colson, and monitored by H. R. Haldeman, who had received the
"take" from the earlier bug planted at DNC headquarters. Dean recounted
how it became necessary to raise large amounts of money to pay for attorneys' fees for the burglars, lest they reveal their connection to the
higher-ups who sponsored them.

After Dean's Senate testimony, the White House spin machine had
explained that Nixon had simply asked questions to "draw Dean out" at
this meeting. But although Dean had expressed his belief, more like a
wish, that Nixon did not already know the facts he was relating, the tape
revealed Nixon's familiarity with many of the details. For example, Nixon
interrupted Dean's account of early fund-raising for the arrested burglars
by Nixon's personal lawyer, Herbert Kalmbach, to add, "They put that
under the cover of a Cuban Committee," a reference to the prior anti-
Castro Cuban activism of the burglars, adding quickly, "I would certainly
keep that cover for whatever it's worth."

Dean immediately added that Haldeman had chipped in $350,000
from a "polling" slush fund, and that he, Ehrlichman, and Mitchell were

all involved in the collection and payment of hush money, "and that is obstruction of justice." Moreover, presidential clemency had been dangled in front of at least one of the burglars. "*As you know,*" Dean added, "Colson has talked directly to Hunt about commutation." Nixon acknowledged that he had, in fact, discussed clemency for Hunt.

And now a larger bombshell, as Dean brought the situation right up to the minute. Hunt was demanding $122,000 for attorney's fees and living expenses, threatening to bring John Ehrlichman, sponsor of the Ellsberg break-in caper, "to his knees and put him in jail" unless the money was paid immediately. This was big news to us. We had been operating under the mistaken belief that this payment to Hunt had *already* been made. Dean hurried along, picking up steam, telling the president that the cover-up was in imminent danger of collapse—they lacked the Mafia's money-laundering tradecraft and could not keep up with the burglary team's demands. Now, to our astonishment, we heard Nixon's response to Dean's plea to end the cover-up before it entangled the president himself.

NIXON: How much money do you need?

This stopped Dean short.

DEAN: I would say these people are going to cost a million dollars over the next two years.
NIXON: We could get that . . . If you need the money . . . you could get the money . . . What I mean is that you could, you could get a million dollars. And you could get it in cash. I, I know where it could be gotten.
DEAN: Uh-huh.
NIXON: I mean it's not easy, but it could be done. But, the question is, who the hell would handle it?

Dean suggested that this should be Mitchell's responsibility, noting that Mitchell had approached Nixon fund-raiser Thomas Pappas with a solicitation. Nixon acknowledged that he knew about the request to Pappas.

Dean gamely returned to his original theme—that laws had been broken and a criminal obstruction of justice case could be made against himself, Haldeman, Ehrlichman, Mitchell, and Colson. It was necessary to determine "how this can be carved away from you, so it does not damage you or the Presidency."

Nixon brushed aside Dean's concern and returned to the nuts and bolts of Dean's immediate dilemma.

> NIXON: The obstruction of justice . . . I feel could be cut off at the pass . . . I wonder if the payments don't have to continue . . . Let me put it this way: Let us suppose that you, you get the million bucks, and you get the proper way to handle it, and you could hold that side. It would seem to me that would be worthwhile . . .
>
> Don't you, just looking at the immediate problem, don't you have to handle Hunt's financial situation damn soon? . . . It seems to me *we* have to keep the cap on the bottle that much . . . Otherwise *we* won't have any options. . . . Either that or it all blows right now.

Bob Haldeman walked in to join the conversation. Nixon, praising Dean for containing the damage, summarized Dean's report: "First you've got the Hunt problem, that ought to be handled right now." And again, "You've got no choice with Hunt . . . You better damn well get that done."

We sat back in utter disbelief. The March 21 tape went far beyond anything we had imagined. Dean's earnest effort to push the president out of harm's way by ending the cover-up and accepting personal responsibility for his role had been rejected by his president in favor of continuing the conspiracy and paying Hunt immediately.

Nixon minimized Dean's concerns about the coming subpoenas from the grand jury and Senate committees, and the likelihood that officials would have to commit perjury if the cover-up were to be continued. Noting that perjury was a tough crime to prove, Nixon advised, "Just be damned sure you say 'I don't remember; I can't recall; I can't give any honest, an answer to that that I can recall.' But that's it."

The implications of this tape were stupendous. *Hunt had not yet been paid.* We went back and forth, rewinding the tape, listening to selected passages again.

Nixon was more than a passive cheerleader for the cover-up; his instruction to Dean to continue the payments to Hunt came *a day before* the delivery of a substantial cash payment to Hunt—powerful evidence of Nixon's *active* participation in a felony.

Each of the other subpoenaed conversations provided helpful pieces of evidence. None of them exculpated any of the targets of our investigation, but none was remotely as dramatic as the "cancer on the presidency" conversation. There could be no doubt of the involvement of Haldeman, Ehrlichman, Mitchell, Colson, and now the president of the United States in a conspiracy to obstruct justice by surreptitiously raising and secretly paying hush money and promising executive clemency to the original burglary team to keep them from revealing the identities of the men who had sponsored the two Watergate break-ins and earlier eavesdropping. The president himself had congratulated his White House counsel for "containing" the investigation so that the burglars' sponsors were not identified before the 1972 presidential election, and had provided advice on how to lie and obfuscate in answering questions under oath.

Given the fact that 18½ minutes of the June 20, 1972, conversation between Nixon and Haldeman had been erased, it was inconceivable that a tape so incriminating would be produced by the White House. Yet here it was. I could only assume that the June 20 tape had contained something even more explosive—a game-ender for Nixon. Perhaps in the obliterated 18½ minutes Nixon had acknowledged receiving a report summarizing the "take" from the illegal bugs at the DNC. After all, Jeb Magruder, deputy chief at the campaign committee, had testified that Liddy had given him typed summaries of the conversations picked up by the electronic surveillance. Magruder said he had passed some of the summaries along to Haldeman's chief aide, Gordon Strachan. Was it conceivable that Strachan wouldn't have kept his boss informed, or that Haldeman wouldn't have told Nixon? I didn't think so. It would have been inconsistent with the "enemies list" mentality at the White House to hide one's light under a bushel when it came to promoting Nixon's tough-guy agenda. And I could imagine Nixon grousing to Haldeman on June 20 that all they had gotten was a "bunch of crap" from the "clowns" that had run the intelligence-gathering operation out of the Committee to Re-elect the President (CREEP). And now, unless they took decisive action to button-up the burglary team, the crime could be traced back to the Nixon campaign.

To say that the tapes had a profound effect on Leon Jaworski only begins to tell the story. Leon was visibly shaken after listening to the March 21 recording. It was not only the discussion of continuing the obstruction of justice that affected Leon; other tapes, in which Nixon displayed a gratuitous meanness of spirit and a penchant for skewering his own supporters with the most venomous language, deeply disturbed the Texas preacher's son. The rock-solid faith he had in the presidency now required an asterisk for Nixon.

If Jaworski were ever inclined to help Nixon survive Watergate when he took the job, the tapes immutably changed his thinking. It was now

apparent why Nixon had gambled so much on pressing the Stennis compromise to the point of the Saturday Night Massacre.

The contrast between Cox's approach, in which the law professor constantly asked us to reinvent the wheel to ensure that every benefit of the
doubt was accorded the White House, and the newly "radicalized" Jaworski was remarkable. It seemed to me that Jaworski quickly made up his
mind that Nixon had forfeited his right to continue as president, and that
he now saw his mission as finding an endgame that least threatened to
tear up the country in the process of showing Nixon the door. It was here
that the generational differences between Leon and his inherited staff
were to be put to the test.

After the tapes hearings were concluded and the first batch of tapes
reviewed, my relationship with Jaworski began to improve. While still
wary of one another, Jaworski began to compliment me on the team's
courtroom performance and loosened his reserve to the point of sharing
war stories of courtroom battles he had fought in years gone by. For my
part, Leon's willingness to pursue the demands of other task forces for
various White House documents and castigate Buzhardt and Haig for
foot-dragging earned my appreciation. Leon's political skills far exceeded Archie's Yankee directness. I had the sense that Leon could evis-
cerate an adversary with a dull carpet knife without mussing his hair. In
trading Cox for Jaworski, Nixon had gone from the frying pan to the
fire.

Having listened to Nixon's tapes, we were now sitting on what was
perhaps the most explosive secret in modern political history. As Nixon
continued his public attack on Jaworski's staff for unfairly targeting the
White House, I am proud of the fact that there was never a leak of what
was on the tapes. We were making serious progress in calling witnesses
before the grand jury and building our case. As we began drafting the
indictment charging Mitchell, Haldeman, Ehrlichman, and others with a
conspiracy to obstruct justice and with individual counts of perjury, the
question of how we would deal with Nixon loomed large.

Because I had been so forceful in challenging the White House's pre-
varications in the tapes hearings, and because of our task force's aggressiveness in moving the cover-up case forward in the grand jury, Leon
worried that I planned to preempt his role and advocate to the grand jury
that it should indict Nixon. This was not true. Although I believed the evidence of Nixon's participation in the cover-up was compelling, I was similarly persuaded that the constitutional remedy of impeachment should
trump the criminal law process in cases where a sitting president had

committed a crime. This was not a view uniformly held, and dissenters, principally among the younger members of the staff, had been open in voicing their disagreement during our internal discussions on the subject. By the same token, I felt it was incumbent on our part not to shy away from an accurate portrayal of Nixon's role in the conspiracy.

For the first time in my career, I felt the need to go beyond simple advocacy to ensure that my boss would do the right thing. This meant I would be walking on eggshells so as not to spook Leon—hardly an easy task for someone used to the directness of the U.S. attorney's office and as diplomacy challenged as was I.

A case in point involved the exercise of prosecutorial discretion in plea bargaining with Richard Kleindienst. Kleindienst, a political appointee to the Justice Department, epitomized to many of us Nixon's politicization of an institution whose independence of action was critical to the reality and perception of fairness in our system of justice. As a federal prosecutor in New York, I had seen firsthand the level of insensitivity to ethical standards Kleindienst had displayed in a political corruption trial prosecuted by one of my more senior colleagues, Robert Morvillo. Robert Carson, the administrative assistant to Republican senator Hiram Fong of Hawaii, had been indicted for conspiracy to commit bribery. The case involved a proposed $50,000 campaign contribution to Nixon's reelection committee in return for Kleindienst intervening in a stock fraud investigation being conducted by our office. Incredibly, Kleindienst, then deputy attorney general, testified that he did not perceive the offer to be a bribe until paperwork summarizing the facts came across his desk in connection with an application for electronic surveillance!

Kleindienst had been targeted for prosecution by our ITT task force, which was investigating the Nixon administration's handling of an antitrust case against the International Telephone and Telegraph Corporation. The task force was headed up by Joseph Connolly, a low-key and keenly intelligent registered Republican from Philadelphia's Main Line. Connolly had focused in on Kleindienst's testimony about alleged political pressure in the ITT case during his Senate confirmation hearing. Kleindienst had repeatedly denied receiving any pressure from the White House concerning the case. In fact, his denials were a lie. Nixon had personally ordered Kleindienst, then assistant attorney general in charge of the antitrust division, to drop the government's appeal of a lower court order favoring ITT. Coincidentally, ITT had promised to donate $400,000 to the Republican Party, essentially underwriting the cost of its 1972 national convention in Miami. An April 1971 telephone conversation between Nixon and Kleindienst had been picked up and recorded by the secret White House taping system. Proving Kleindienst had lied would be shooting fish in a barrel. Connolly and his task force wanted no less than a felony guilty plea from Kleindienst. But Jaworski found extenuating circumstances in Kleindienst's actions and his decision to come forward and confess to lying to the Senate. He was determined to offer Kleindienst a misdemeanor, which would allow him to avoid serving any serious jail time or forfeiting his license to practice law in disbarment proceedings.

To my thinking, Kleindienst, who had been appointed by Nixon to succeed John Mitchell as attorney general after Mitchell left to become Nixon's campaign chairman, represented everything that was wrong about the Department of Justice under Nixon. If the ITT matter were an isolated incident, I would have been less troubled by a misdemeanor plea. But in addition to the Carson case, there was Kleindienst's role in the immediate aftermath of the Watergate break-in to consider. Gordon Liddy, the wildly eccentric chief operating officer of the Watergate burglary and bugging team, reportedly an aficionado of Nazi propaganda films and recordings, had tracked down Kleindienst at the Burning Tree Country Club hours after the burglary team had been arrested at the Watergate. Liddy explained that he was there to convey a request from John Mitchell that Kleindienst assist in securing James McCord's release from jail before it became known that McCord was the chief security officer for CREEP. Although Kleindienst never acted on Liddy's lunatic request, he did not report the incident to the FBI or federal prosecutors, who would spend enormous time and resources linking Liddy (not to mention Mitchell) to the arrested burglars.

I had called Kleindienst's lawyer to see whether his client was amenable to an interview in my office about the Burning Tree episode. Kleindienst was all hail-fellow-well-met bonhomie as he sat across the desk from me. Kleindienst had done some homework and proceeded to blow smoke up my ass about what a great job I had done in winning certain cases back in New York. Consistent with his "we're all colleagues from the good old Department of Justice days," Kleindienst put his feet up on my desk to demonstrate his comfort level. I smiled and suggested that we ought to get down to the reason for my invitation. Grinning broadly, Kleindienst agreed.

"You have the right to remain silent," I said. "You understand that anything you say may be used against you . . ." The former acting attorney general's expression changed like a sudden thunderstorm on a summer afternoon. He didn't like having his Miranda warnings recited to him any more than I liked how he had disregarded his oath of office in favor of his political cronies.

But I did not openly side with Joe Connolly against Jaworski on the Kleindienst plea issue, although I agreed that a slap on the wrist to a high DOJ official who had committed perjury and had kept quiet on June 17 was the wrong message for us to send. Was Jaworski's decision affected by self-protective courtesy from one member of the legal establishment to another? Jaworski was dug in on his decision to give Kleindienst a misdemeanor, and I felt that I couldn't expend any capital disagreeing with Leon on tangential issues while the Nixon decision was yet to be made. Applying this kind of balancing was a new experience for me. Connolly resigned in protest over the Kleindienst misdemeanor plea. The negative publicity stung Jaworski deeply.

As we approached the time for presenting our indictment of the Big Three—Mitchell, Haldeman, and Ehrlichman, the most powerful and influential men in Nixon's administration—the decision on what to do about the president loomed large. The evidence pointed unmistakably to Nixon's participation in the cover-up, but the law was uncertain as to whether a sitting president could be subjected to a criminal indictment while in office. The combination of the potential chaos such an action might bring and the availability of the constitutional remedy of impeachment in the wings solidified Jaworski's determination that indictment of the president was not an option. I agreed, at least while impeachment remained a viable alternative. But a number of issues related to Nixon's role had to be resolved. As time passed, it became clear that Jaworski was unwilling to have the grand jury characterize Nixon's role in any way. Ordinarily, prosecutors either identified unindicted coconspirators in the body of the indictment used to charge those named as defendants, or deferred naming unindicted coconspirators until a "bill of particulars" filed at some point before trial. While Jaworski agreed with us regarding the sufficiency of the evidence against the president, his conservative instincts led him to the unshakable conclusion that he would not get ahead of the curve in characterizing Nixon's role. This should be left to Congress, once it got up to speed on the evidence supporting impeachment. But the courts had denied Congress access to the tapes, the contents of which remained secret, since we had obtained them pursuant to a grand jury subpoena and because we had stringently observed the requirement of grand jury secrecy.

Numerous meetings, accompanied by voluminous written memoranda discussing these issues, took place among various factions within the office. Finally, we were able to persuade Leon that transmittal of the tapes and other evidence we had obtained, assembled in the form of a nonaccusatory "road map," could be presented by the grand jury to Judge Sirica with the request that he allow the package to be transmitted to the House Judiciary Committee while it considered articles of impeachment.

The issue of grand jury action regarding Nixon was more difficult. Jaworski bristled whenever I sought to bring up the subject of Nixon as co-conspirator. But under the rules of evidence, the tape recordings of Nixon and his coterie, which were essential to our proof against the Big Three, would be inadmissible hearsay unless Nixon's role as a coconspirator were accepted by the trial judge as an exception to the hearsay role. Under settled rules of evidence, once the prosecution established the existence of a criminal conspiracy, the statements of any of its members in furtherance of the conspiracy are admissible in evidence against all other members of the conspiracy. This argument appealed to Jaworski the trial lawyer, but Jaworski the establishmentarian was adamant: There would be no mention of Nixon as a coconspirator in the indictment.

After many sleepless nights, I came up with a solution that I thought we might be able to sell to Leon. At some point before trial, a judge would order us to provide a list of unindicted coconspirators in a bill of particulars. At that juncture, we would have to identify Nixon as a member of the conspiracy or risk having the tapes—all of which involved Nixon as an active participant—deemed inadmissible. Jaworski would then be subject to an attack from the White House that he had supplanted the grand jury to brazenly name Nixon when the grand jury itself had done no such thing. Instead, how about allowing the grand jury to vote *now* to authorize the special prosecutor to name a designated list of unindicted coconspirators *later*? There were at least a dozen men who had entered plea bargains or otherwise agreed to cooperate who would eventually be named as unindicted coconspirators. If the grand jury had the opportunity to vote on authorizing Jaworski to name Nixon later, this would accommodate Leon's desire to avoid getting ahead of the curve now and provide cover for him later when the time came to name the coconspirators. I had never heard of any such procedure being employed before, but the circumstances called for some level of creativity. It would also provide us peace of mind that Jaworski wouldn't get cold feet when the time came to speak up.

I put the proposal to Jaworski at a mid-February dinner party Jill Wine hosted at her home, which we had planned several weeks before to welcome the Jaworskis to Washington. I omitted the part about cold feet. Leon listened impassively and said he would get back to us. We waited on tenterhooks for forty-eight hours before Leon gave his assent.

Leon addressed the grand jury personally to explain why Richard Nixon was not included as a named defendant in our proposed indictment. He then explained the procedure for the jury to vote on authorization for him to name specific unindicted coconspirators at the appropriate time prior to trial. As I read the names of the list of proposed unindicted coconspirators, arranged in alphabetical order, the stenographer's eyes opened wide when I got to Richard M. Nixon.

As it turned out, the grand jury's authorization came into play earlier than expected. Following the return of the indictment, we issued a trial subpoena for an additional sixty-four specific tape-recorded conversations. Included in the subpoena was the June 23, 1972, conversation between the president and H. R. Haldeman in which Nixon had orchestrated a plan to have the CIA derail the FBI's investigation into the provenance of the dozens of hundred-dollar bills found on the burglars when they were arrested—bills that had been laundered through a bank in Mexico and would ultimately be traced back to CREEP. Ultimately, the revelation of this "smoking gun" tape proving Nixon's obstruction of the investigation only days after the burglars were caught crushed any remaining political support for Nixon and forced the president to choose between certain impeachment and conviction, or resignation.

But now, two months after the indictment was returned, another court battle loomed over enforcement of our new subpoena. Nixon vowed that he would not turn over more tapes. One of the main arguments put forward by the president's new criminal lawyer, James St. Clair of Boston, was that the tapes failed to meet the legal requirement that subpoenaed materials be "evidentiary" in nature. The tapes we had subpoenaed could not be used at trial because they would be deemed inadmissible hearsay. It appeared the president's strategy was based on the fact that Nixon had not been named in the indictment as a coconspirator. The savvy and experienced St. Clair assumed he had trapped Jaworski. If the special prosecutor sought to counter Nixon's argument by now announcing that Nixon *was* a member of the conspiracy, it would look like he was overreaching the grand jury. But our ability to keep secret the grand jury's vote on the unindicted coconspirators had instead trapped Nixon.

Jaworski's tolerance for White House provocation was already growing thin. Haig had tried an end run around compliance with the new subpoena in a private meeting with Jaworski at the White House that left

Leon with a bad taste in his mouth. Incredibly, Haig had pressed Jaworski to accept a White House *summary* of the sixty-four conversations in lieu of the tapes themselves, and then vouch for the fact that the conversations exonerated Nixon! It was the Stennis compromise on steroids. Referring to unspecified threats and Haig's description of St. Clair as a tough lawyer, Jaworski responded that he had "dealt with tough guys all my life," and that St. Clair was unlikely to scare him. Indeed, I had often thought of how tough it must have been for Jaworski to make his mark in the rough-and-tumble world of Texas law and politics, the son of a preacher with a foreign-sounding name.

Leon was reluctant to spring the grand jury's unindicted coconspirator vote on Haig without first alerting him to the facts that would support our counterargument. So on Sunday afternoon I accompanied Jaworski and Phil Lacovara to the White House. I carried with me the February 25 transcript of the grand jury's vote authorizing us to name Nixon. We arrived at the diplomatic entrance and were ushered into the Map Room. Both Haig and St. Clair had appeared on that morning's talk shows, reiterating Nixon's determination to resist producing more tapes. The decision was final.

I handed the transcript to St. Clair. The color drained from his normally ruddy cheeks as he realized he had been outmaneuvered. Perhaps they would be willing to give us a subset of the sixty-four taped conversations, which we could prioritize, Leon suggested. Then we wouldn't be obliged to disclose Nixon's coconspirator status immediately, although we might have to later, if and when the trial of the Big Three went forward. Haig and St. Clair said they appreciated Jaworski's offer and would like to think about it.

In a public about-face, the White House announced without elaboration that it was considering turning over some additional tapes. We scrambled to cut down our list of sixty-four conversations and provide St. Clair with a list of priorities. We included the June 23 tape on our reduced list. Nixon rejected our proposal. We then proceeded to destroy St. Clair's arguments in our legal briefs.

Personally galling to Jaworski was a newly minted White House legal argument that the special prosecutor lacked legal standing to subpoena the tapes since he was part of the executive branch and, therefore, could not overrule the chief executive. Of course, Jaworski had specifically demanded, and had been granted, the right to go to court to obtain evidence from the White House as a condition of accepting Haig's job offer. Leon saw the White House argument as a personal betrayal by Haig, whom he had always treated as an honorable man. I saw it as par for the course. First Judge Sirica and then the Supreme Court, in a crushing unanimous decision, determined that Richard Nixon was not above the law and would have to turn over the tapes.

The House Judiciary Committee, chaired by Peter Rodino of New Jersey, had Nixon in a vise grip of evidence demonstrating high crimes and misdemeanors warranting impeachment. The president, trapped by his own mendacity, resigned in disgrace on August 9, 1974, fewer than eleven months after the Saturday Night Massacre. Nixon's cynical plan to use the selection of the affable Gerald Ford as his vice president (after Spiro Agnew's resignation in disgrace) as a buffer against his own impeachment proved to be another miscalculation. Congressional leaders, Nixon believed, would conclude that Ford was unqualified to assume the presidency. Given the alternative of permitting Nixon to continue in office, Congress chose Ford.

We were now confronted with the question of what to do with private citizen Nixon. Should the cover-up indictment be superceded to include Nixon along with his former lieutenants? Talk of a presidential pardon was in the air, especially heightened by reports of Nixon's severe depression and deteriorating physical health. Jaworski saw the pardon decision as the monkey on President Ford's back. Leon was unwilling to "adopt the monkey" by initiating action against Nixon. But Ford responded to a question at a press conference three weeks after assuming office, saying he would not make a pardon decision while the matter of Nixon's fate might be determined by the criminal justice system. Jaworski "had an obligation to take whatever action" he deemed appropriate in "conformity with his oath of office," Ford continued. Jaworski reacted with agitation. The monkey had quickly grown to a five-hundred-pound gorilla. Why should he have to make a decision about charging Nixon with a crime if Ford was eventually going to pardon the man who had handed him the presidency? Could Ford be stimulated to show his hand?

A week after Ford's press conference, Jaworski met alone with the new president's White House counsel, Philip Buchen. Leon did not see fit to provide advance notice to anyone on the staff of this meeting. He made clear to Buchen his view that pretrial publicity would preclude any attempt to put Nixon on trial for at least a year. Based on internal memoranda and comments made to staffers, I believe Jaworski also urged Buchen to counsel Ford that if he intended to pardon Nixon he do so immediately, and that if Ford's decision were to be based on the difficulty of Nixon getting a fair trial, Jaworski would not oppose it. Four days after

Jaworski's meeting with Buchen, Gerald Ford announced he was pardoning Nixon. The president gave two reasons—national reconciliation and massive pretrial publicity, which would make a fair trial for Nixon impossible for many months or years. Senator Barry Goldwater of Arizona was among the first to comment publicly, praising Ford's decision as wise and courageous, and noting that Leon Jaworski had serious doubts about whether Nixon could ever get a fair trial.

Incredibly, Ford had not made it a precondition of the pardon that Nixon acknowledge his involvement in a criminal conspiracy. A statement issued from Nixon's San Clemente compound referred only to "mistakes" and "misjudgments," and that Nixon had been wrong not to act "more decisively and more forthrightly" in dealing with Watergate. What a load of crap. Nixon had been forthright and decisive from the beginning—have the CIA block the FBI's investigation of the money chain with a bogus concern over national security, continue hush money payments to the burglars, promise them clemency, lie to the investigators.

I had no argument with Ford's right to pardon Nixon—that was specifically within his constitutional prerogative, for whatever motive. This was a decision for which Ford, for better or worse, would be accountable to the electorate. Indeed, I had no particular interest in seeing a former president stand trial, much less serve a prison sentence if convicted. But the special prosecutor's involvement in accelerating a pardon bereft of accountability was deeply disturbing to me. The cover-up trial was less than two months off. The jury would be sequestered. Had Ford not reversed course from his pledge not to intervene until the system brought a decision to his desk, an indictment could have been presented after the jury was sequestered. Then it would have been up to Nixon whether to accept Ford's pardon in the face of specific charges against him. Instead, decades of Watergate revisionists have denied Nixon's culpability, claiming he was simply driven from office for specious "political" reasons.

Following the pardon, we faced the prospect of trying Nixon's subordinates for the same crime for which their boss had just been pardoned. Jim Neal had returned to the task force and immersed himself in pretrial preparation. Jim was particularly affected by the content and tone of the discussions on the tapes. Nowhere was there any suggestion of taking responsibility for the crimes that had been committed. All we heard was the desperate attempt to choose a scapegoat on whom the others could pin the blame. I was struck by the paralysis that gripped Nixon and his chief lieutenants. The tapes portrayed a seemingly endless series of conversations where the participants, obsessed with Watergate, went round and round searching for a way out.

Neal made good on his earlier promise to share responsibilities at trial, and he allowed me to give the opening statement to the jury and final rebuttal argument. Jim's closing argument was brilliant, the best I have ever seen. The defense lawyers never laid a glove on John Dean. The tapes made him the most thoroughly corroborated witness of all time. All the defendants took the stand in their own defense. Neal expertly cross-examined Mitchell and Ehrlichman and I cross-examined Haldeman. Jill did a great job with Robert Mardian, a political appointee to the Justice Department and hard-core crony of Mitchell's. George Frampton, Gerry Goldman, and Larry Iason provided the same consistently outstanding preparation that they had from day one—giving the courtroom players the wherewithal to maximize our effectiveness.

In fact, once we got the tapes, the evidence was so overwhelming the only chance the Big Three had was if we screwed up. We didn't. Jaworski felt that matters were so well in hand that he returned to Texas, resigning as special prosecutor two days after the jury was selected, a decision for which he took some heat. But Leon's decision to resign didn't shock me. At sixty-nine years of age, he had given a year of his life to return to public service. He had accomplished what he had set out to do. All in all, he had overseen a definitive, if not a perfect, conclusion to an extraordinary assignment. The jury had no trouble finding Haldeman, Ehrlichman, and Mitchell guilty of conspiracy to obstruct justice and perjury, and Judge Sirica sent them to prison.

I resigned after the briefs for the appeal were finished and then coauthored *Stonewall*, with my colleague and friend George Frampton. The title came from Nixon's tape-recorded conversation with John Mitchell, on March 22, 1973, in which he admonished his former attorney general:

> *I don't give a shit what happens. I want you all to stonewall it, let them plead the Fifth Amendment, cover-up or anything else, if it'll save it—save the plan. That's the whole point.*

———

THE TAPES THE WATERGATE Special Prosecution Force pried from the White House in 1973 were only a sampling, albeit a well-informed one, of Watergate-related conversations among the president and his closest aides. The voice-activated taping system captured conversations not only from hidden bugs in the Oval Office, but also in Nixon's hideaway office in the Executive Office Building next door to the White House, in the Cabinet Room, at Camp David, and on various telephones the president used regularly. Under the terms of an agreement reached with the Ford administration at the time of his resignation, and for the next two decades, Nixon waged a protracted legal battle to keep the remaining tapes from public scrutiny. Had they been released sooner than the 1996 date eventually mandated by Congress, Nixon's attempt to rehabilitate himself as a "senior statesman" would have been a nonstarter.

The focus by the media in reporting on titillating new information in subsequent releases of tapes over the years resulted in headline stories focusing on Nixon's penchant for making anti-Semitic remarks, including a conversation with the Reverend Billy Graham, of all people, in which the two men discussed their perception of Jewish influence in the media and Nixon's intention in his second term to take action to lessen that influence. The new tapes showed Nixon's preoccupation—abetted by Haldeman and Colson—with Jewish employees of federal agencies and Jewish contributors to the Democratic Party.

But it was left to serious scholars, notably Professor Stanley Kutler of the University of Wisconsin, to identify and laboriously transcribe a trove of additional Nixon recordings held at the National Archives. President Ford's unconditional pardon of Richard Nixon left the door open for a variety of Nixon apologists to continue to minimize Nixon's role in the Watergate cover-up. But the new tapes transcribed by Kutler and others who followed will forever slam the door on such revisionists for anyone who has the time or inclination to look at the evidence.

Even with my high threshold for surprise—the product of decades of being immersed in the Washington scene—there was a plethora of jaw-dropping material contained in the newly released tapes. For example, only an hour after Nixon's March 21, 1973, meeting with Dean and Haldeman, the president met in the Oval Office with Rosemary Woods, his devoted personal assistant and secretary. Nixon told Woods, "We at the present time may have a need for substantial cash for a personal purpose," and asked her how much cash she had on hand. Using a shorthand they both plainly understood, Woods referenced a cash hoard, the exact amount of which was uncertain. "I would have to look . . . I'd have to get in the safe [which Woods revealed in a later tape was in her home]. I don't remember." Later on, Nixon used Woods as an intermediary to get a message to Tom Pappas, a prominent supporter of the Fascist colonels who had seized power in Greece and now a reliable Nixon contributor, who had chipped in a healthy sum in cash to the hush money pot. Nixon had met with Haldeman in early March to discuss Pappas's request that the "pro-colonels" U.S. ambassador to Greece not be removed, as the administration had planned to do. Haldeman reports that John Mitchell, who is depending on Pappas for cash, says it would be "a very useful thing not to disrupt" the status quo. Nixon responds, "Good. I understand. No problem. Pappas has raised the money for his other activity or whatever it is. How's he doing?" Haldeman relates how Pappas's business dealings in Greece are making him fabulously rich.

"Great! I'm just delighted," Nixon said.

Haldeman added, "And he's able to deal in cash."

Of particular concern to Nixon was the fact that he had met with Pappas in the Oval Office on March 7, 1973, to personally thank him for his help. "I'm aware of what you are doing to help us," Nixon told his Greek-American benefactor. Pappas related how he made a dozen trips since January, presumably from Greece to the United States, carrying cash. Later, on June 6, fearful that his connection to Pappas could be revealed, Nixon reminded Rosemary Woods that he had met with Pappas on March 7: "On that occasion I thanked him for raising money . . . but I just want to make damned sure that Pappas, Jesus, . . . I don't want anything indicating that I was thanking him for raising money for the Watergate defendants. I think he's smart enough to know that, . . . but you just never know." Woods dutifully agreed to meet with Pappas to convey the message.

The newly released tapes showed that the firing of Archie Cox was foreshadowed well before the existence of the taping system was revealed by Alexander Butterfield. Cox's stature in the eyes of Nixon, Haig, and Buzhardt quickly evolved from Nixon's "he's not a mean man," "a good man," and "believe me, if [Richardson would] get Cox [to be special prosecutor], that'd be great. Fine. Fine," and Haig's "he's not a zealot," during their May 18 conversation, perhaps because they believed the professorial Cox didn't have the skill set to unravel the conspiracy. A week later, Haig expressed his belief that Cox would be "ineffective"; "he'll have these cases so screwed up nobody will ever be brought to court." But as soon as it became clear that the special prosecutor was determined to subpoena White House documents if they were not furnished voluntarily, Nixon instructed Buzhardt to get tough: "We've just got to be ready to kick him right in the teeth." By June 7, 1973, more than four months before the Saturday Night Massacre, Nixon confided to Haig, "I think it might not be beyond the pale, Al, to think in terms of it's maybe in our interest to get him out of there. You understand?" Haig: "He's a sonofabitch." Henry Kissinger fanned the flames on June 19: "[Cox] is a *fanatic* liberal Democrat and all his associates are fanatics."

By July 11, Cox's first name had been replaced by sonofabitch. "That sonofabitch Cox . . . ," Nixon groused, "we gotta get a case on him, that's the point."

And on July 12, the day before the taping system was turned off, Nixon again turned to the strategy of firing Cox, telling Haig, "But, by God, Buzhardt or somebody . . . gotta get off their ass and get up to chapter and verse on what Cox and his colleagues have said, which indicate, you know, 'We're out to get the President' and all that stuff." One can only imagine the invective that Nixon and his new team of enablers, Haig and Buzhardt, would spew against Cox in the ensuing months as Archie made known his intention to follow the evidence wherever it might lead.

THIRTY-FIVE YEARS HAVE PASSED since Richard Nixon's resignation. Watergate is the iconic political scandal of our time. The suffix "-gate" has been appended to all manner of scandals and pseudoscandals that have arisen in the ensuing years in the United States and overseas. At the time, the common wisdom was that Watergate demonstrated that "the system worked" and showed that "no man is above the law." The nation was able to rid itself of a president whose obsessive desire to punish his critics and political enemies led to the criminal misuse of the power of his office. Nixon's philosophy—"It's not illegal if the president does it"—was soundly rejected by the public, the press, the judiciary, and Congress. Having surrounded himself with sycophants who catered to his darker impulses, men who competed for the president's favor by demonstrating their commitment to the bare-knuckled, tough-guy approach Nixon savored, Nixon could not escape the consequences of their actions. Nor could his closest aides. His chief of staff, attorney general, chief domestic adviser, White House counsel, personal attorney, and a squadron of lesser White House and campaign officials all went to prison.

It could be said that the institutions of government functioned just as the Framers of the Constitution had intended, and the nation's most powerful leader, had he not taken preemptive action by resigning, would have been removed without bloodshed or chaos. This was rightly deemed a great accomplishment, and I was proud to have played a role in bringing the facts to light.

But the system almost didn't work. Had Nixon not tape-recorded his conspiratorial skullduggery, it is a fair bet that his top underlings would have been able to escape punishment, and the plan to stanch the bleeding at Dean's level would have succeeded. I have no doubt that without the incriminating tapes, Nixon would have served out his term.

Had Nixon destroyed the tapes after presidential assistant Alexander Butterfield revealed their existence, particularly had he done so before any subpoenas were issued by the special prosecutor or Congress, it is also likely he would have been able to serve out his term of office. While claims of obstruction of the investigation would have accurately portrayed his defiance, without the actual incriminating evidence on the tapes, I believe there would not have been sufficient congressional will to sustain impeachment, much less conviction by the Senate. Nixon could have argued plausibly that he needed to destroy the tapes because disclosure of their contents would have been a betrayal of the trust of the many individuals who spoke with him, unaware they were being secretly recorded.

In retrospect, it seems that Nixon miscalculated at every important fork in the road during Watergate. Had he not named an outsider, L. Patrick Gray, to succeed J. Edgar Hoover, he would not have created the enmity of Mark Felt (aka Deep Throat), who expected to be tapped as the next FBI director and began to leak information to Bob Woodward. Had he not sought to make Elliot Richardson attorney general, he might not have had to endure appointment of a special prosecutor, and certainly not Archibald Cox. The ham-fisted use of force in the Saturday Night Massacre brought about a dramatic shift in public opinion from which Nixon never recovered. Nixon also misjudged Leon Jaworski—whose establishment credentials and willingness to negotiate privately with the White House did not overcome his determination to see the president removed from office, once he was persuaded of Nixon's active participation in a criminal conspiracy.

Watergate also demonstrated that while we are a nation governed by the rule of law, the identity of the individuals charged with carrying out those laws may determine whether the ultimate result is righteous. Without the courage and independence of Judge John Sirica, a seventy-two-year-old Republican who would not tolerate his courtroom being used for obstruction of justice, or his grand jury being denied the right to obtain evidence—even from a sitting president—Watergate might well have had a truncated ending. Senator Sam Ervin and Congressman Peter Rodino, each in his own way, provided essential leadership at critical points in the process. The courage and integrity of Katharine Graham and the experienced journalists at the *Washington Post* who supervised two young and aggressive reporters, Bob Woodward and Carl Bernstein, who were willing to defy the very real threats of economic retaliation by the White House and print the truth, were critical to moving the investigation forward.

And of course, the one-two punch of Archibald Cox and Leon Jaworski, so different in many ways, was critical. Each played a unique role in pursuing the evidence that made the denouement of Nixon's resignation in the face of certain impeachment seemingly inevitable. But was it?

With the benefit of three more decades of Washington experience since Watergate, I'm convinced that the most significant factor in Nixon's eventual demise was that the Democrats had majorities in both houses of Congress. Had the Republicans been in control, there would have been no bargain to appoint an independent prosecutor as a condition of confirming a new attorney general. With the political appointees at the Justice Department still in control, there would have been no decision to subpoena the tapes. And the existence of the secret tapes would not have been revealed but for the creation of a Senate investigatory committee with subpoena power and the willingness to ferret out the truth. Under a Republican-controlled Senate, any impulse to conduct a vigorous investigation of misconduct in the executive branch would have been sharply curtailed.

———

WATERGATE REPRESENTS THE END of American innocence and the beginning of a new cynicism about our national leaders. Combined with Lyndon Johnson's lies and misrepresentations about the Vietnam War, Nixon's barefaced exploitation of an American public that wanted to believe their president would not lie to them destroyed the bonds of trust that we held as part of our contract with our highest elected official.

The post-Watergate reforms aimed at curbing the corrosive effects of money in politics lasted for a decade or so, until the combination of creative lawyers exploiting loopholes in campaign finance laws and congressional lack of will to plug the loopholes essentially nullified the temporary fix. The public's outrage over excesses in presidential power proved to be short-lived as well. The Reagan administration's sorry record in the Iran-Contra affair never generated the same outcry as Watergate, perhaps because the nation was still reeling from the trauma of Watergate, and certainly because Ronald Reagan's popularity insulated him from true accountability. Aspects of that scandal, particularly the revelation of a secret, off-the-books paramilitary operation being run out of the White House and funded by personal contributions by autocratic heads of state, were deeply troubling.

The march toward a dominant and largely unchecked executive branch was dramatically demonstrated by the first six years of George W. Bush's administration, where Republican majorities in the House and Senate resulted in a feckless Congress that was AWOL when it came to meaningful oversight. The lessons of Vietnam proved heartbreakingly forgotten; the elimination of the draft has resulted in a far more docile electorate, slow to react to shortsighted and unprincipled use of force abroad. Changes in the economics of the news business showed the press to be largely out to lunch, except when it came to the all-important tracking of celebrity-related scandals or the sexual peccadilloes of elected officials.

In the end, I look back on Watergate as an aberration. We saw a deeply flawed and fundamentally unlikable president, congressional leaders of the opposition party empowered and willing to investigate excesses of executive power, a nationally respected newspaper willing to investigate and print, notwithstanding the risk of threatened reprisals, two special prosecutors determined to carry out their sworn responsibilities efficiently and capably, and a federal judge who, in the twilight of his career, decided that the president of the United States was obliged to obey the law and provide evidence to a grand jury, backed up by a unanimous Supreme Court, including four justices appointed by that same president.

Memo to future presidents: Don't tape yourself committing a crime.

CHAPTER TWO

United States v. Sweig and Voloshen

W ho was this brash young lawyer who had gone toe-to-toe with the Nixon White House in the aftermath of the Saturday Night Massacre?" you may be asking. Even if you're not, here is the obligatory biographical interlude.

I was born in Brooklyn—America's "fertile crescent," if those of us who share such provenance do say so ourselves. In 1945, my dad returned from service in the Army Air Corps in the European theater. Until then, it had just been my mother and me for my first two and a half years, in a third-floor walk-up apartment on Avenue N and East 3rd Street. My mother imbued in me her sense of fairness—learned during a tough time as a foster child from the age of five, at a time when families took in foster children for the extra few dollars it would bring. Sylvia went through life by her childhood nickname of Toby, given when she was placed with a family that already had one Sylvia. She had a keen awareness of inequality of treatment and a well-honed skepticism of people who promised one thing but delivered another. Toby taught me to stand up to bullies and to root for the underdog.

My mom's opinionated, in-your-face personality allowed me some poetic license in describing her to friends. By the time I was in college, I had invented an early career for her as a roller derby queen—Tuffy Schultz (her maiden name) of the New York Chiefs. Somehow, this description found its way into a newspaper profile of me during Watergate. Toby took to the notion of being a former roller derby queen, and in later years would embellish the joke with reminiscences of her days with skates flashing and elbows flying.

My dad, Isaac, returned from the war in a hurry to resume his job as a salesman for a textile importer in Manhattan's garment district. Although the GI Bill was available, the immediate challenge of supporting a family took priority. It was left to me and my younger sister, Lorraine, along with the cousins of my generation to be the first in our family to graduate from college.

The postwar years were a time of exuberant celebration of America's values and power. We had saved Europe (and the Far East) from the rapacious Axis powers bent on world domination. We had fought a just war and won. Our public school civics lessons taught us the blessings of living in a democracy created by our revered Founding Fathers. There was nothing beyond our reach—we were a "can-do" nation willing to make sacrifices when the chips were down. President Eisenhower was an easygoing war hero who focused the nation on peace and prosperity.

I don't remember how old I was when I first learned about the Holocaust. The knowledge of what had happened in Europe had a profound effect on how I viewed the world and those who run it. But for the "accident" of my grandparents immigrating to the United States, it was more likely than not that I would have been murdered as a small child—simply by reason of my identity as a Jew. The fact that these crimes resulted from official policy of a German government that came to power through manipulation of the democratic process—carried out against men and women who were loyal citizens, in some cases war heroes of their own country—was a lesson seared into my psyche. Could something similar ever happen in the United States? No matter what constitutional protections were in place, who had the responsibility to make sure our political leaders and institutions protected those least able to protect themselves?

Perhaps the most important event in my young life was being admitted to Stuyvesant High School, one of New York City's premier public schools. Admission to Stuyvesant was open to all boys (girls were not admitted until 1969) in the five boroughs of New York. The single criterion for admission was a pupil's score on a citywide test. Housed in its original decrepit 1904 building on the edge of Manhattan's Lower East Side, Stuyvesant was a nightmare to get to from Laurelton, the middle-class enclave of single-family homes on the Queens border with Nassau County where we moved in the mid-fifties. My school day began and ended with an hour-and-a-half bus and subway ride. The school's athletic facilities were nonexistent and—did I mention?—no girls. I was beginning to feel my teenage oats—interested in girls and in running track. And I certainly had no interest in spending more than three hours every day commuting. But Stuyvesant offered academic opportunities comparable to the best private schools, to study under teachers who themselves competed to be able to teach in an atmosphere free from discipline problems or other distractions. Stuyvesant boys were there to learn, to advance themselves beyond the station of their parents' generation through rigorous academic achievement and the opportunities that would follow. I was encouraged to open my eyes and ears—to think on my own and not be afraid to ask questions.

The jump from challenging received wisdom to challenging authority was not difficult. I was becoming aware that platitudes about equality and opportunity did not apply to all sectors of our society, most notably to people of color—then called Negroes. Being an avid Brooklyn Dodgers fan, I could identify with the egalitarian justice of giving Jackie Robinson and Roy Campanella and Junior Gilliam the opportunity to compete— literally on a level playing field. I began to ask questions: Why shouldn't Negroes be allowed the same chance as others? Why were there no Negroes on the (hated) Yankees? Where was the justice in Jim Crow laws in Southern states that discriminated against Negro soldiers returning from World War II battlefields?

Rock and roll was sweeping New York, a challenge to our parents' generation of music. Black artists were in the vanguard of the doo-wop sound of the 1950s, further breaking down barriers between race and class. *MAD* magazine skewered the establishment with devilish accuracy.

I had a summer job every year from the age of twelve. Caddying, running a hotel elevator, busing tables, parking cars at a beach club (three years before I was old enough for a driver's license), pushing a hand truck in the garment center, working beer and laundry delivery routes, and a variety of office jobs put me next to a wide variety of workingmen and -women. As much as anything else, these summer jobs provided me with a valuable advantage in my chosen profession as a courtroom lawyer. When it came time to pick a jury and make a closing argument, I knew whom I was talking to.

THE CULMINATION OF ACADEMIC achievement from Stuyvesant High School, on through Muhlenberg College, Columbia Law School, and

Northwestern (where I had earned a postgraduate law degree on a Ford Foundation fellowship)—everything I had worked for—arrived in the form of an offer by Robert Morgenthau to join his office and become a federal prosecutor in New York. Officially known as the United States Attorney's Office for the Southern District of New York, Morgenthau had established that office as the most professional, independent, and aggressive of all the U.S. attorneys' offices in the country. In the seven years since his appointment by President Kennedy, Bob, son of Henry Morgenthau, FDR's legendary secretary of the treasury, had built a prosecutorial juggernaut. Breaking with tradition, Morgenthau hired young lawyers without regard to political affiliation—indeed, it was an article of faith that no question regarding political persuasion would be asked of the applicants to the office.

The political independence of the office was underscored by a story told and retold about how one of New York's powerful political leaders had contacted Morgenthau soon after he took office. It seemed that the leader's law firm had a client who was under federal investigation. The politico settled into an easy chair in Morgenthau's commodious office, lit up a cigar, and explained that he was not asking for any favorable consideration regarding the outcome of the client's case. He only wanted a brief delay in any decision to indict the man, as certain questions regarding payment of fees still needed to be worked out. The leader thanked Morgenthau for his understanding, wished the new U.S. attorney well, and left with a smile on his face.

Morgenthau immediately found out which of his assistants was handling the case and summoned him to his office.

"Where are you in the Jones investigation?"

The assistant U.S. attorney stammered that he didn't regard the Jones matter as a priority and hadn't done much work on it lately.

"Does the evidence warrant presenting the case to the grand jury for indictment?"

"I believe it does," answered the puzzled assistant.

"Then I want the case presented ASAP. Is next week doable?"

The answer was yes.

"Then do it."

It was only sometime later that the reason for Morgenthau's interest became known to his staff. But news of what that SOB Morgenthau had done traveled like wildfire through the community of politicos, hacks, and influence peddlers. Anyone who expected Morgy to play ball would be in for a nasty surprise.

At not yet twenty-five years of age when Bob Morgenthau swore me in, I was the youngest lawyer to join the office in anyone's memory. Normally, a lawyer had to have two or three years' experience in private practice or have clerked with a federal judge to be considered. I was sure that the recommendations of my two Northwestern mentors—James Thompson and Joel Flaum (incidentally, both Republicans)—had swayed Morgenthau to accept my year of postgraduate legal studies as meeting the "practice" requirement.

To be working for a man whose only requirement was that we "do the right thing" was the closest thing to professional heaven for a young, idealistic lawyer determined to make a difference. My five years at the U.S. attorney's office were the most important of my career, for it was there that I learned the meaning of public service, while at the same time began to learn to be a trial lawyer. The friendships I made with colleagues during those years have been among my most treasured. I can never repay the debt of gratitude I owe to Bob Morgenthau for giving me that opportunity and to his Republican successor, Whitney North Seymour Jr., for promoting me up the ranks.

Young lawyers' training consisted of a period of informal apprenticeship to more senior prosecutors, while at the same time cutting their teeth on straightforward and uncomplicated cases involving less serious federal crimes—forged checks, thefts from the mail, interstate transportation of stolen vehicles, and the like. The philosophy of the office was to give young prosecutors as much responsibility as they could handle.

From the moment of my first jury trial, I realized that this was something I could do and enjoy. All of my doubts about law school and choosing the legal profession vanished. Everything before was part of the ticket of admission to becoming a courtroom lawyer. It seemed that all of my summer job experiences, the self-confidence I had gained from being on my own, the understanding and empathy I had gained from men and women who struggled to make ends meet, had all come together. I relished the opportunity to question witnesses and to put my case before the jury in opening statements and final arguments. And I quickly began to appreciate the power that a federal prosecutor has over the lives of individuals and their families who would be affected profoundly by their entanglement with the criminal justice system. I learned that federal prosecutors have enormous discretion in making decisions about whether to file charges and who should be charged. "Do the right thing" was our only marching order.

From my point of view, the most interesting cases in the office involved organized crime and labor racketeering. After long neglect, and under the prodding of Attorney General Bobby Kennedy, the FBI had begun to focus on the deadly grip the Mafia had over certain industries and their related labor unions—refuse carting, transportation, the docks, to name a few. I sought out my more experienced colleagues who were handling these cases to see if I could make myself useful, hoping to get a second or third chair in a big trial. Paul Rooney, a dapper redhead who sported a goatee, took a liking to me and gave me my first chance. In *United States v. Plumeri et al.*, the defendants were charged in a kickback scheme involving corrupt union officials and a capo in the Genovese Mafia family, James "Jimmy Doyle" Plumeri. We won the case, or rather, Paul Rooney won the case—he let me question a few witnesses—against some of the most experienced and successful criminal defense lawyers in New York.

I began to get the reputation as a streetwise kid who was not intimidated by the courtroom or big guns in the defense bar. This was heady stuff, perhaps a bit much for a twenty-five-year-old to handle gracefully. I had just gotten my picture in the *New York Daily News* in connection with a Mafia case I was prosecuting. That evening, my cousin Stan telephoned me from his apartment in Brooklyn.

"Hey, cuz, I saw your picture in the *News* today." Stan is the most family-minded of my cousins and has made keeping close tabs on us an avocation.

"Yeah," I began, "it's quite an interesting case—this Mafioso . . ." I went on, about to launch into a soliloquy on fighting crime in the federal courthouse.

"I was riding on the subway," Stan interrupted, "and I looked down, and I was standing on your face."

Stan's observation, quite sincerely made, provided a rare moment of epiphany. Getting my picture in a newspaper was not really that big a deal, and I had better keep a rein on my ego, lest I find myself counted among the pompous, self-important characters I found so insufferable. Years later, during Watergate, when I got a good bit of press attention, a reporter asked me how I was able to handle so much publicity without getting a swelled head. I smiled, thinking of Cousin Stan's timely comment. I have made a conscious effort not to take myself too seriously, while not detracting from the seriousness of my professional pursuits.

I continued to work with Rooney and his colleagues, Elkan Abramowitz, Paul Galvani, and Paul Perito, all members of the organized crime and special prosecutions unit. Soon, I made the transition from the short trials unit to special prosecutions. It was here I got my chance to work on an investigation that tested Bob Morgenthau's political independence and became the biggest case in the office. Rooney and Abramowitz were working on an investigation that grew out of information from a shadowy private investigator who had a falling-out with a disreputable client. The PI talked about secret tape recordings and claims that a Manhattan state court judge was on the take and was fixing cases. My eyes must have grown as big as saucers. Secret recordings, a microphone disguised as a tennis racquet tie tack, a corrupt New York Supreme Court judge!

The investigation implicated a New York lawyer named Nathan Voloshen. Voloshen, a diminutive, balding man in his late sixties, had a stable of clients from organized crime figures to stock swindlers under investigation by the SEC. According to the information we were receiving, Voloshen was able to get results—for which he charged handsome fees—by pulling strings not only in the New York State courts but with federal authorities as well. Where did Voloshen get his juice?

The answer was not long in coming. FBI surveillance showed that Voloshen took the 7 A.M. Eastern Airlines Shuttle from LaGuardia to Washington, DC, every Tuesday and Thursday. He was picked up by a limo with official government plates. His destination: the office of Speaker of the House John W. McCormack, the most powerful elected official in the United States after the president himself.

PAUL ROONEY POKED HIS head into my office on the fourth floor of the federal courthouse in Foley Square. "I want you to sit in on an interview with me. Some guy just called me from a pay phone in the Nedick's across the street. He claims to have highly sensitive information about judicial corruption in the state courts, and doesn't trust the FBI or anyone other than Morgenthau to give it to. I don't want to talk to this guy alone—you need to be a witness."

"Lucky I was in my office," I thought as I jumped out of my desk chair and hurried to keep up. "All Rooney needs is a body to sit in. If not me, then the next guy down the hall."

Ted Ratnoff was one of the least attractive people I had ever met. Bald, overweight, and with a complexion so sallow he appeared never to have ventured out of doors. From his thick, horn-rimmed glasses and mismatched clothes, his appearance shouted "nerd." In a nasal, New York accent, Ratnoff explained that his genius for developing eavesdropping equipment was so far superior to what the feds had available that it had put him crossways with the FBI, who showed an unwelcome interest in his activities as a private investigator. To emphasize his point, he displayed a gold-colored tie tack in the shape of a tennis racquet, which he claimed concealed a microphone that could broadcast conversations to a tape recorder in a suitcase several blocks away. Rooney and I glanced at each other, conveying the unstated opinion that we were dealing with a rattlesnake who might easily be recording us at that moment.

Finally, the well-named Ratnoff got to the point. He had heard from sources he had in the legal community (we later learned it was from a lawyer named Richard Wels for whom he had done investigative work) that Morgenthau's office was investigating Mitchell Schweitzer, a justice of the New York Supreme Court. Ratnoff claimed to have information about Schweitzer's relationship with a lawyer in town named Nathan Voloshen who was able to get favored treatment for his clients from Schweitzer. He wanted to make clear he would not be a witness. As we silently pondered when Ratnoff would get around to revealing what he wanted in return for providing information, Rooney pressed on for details. Ratnoff was obliging. As he rattled off names, I scribbled notes, trying to keep up.

Finally, Ratnoff suggested that we could really benefit from employing his electronic surveillance equipment as we pursued our investigation. It also seemed apparent that Ratnoff had had a falling-out with one of his clients and wouldn't mind seeing him bloodied in the investigation. Such is the business of investigating corruption. It is unlikely (though not out of the question) that those in possession of damaging information come by it strictly by honest chance. Human nature being what it is, information becomes a tradable commodity, favorable treatment excusing a witness's own misdeeds being the most common request. But sometimes revenge can be a strong motivator to drop the dime (that's what it used to cost to place a call on a pay phone) on an enemy or rival.

Paul was cordial but noncommittal. He would see what he could do. Ratnoff provided a byzantine method of getting in touch with him and bid us good-bye. I could not wait to wash up after shaking his clammy hand.

I waited expectantly for Paul to fill me in on what was going on. "We've got a lot of leads to follow up. I hope you've got some time to put into this." He didn't have to ask twice. Just like that, I was in on the hottest investigation in the U.S. attorney's office. Rooney and Ekan Abramowitz of the special prosecutions unit were working on a hush-hush investigation that started from information provided by Herbert Itkin, a star informant with reputed CIA connections who had worked as an undercover informant for the FBI. Itkin, a labor lawyer, had been able to gain the trust of labor racketeers and their Mafia henchmen, all the while reporting to his handlers at the FBI. A number of high-profile cases resulted, among them the prosecution of the powerful Tammany Hall leader Carmine De Sapio and Mafia don Anthony "Tony Ducks" Corallo. Elkan Abramowitz, a tall, outgoing, and accessible fellow, had successfully prosecuted labor racketeer Jack McCarthy, one of Voloshen's clients, and sent him to jail. Rooney, physically fit and always impeccably dressed, from wingtips up to his homburg, was more reserved than Elkan, but he had a sharp wit and, like Elkan, a well-developed sense of the absurd. I had learned a great deal from second-chairing Paul in the Plumeri trial and was eager to work with him again. Only six or seven years older than I, both struck me as grown-ups. I was still a kid.

Because of the obvious sensitivity of the investigation, the team would regularly brief Bob Morgenthau. This provided my first invitation into the inner sanctum. I was in high cotton. I would never have dreamed of calling this older man (almost fifty!) Bob, and since "Mr. Morgenthau" was too formal, I followed the lead of my colleagues, who addressed him as "Boss." He didn't seem to mind. In fact, I think he enjoyed it.

Morgenthau gave us the green light to take the investigation wherever it might lead. With the benefit of the intervening years, I can only marvel at the commitment to independence and integrity that Bob Morgenthau displayed in giving his young assistants the discretion to pursue an investigation that might implicate a top national figure in his own political party. Many alumni of Morgenthau's eight-year stint as U.S. attorney have gone on to prominence as judges, practicing lawyers, and teachers. Bob Morgenthau stayed true to his natural calling as a tough, independent-minded prosecutor of unimpeachable ethics. Elected district attorney for New York County in 1974, he is still in office.

As we began to develop the evidence, we learned what a busy little bee Voloshen had been. Ratnoff's and Itkin's leads had only scratched the surface. We were finding that the Speaker's name had been invoked on behalf of Voloshen's clients in a wide variety of matters ranging from helping convicted mobsters get out of jail early to granting high-rolling corporate executives unprecedented access to the chairman of the Securities and Exchange Commission.

Once the role of the Speaker's office surfaced, the FBI agents assigned to the investigation became suddenly unavailable. J. Edgar Hoover, it seemed, was not about to involve the bureau in investigating the most powerful man in the U.S. Congress, which, not incidentally, controlled the FBI's budget. In place of FBI shoe leather, we used the power of grand jury subpoenas to continue the investigation, compelling witnesses to testify upon threat of prosecution for contempt if they refused and perjury if they were untruthful.

We learned that Voloshen's principal juice came from the Speaker's office, and that the Speaker's longtime administrative assistant, Martin Sweig, acted as Voloshen's facilitator and right-hand man. Not only was Voloshen picked up from the airport by the Speaker's driver and taken to McCormack's district office in the Rayburn Office Building, he actually sat behind McCormack's desk while making and receiving phone calls and greeting clients—all with Sweig's active support. Meanwhile, John McCormack operated out of the lavish suite of offices set aside for the Speaker's use in the Capitol. Voloshen would make calls to the Bureau of Prisons, the SEC, and the Department of Justice, expressing the Speaker's interest in this matter or that. Sweig would invariably follow up, confirming Voloshen's representations. We needed to find out the level of McCormack's personal involvement in and awareness of what was going on in his office. As the investigation progressed, we saw patterns develop of calls being placed opening doors, asking for specific action—all with the invocation of Speaker McCormack's personal interest in the matter.

Voloshen, however, was not always successful. Imperiously, he made the mistake of refusing to return the up-front money he had taken in a number of cases, creating a subclass of very unhappy customers. Among these were a Frenchwoman who had paid Voloshen $2,000 to fix a forgery case, and a convicted swindler named Eddie Gilbert whose family had paid Voloshen upward of $25,000 to reduce his sentence with little to show for it. With these and other former clients willing to come forward and testify about being cheated by Voloshen, we decided to open a second front—charging Voloshen with mail and wire fraud for falsely claiming to have paid off various officials. Let him counter with a defense of bribery, we reasoned.

Various witnesses claimed that Sweig could and did mimic his boss's voice on the telephone, and that he could and did sign McCormack's name to official correspondence. Other witnesses overheard Voloshen imitating Sweig's voice on the telephone. Thankfully, no one claimed that anyone was pretending to be Voloshen.

The big question was why the Speaker gave Voloshen the run of his office, and why Sweig and/or McCormack were extending themselves for Voloshen. Clearly, Voloshen was raking in substantial amounts—$10,000 here, $25,000 there, and as much as $50,000 for arranging a meeting for the chairman of the Parvin-Dohrmann Corporation with Hamer Budge, head of the Securities and Exchange Commission. Was Voloshen bribing McCormack, Sweig, or both?

The time had come to pay a call on McCormack. Arrangements were made for us to interview the Speaker in Washington. At the last moment, Morgenthau decided to add some gravitas to our team by asking one of his most senior assistants, Peter Fleming, to lead our expedition and serve as chief of protocol. Fleming, already well on his way to becoming one of the preeminent trial lawyers in the nation, got a quick synopsis of the investigation as we traveled from New York to Washington.

The four of us met the Speaker in his office in the Capitol. No one could fail to be impressed by the grandeur and history of that building. I had never before been inside the Capitol. Now I had the Speaker of the House as my tour guide. McCormack could not have been more gracious, treating our visiting delegation as though we were simply curious tourists. He explained that Nat Voloshen was a dear old friend who was very thoughtful and courteous. Yes, he would have no problem extending him the hospitality of his office, but he was sure that Nat would do nothing improper. Moreover, Voloshen spent his time at McCormack's district office in the Rayburn Building, which McCormack assured us he rarely visited himself, as his duties as Speaker kept him exclusively in the Capitol.

Tall, rail thin, and grandfatherly, he showed us the memorabilia in his office and escorted us to see his district office where Voloshen held court. Fleming pointed to a beautiful replica of a sailing ship and engaged the Speaker in a discussion of the merchant trade from Boston harbor. "You must have many fond memories surrounded by all these mementos," Fleming ventured. The Speaker stayed right on message. "Mr. Fleming, I spend almost no time in this office." We politely inquired about McCormack's recollection of the laundry list of Voloshen clients whom we had learned supposedly had the backing of the Speaker's office. None rang a bell. We told McCormack we would probably have to take his testimony under oath at some point in order to formalize his recollection for the grand jury. The Speaker responded as though nothing would give him greater pleasure than to help us.

We made our way back to New York and reported on our meeting to Bob Morgenthau. Our marching orders were to push on with the investigation, focus on the relationship between Voloshen and Martin Sweig, and be on the lookout for any signs of Voloshen funneling money to McCormack or Sweig. Clearly, the Speaker's office was at the core of Voloshen's influence-peddling operation. But had a crime been committed?

Meanwhile, another drama was playing out that would have a profound effect on the U.S. attorney's office. Richard Nixon had defeated Hubert Humphrey in the November 1968 presidential election. Traditionally, each U.S. attorney throughout the country would submit his or her resignation coincident with the inauguration of a new president. Morgenthau chose not to follow tradition. Technically, Morgenthau's four-year term of office extended until June 1971. And rumor had it that Nixon wanted to select a political crony for the U.S. attorney's position in the Southern District of New York. Morgenthau had created what was regarded as the premier federal prosecutor's office in America; he was not about to turn over the keys to a political hack. Moreover, there were pending trials against Tammany Hall leader Carmine De Sapio and former Joe McCarthy apparatchik Roy Cohn to see through. Morgenthau received support from both Republican senators from New York, a ringing endorsement for the nonpartisan record he had achieved.

Nixon, and his new attorney general, John Mitchell, proceeded gingerly, mindful of Morgenthau's stellar reputation for prosecuting financial swindlers and organized crime kingpins. Morgenthau would have to be dealt with carefully. Nixon and Mitchell chose the power of the purse as their primary weapon, launching a war of attrition against the boss. No new hires were authorized. Not only was normal growth stunted, but the usual turnover of people leaving the office was beginning to leave us understaffed. Then, normal operational funds were dramatically cut back. We responded by launching paper clip drives and buying our legal pads and pens with our own money. The effect was obvious. Espirit de corps among Morgenthau's assistants, while normally high, soared to an unprecedented level.

Meanwhile, the Voloshen investigation proceeded full bore, as we put scores of witnesses under oath before the grand jury. The more evidence we compiled of blatant influence peddling, the more puzzling the mystery of why the Speaker had allowed it to happen.

By all accounts, John McCormack lived an exceptionally modest lifestyle. He was first elected to Congress in 1928, when Calvin Coolidge was in the White House. He and his wife moved into a three-room suite at the Hotel Washington, where they stayed for the next forty-two years, as he was reelected from his South Boston district in the next twenty elections. The seventy-eight-year-old McCormack was utterly and totally devoted to his wife, Harriet, who was eight years older than he. Other than a personal automobile, the couple owned no property or investments. Their official residence was a leased second-floor flat in Boston's Everett Square. The childless couple shunned the Washington social scene. McCormack prided himself on dining with Harriet, usually alone, every evening of their married life.

McCormack had been elected Speaker in January 1962, following the legendary Sam Rayburn's death. True to his working-class district and his personal story of growing up in poverty, McCormack had been an ardent supporter of the New Deal, the Fair Deal, and progressive social programs throughout his long career. The nation's attention had focused upon him most acutely following President Kennedy's assassination when he became next in the line of succession for the presidency behind President Lyndon Johnson, until Hubert Humphrey was elected vice president in 1964. With no ambition to become chief executive, McCormack had modestly commented that being a heartbeat away from the presidency was the most stressful period of his life. This was hardly the profile of a politician on the take.

Equally perplexing was the role of Martin Sweig. We learned that Sweig, a forty-seven-year-old bachelor, had begun working for McCormack when he was twenty-two years old. He continued his studies in Washington by night, earning his doctorate in history at Georgetown University. Dr. Sweig, as he insisted his subordinates address him, was the son of German immigrants, whose father ran a kosher meat market in Winthrop, Massachusetts. Balding, bespectacled, and somewhat stooped, he presented himself as the prototypical career staffer—knowledgeable about the rules of the House and personalities of those who held office, as well as those who served them. Although soft-spoken and deferential when we questioned him in the grand jury, we got reports from others that Sweig could be quite the martinet, barking orders and acting as though he, and not his boss, were the lord of the manor. Still, hardly the type one would take for a wheeler-dealer out to make an illegal score.

To sum it up, there was plenty of action in the office on behalf of sketchy, if not downright shady characters, but no evidence that money had changed hands for the favors received.

In 1969, when the Parvin-Dohrmann Corporation was hit by the SEC with a trading suspension, its chairman turned to Voloshen for help. The company, which invested in Las Vegas casinos, allegedly inflated the value of its stock by issuing false and misleading statements. Voloshen was brought in to open doors for the company at the highest level of the Securities and Exchange Commission. Sweig, asserting the Speaker's interest in the matter, arranged for Voloshen and the company executives to meet on short notice with SEC chairman Hamer Budge. Voloshen started the meeting by advising Budge, "I bring you warm greetings from

Speaker of the House McCormack." Delbert Coleman, the company's chairman, made the case for lifting the suspension. Budge said he would take their arguments under advisement.

This wasn't good enough for Coleman. The next day, Voloshen and Coleman were joined by Sweig for lunch at Duke Zeibert's restaurant. Voloshen proposed that they drop in again on Budge, this time accompanied by Sweig. Despite the fact that no prior appointment had been made, the SEC chairman received the small delegation, which arrived via the Speaker's official limousine. Sweig duly introduced himself as the Speaker's administrative assistant and sat quietly while Coleman and Voloshen pressed Budge to lift the trading suspension. The heavy-handedness of this attempt to use influence was breathtaking. The strategy worked: Budge arranged for Coleman and his lawyer to meet with Budge's staff that afternoon. The suspension was soon lifted.

We questioned Sweig at length about the circumstances of his involvement. He had set up the appointment without the Speaker's knowledge as a favor to Voloshen. He made an error in judgment—"It was a darn fool thing" to accompany Voloshen and Coleman to the SEC—but had received nothing in return from Voloshen or others. He had no idea how much Voloshen had charged, and when pressed to explain why he went with the others to the meeting, Sweig lamely responded that he had never visited the SEC building before and he went out of curiosity. Chairman Budge was hardly more convincing when he claimed it was not unusual for people with cases before to the SEC to see him personally and without an appointment.

The most glamorous witness before the grand jury was Jill St. John, who had been touted to buy Parvin-Dohrmann stock by one of the company's insiders. The movie star had made a bundle on a modest investment. Had she overheard any of the discussions surrounding Voloshen's ability to get Sweig to attend the SEC meeting?

I was assigned the task of questioning the redheaded beauty. Someone had to do it. Represented by the legendary Edward Bennett Williams, St. John told the grand jury she knew nothing of the machinations involving the hiring of Voloshen. I reported back to Rooney and Abramowitz (whose curiosity did not overcome their good judgment in not packing the grand jury room) that she had no useful information to contribute to our investigation, but that I did get her unlisted phone number in case we needed to get in touch with her later. Paul and Elkan rolled their eyes.

One of the examples of Voloshen's fraud involved California governor

Pat Brown. Voloshen had claimed to the girlfriend of a convicted armed robber he had made a $10,000 campaign contribution to Brown, to assure her boyfriend's parole. I arranged to bring Brown before the grand jury, explaining his testimony was necessary to prove the fraud. Brown balked, claiming he would be smeared in the press when stories about his being "hauled before a grand jury" leaked out. I assured the skeptical governor that our office did not operate that way and that he could be assured of grand jury secrecy.

From the first day in the office we had it drilled into us that leaking to the press about our investigations was both ethically and legally wrong. It was a rule I would follow for the rest of my career—much to the bemusement of my future colleagues in Washington, where leaking to the press is considered an art form. At any event, Pat Brown came to New York, testified in the grand jury, and returned to California without a word in the press.

John Donato, a young man who for a time worked with Voloshen, told us that Voloshen was called to help a defense-contracting firm in Alabama avoid a crisis. It seemed the expanding company was poaching engineers and scientists from the nearby Huntsville Arsenal. The company became the target of noted rocket scientist Dr. Wernher von Braun, who warned that any contractor "raiding" the arsenal would be denied government contracts. Voloshen, using the Speaker's entrée, visited von Braun and came back with a press release signed by von Braun praising the company.

Not many of Voloshen's clients were so mainstream. Indeed, he had a thriving business in getting convicts paroled, having their prison sentences commuted, or at least assuring them better prison accommodations—all with the assistance of the Speaker's office. Why was the Speaker's office intervening with prison officials and parole boards?

I was surprised to learn that one of the clients on Voloshen's roster was Salvatore "Sally Burns" Granello, a reputed member of the Genovese crime family, who was serving a stretch at Danbury federal prison in Connecticut. I had prosecuted Granello and put him there. Apparently, Granello was giving the warden trouble and was slated to be transferred to the higher security prison at Lewisburg, Pennsylvania. When Granello's lawyer's request to stop the transfer was denied, Voloshen was brought in. For a mere $5,000 fee, Voloshen had Sweig call the Federal Bureau of Prisons with the same request. The transfer was immediately countermanded and Granello stayed put.

We had accumulated more than a dozen of these interventions, all following more or less the same modus operandi. None of the beneficiaries were actual constituents of the Speaker's home district, none of the objects of the influence could be certain he or she actually spoke with John McCormack, and no money was traceable to McCormack or Sweig.

Some of the episodes were brazen to the point of chutzpah. Voloshen's client Jack McCarthy was a "labor consultant" who from time to time had run afoul of the labor-racketeering laws. Voloshen/Sweig had tried to assist him in various ways—with a federal charter for a Florida bank in one instance, and with a federal prosecutor in Washington in another. Sweig had called the prosecutor on McCarthy's behalf, saying the Speaker wanted him to know he was a friend of the person the prosecutor was investigating. But the attempt to get McCarthy's son into college took the cake.

Robert W. Mayer, the director of admissions at the University of Delaware, told us about the calls he had received from the Speaker's office. In the first, Mayer said he took a call from Dr. Sweig, who explained that the Speaker was interested in the application for admission of the younger McCarthy. Mayer replied that he was familiar with the application and that the decision was not favorable. The phone was then turned over to a man who identified himself as Speaker McCormack but whose voice sounded the same as that of the first caller. The "Speaker" reiterated support for the McCarthy application.

Soon thereafter, the admissions director received another call from the Speaker. This time he turned the phone over to someone who identified himself as a scientist for NASA (possibly Voloshen, who no doubt felt sufficiently tutored by his earlier interaction with von Braun). The "scientist" said he had been reviewing the NASA file on the university's contribution to space research and found it impressive. The Speaker's voice then came on to say he was delighted to hear such a favorable report and was hopeful Congress could increase NASA's grant to the university. He then reintroduced the subject of McCarthy's application for admission.

The admissions director did some checking around regarding the university's grant from NASA. Young McCarthy was admitted.

Voloshen apparently had made college admissions a subspecialty, a nice balance to his thriving prison practice. Peter Bratti, a very successful tile and terrazzo contractor, who was to become an important witness at trial, told of his encounter with Voloshen in the field of higher education. Bratti was a friend of Speaker McCormack's and a fellow Knight of Malta. Over the years he had often met Voloshen in McCormack's company and was well aware of the close friendship between the two. One day Voloshen approached Bratti with a request for a favor. "Sure, Nat, whatever I can do," Bratti proclaimed, exuding the fraternal spirit of those in proximity to the powerful.

"Peter, you are a member of the Board of Trustees at Marymount College, if memory serves, is that correct?"

"Yes, proudly so."

"I have a dear friend whose daughter has applied there and who may need some help."

"Sure, I'll help if I can. What's the name?"

"Genovese."

"What?" Bratti exclaimed. "Vito Genovese, the narcotics king?"

"No, no," the dapper Voloshen assured him quietly, "Not *that* Genovese. This is for Michael Genovese, his brother, a real sweetheart—in the tomato business in Philadelphia. Very successful." Overcoming a moment of rational thinking, Bratti agreed to meet the girl and her father at Bratti's posh New York office near the United Nations.

At the appointed hour, as Bratti recounted, the student, dressed in her parochial school uniform, arrived with her father—and five very large men who were introduced as her uncles. Some of them, according to Bratti, had to turn sideways in order to fit through the doorway to his office. He feared that his office furniture, some antique chairs in particular, might splinter under their weight. In Bratti's telling, Michael Genovese did not appear to be a native English speaker.

"My daughter wants to go to Marymount College," the tomato magnate began. "I give ten thousand dollars." Somewhat taken aback by the directness of the man's opening remarks, Bratti explained that it was not customary to make a donation *in advance* of matriculation. Of course, such generosity would be much appreciated later on—if she were admitted. Bratti now turned to his prepared remarks about how Marymount had very high academic standards and was a very difficult school to get into.

"My daughter is a very good girl, she's in the house every night, nine o'clock. No exceptions. And works hard, gets good reports. Show your report card," the tomato king ordered.

The young girl stood up demurely and handed Bratti a report card. All Cs and Ds. Was it possible the father couldn't read? Bratti carefully considered this possibility as he chose his next remarks.

"So this is your report card?"

The young girl nodded.

"Very nice." Bratti stood up, handing back the incriminating document and moving to wind up the meeting. "I'll be happy to speak to the mother superior at Marymount and see if I can help."

None of the visitors moved to get up.

"Okay, you go now," Genovese commanded. "We wait here."

Bratti briefly pondered the situation and left the Genovese college application committee chatting amiably in his office while he made the hour drive north to Westchester County.

"Hello, Mother Superior, how are you?"

"Well, Peter, thank you. To what do we owe this surprise visit?"

"I've been thinking, Mother Superior, that the admissions standards for Marymount are too inflexible. I mean, there's more to gauge a young woman's potential than just high school grades."

"Peter, what is it, what do you really want?"

"I would like to help a very lovely girl come here, but her grades are not the highest."

"What's her name?"

"Genovese, but not *that* Genovese."

"Peter, you know it means nothing to us who the parents are. But I remember that application; we already turned her down. She just doesn't have the academic background to succeed here."

"Mother Superior, who built the gymnasium?"

"You did, Peter."

"Who built the swimming pool?"

"You did, Peter."

"Do I have to go to the head of the Order, or will you give this nice young girl a chance?"

Bratti was able to convey encouraging news to the occupation forces resident in his office. Miss Genovese's application would receive favorable treatment.

While the investigation provided its fair quotient of memorable characters and some good laughs, there were far more serious aspects. The Vietnam War was going full steam, and the draft was catching tens of thousands of young men—including the sons of the rich and well connected—in its net. Enter Nathan Voloshen, the man with a plan, who could fix that kind of a problem too—with a little help from his friends in the Speaker's office.

For me, this was among the most cynical aspects of the influence-peddling scheme. John McCormack was an outspoken supporter of the war. He had compared fighting the communists in Vietnam to fighting the Nazis in World War II. How could he tolerate his name being used to secure the discharge of privileged young men from military service while others were being slaughtered and maimed in the killing fields of Southeast Asia?

We called Voloshen and Sweig to the grand jury, advising them of their constitutional right not to testify. Not surprisingly, Sweig agreed to testify and denied wrongdoing. Public servants, elected and appointed, realize that taking the Fifth may spell the end of their careers. More surprisingly, Voloshen answered our questions instead of invoking his Fifth Amendment privilege. With Voloshen it was an act of hubris. He should have known better. Both men were now vulnerable to perjury charges if anything they said in front of the grand jury was found to be untrue.

John McCormack was the last witness from whom we would take sworn testimony. In deference to his position, and to reduce the possibility of publicity, we agreed to take the Speaker's testimony in his Capitol office rather than having him come before the grand jury in New York. His familiar visage would have been recognized in a nanosecond had he appeared in the Manhattan courthouse. Instead, we would read the transcript of his testimony to the grand jury.

The Speaker acknowledged his long-standing relationship with Nathan Voloshen, but he had no idea Voloshen was using his office as the hub of an influence-peddling scheme. And, along with asserting that he was unacquainted with any of the clients on Voloshen's fix-it list, much less intervening on their behalf, McCormack denied taking so much as a dime from Voloshen. As for Dr. Sweig, the Speaker reaffirmed his confidence in the man who had served him for nearly a quarter century, while acknowledging that he had acted beyond his authority in contacting "sensitive" agencies like the SEC and Department of Justice without his specific authorization.

Indeed, the Speaker had been obliged to suspend Sweig without pay after the SEC had filed a civil suit against Coleman and the Parvin-Dohrmann crowd after they learned that Voloshen had been paid at the rate of $10,000 an hour for his "work" in arranging the two meetings with Budge. At the time, the Speaker proclaimed his innocence of any wrongdoing and vowed he would run for another term, with no intention of giving up the Speakership.

Meanwhile, *Life* magazine's investigative reporter, William Lambert, had written an extensive article exposing the Voloshen-McCormack relationship and focusing on the characters who were allegedly helped by McCormack's and Schweitzer's intercessions. Lambert wrote that he had

been offered a $50,000 bribe (in two installments) by a Voloshen interme-
diary not to publish his exposé.

Accordingly, the Speaker's office was being staked out by reporters
such as the nationally syndicated Jack Anderson, who advised readers
that he had performed his own undercover investigation of the Speaker's
office and pronounced the Speaker clean. Our deposition team of Rooney,
Abramowitz, and myself was spotted by a reporter as we left the Speaker's
office—not because any of us (me, least of all) were particularly recognizable but because the grand jury stenographer we brought along with us
had carried her stenotype machine in a distinctive Fifth Avenue department store shopping bag. Our cover was blown and the Speaker's office
confirmed to the press the reason for our visit—to help the U.S. attorney's
office complete its investigation, with the Speaker's full cooperation.

Back in New York, we reassessed what we had: a lucrative influence-
peddling business run out of the Speaker's office by a longtime friend of
the Speaker, benefiting individuals whom the Speaker denied knowing
and who were not constituents from his district, all actively aided by the
Speaker's principal assistant who was known to perfectly mimic his boss's
voice. And, oh yes, no evidence that Voloshen paid off either McCormack
or Sweig.

That isn't to say John McCormack didn't have his weakness. Although
a teetotaler, he liked a game of poker and he liked a good cigar. But his
principal weakness was his beloved wife, Harriet. And, we learned, there
was no kindness Voloshen would not bestow upon her. Indeed, as the
story went, the elderly Mrs. McCormack became virtually addicted to a
certain face cream Voloshen delivered every two weeks in a small unmarked jar, which he supposedly received from a special source in Swit-
zerland. In fact, the cream was apparently the readily available Oil of
Olay, which the crafty Voloshen transferred from its original container
into the mysteriously unmarked jars. "Voloshen's lotions," those in on
the scam called it. But as grounds for a charge of bribery? Please!

Many years later, a former acquaintance of Voloshen's told me a story
that highlighted how much the McCormacks relied on the dapper lawyer.
One day in a New York restaurant, Voloshen spotted a friendly Irish
Catholic labor lawyer with whom he had some business. "James, you have
to do me a favor," the visibly agitated Voloshen exclaimed. "Where can I
find nuns' underwear?"

"Are you going dotty on me, Nat?"

"No," Voloshen replied. "It's the only kind Mrs. McCormack will wear,
and I've got to get some for her."

We had no basis to bring a charge of bribery. We decided to charge Voloshen and Sweig under a little-used interpretation of the federal conspiracy statute that made it a crime to conspire to deprive the government of the honest services of its employees. The indictment would charge that Sweig misused his position by exerting pressure at the Departments of Justice, Treasury, Labor, Defense, and Post Office, as well as the Securities and Exchange Commission and the Selective Service—all on behalf of Voloshen's clients. To that we added several counts of perjury for false statements Voloshen and Sweig had made before the grand jury. Finally, we would charge Voloshen separately with defrauding the dissatisfied customers who had paid for a fix to be put in but got no return for their money. If money had somehow been funneled to McCormack, we would need to convict Voloshen and/or Sweig, and then see whether they would try to bargain down their jail time by turning state's evidence.

The indictment received front-page attention in New York, Boston, and Washington. Despite the fact that John McCormack was not charged with any violation of law, editorial writers throughout the land questioned whether the time had come for the seventy-eight-year-old Speaker to surrender his position. After all, if he was unaware of an influence peddler conducting business from behind the desk of one of his government offices, how much confidence could the nation's leaders have that the "oblivious" Speaker was competently satisfying the burdens of his important office?

Four days after the indictment was returned, Bob Morgenthau, facing an ultimatum from Nixon and Mitchell to resign or be fired, resigned as U.S. attorney for the Southern District of New York. He had accomplished much in his eight years of leadership, and many of the lawyers he had hired as his assistants figured this would be a natural point to move on with their careers. Normally, an assistant U.S. attorney makes an unwritten commitment to stay for three years. Many of Morgenthau's assistants had chosen to stay much longer. Among those who left were my mentors Paul Rooney and Elkan Abramowitz, as well as most of the members of the organized crime and special prosecutions unit. The sometime diplomat Peter Fleming left as well. So, at twenty-six years of age and with fewer than two years' experience under my belt, I was catapulted to the top of the food chain as the only remaining assistant U.S. attorney who had a working knowledge of the most important case in the office.

The fears of President Nixon appointing a political hack to replace Morgenthau were put to rest when Whitney North Seymour Jr. was named to take over. Apparently, the heat and light generated by Morgenthau's holdout campaign had dissuaded the president from any notions he might have had about politicizing the office. The son of a distinguished former president of the American Bar Association and head of a major Wall Street law firm, Seymour had impeccable credentials of his own as a lawyer committed to public service. Having served as an assistant U.S. attorney in the midfifties, Seymour quickly reiterated the core ideals of the office in word and deed, filling his executive positions with high-quality lawyers, some of whom had served as assistant U.S. attorneys earlier in their careers. None of the lawyers Morgenthau had hired were terminated—many were promoted.

My best friend in the office, Tom Fitzpatrick, and I contemplated the changing of the guard from our vantage point as groundlings. Tom and I had been sworn in on the same day and had shared space for our first several months on the job in the office library until normal attrition opened up private offices. Fitzpatrick had graduated from Fordham University, undergraduate and law school, and had practiced law for a couple of years in a Wall Street firm before being hired. We found an inexhaustible source of entertainment in the parade of hapless crooks, stereotypical law enforcement agents, and irascible and sometimes lunatic judges that comprised our daily diet. We have remained best friends to this day.

Deeply interested in the ethnic melting pot that made up most of the city we knew, we would compare notes from our personal perspectives. Tom was expert on Irish immigrants and was quick to predict the biases of a potential juror of Irish heritage based on a few variables. For example, he seemed far less nonplused than I about the attitudes of our office librarian, whose domain we shared, a sweet, elderly woman named Helen McKnight. As various defendants were frog-marched into our office in handcuffs by their arresting agents for intake interviews, Mrs. McKnight would size them up. Invariably and no matter what the alleged infraction— after all, Tom and I were lowest on the totem pole and were assigned the least serious cases: postal embezzlers, check forgers, car thieves, and the like—the diminutive librarian would volubly proclaim, "They ought to stand him up against the wall and shoot him."

I, on the other hand, was slightly more cosmopolitan than Tom in my reach. On a lunch excursion early on in our budding friendship, we found ourselves in a small Italian restaurant, Vincent's Clam Bar, in Little Italy near our office. The crowded restaurant was filled wall-to-wall with large individuals, many of whom would not have flirted with legitimate employment. Looking up at the chalkboard that substituted for a menu, Fitz read off a list of choices not then recognizable to his Irish palate, "calamari, scungilli, polpi—what do guys usually get here?" he asked.

"Three to five," I replied, quickly realizing that maybe my remark was not as funny as I thought, as heads on thick necks began to turn in my direction.

Whitney North Seymour Jr. was a new commodity. Despite his famous lineage, Bob Morgenthau could shoot the bull (in a limited hangout sort of way) with his assistants. He liked smoking good cigars (and kept a box of cheap cigars around in case he was feeling particularly generous and wanted to treat an assistant to a stogie). He displayed a wry sense of humor and never put on airs.

For starters, at six foot eight, Seymour couldn't help looking down at most people. He insisted that we call him by his nickname, "Mike," which his parents had tagged him with since before he was born—referring to the fetus as the "microcosm" and then "mike" for short (which he definitely wasn't). He had a booming voice to match his size and spoke in perfect paragraphs—much like the legal briefs he was expert at writing. He filled his office with memorabilia of his hero, Teddy Roosevelt, meticulously arranged and seemingly covering every visible surface. We had gone from Super-Jew to Super-WASP in the blink of an eye.

Soon after he was ensconced in "Teddyland," Mike called me into his office to discuss the Voloshen/Sweig case. I had already briefed the new chief of the criminal division, Harold Baer, on the investigation. Gruff and to the point, Baer had previously served a stint in the office. He had gotten a scouting report on me from friends of his who had left the office along with Morgenthau. Also, I knew that Silvio J. Mollo, a career prosecutor who had been in the office longer than anyone could remember, liked how I had performed in the courtroom. Sil was no pushover. The new chief made some noises that sounded complimentary. I waited. Baer wanted to hear the strengths and weaknesses of the big case. I gave them to him.

Harold got quickly to the point. "I don't care if you're the greatest thing since sliced bread. You are only twenty-six years old, and—"

"I just turned twenty-seven," I interrupted.

"Happy freaking birthday!" Baer thundered. "There is no way you are going to try the Sweig case! You have been a trial lawyer for all of sixteen months." This time the math was correct. Only a crazy person would suggest I be put in charge of a case of this importance. I looked across the desk as my new chief glared at me. Baer was not crazy. Eccentric maybe, but not crazy.

"Okay, now tell me something I don't know," I replied.

Baer looked at me silently for a moment and then exploded into a raucous laugh. "I'm glad we understand each other. But since you know the case and the witnesses, you are going to stay with it and help Mike Seymour prepare to try it."

Now, that was a surprise. In his eight years as U.S. attorney, Morgenthau had never ventured into a courtroom to try a case. He was not a trial lawyer; his talents lay elsewhere. An attempt by the boss to try a case would have been a disaster. I had heard that Seymour was an accomplished appellate and civil practitioner but had no idea how he might fare in a criminal jury trial.

Nevertheless, I was elated. I would stay on the case, make myself useful, and possibly get some role to play in the courtroom. Plus, I would have the opportunity to work closely with the U.S. attorney.

I told Mike Seymour it was an honor to be able to work with him on the Sweig/Voloshen case. The way Voloshen had been able to use the Speaker's office to influence the wheels of government, with Sweig's ready assistance, was an affront to good government. Perhaps this case would send a message to political fixers and corrupt officials alike that there would be a serious price to pay for illegal conduct. I was no match for Mike Seymour in the "good government" department. He was fully steeped in the credo that public officials must "turn square corners" and that corruption needed to be yanked out of the system by its roots. That was why he would take the lead in trying this case. I collected all the relevant grand jury transcripts and memos for Mike's review and set about to help prepare the case for trial. Bill Gilbreath, an immensely likable and talented assistant attorney several years my senior, was added to the trial team.

Meanwhile, questions were being raised about McCormack's future as Speaker. In February, a "no confidence" resolution put forward in the Democratic caucus by Representative Jerome Waldie of California was beaten back by a vote of 192–23. The vote showed the Speaker to have a significant reservoir of support. But a growing group of younger, progressive members were joined by the Washington Post and others in asking rhetorically whether the twenty-term congressman was "fully alert" to what had been going on under his nose, and whether he was up to the dynamic demands of national leadership in the 1970s.

At the same time, Voloshen faced another indictment from Baltimore federal prosecutors investigating a bogus letter on McCormack's official stationery used to defraud a defense contractor, while the IRS was on his tail for underreporting his 1962 income by $92,000.

The drumbeats grew louder as each new misuse of the Speaker's office came to light. McCormack's denials of knowing what Voloshen and Sweig were up to seemed increasingly like Inspector Louis Renault expressing shock that gambling was going on in the back room at Rick's. Finally, in May—only a month before the trial was scheduled to start—John W. McCormack announced that he would not seek reelection.

We were now in final preparation mode for the trial. Mike Seymour was generous in assigning me responsibility for making the opening statement and taking several witnesses. Mike would make the closing argument and take the main witnesses, including Speaker McCormack, whom we would call as a government witness. Although McCormack had done nothing publicly to denounce Sweig or Voloshen for misusing his office—other than to suspend Sweig for his "mistake in judgment" regarding the SEC meeting—we would need his testimony to prove to the jury that he had not authorized Sweig to use his name to intercede for Voloshen's clientele.

The news media was pressing our office for spicy details or at least a preview of what was to come at trial. Mike made it clear that we would not try this case in the press, that there would be no leaking of the government's evidence in advance of trial. And there wasn't. The prosecution would do all its talking in the courtroom. Seymour was fond of quoting the laconic Calvin Coolidge: "You don't have to explain something you never said."

Presiding over the trial was Judge Marvin E. Frankel, a brilliant jurist who had sustained our legal theory against pretrial motions filed by the defense seeking to dismiss the conspiracy count for failing to state a crime. Due to the high level of publicity surrounding the case, the prospective jurors were interviewed by the prosecution and defense lawyers individually. Just as we were about to start the process, Jules Ritholtz, Voloshen's lawyer, announced that his client was changing his plea from not guilty to guilty. In the six months since his indictment, Voloshen's health had declined rapidly. Literally, his heart had failed him and, faced with assaults on several fronts, he decided to throw in the towel. He sought no plea bargain to reduce the charges against him. He pleaded guilty to the conspiracy charge and all three counts of perjury against him in the indictment.

I was shocked to see the tough, dapper operator who had appeared before the grand jury transformed into a frail old man with trembling hands, a shuffling walk, and slow halting speech. This was no acting job—Voloshen was a sick man. No offer was made to testify against his

codefendant, Sweig. No offer was made to provide any help to the prosecution in return for leniency. Sentencing was set for four months later,
well after the trial would be concluded. The judge would advise the jurors
of Voloshen's plea but admonish them to consider Sweig's guilt or innocence solely on the evidence presented against him. We returned to the
task of jury selection and picked a jury in less than a week.

Sweig's lawyer, Paul T. Smith, was in many ways the antithesis of Mike
Seymour. He was overweight and rumpled, with a pronounced Boston
accent and the florid facial features of a man reputed to enjoy strong
drink. He was also one helluva good trial lawyer.

I laid out the prosecution case in my opening statement to the jury,
detailing the lineup of convicts, fraudsters, hoods, fast-buck artists, and
conscripted sons of the wealthy, who, simply because they paid Voloshen
handsome sums of money, had the influence, power, and prestige of the
Speaker's office extended on their behalf. None of this would have been
possible without Martin Sweig's fraud and dishonesty, unbeknownst to
his boss, Speaker of the House John W. McCormack. Showing the jury a
diagram emphasizing the distance between the Speaker's ceremonial office in the Capitol and McCormack's district office in the Rayburn Building, I explained how Voloshen and Sweig were able to carry out their
influence-peddling racket at some remove from McCormack's ability to
observe. I tried to defuse Smith's central argument by acknowledging that
we would offer no proof that Sweig took any money for his efforts, nor
were we obliged to under the law, as Judge Frankel would instruct them
when it came time for them to deliberate on their verdict.

Paul Smith countered by telling the jury that the evidence would establish that McCormack and Voloshen had been fast friends well before
Sweig even joined the Speaker's staff and that McCormack had instructed
Sweig to give Voloshen—and others of his friends—the "red carpet" treatment. Sweig had done nothing but follow the Speaker's instructions. His
calls to various agencies of the federal government were not illegal in and
of themselves. And most important, the prosecution would be unable to
prove Sweig took a single dollar for helping Voloshen.

Smith was clearly energized by not having the smarmy, money-
grubbing Voloshen sitting next to his client in the courtroom. His chances
were much better portraying Dr. Sweig, sitting downcast and quiet at the
defense table, as the obedient staffer, somewhat bookish in his clear-
framed eyeglasses and stooped posture. Nowhere to be seen was the
gruff, Teutonic martinet former staffers had described, lording it over the
lesser vassals in his congressional domain.

Smith had what I would come to describe in my subsequent career as a defense lawyer as a very "triable" case.

We were hoping that the crassness of the influence exerted, coupled with the unattractiveness of Voloshen's seedy clientele, would trump the lack of evidence that Sweig was on the take. As the days went by, it seemed less and less likely that Voloshen would offer to trade information for consideration in sentencing.

The heart of our case of perversion of high office was captured in the testimony of Michael Hellerman, chairman of a mob-connected company seeking SEC approval for a stock issue. Hellerman had paid Voloshen a $10,000 advance after Voloshen took him to lunch at the exclusive House dining room in the Capitol and had him chauffered to the airport in the Speaker's official limousine. Voloshen told him, "We can do anything in Washington short of murder," Hellerman testified.

The major event at trial was the appearance of John W. McCormack. Mike Seymour had prepared carefully for the Speaker's testimony, which could make or break our case. We would emphasize that while McCormack had long been friends with Voloshen, he had no idea of what was going on, much less did he authorize Sweig to allow Voloshen to operate an office within an office for customers who could and would pay cash on the barrelhead for the Speaker's influence.

McCormack was to be our last witness, a function of his schedule rather than ours. He followed a parade of forty-five witnesses of two categories: clients of Voloshen who testified of fees charged and promises made, and officials who were on the receiving end of the pressure. Three of them—chairman of the New York parole commission, a U.S. Army major in Fort Jackson, South Carolina, and the University of Delaware admissions director—testified they had spoken directly with Speaker McCormack. While Smith never acknowledged Sweig's ventriloquism, he suggested in questions to several witnesses that the absent Voloshen could himself impersonate the Speaker's voice.

All eyes were on John McCormack as the pallid, frail-looking Speaker made his way deliberately to the witness stand, stumbling and then catching himself, to audible gasps from some in the packed courtroom. First acknowledging the jurors, the Speaker peered through severe rimless spectacles until he located Sweig at the defense table. Raising his clasped hands over his head in the boxer's universal salute of victory, McCormack smiled at his former aide and nodded his white-haired head. Sweig, in turn, stood up and bowed slightly.

The jurors had followed this silent kabuki performance with rapt attention. "Holy shit," I thought. "We've lost the case before the Speaker even takes the oath."

Mike Seymour gamely tried to evoke some indignation from the septuagenarian congressman—to no avail. "Did Dr. Sweig at any time discuss with you the affairs of any of the people we have referred to here today?" Seymour asked.

"No, not to my knowledge."

Eliciting that McCormack considered Voloshen a friend of more than twenty years' standing, Seymour continued: "Did you know Voloshen was using your congressional office extensively for his business?"

"No."

"That he was using it for conferences with his clients?"

"No."

Politely, but firmly, Seymour pressed McCormack as to whether he had made a series of calls about which the earlier witnesses had testified. McCormack did not recall placing the calls or authorizing anyone on his staff to do so, using his name. Nor did he know Voloshen had collected $50,000 for arranging the SEC meetings on the Parvin-Dohrmann suspension. Then, acknowledging that he had met Voloshen's young business partner, John Donato, in his office on occasion, the Speaker added that he was unaware of Donato's business. "I'm not an inquiring fellow," the Speaker said. No kidding. As a reporter covering the trial for the *New York Daily News* wrote, "McCormack gave himself a clean bill of ignorance."

The most McCormack would say was that Sweig had made an "error of judgment" in contacting sensitive agencies like the SEC and Department of Justice. Seymour and the trial team were cornered. There was no way to attack McCormack for not sharing our outrage at his chief aide allowing a New York lawyer to make a congressional office his personal operations center for selling the old man's influence.

Smith's "cross-examination" only gilded the lily. McCormack acknowledged Sweig as a "dear friend" as well as loyal employee of twenty-four years. "He was very devoted. He worked hard. He studied hard. He was very devoted to me. He worked long hours." McCormack finished up with a ringing endorsement of Sweig's penchant for fighting injustice and his reputation for truthfulness, honesty, and veracity. What a performance! Unauthorized things had happened without his knowledge, but nobody was responsible. Is this the way a man compelled by circumstances to give up one of the most powerful positions in government would logically act toward those responsible for his undoing? Logic dictated there was more to the story.

But now was the time to see whether we could salvage any of the counts against Sweig. After McCormack's testimony, I thought there was little chance of the jury finding him guilty of conspiracy to defraud the United States, even though Voloshen had pleaded guilty to it. Indeed, Smith was recalibrating his defense tactics. He had earlier advised the judge and jury that Sweig would take the stand and testify in his own defense. Given the impact of McCormack's performance, he scotched that idea, calling only three character witnesses, among them Thomas P. "Tip" O'Neill, who would succeed McCormack as Speaker of the House. Then the defense rested.

We had one final witness we had been holding back for rebuttal. Peter Bratti, the tile and terrazzo contractor who served on the board of Marymount College, testified that he had personally overheard Sweig on a number of occasions identify himself on the telephone as Speaker McCormack. Despite his contention throughout the trial that Sweig had never impersonated his boss, Smith declined to cross-examine Bratti. I was hoping to lure Smith into tangling with Bratti, thereby highlighting the contradiction. Smith wasn't biting. Had the wily Smith been tipped off about Bratti's testimony in time to save Sweig from committing himself on the witness stand to a denial of impersonating the Speaker? Probably. Did I think Bratti's testimony would be enough to turn the tide in our favor on the conspiracy charge? Probably not.

Instead, I pinned our hopes for a conviction on one perjury count. In his testimony before the grand jury, Sweig had flat-out denied knowing anything about efforts emanating from the Speaker's office to obtain a hardship discharge from the army for one PFC Gary Roth. Mike Seymour had assigned me responsibility for presenting evidence that Sweig deliberately lied. Roth's father-in-law, a New York manufacturer who was a client of Voloshen's, testified at trial that he had paid Voloshen $1,500 in cash to "see what he could do" for Gary. Several calls were made from the Speaker's office urging that a hardship discharge be granted to young Roth, including one purportedly by the Speaker himself, according to the testimony of the earnest army major who was at the receiving end of the pressure. Roth's father testified that at Voloshen's urging he signed a letter to the commanding officer at Fort Jackson, where Roth was stationed, saying, "My very dear and good friend, House Speaker John McCormack, has told me that his office has discussed with you the case of my son." When Roth Sr. told Voloshen he had never met the Speaker, Voloshen told him to sign the letter anyway. A copy of that letter together with other information about Roth was found in the files of the Speaker's office.

In his closing argument, Mike Seymour eloquently reviewed the evidence of how the Speaker's office had been transformed into a "Trojan horse" by a conspiracy of Voloshen and Sweig, where the "easy morals of shadowy figures" had penetrated into the hallowed halls of Congress. He pointed to the "sorry spectacle" of Voloshen trading on the Speaker's prestige and reaping hundreds of thousands of dollars in the process. He refuted the notion advanced by Paul Smith in his examination of witnesses that such calls to various agencies as the prosecution had proved were routinely made on Capitol Hill. By doing so, Seymour contended, Smith was "putting the integrity of the whole Congress on trial."

Mike's closing had begun to morph into a civics lesson. Quoting from Abraham Lincoln and other American icons, Mike's argument seemed to sail over the jurors' heads.

Closer to the ground, Paul Smith wasted little time in restating the same theme that had permeated the defense from the get-go. The contacts were not per se illegal, and there was no evidence that Sweig was motivated to violate the law. After all, he had not received a dime in payment. Whatever the jury might think about whether it was "unfair" for these contacts to be made, these were philosophical matters, not legal ones. If there was a conspiracy—and Smith was prepared to accept that proposition—its members were Voloshen and his partner, Donato. Dr. Martin Sweig was clean.

The only place I sensed vulnerability in Smith's argument was when he addressed the perjury counts. If Sweig had merely testified he couldn't recall the Roth matter—instead of making a flat statement that he had no knowledge of contacts on the young soldier's behalf—he might have avoided a perjury charge. That "if" might prove to be Sweig's undoing. Mike Seymour had assigned me responsibility to make the government's rebuttal argument. I hammered on the evidence of the perjury charge regarding the Roth file and how the government and honest citizens are harmed when our military is subject to political pressure to discharge a young soldier because of whom he can pay. I reminded the jury of the chicanery that Peter Bratti had witnessed, of Sweig claiming on the telephone that he was the Speaker, and how McCormack had denied he had made or authorized any call on Roth's behalf. Yet, the army major in South Carolina had received repeated calls from the Speaker's office, including one supposedly from the Speaker himself. Martin Sweig had deliberately lied about his involvement, and a privileged young man was discharged from the army because Sweig and Voloshen had misused the

Speaker's authority. I sat down, hoping the jury would not give Sweig a complete pass.

The hardest time for a trial lawyer is when the jury is deliberating. There is nothing more you can do to advance your cause—although something always comes to mind (at least to me) as to how you might have improved your presentation. We didn't have long to wait, relatively speaking. Although the jury had requested that certain parts of the judge's instructions on the law regarding conspiracy be reread, we heard nothing further from them during their nineteen hours of deliberations.

The verdict was returned on July 9, twenty-three days since we had first picked a jury, seven months after the grand jury had returned its indictment. We listened nervously as the court clerk read from the verdict form handed up by the jury foreman: On Count 1, the conspiracy charge, not guilty. Not guilty on all the other remaining charges except one. The jury found Martin Sweig guilty of one count of perjury on the Roth matter.

Paul Smith was elated, bounding up to shake hands with the jurors after Judge Frankel had excused them. The jury had bought almost all of Smith's arguments. I could understand. If John McCormack didn't feel betrayed by Sweig, had the government really been defrauded? We hadn't proved our conspiracy case against Sweig beyond a reasonable doubt.

It was hard to tell who was more disappointed, Sweig or Seymour. Despite his lawyer's ebullient reaction, Sweig had been convicted of a felony charge and might well go to prison. Judge Frankel immediately set a sentencing date for six weeks hence. Seymour, on the other hand, was devastated that the jury had not agreed that Sweig's role in the influence-peddling scheme was enough to warrant a conviction on our main conspiracy charge. I tried to console him: "Tomorrow's headlines will say, 'Sweig convicted,'" I predicted—correctly, as it turned out. Seymour would get over his disappointment. Sweig would not.

A couple of weeks before Voloshen's sentencing, Jules Ritholtz made an appointment to bring his client in to see us. I was shocked at the additional physical deterioration Voloshen had undergone. The sharp, glittery-eyed fixer whom we had questioned in the grand jury was a very sick man. One did not need to review the doctors' letters that Ritholtz had brought along to see that Voloshen was close to death's door. I could see no way Judge Frankel would send this man to prison. But Ritholtz wanted the added security of a statement that his client had "cooperated" with the prosecutors. In a croaking voice, Voloshen repeated his previous denials of having bribed either McCormack or Sweig. Pausing to take a nitroglycerin pill with a trembling hand, Voloshen went on to say that the Speaker's nephew, Edward McCormack, had been referred a lot of legal business by and through his uncle. Eddie, who had served a term as Massachusetts's elected attorney general, was the Speaker's closest blood relative.

Were any of these referrals shams, indirect payments to the Speaker? Voloshen had no proof to offer. Great. Eddie McCormack had been out front in the press, as might well be expected, denouncing Voloshen's betrayal of the Speaker's friendship while proclaiming his uncle's honesty and integrity. Here was Voloshen striking back at Eddie with no facts to support him. Referring business to a nephew was perfectly legal—there was no way this would pass muster as cooperation.

Voloshen could tell he wasn't making any headway. He put another tiny nitro pill under his tongue. There was a lobbyist named Mike Silbert whom he knew to be a frequent visitor to the Speaker's office. We pressed for details. Voloshen said that Silbert represented a manufacturer of ladders and aluminum products in Florida named Keller. He thought Sweig may have helped Keller's son with the military. The other things Voloshen mentioned were useless from any investigative standpoint. The meeting had lasted little more than an hour before Voloshen shambled out.

Neither Mike Seymour nor I had any stomach for seeing Voloshen receive what would amount to a death sentence, due to his precarious health. Judge Frankel lectured Voloshen on the seriousness of the crimes of which he stood convicted. They were "crimes of the utmost heinousness; crimes that tend strongly to corrupt the democratic process." But Voloshen's health was the determining factor in Frankel's decision to sentence him to one-year probation and a $10,000 fine. With the aid of a cane, Voloshen slowly made his way out of the courtroom.

Nine months later, Voloshen was dead. The episode had a lasting effect on me. I had seen a vigorous man, seemingly in good health, go down the tubes. Sweig's sentencing followed Voloshen's by a month. "If I have done wrong, I didn't mean to," Sweig pleaded. Again the "if." His lawyer asked for leniency, saying that Sweig had been punished enough. Judge Frankel disagreed, observing that the evidence showed "a picture of a corruption of a very profound kind" and "a grievous case of perjury . . . linked to an abuse of government trust." He imposed a sentence of thirty months at the minimum-security prison at Allenwood, Pennsylvania, and a $2,000 fine.

By this time, I had a full dance card of cases to try and additional grand jury investigations to pursue. John McCormack would be retiring in January. But there was still the matter of Voloshen's lead regarding Mike Silbert. I was quite sure we had not gotten the full story on what had been going on in the Speaker's office. With Seymour's approval, I set out to pursue the matter.

I learned that Silbert was seventy-two years old and living in Florida. I was fast becoming one of America's foremost experts on geriatric fixers. After verifying some basic information, I soon paid a call on Speaker McCormack in Washington. The Speaker greeted me warmly. I asked whether he was willing to continue cooperating with our office by voluntarily producing any files he might have relating to Silbert or Keller. There would be no need for a subpoena, the Speaker told me. He had already begun moving his files to Boston University in anticipation of his retirement. Although he had no recollection of Keller, I would be welcome to review any Keller files at BU. Would he mind writing a note to that effect? I asked. On the spot, McCormack dictated and signed a letter on his official stationery giving me permission to review and copy any such files.

Before anyone had time to countermand my permission slip, I was up at Boston University. I brought with me an IRS revenue agent, Anthony J. Passaretti, to help cull through the files. After our experience with the FBI's reluctance to assist in investigating Voloshen's involvement with the Speaker—the Hoover FBI's reaction being more or less akin to Dracula greeting the sunrise—we deemed it prudent to look elsewhere for investigative assistance. Tony Passaretti had worked with me on the Granello prosecution and was known by other assistants as a knowledgeable and indefatigable investigator. Harold Baer cashed in some chits with the IRS and had Tony assigned to work with me. For his part, Tony was happy to escape the IRS bureaucracy for the more lively and varied kinds of cases we were working on.

From that point on, Passaretti worked with me on every case I had in the U.S. attorney's office, whether or not there was any alleged violation of the tax laws. No one ever had a more dedicated partner or a better friend. In addition to his other skills, Tony had a particular talent for making witnesses feel at ease. He carried a supply of small rosaries with him at all times to calm the usually agitated witnesses who found themselves entangled in criminal trials.

Herbert Itkin was on the witness stand testifying in a political corruption case I prosecuted years after the Sweig case. The defense lawyer, engaged in a largely ineffective cross-examination of this experienced witness, noticed that Itkin was glancing down from time to time at something he appeared to be holding in his hand, obscured from view by the wood-paneled witness stand. Suspecting that Itkin was surreptitiously referring to some kind of cheat sheet, the lawyer demanded loudly that Herbie show the jury what he was secretly holding. As Itkin promptly displayed one of Passaretti's signature rosaries, the defense lawyer reacted as though he had been struck with a mallet.

Our trip to Boston proved highly rewarding. As the Speaker's files had not yet been cataloged, it took us a few hours to find what we were looking for. A file showed that Keller's son had been granted a hardship discharge from the navy, apparently after repeated calls from McCormack's office. The file gave us all the information we needed to track down the naval officers who were contacted by the Speaker's office. Methodically, we established what the existing rules were for the granting of a hardship discharge, and then questioned the navy officers who made the decisions. The Keller episode represented the heaviest handed exercise in applying improper pressure by the Speaker's office I had seen yet.

Henry A. Keller Jr. was a yeoman assigned to Jacksonville Naval Air Station in February 1969. Commander Lawrence Weber, a twenty-year navy veteran, was the ranking administrative officer at the base. He explained that Keller told him he wanted a discharge because his wife had psychological problems, was seeing an analyst twice a week back home in Miami, and that he could not afford to continue her treatments. Weber advised Keller that the navy would supply psychiatric care for his wife, but if he wanted a discharge he would have to fill out a formal application.

Some weeks later, Weber received a call from a Lieutenant Commander. Jones of the navy's Bureau of Personnel who told him that Speaker McCormack's office was asking why there was a delay in processing Keller's discharge. Weber replied that Keller had never filled out the papers.

Incensed, Weber called Yeoman Keller into his office and told him he didn't appreciate his using political pressure, and that his papers would be processed in the regular course—when he filed them. Weber immediately received a second call from Jones at the Pentagon, who asked why he had told Keller, "I don't give a damn what the Speaker of the House had to say." Sputtering, Weber tried to explain what he had told Keller, but he saw the handwriting clearly on the wall. Weber told me he hopped to and quickly got an aide to help Keller fill out the application papers for a hardship discharge. Nevertheless, Weber recommended against granting the discharge on the grounds that Keller apparently had substantial resources to pay for his wife's treatment and was living far above his navy pay.

To Weber's astonishment, Keller was ordered discharged on grounds of hardship a mere six days after the application went in! Pressure had come from the head of the Bureau of Naval Personnel (BUPERS) to get the lad out, pronto. Not surprisingly, the normal steps for processing a hardship application had been bypassed.

After questioning both Keller Jr. and Sr. under promises of immunity, I learned something that no other witnesses had given us before: Mike Silbert had claimed that Sweig wanted $5,000 cash for his services. Keller Sr. gave him the green light and had bank records corroborating how the cash he gave Silbert was generated. The timing of the cash withdrawal matched perfectly with Keller's discharge.

Now it was time to bring Silbert in. My experience with Voloshen's dramatic decline had made me think hard about what I was doing. Sweig had reported to Allenwood Federal Prison in July to begin serving his sentence. Was I some sort of Inspector Javert, implacably pursuing my prey beyond reasonable bounds? Or was I representing an honest effort on behalf of the public to expose and prosecute corruption?

If Mike Silbert could confirm that Sweig asked for and received a bribe for using the Speaker's influence to get a millionaire's son out of military service, I would go forward and seek a new indictment of Sweig—this time for bribery. But what if Silbert had lied to Keller? What if Sweig had not asked for money and Silbert had simply pocketed Keller's cash? This would hardly have been an unlikely scenario, given the general moral tone of the people involved.

I decided to deal gently but firmly with the seventy-two-year-old Silbert. Wisely, he had retained a very capable defense lawyer when I subpoenaed him to testify before the grand jury. Herald Price Fahringer could have had a career in Hollywood as easily as one in the courtroom. Tall, prematurely silver haired, and impeccably dressed, Fahringer was an experienced defense lawyer from Buffalo, New York, who often tried cases and argued appeals in the federal courts in New York City. Fahringer told me Silbert would assert his Fifth Amendment right not to testify. It would be pointless to drag the old man before a grand jury. Why wouldn't we just go away?

I candidly explained the facts I had. All we wanted from Silbert was the truth; I was not seeking to prosecute him and would grant him immunity for his truthful testimony. We could do this the hard way or the easy way.

Fahringer knew that there were two possibilities: His client had bribed a federal official or he had defrauded his employer out of $5,000. Either way, this was the right time for him to retire. Silbert was undoubtedly aware of Voloshen's plight. Immunity for truthful testimony must have appealed to him as the best option for a bad situation. After much back-and-forth, Fahringer brought Mike Silbert in for a proffer—an off-the-record opportunity for me to hear what he had to say firsthand, question him, and evaluate his demeanor and credibility as a witness. Only then would I decide whether to grant immunity. As always, Tony Passaretti, older (he was a couple of years older than my father) and reassuring, helped put Silbert in a more cooperative frame of mind. Fahringer had done his job well. Cooperating under a grant of immunity ought not be a halfway measure. If a witness tells only part of the story and is later found to be holding back or lying, he could wind up losing his immunity and being prosecuted—truly a lose/lose proposition.

To my relief, Silbert appeared to be in excellent health, tall, stocky, and avuncular. His story was convincing. Silbert approached Sweig about helping his boss's son shortly after Keller had received his 1A classification and army induction notification. Sweig counseled that rather than hassling with the draft board, Keller should join the navy instead, as a first step in the plan to get him out. Sweig told Silbert his connections were better in the navy than any other branch. When Silbert reported later that young Keller had joined the navy and been assigned to duty in Jacksonville, Sweig told him it would cost the Kellers $5,000 to work out a discharge. After getting the cash from Keller Sr., Silbert had the $5,000 mailed to Sweig, as the Speaker's top aide had directed. The kicker was that Silbert had a witness to mailing the cash to Sweig! Concerned that the $5,000 might somehow get lost, Silbert had a friend watch him put the cash into an envelope addressed to Sweig, which the friend, at Silbert's request, actually put in the mail.

I pressed Silbert on his prior dealings with McCormack and Sweig. The Speaker had never asked for money and Silbert had given him none. But Martin Sweig was another matter. Keller Industries, a manufacturer of aluminum window frames and ladders, enjoyed access to the Speaker's office as it grew to be a $100-million-per-year business. Silbert handled the company's labor relations. What he told me next made my jaw drop. At Sweig's request, for years Silbert had directly paid the rent on Sweig's Washington apartment. And he had the canceled checks to prove it!

I reported Silbert's tale to a wide-eyed Mike Seymour. The taunting and sanctimonious words of Paul Smith's closing argument still reverberated: "The prosecution cannot prove Martin Sweig took a dime." Seymour authorized me to seek an indictment for bribery. But there was one small problem. Nothing having to do with the Keller episode had any connection to the Southern District of New York. Everything had occurred either in Florida or Washington. We had no jurisdiction to bring this case in New York. We could refer the matter to the U.S. attorney's office in Washington or Miami. Or perhaps there was an alternative. Within a week the chief of the criminal division of the Department of Justice approved a request from Seymour that I be appointed temporarily as a special assistant U.S. attorney for the Southern District of Florida. In that capacity, I could convene a grand jury in Miami and prosecute the case there myself.

There were still two witnesses to consider: Martin Sweig and John McCormack. I wrote to Paul Smith, advising him that Sweig would have the opportunity, if he chose, to testify in the grand jury about Keller. This was little more than a formality. After Sweig's conviction for a single count of perjury before the grand jury in the Voloshen case, there was no way he was going to testify again.

That left Speaker McCormack. McCormack had since retired from Congress after a farewell party in December that was widely reported for the effusive praise heaped upon the Bostonian by colleagues from both parties. In addition, as a parting gift, Congress had voted him a stipend for two years' paid office space in Boston as well as salaries for a secretary and administrative assistant.

I wanted the Speaker's testimony locked in on the record. After his performance in the New York trial, I was wary of how he might try to protect Sweig. It would be interesting to see his reaction to the new revelations about his trusted aide taking cash from Silbert. Again, out of deference to McCormack's age and former position, we would not require him to appear before the grand jury in Miami, but would take his sworn deposition at a location convenient to him and then read the transcript to the grand jury. The Speaker requested that the deposition be taken in the law office of his nephew, Edward McCormack. Our ground rules permitted Edward to observe but not to confer with his uncle or otherwise participate in the conduct of the deposition.

The Speaker, dressed as always in a gray suit and vest, seemed to have aged in the few months since I had last seen him in Washington. After some initial pleasantries—"Call me Eddie," said the younger McCormack— the Speaker slid his tall, lanky frame into a chair at a conference table in Eddie's spacious office. Grayer, even gaunt, McCormack raised his right hand and swore that the testimony he was about to give would be the truth, the whole truth, and nothing but the truth.

I took a moment to reflect on the momentousness of the occasion. How was it possible that a twenty-seven-year-old kid from Brooklyn was now representing the full authority of the United States of America in taking sworn testimony from the former Speaker of the House of Representatives? I caught myself and began to put on the stenographic record the purpose of the inquiry. I then explained that the Speaker, like any other witness before the grand jury, had certain constitutional rights, including the right to refuse to give self-incriminating testimony. The Speaker acknowledged that he understood his rights, and I spent the next two hours probing every aspect and possible connection that McCormack might have to the brief navy career of young Keller and the strings that were pulled to secure his discharge.

McCormack denied any knowledge of the Keller matter or of Sweig's involvement in it, much less any active role. By this time, I had learned a great deal about Sweig's controlling grip over the operation of the Speaker's office, his mendacity, and his incredible hubris in having his rent paid directly by a lobbyist. It was easy to see how return phone calls or correspondence relating to Sweig's pet matters would be shunted directly to Sweig. I had no evidence to suggest that McCormack had made any calls or written any letter on Keller's behalf. Laconically, McCormack allowed as how he neither knew of nor would have approved of Sweig being paid for doing Silbert's bidding. But where was the outrage?

At the conclusion of the deposition, while the stenographer was packing up her notes and equipment, the Speaker motioned me over to a corner of the office. Eddie moved to join us, but his uncle waved him off.

Throwing his lanky arm over my shoulders, McCormack towered over me. "Richard," he began in a hushed, almost conspiratorial voice, "you don't really believe I had anything to do with this?"

I looked the old man in the eye. "Mr. Speaker, I have seen no evidence to suggest you knew what was going on." My answer was truthful but perhaps could have been phrased more diplomatically. No matter. The Speaker, tightening his grasp on my shoulder and revealing his true colors as an old-time Boston pol, pressed on, hardly drawing new breath, "because, I want you to know that more than any person in the United States, other than President Truman, I was responsible for the creation of the State of Israel." The brazenness of this statement left me speechless. The sheer chutzpah of taking a shot at influencing me with it was mind-boggling. I finally replied, "Gee, I didn't know that, very interesting, Mr. Speaker," as we shook hands and said good-bye.

Our deference to the Speaker did not extend to cutting him any slack in subpoenaing and reviewing his financial records. But we could find nothing that contradicted the picture of a man who had accumulated little in the way of assets or net worth. We were rewarded with a story in Jack Anderson's nationally syndicated column headlined, "McCormack Hounded Despite Denial." Anderson, who had staunchly defended McCormack from the time the first publicity over the Parvin-Dorhmann SEC intervention broke, labeled me a "Nixon gumshoe," harassing an old man about a hardship discharge for a navy enlisted man. According to Anderson, the locus for the interview in Eddie's office was accomplished only after we "finally agreed not to bait the grieving McCormack at the hospital where he is keeping a lonely vigil at the bedside of his beloved wife, Harriet. McCormack balked at answering the gumshoe's questions at the hospital, Anderson continued, "for fear it might upset his wife." Pure bunk. And me, a Nixon gumshoe? Only time would demonstrate the irony of Jack Anderson's assertion. Anderson went on to vent his spleen at Nixon and his attorney general, John Mitchell, for engineering this outrage. First the president honors the man at a White House luncheon, and then this! A sputtering Ron Ziegler, Nixon's press secretary, denied any White House involvement in directing the investigation. This was to prove to be one of the standout truthful assertions of Nixon and his press secretary insofar as it dealt with matters that concerned me directly. There would be no reply from us to Anderson. I would just keep my head down and try to do the right thing.

I presented my evidence to a Miami grand jury, which promptly voted to indict Sweig for bribery. As the trial date approached, Tony Passaretti and I checked into the Everglades Hotel in downtown Miami near the courthouse, an establishment that clearly had seen better times. We were given the use of an office in the U.S. attorney's office. Other amenities like secretarial help and supplies magically appeared courtesy of Passaretti's foraging skills, first honed as an army sergeant during World War II. Even minus the Thompson submachine gun he carried in combat throughout the European campaign, Tony's skills were notable, replacing rank and the threat of violence with sweet talk and charm.

The judge who had been assigned the case was a tough old bird named William Mehrtens who reputedly carried a sidearm at all times— more of an unusual characteristic in Miami then than it is now. Mehrtens had a well-earned reputation as a law-and-order conservative, usually favoring the government in criminal cases. It would remain to be seen how he would react to seeing a Washington insider tried on criminal charges.

Sweig was brought from prison to attend the trial. He actually looked better than when I had last seen him at his sentencing. Perhaps the rest had done him some good. Paul Smith, feisty as ever, came down from Boston to defend him. I was the sole lawyer for the prosecution.

The evidence went in as well as I could have expected. The testimony of the navy men, Silbert, and the Kellers was reported daily in the Miami papers, often on the front page. Something of a flap occurred when two top navy brass testified about the effect of political pressure on the decision to cut Keller loose. One, the chief of naval operations, was appalled by the shortcuts. The commander of the Atlantic Fleet, who had headed BUPERS when the Keller decision was made, had a different take. The judge began to perceive this was no run-of-the-mill prosecution. My only setback was the court's ruling that Silbert's other payments to Sweig for his rent and the like would not be admissible, as they were unrelated to the bribery charge involving young Keller's discharge.

There was no need for me to call John McCormack as a government witness. If Sweig wanted him in the courtroom, he would have to call him as a defense witness. And he did.

McCormack's appearance in the Miami courtroom followed only a month after his wife of fifty years passed away. Surely he could have easily avoided testifying if he had so desired. But Smith was counting on the Speaker to rescue Sweig from what looked like an open-and-shut case of bribery. This time there was no pantomime for the jury's benefit as the Speaker, looking every bit his seventy-nine years, took the stand. Under Smith's questioning, McCormack told the jury of Sweig's hard work and dedication. While he did not recall any matter involving Henry Keller Jr., it would not have surprised him if Sweig did help him, as it was standard procedure in his office to "perform favors covering the whole spectrum of human activity."

"Sure," I thought. "As soon as the military could draft young men, McCormack's office would apply pressure to get them out. All requests for discharge cheerfully granted. The whole process would be a big revolving door."

Of course, the Speaker went on, Sweig had authority to use his name and sign letters on his behalf. And it was Sweig's duty to help friends and constituents obtain services from government agencies, including applications for compassionate or hardship military discharge. Yes, it was acceptable for Sweig to take such steps without his specific knowledge, the Speaker agreed. He was far too busy with other important matters to involve himself with such things. And finally, it was clearly within Sweig's authority for him to make telephone calls to naval officers using McCormack's name.

But there would be no vouching for Sweig's honesty and integrity by the Speaker at this trial. That would have opened the door to examination of Sweig's prior perjury conviction and Silbert's rent payments—facts Smith needed to keep from the jury.

Perhaps Smith was counting on me to undertake a vigorous cross-examination of the Speaker. Not a chance. There was no way I would alienate the jury by treating the kindly old man as anything but a favored uncle.

Of course, I began, McCormack would never have countenanced a member of his staff demanding, much less receiving, cash in return for these favors. The Speaker was quick to agree. That, he knew, was not only wrong but also against the law. Under gentle leading, McCormack acknowledged that he had never heard of Keller, much less did he make any calls to the navy on his behalf. Indeed, he was unaware of having a Keller file in his office until I visited him in Washington and asked if I might review his files. While McCormack acknowledged knowing Silbert, whom he recalled had been introduced to him by another member of Congress, he categorically denied knowing that Silbert, who had testified as an unindicted coconspirator, paid Sweig $5,000 in cash. Having accomplished what I needed to do, I sat down, thanking McCormack courteously. If we were to lose the case, it would not be because I had snatched defeat from the jaws of victory by overzealous cross-examination.

Smith, looking desperately to create some doubt in the jury's mind as the case was coming to a close, took a last shot on redirect examination. Why, he asked McCormack, if doing favors were part of the office routine, was it necessary for anyone to pay Sweig to have him make calls to the navy to push for a hardship discharge? I could think of a few reasons, starting with Sweig's greed and hubris, but I was not about to listen to any answer the Speaker might have rehearsed with Smith. I objected, as the question was improper on several grounds, and the judge sustained it, directing McCormack not to answer.

As the Speaker left the courtroom, Smith rested his case, having called only one witness. Final arguments were straightforward. I had the evidence and held all the cards. All Smith could do was ask the same question he had put to McCormack. Why would anyone pay Sweig? In final argument I could supply my own answer—because Sweig had put the Speaker's influence up for sale and that was his price.

The jury had little trouble reaching a verdict. Guilty on all three counts of conspiracy and bribery as charged in the indictment. At sentencing, Sweig denied he had done anything wrong. Judge Mehrtens sentenced him to three years in prison, to run concurrently with his prior thirty-month sentence on the perjury conviction.

I found it hard to understand then how McCormack could have been both unaware of what had gone on and still willing to stand up for Martin Sweig. Where was the outrage, or at least the disappointment and disapproval? Had Sweig's service to him over so many years canceled the normal sense of betrayal one in McCormack's position might harbor toward Sweig and Voloshen, who together ruined the Speaker's last act on the public stage? Was it simply loyalty that brought McCormack to Miami to testify on Sweig's behalf, or did the old man have something to fear if Sweig felt abandoned? I didn't know the answer then, and I don't know the answer now.

John W. McCormack died on November 22, 1980, at the age of eighty-nine. The building housing the Post Office and Federal Courthouse in Boston was named after him.

MARTIN SWEIG WAS PAROLED from prison after serving one year of his three-year sentence. "I was a model prisoner," Sweig said to reporters upon his release.

Judge Mitchell Schweitzer, sixty-six, resigned from the New York State Supreme Court on December 22, 1971, one day before he was scheduled to appear before a judicial panel deliberating on his removal from the bench. Some of the charges Schweitzer faced related to his relationship with the deceased Nathan Voloshen, whom he allowed to entertain him publicly on a weekly basis for seven years, while at the same time interceding on behalf of Voloshen's mobster and swindler clients, one of whom, Michael Raymond, referred to Schweitzer as the "best judge money could buy." Schweitzer gave ill health as the reason for his resignation.

Ted Ratnoff was arrested by detectives under the direction of Manhattan DA Frank Hogan, seizing a large quantity of tapes and electronic recording equipment from the "bug master's" home in Pound Ridge, New York. It was suggested that Ratnoff was extorting money from patrons of the notorious Eastside Madam, Xaviera Hollander.

When Salvatore "Sally Burns" Granello got out of jail, he swore revenge against the members of his Mafia family who had whacked his son while he was behind bars. Apparently, the young Granello had slapped a "made" member of the family in public, and his death sentence was swiftly carried out without notification to or right of appeal by Sally. Granello's threats of retribution reached the ears of the bosses. The decision "to put an X through Granello" was picked up by an FBI bug. In accordance with FBI protocol, two special agents picked Sally up, played him the tape, and offered to put him into protective custody. Nothing doing. Passaretti and I were briefed on the situation because of our earlier work in prosecuting Granello. We hit him with a forthwith subpoena (which requires the person to appear immediately) and he agreed to come in to talk. Tony and I gave it our best shot, trying to convince Sally to leave the dark side and work with us to get the men who had murdered his son. Granello was courteous but firm. No dice. Six weeks later, Granello's body was found stuffed in the trunk of a stolen car, a bullet in his brain. Murdered gangland style, as the tabloids put it.

CHAPTER THREE

Abscam

Watergate had provided a watershed point in my career. Many opportunities were available. Would I go back to the U.S. attorney's office in New York? Would I take another job in the public sector? Mario Cuomo, then lieutenant governor of New York, wrote to ask whether I might be interested in leading an effort to investigate nursing home abuses in New York State. I felt that I had learned and accomplished much in my seven years as a prosecutor. If I were going to have a career in the private practice of law, this would be the right time to make the transition.

I was greatly flattered to receive offers from two legendary figures in the law—Louis Nizer and Edward Bennett Williams—to join their law firms. In a sense, these offers gave me the self-confidence to believe I could build a law practice on my own. In the eighteen months I had lived in Washington, I had grown to appreciate the easy accessibility of Georgetown, with its leafy trees and beautiful gardens, to the downtown business center. The people were friendly and I had earned something of a reputation as a tenacious, if still inexperienced, courtroom lawyer. And I was intrigued with life in America's political capital. I decided to accept the offer of partnership in the midsized commercial firm of Melrod, Redman & Gartlan, known for its real estate and banking practice. They offered a chance to earn a substantial multiple of my government salary and the financial support and backup to launch my career in private practice.

Since all my prior experience was in the prosecution of white-collar crime, it was logical that I would begin as a criminal defense lawyer. Civil litigation would come later, over time. My first trial came as a referral from Jack Bray, an outstanding lawyer who had successfully defended one of H. R. Haldeman's principal deputies, Gordon Strachan, in the Watergate cover-up case. I was drawn to Jack's quick wit and sunny disposition. We have been close friends for more than thirty years.

My first client had been indicted for insurance fraud and was scheduled to stand trial in federal court in St. Louis. I was able to get the case dismissed after discovering improper contacts between the prosecutors and the private insurance industry association that investigated the case. I was off to a good start.

I was fortunate to win a succession of criminal cases that followed, some by jury verdict and some on technical and procedural arguments before trial. My familiarity with prosecutorial thinking and procedure served me well. I was starting to get bigger cases and more opportunities to showcase my ability.

The first nationally publicized criminal defense case I was involved with after Watergate was Abscam—the FBI sting operation that resulted in the convictions of six congressmen, one senator, and three members of the Philadelphia city council. And while the conduct of the politicians who took money from the make-believe representatives of a make-believe, fantastically wealthy Middle Eastern businessman was cravenly avaricious, repugnant, and ultimately judged illegal, the conduct of those who dreamed up and executed the scheme pushed the limits of aggressive law enforcement over the line into a zone threatening fundamental restraints on police powers.

A sting operation can be a useful and effective law enforcement technique. Take, for example, the "granny cop" scenario. To combat a wave of muggings in a particular neighborhood, an undercover police officer is disguised as an elderly woman and sits with her purse in plain sight on a park bench. With the proper backup, the police will apprehend predators who attempt a purse snatching or worse. That's legitimate.

But sting operations, to be fair, must mimic real-life situations. And once a sting operation is set in motion, it is difficult, under the best of circumstances, for the police to be in complete control over how things develop.

Unlike solving a crime that has already been committed, injecting a police element into an ongoing scenario can have unforeseen consequences. For example, in a Midwestern "fencing" sting years ago, police set up an undercover operation to buy stolen cars, videotaping the thieves for later identification and prosecution. In order to snare the largest number of thieves in the area, the police offered prices for the stolen vehicles substantially above the going rate. As anticipated, with the higher prices the sting's business took off. Then tragedy struck: Two innocent car owners were murdered in the course of the thefts. Did the inflated prices "create" more crime by encouraging a more violent element into car theft?

Few who have been involved in running undercover investigations—myself included—can honestly deny the adrenaline rush that comes from hearing the target incriminate himself on tape to a supposedly trusted accomplice, particularly when the target brags about how smart he is in avoiding detection. Yet, once set in motion, the potential for surprise in an undercover operation is boundless.

One benign example. The Knapp Commission's New York City police corruption investigation provided many promising leads to follow up. During the time I was chief of the special prosecutions unit at the U.S. attorney's office, we devised a sting operation to investigate allegations surrounding a crooked lawyer fixing cases before a state court judge. A bail bondsman who "rolled over" when caught in a police bribery case gave us the information necessary to open an investigation. We proposed to stage a "controlled" arrest of an undercover law enforcement officer who would seek out the lawyer. Would the lawyer solicit bribe money and steer the case to the allegedly corrupt judge, as the bondsman assured us was the lawyer's modus operandi?

To ensure that the undercover cop would be unknown to our targets, the Drug Enforcement Agency representative to our state/federal anticorruption task force recommended we use a rookie DEA agent from Detroit who had never even been to New York. Because the DEA agent was a young woman, great care was taken to ensure that the staged arrest and subsequent processing would take place early enough to absolutely guarantee that she would not, under any circumstance, be held overnight in jail. We went over the simple plan several times: The DEA agent would be "arrested" by Vinnie Murano, one of the NYPD officers assigned to the task force, at eight o'clock in the morning. The charge would be possession of a concealed handgun our cop would observe as our decoy opened her purse in a restaurant. She would be processed immediately at the precinct and brought to the criminal court building for arraignment. Bail would be arranged by our cooperating bondsman. Guaranteed, this could all be accomplished by two P.M. She would then be wired with a recording device and introduced to the lawyer targeted by the bondsman. Two other officers would provide surveillance. Foolproof, right?

As I waited in my office in the federal courthouse in Foley Square, I received reassuring reports on the progress of the controlled arrest. Everything was going as planned. Once she was back at my office, our newly minted criminal defendant would be prepped for the tricky next steps of her meeting with the lawyer. She would make absolutely no suggestion of a bribe—it would come from the lawyer or not at all.

Tom Doonan, one of our in-house investigators, was the first to return from the New York County courthouse at 100 Centre Street. "Rick [my nickname then], you better sit down."

"What? They denied her bail?" My mind raced. What could screw up such a simple plan?

"She pleaded guilty."

"Are you fucking nuts? The whole idea is that she goes into the system—fighting the case! You can't be serious!"

"I only know what I saw," Doonan reported in a Joe Friday monotone. "She pleaded guilty."

Ten minutes later the rest of the contingent, including our undercover prodigy, was in my office. Considering the amount of time and effort that had gone into establishing the predicate for the sting, I tried to restrain my incredulity.

"I'm told you entered a guilty plea. Yet the whole idea for the sting was based on your pleading *not* guilty. How could you plead guilty?"

The young DEA agent wiped away a tiny tear with her finger.

"Once I got to the courthouse they assigned me a Legal Aid lawyer. He told me that he thought he could get me a suspended sentence for the gun charge. He was so persuasive, I felt stupid saying I wanted to go to trial. So I agreed to plead guilty."

Astonishing. Our careful plan defeated by the press of business at the criminal court plea bargain bazaar and an impressionable rookie agent.

"Go back to Detroit," was all I could muster.

———————

THERE HAD NEVER BEFORE been a case like Abscam, and I hope never to see a repetition of such unbounded expansion of federal law enforcement authority. At its core, Abscam was an honesty test, imposed essentially on a random basis, to see whether members of Congress and other politicians would bite at the opportunity to take large cash payments from an oil-rich Arab sheikh in return for a promise to help the sheikh at some later date.

Among the most glaring defects in the investigation was the selection of the FBI's undercover operative, a convicted confidence man and life-long hustler named Mel Weinberg. A crude-talking "deez and doze" guy from the Bronx, Weinberg was as street-smart and fast on his feet as any con man I had seen before or since.

A career swindler, Weinberg had been nabbed for perpetrating a scheme in which he collected hundreds of thousands of dollars in "front fees" from gullible businessmen on the promise of securing financing for their ventures. Of course, the financing never came through because Weinberg's promises were lies. Weinberg then talked the FBI into using him as an undercover operative to buy stolen securities and artwork in a fake fencing operation. In return, the FBI went to bat for Weinberg, convincing the sentencing judge to reduce a three-year prison term to a suspended sentence and probation. As part of the sting, Weinberg employed the same scam he had used in fleecing his businessmen victims—that he represented a Middle Eastern sheikh who would pay top dollar for stolen securities and works of art. An indication of Weinberg's single-minded determination to please his new masters and save himself from jail was that one of his early victims was his friend and personal lawyer.

Weinberg soon convinced his handlers that to make his cover more credible, he should have opulent surroundings and the accoutrements of wealth. Weinberg was paid a starting salary of $1,000 a month, later raised to $3,000, plus expenses. An inkling of what was to come might have been gleaned from the justification his FBI handler gave for recommending the increase in pay—that Weinberg would "try and con other people on the side" if his lifestyle was not kept up.

Several months later, the ruse shifted to Weinberg playing the role of a trusted aide to the sheikh in charge of "making friends" with powerful government officials to facilitate the sheikh's U.S. business operations or, due to political instability in his supposed home country (the United Arab Emirates was mentioned along with a handful of other countries), in case he needed to seek refuge in the United States. The FBI set Weinberg up with a headquarters on Long Island for the sheikh's company, Abdul Enterprises, Inc. Weinberg's FBI salary would be supplemented by substantial bonuses based on his performance. A yacht in Florida, a Washington town house, and posh hotel suites in New York and Philadelphia—all wired for sound and video—were supplied to add authenticity. Thus had the wily con man parlayed a three-year prison term into a salaried position, cushy benefits, and a bonus arrangement—all under the protection of the FBI.

Most important, the FBI arranged with Chase Manhattan Bank to provide Weinberg an extraordinarily valuable tool, beyond the dreams of any con man—confirmation that the fictitious sheikh had $400 million on deposit at Chase. Anyone questioning whether this portly, bearded, half-Jewish skell was really connected to a multibillionaire Arab oil baron could check it out with the Chase banker Mel was only too willing to provide as his reference.

How was Mel supposed to meet members of Congress? The concept was that middlemen with prior corrupt connections would be lured to the FBI's honeypot by the smell of ready cash and big paydays. But Weinberg's performance bonuses, coupled with his natural proclivity to lie and cheat, plus the FBI's failure to investigate whether the middlemen actually had the prior dealings they professed to have, completely skewed the investigation. Instead of reviewing evidence of these middlemen's prior corrupt activities, it would be proof enough for the FBI if they were able to produce politicians willing to take the sheikh's cash.

Enter Howard Criden, a middle-aged lawyer who was the lead partner in a small Philadelphia commercial law firm. Criden telephoned me after meeting with the chief prosecutor in the case, Thomas Puccio, head of the Brooklyn federal organized crime strike force. Puccio had tried to convince Criden to throw in his lot with the prosecution by pleading guilty and turning state's evidence. Puccio had played incriminating videotapes of Criden's meetings with Weinberg and others to bring home the point that the Philadelphia lawyer had no choice but to plead guilty and testify for the government. Criden was at the point of surrender. All he wanted was a few days of anonymity before his arrest so that he could explain the situation to his two sons and set his affairs in order. Puccio readily agreed. On his way to the restroom, Criden passed an FBI agent who was photocopying a newspaper article. Quickly scanning the article, Criden realized Puccio must have known his promise was impossible to keep. Criden's name was prominently mentioned in the story. In fact, the national media were all over the case—the result of a deluge of leaks emanating from government sources. Furious, Criden told Puccio the deal was off.

A large and generally affable man, Criden believed he had been manipulated into producing a half dozen congressmen who met with the bogus sheikh and his supposed representatives. His initial dealings with the prosecution convinced him not to do his victims further harm by becoming a witness for the prosecution against them. Criden asked if I would defend him and try the case. I said I would. The more I learned about Abscam, the less I liked what the government had done.

From the outset, our defense strategy was fraught with risk. Could a jury be persuaded that the government's conduct was so extreme and overreaching, creating crime where none existed before, that it would excuse the defendant's sleazy conduct, immortalized on videotape? Even if the jury voted to convict, would the federal courts find that governmental violations of due process of law were so outrageous as to justify overturning any guilty verdicts?

In the beginning, I had only Howard Criden's version of what had occurred. The trick would be to develop evidence admissible in court of what had gone on behind the scenes in the Abscam investigation to prove a pattern of governmental manipulation and misconduct. Despite the government's obligation to make potentially exculpatory facts known to the defense, it was clear from the outset that getting the straight story would be a challenge. In essence, I would be investigating the investigators.

The initial, devastating publicity about the case was the first objective indication that there were serious problems with the fairness of the investigation. Compared to an ordinary leak in a criminal case, Abscam was a tsunami. NBC reporters had identified the location of one of the Abscam meeting places—a rented house on W Street in Northwest Washington—and had staked out the house with its own hidden surveillance team for nearly two months, recording Abscam targets entering and leaving. In addition, both the *New York Times* and *Newsday* immediately ran extensive details of the investigation that could have only been the product of a massive leak, contrary to explicit Department of Justice rules.

A second indication that Criden's concerns might have merit was that the prosecutor in charge of the investigation was Thomas Puccio. While I had no prior dealings with Puccio, his reputation among my former colleagues in the Southern District of New York was terrible. Even discounting for the natural rivalry between offices in close proximity, I knew of no other federal prosecutor about whom my colleagues held such a jaundiced view. Walter Phillips, one of our most talented prosecutors, had dealt with Puccio on a number of cases involving international narcotics traffickers. Usually unflappable, Wally became near apoplectic at the mere mention of Puccio's name. Robert Morvillo, chief of our criminal division (who has since become one of the premier white-collar criminal defense lawyers in America, most recently defending Martha Stewart), once returned from a meeting with Puccio and immediately issued orders that no one in the office was to talk to Puccio without a corroborating witness present. As events unfolded, I found no reason to disagree with my colleagues' judgment. It would take extraordinary efforts to extract reliable information from the government about the conduct of the Abscam investigation—much of which was not disclosed until years after the trials were over.

Criden claimed that Mel Weinberg convinced him (in conversations that Weinberg had either deliberately failed to record or had recorded and then destroyed) that none of the politicians would ever be called upon actually to do anything for the sheikh. As bizarre as it sounded, Weinberg told him that his boss, who was fabulously rich—"Hey, the man's got four hundred million sitting in a fucking *checking* account for crissake"—simply liked to make friends with politicians in countries where he did business. "Fifty thousand for a multibillionaire is like a twenty-dollar tip that me or you might leave for a waiter."

It was 1979, and America still remembered the oil embargo that had begun in 1973, with huge lines at gas stations throughout the nation and soaring prices. Why not help relieve this fat cat sheikh of some of his petrodollars? Of course his boss was eccentric. Why else would a prominent Arab entrust a knock-around guy from the Bronx—named Weinberg, no less—to spread around his cash? Mel made it clear to Howard that he was making a big score. He had locked onto the proverbial golden goose and anyone checking on Weinberg's background would find nothing inconsistent with his story—Mel's reputation as a grifter was well established.

Every time the sheikh made a new political friend, Mel would get a handsome payment himself. Any questions? Just check with our banker at Chase Manhattan. And as the politicians were introduced, it was cash on the barrelhead—$50,000 a pop. Criden could confirm that Weinberg's description was true. None of the pols actually had to *do* anything. They simply needed to *say* that they would be helpful, if necessary, at some unspecified future date. What more did Criden need to see?

Abscam was powerful proof that when something seems too good to be true, it usually is.

Weinberg was fiendishly clever in reengineering the sting for his own benefit. He knew that the congressmen would never be called on to introduce a bill or vote on a proposal favoring the sheikh or one of his companies. Such invasion of the legislative province was well beyond the FBI's reach. And Weinberg's boast to Criden of being rewarded whenever the sheikh made a new friend was not far from the swindler's bonus deal with the FBI.

Should the FBI "supervisors" from the bureau's sleepy Long Island office, not to mention Puccio, have been suspicious that Weinberg was running a somewhat different sting operation from the one his putative handlers described to their superiors at the FBI and Department of Justice? Using an experienced con man as an undercover operator poses far more difficult issues for law enforcement than the typical scenario where a criminal who has been turned introduces an undercover cop into a drug ring. It is then the undercover cop who has the principal dealings with the targets of the investigation, and it will be his or her credibility—backed up by electronic recordings if feasible—when it comes time to testify. Yet in Abscam, it was Weinberg—not his FBI minders who were later introduced to the targets as other employees of Abdul Enterprises—who maintained the principal contacts and made the arrangements for the payoffs. So if Mel let on to Howard that he was happy to cut corners in order to earn his commission from his eccentric boss, how difficult would it be to warn Criden not to be too candid about their arrangement in front of the other employees of the sheikh who might show up from time to time?

In order to maintain the integrity of an undercover operation, all contacts between the government operative and the targets must be monitored and reported. Yet instead of closely supervising Weinberg to ensure that his every contact with the targets was tape-recorded, Weinberg had had hundreds of telephone conversations as well as face-to-face meetings with targets of the investigation for which no recordings were produced. Moreover, when it came time for the prosecution to turn over the FBI reports chronicling the investigation, it turned out that only a single summary report—instead of the scores one would expect to have been generated contemporaneously—was produced by the FBI.

Howard Criden's law practice centered on real estate transactions. He met Angelo Errichetti, mayor of Camden, New Jersey, through Criden's interest in finding financing for an Atlantic City casino deal. Errichetti had been introduced to Weinberg by a neighbor who learned that the portly con man represented foreign investors looking for real estate opportunities in Atlantic City. Errichetti introduced Criden to his new friend, Mel Weinberg. Holding out to Criden and Errichetti the possibility of earning millions of dollars in fees if they could secure financing from Abdul for legitimate multimillion-dollar ventures, Weinberg made it clear that their esteem in the eyes of the sheikh would be substantially enhanced if they were able to introduce the sheikh to friendly politicians.

Mel Weinberg's fertile mind soon came up with the hallmark twist of the Abscam ploy—the seemingly irrational permutations of the "Arab mind," chief among which was that Middle Eastern businessmen such as his boss would not do business in a foreign venue unless they could make gifts of cash to the politicians of the region. To this, Weinberg added the proposition that in case the sheikh ran into political difficulties at home, he wanted to be able to call upon "friends" in the U.S. government to sponsor legislation allowing his immigration to America (as if this would have been a problem for a billionaire businessman). Of course, Weinberg was quick to assure Criden and Errichetti (in conversations that he apparently did not bother to record) that the sheikh and his friends were somewhat paranoid and faced no real threat in their home countries.

According to the FBI, the essence of the Abscam sting was for corrupt middlemen to bring in politicians with whom they had done crooked deals before. Yet Criden—who was responsible for bringing at least five different congressmen into the scheme—had met none of them, much less had corrupt dealings with them, before Abscam. He simply drew on acquaintances to get a reference, often cold calling, to let the congressmen know a very wealthy Arab businessman wanted to make investments in their districts. Even without doing a full background investigation on Criden before employing him as their de facto search committee (it *was* the FBI, after all), there were abundant clues that Criden was not some master fixer. For example, Criden talked about bringing in a New York congressman who was chairman of the House Maritime Committee. On October 10, 1979, Weinberg and Criden discussed a "heavy hitter":

WEINBERG: Who's that? The guy from New York?
CRIDEN: Yeah
WEINBERG: I think I know his name. Is it an Irishman?
CRIDEN: Yup. Begins with an "R."
WEINBERG: An "R"? I thought it begins with an "M."
CRIDEN: Well, the guy's got a lot to do with boats and maritime.
WEINBERG: Murphy?
CRIDEN: No. Ryan . . . Chairman of the Maritime.

Thus, despite Weinberg's prompting, Criden flunked the quiz on the identity of the Irish-American congressman and chairman of the House Maritime Committee with whom he was supposedly on intimate and corrupt terms.

It was not until a full week later that Criden repaired his recollection.

WEINBERG: Who the fuck is coming?
CRIDEN: Murphy

WEINBERG: You dumb fuck, you gave me "Ryan."

CRIDEN: I know I gave you the wrong guy. Murphy, you know who Murphy is? Murphy is the Chairman of the House Committee on Immigration. Not Immigration, Maritime. Ships . . .

How was it possible to ignore Criden's unfamiliarity with the very individuals he supposedly dealt with in past corrupt deals?

There was one incident that had to put the FBI on notice not only that Criden did not have the relationships he purported to have, but that he must have had some side understanding with Weinberg. Criden had quickly forged a working relationship with Angelo Errichetti. Having compared notes on their private conversations with Weinberg that public officials could receive cash payments without ever being called upon to deliver any benefit to the sheikh, Errichetti and Criden embarked upon their own variation of the scheme to help relieve the sheikh of his petrodollars.

If no actual official act need ever be performed, why go to the bother and expense of producing an actual public official? And so it came to pass that one Ellis Cook, a young partner in Criden's law firm, was persuaded to impersonate an unwitting high-ranking official of the Immigration and Naturalization Service named Mario Noto. The scam on the scammers was uncovered when an alert FBI agent noticed that Criden's young partner bore no resemblance to a photo he had obtained of the much older Mario Noto. It was sealed when the bumbling Cook misspelled his own name, "N-O-P-O," in a meeting with the sheikh's representative.

One might imagine that such an event would cause a reevaluation of Abscam's investigative premise and a quick decision to discontinue using Criden or Errichetti as middlemen. And wouldn't Criden and Errichetti—absent a secret arrangement with Weinberg—have had reason to fear retribution from the powerful sheikh for trying to pull off such a brazen fraud?

Not only did Criden and Errichetti go unpunished for their little frolic, they soon became the exclusive middlemen for Abscam. Criden went forth making telephone calls to lawyers he knew in distant parts of the nation to see if they could introduce him to congressmen from their regions.

Another episode, captured on videotape, demonstrated that the Camden mayor was operating under rules consistent with the notion that the sheikh was merely a cog in a divine plan to reverse the imbalance of foreign trade in Errichetti's favor. In this case, New Jersey senator Harrison "Pete" Williams was the target. All the senator needed to do was say yes to whatever the sheikh wanted to talk about and then leave with the cash.

No further obligation. Errichetti and Weinberg would both earn a pay-day, and Errichetti would ingratiate himself closer to making the big score he dreamed of in getting the sheikh to finance his project.

The evidence of Weinberg having skewed the sting into a scam was clear to me—but so was the Camden mayor's penchant for prodigious use of profanity crammed into every conceivable (and many inconceivable) nook and cranny of conversation. How would a jury react to hearing such language, as when the mayor described to Weinberg how he had prepped Williams for his meeting with the sheikh?

> ERRICHETTI: In other words, with Pete Williams, ok. When I went there he didn't say two fucking words. I got Pete by the fucking throat, I tell you as close as I came in his office. "Let me tell you something, cocksucker, don't you go fucking this thing, up. I got a chance to make a fucking million dollars, you prick. All you're gonna do is give a speech like you never gave in your life. Not much left to say. You're gonna fucking guarantee that fucking contract." He said, "No way." . . . I said, "You're gonna fucking say it. I don't give a fuck. *Never mind about doing it. You're gonna fucking say it.*"

On the eve of the anticipated meeting, Weinberg suggested to Errichetti that in order to stimulate the naturally low-key Williams into a more ro-bust performance, they "pep him up" by giving him some marijuana to smoke. And in a prep session with Senator Williams and Errichetti min-utes before the FBI-videotaped meeting with the sheikh, Weinberg ex-horted the senator to view the impending conference as "all bullshit" and "all talk."

In order for our trial strategy to succeed, we would need a judge who understood the difference between a vigorous federal investigation and one tainted by overreaching and impropriety. The evidence was over-whelming as to Criden's greed and willingness to inveigle public officials to meet with Weinberg and the fictitious sheikh. At most, he was guilty of attempting to fleece Weinberg's eccentric boss. But that wasn't the charge he faced. Criden had been indicted in both Brooklyn and Phila-delphia on charges of conspiracy to commit bribery in a total of five sepa-rate cases. In order to prove a conspiracy to commit bribery, the government would have to prove a quid pro quo—that is, that the public official re-ceived a payment in return for a promise to perform an official act. It was our contention that if the public official never intended to perform, it followed that the crime of bribery could not be proved. Key to the defense was the willingness of the assigned judge to accept our premise, at least to the extent of ordering the government to produce its files and answer questions about its methods. My hopes for the assignment of a sympathetic judge were only half realized. In the first of the Brooklyn federal court cases, Criden was indicted together with Errichetti, Representative Michael "Ozzie" Myers, and Louis Johanson, another of Criden's law partners, who actually knew Myers and was instrumental in inviting Myers to join in soaking the sheikh.

In Philadelphia, Criden was indicted along with Johanson, George Schwartz, president of the Philadelphia City Council, and Harry Jannotti, another councilman. While the Myers case was premised on helping the make-believe sheikh with a possible immigration problem, the Schwartz sting was based on an even more bizarre proposition. Here, Criden was informed that the sheikh and his partners wanted to build a luxury hotel in South Philadelphia. Could he line up City Council members who would be willing to help? Since a councilman was lower in the pecking order than a member of Congress, the reward for meeting with the sheikh's agents would be "only" $25,000. Of course, the predictable reaction to anyone wanting to spend tens of millions of dollars building a luxury hotel in that economically depressed area of Philadelphia would be welcomed with open arms and the key to the city. One of the councilmen told Weinberg just that. There was no need to pay him anything. He would gladly sponsor such a project, which would provide hundreds of new jobs and significant tax revenues for the city.

Mel's response was a new invocation of the vicissitudes of the "Arab mind." Unless his bosses could be sure that no problems with zoning, etc., would pop up (Criden observed that the area was at present zoned for urban warfare), they would not be comfortable making the investment. When the councilman reiterated that he wanted no payment for his support of such a project, Weinberg made it clear that unless such payments were accepted, the sheikh would simply look to another city to build his hotel. Ultimately, the council members lined up to receive payments, and Criden happily took his cut as facilitator.

The judge assigned to the Philadelphia case was John Fullam, a crusty veteran of fourteen years on the federal bench. He demanded that the lawyers appearing before him be fully prepared and would suffer no fools. That was fine with me.

On the other hand, the judge assigned to the Brooklyn case was the tall, square-jawed George C. Pratt, a law-and-order Republican appointee who had only four years' experience on the bench. I didn't mind the law-and-order part—indeed, I would have welcomed a former prosecutor who would see how far the Abscam investigation departed from established norms of procedure. But, as I quickly learned, Judge Pratt had the unfortunate combination of no practical criminal law experience and an unshakable willingness to accept at face value all of the prosecution arguments.

Puccio and the FBI wanted the Brooklyn case to be tried first. The Philadelphia prosecutors acceded, but not before Judge Fullam scheduled a hearing on the government leaks of prejudicial pretrial information. As depressing as watching the videotapes had proved to be, at least we would have the opportunity to seize the initiative and the moral high ground (think of trying to find the high ground in a swamp) by holding the first hearing in the case on the subject of the government's misconduct.

Judge Fullam was deeply troubled by the unprecedented leak of information that obviously came from government sources. As *Time* magazine reported, "Investigators leaked their findings to an overeager press, irreparably damaging the reputations of public officials before anyone had ever been formally accused of a crime . . . the massive and apparently deliberate leaks to the press were all legitimate topics of ethical concern and growing controversy."

Ordinarily, pretrial publicity is a big headache for a judge concerned about giving a defendant a fair trial. But when the prejudicial information comes from blatant leaks by the government, the court may fashion sanctions to punish the offenders. As Weinberg was himself a key suspect in leaking information, I subpoenaed him to appear at the hearing. The Philadelphia leaks hearing allowed me to take Mel Weinberg for a little road test, to see how he would respond to questions. I was interested in his demeanor. Would he become angry, defensive, combative if he were pushed? Did he have a hot button? Did he have "issues"? Most important, how would he play before a jury? Did he have a manner that was likable? Some of the professional con men I had met could charm the birds out of the trees.

On the stand, Weinberg seemed unprepared, tentative, unsure of himself. He was the same "deez and doze" character I had seen on videotape but without the self-confidence and swagger. I wanted to test his recollection of events without straying into the specifics of the upcoming trials. It was only jabs and feints—no haymakers until a jury was in the box. When Weinberg tried evasion or double-talk, Judge Fullam was quick to sustain my objections and insist that he answer the questions. Clearly, the judge had sized Mel up for what he was.

Weinberg steadfastly denied he was the source of any leaks to the media. But it turned out he was working on a book project with a journalist, providing the defense the opportunity to seek a subpoena for the manuscript. Coincidentally, his partner on the project was an editor at *Newsday*, one of the papers that broke the Abscam story, replete with details that could have come only from a government source.

I felt good about the first encounter with Abscam's chief operating officer. There were no knockout blows, but we had scored some points and had touched Mel up a bit. Only later did I learn the reason for Mel's lack of preparation. Puccio and his team had not made Weinberg available to the Philadelphia prosecutors handling the case before Judge Fullam. Until the last minute, they believed they could avoid producing the con man for the leaks hearing. As we were later to learn, the level of dissension among the prosecutors who had been involved in the investigation was virtually unprecedented. Judge Fullam opted to adjourn the hearing rather than conclude it, waiting until after trial to resume, if necessary, further inquiry into the leaks and other alleged violations of due process of law.

Weinberg was not alone in contemplating an Abscam book. It turned out that a close friend of Puccio, Jack Newfield, a writer for the *Village Voice* who had shared a Fire Island summer rental with the Brooklyn prosecutor while the Abscam investigation was under way, had negotiated a contract to write a book about Abscam. Puccio denied involvement in the project. Yet the facts showed that Newfield had locked up the deal prior to any Abscam indictments being returned. And Newfield's contract, which referred to the subject of the book as "Project X," provided for a hefty payment by the publisher to an unspecified "collaborator," if one were to be selected.

In a post-trial hearing on due process, probing whether the Abscam prosecutions satisfied basic standards of fairness, Puccio was called by lawyers for the defendants and questioned under oath about the Newfield book deal. The stakes were high, as a subsequent Senate report observed. If the allegations of Puccio's hidden interest were true, he would be guilty of violating American Bar Association standards relating to the administration of criminal justice, the ABA Code of Professional Responsibility, and, possibly, conflict-of-interest statutes. In addition, these ethical breaches would taint the fairness of the trials Puccio prosecuted and, by implication, the fairness of the entire investigation.

At the hearing, Puccio admitted that he was aware of Newfield's contract to write a book about Abscam but denied talking to him about possible collaboration. Later in the proceedings, Puccio requested permission to provide further testimony after "reflecting" on the questions about Newfield's book. Puccio then testified that he and Newfield had in fact discussed collaborating on a book in the future, but it had nothing to do with Abscam. The conversation occurred while Puccio was supervising the Abscam investigation, as did a dinner meeting Puccio attended with Newfield and Newfield's literary agent, Esther Newberg. But, according to Puccio, Abscam was never mentioned. Puccio admitted he was aware that Newfield had negotiated a contract for an Abscam book that provided for a potential coauthor. Indeed, the March 1980 contract provided for an advance to Newfield of $40,000; if a coauthor were selected, his or her advance would be $100,000. In later testimony, Newfield acknowledged that the only coauthor he would have considered was Puccio. And Puccio admitted that Newfield showed him the contract, and that it was obvious to him who the coauthor was supposed to be. Yet he had not discussed with Newfield who that coauthor would be. And still more interesting was this exchange during Puccio's examination at the Myers due process hearing:

Q: There's never been any discussion between you and Mr. New-field or Mr. Newfield's agent or any of the officials at Berkely or Putnam Press about your possible collusion as that coauthor or collaborator?
A: It might have been discussed but not by me.
Q: Was their discussion with authority, your approval?
A: Yes.

Ultimately, Judge Pratt ruled that the saga of "Project X" did not demonstrate that Thomas Puccio had either a conflict of interest or an undisclosed financial interest in the outcome of the prosecution.

THE BROOKLYN FEDERAL COURTHOUSE in Cadman Plaza is a stolid, unremarkable building across from a park. The trial began in August 1980, the tail end of a long hot summer. The courtroom in which the Honorable George C. Pratt presided was a windowless affair, outfitted with a dozen television monitors, portending the focus on the videotaped evidence of Howard Criden and his codefendants.

Sometimes the lawyers in a multidefendant case make the prosecution's work easier by disagreeing on tactics or strategy, or pointing fingers at each other. Such was not the case in *U.S. v. Myers, et al.* There were obvious differences among the four defendants on trial. Errichetti and Criden were involved in several Abscam transactions; Myers was the congressman who took money; Johanson, Criden's former law partner—a tall, introspective man who barely spoke—was the least involved, having merely facilitated the Myers introduction. Notwithstanding the differences, the defense lawyers acknowledged that our clients' fates would depend on whether the jury believed the government's conduct was so offensive as to outweigh the avarice and lack of moral compunction they were about to witness on videotape. If Criden prevailed in the first trial, the government might drop the cookie-cutter follow-on cases against him. Our odds were slim at best.

A silver lining was the opportunity for me to work alongside three top-notch defense lawyers. I already knew Myers's lawyer, Plato Cacheris, as the talented cocounsel (with Bill Hundley) who had represented John Mitchell in the Watergate cover-up trial (and, more recently, Monica Lewinsky). John Duffy, a seasoned Philadelphia criminal lawyer with a quick wit and ribald sense of humor, represented Johanson, while Angelo Errichetti had chosen one of the truly great courtroom lawyers of our time—Ray Brown of Newark, New Jersey. I had known Ray Brown only by reputation as a brilliant and indefatigable cross examiner who had made the difference between almost certain conviction and acquittal for scores of criminal defendants lucky enough to secure his services. At sixty-five years of age, he was still near the top of his game.

Although I was the kid among the defense lawyers, we quickly bonded into a team. Ray Brown was generous in complimenting me for the work I had done in Watergate and treated me as an equal. Ray (his son was Raymond, also a talented lawyer, so the old man was always "Ray") wanted to make sure from our first meeting that I knew he was black. Because he was so light skinned—the product of a Spanish and Carribean-African melting pot on the Carolina coast—people had often assumed him to be Caucasian. Indeed, as a young World War II officer in the still segregated army, Ray had been assigned to an all-white unit. He quickly let it be known he was a black man, proud of his heritage, who would not serve in a segregated white unit. Ray Brown served with distinction, rising to the rank of colonel, and has fought against racial injustice all his life.

Judge George Pratt was all business, with no discernible sense of humor. His law practice prior to his appointment to the bench was as partner in a Long Island corporate firm. A story about him related that he had found the pleasant view from the window of his suburban office too distracting, so he had ordered the window bricked up. Apocryphal or not, the tale seemed to capture Judge Pratt's no-nonsense, slightly Calvinistic style.

Our first big test would be whether we could obtain tapes of the conversations in which Errichetti and Criden claimed Mel had schooled them on how no one would ask the congressmen actually to *do* anything, and other ways to cheat his boss, the sheikh. By the time we were set for trial, we had received a tape of the prep session for Senator Williams—a powerful indictment of Weinberg's modus operandi, but no similar tapes of conversations between Criden and Weinberg. Either Criden was lying or Weinberg had failed to record or had recorded and then destroyed tapes of the conversations we needed to prove our defense directly. But Criden had recounted his recollection of events well before we learned of the similar episode with Williams. The best evidence we had on tape of Weinberg's signal that he was on the same side as those willing to relieve the sheikh of his pin money was his aside to Myers, "We got the goose that lays the golden egg; we all like to make a buck." The prosecution argued that all relevant conversations had been faithfully recorded by Weinberg under the FBI's watchful supervision.

As the failure to make regular reports or supervise and account for contacts with the targets became evident, I argued to Judge Pratt that the Abscam investigation departed significantly from normal standards of control and supervision. Coupled with the government's leaks and prejudicial publicity, the defense argued the case should be dismissed. Neil Levy, my associate working on the case, wrote detailed legal briefs supporting our position. Judge Pratt, unpersuaded, denied all motions to dismiss.

As the first of the Abscam trials, the Myers case commanded the full attention of the national media. As we filed into the courtroom, John Duffy pointed to Puccio, dressed in a rumpled and ill-fitting suit, remarking that the balding prosecutor with the bad comb-over would miss the *GQ* best-dressed list again that year. There was something about Puccio's smug officiousness that got Duffy's Irish up. I began calling the Philadelphia lawyer "Diorfy" to highlight his offended fashion sensibilities.

"Do you see that thread hanging down from the Pooch's coat jacket?" Duffy remarked during one of our many sidebar arguments at the bench.

"Ever alert to fashion trends, Diorfy," I replied. "Why not give the Pooch some tips?"

"How about this for a tip?" Duffy walked behind the prosecutor, who was intently making his point to the ever-receptive judge. Carefully, he began pulling on the thread, while appearing to give his rapt attention to the colloquy at the sidebar. As Puccio returned to the prosecution table, the result of Duffy's tailoring became apparent. Half the lining of Puccio's suit jacket was hanging down.

The prosecution led off with a barrage of tapes. On the profanity meter, exposure to an hour or two of Errichetti on tape was equivalent to a four-year hitch in the navy. Moreover, there seemed little that Errichetti would not agree to do to separate the sheikh from some of his oil wealth. But it was Ozzie Myers, the congressman-cum-longshoreman and bartender from South Philly, whose concise philosophy of life in the corridors of power became the anthem of Abscam. In Washington, Myers explained, "Money talks and bullshit walks." The defense table took these incoming fusillades of videotape stoically, feigning nonchalance as though such horrifying evidence of greed was unremarkable.

> ERRICHETTI: I will naturally talk to Ozzie first; I was just trying to grasp as to what he'll say. Ozzie's got balls, that's for openers.

There was no doubt that Myers fulfilled Errichetti's prediction that Ozzie would say whatever was required. In the meeting, Myers promised to support legislation to help the sheikh immigrate to the United States in the event that he later wished to do so.

The power of these tapes could not be overstated. Clearly, the effect on the jurors hearing an elected official respond with such vulgar alacrity to what appeared to be an unvarnished bribe was profound. Were we nuts in thinking that the jury could follow a court instruction to acquit on the charge of conspiracy to commit bribery because the defendants thought they were engaging in a fraudulent scheme with Weinberg to bilk the sheikh? Perhaps we were drinking the Kool-Aid of self-delusion. But even if the jury found our clients guilty, there was hope that the court of appeals would overturn a jury verdict if we were able to produce enough evidence to support our claims of prosecutorial misconduct.

Weinberg's idea of projecting credibility in his Brooklyn courtroom debut was to dress in a cream-colored three-piece suit with a pinkie ring on *each* hand, a large Rolex watch, and oversize, tinted aviator glasses. With his hand on the Bible, the career liar and swindler swore to tell the truth, the whole truth, and nothing but the truth.

One of the leads we gleaned from the hearing before Judge Fullam paid a big dividend. On the night before Weinberg's cross, I obtained a draft of the scam artist's autobiographical notes. Mel saw himself as a character straight out of Damon Runyon. And indeed, many of the anecdotes were hilarious—so long as you weren't on the receiving end of one of his swindles. By his own account, Mel had started down a crooked path of lies and cons at the tender age of seven, when he swiped gold stars for his report cards from his first-grade teacher's desk. By the eighth grade he was done with formal education, dropping out of school. Working for his father's glazier business, young Mel drummed up commerce by breaking storefront windows with a slingshot in the dead of night. Later he expanded this into a more lucrative insurance fraud operation.

My personal favorite involved the time Weinberg, believing he was suffering a heart attack, was rushed to the hospital. Feeling better by the time he was examined by a cardiologist, the tough-talking con man somehow got the heart specialist discussing hit men and the mob. By the time he left the hospital, Weinberg had swindled the doctor out of $10,000 on the bogus promise to have a hit placed on the cardiologist's wife.

But the jury also needed to see that the sine qua non of confidence artists is an utter heartlessness toward their victims and a disdain for their weakness and gullibility. It was this side of Weinberg's character I wanted to show the jury. How Weinberg boasted of screwing his own cousin out of tens of thousands of dollars in a series of scams. How Weinberg had bought up a quantity of defective socks for pennies and then sold them to workers as they rushed past the factory gates where Mel had set up his itinerant business. It was not until well after the fraudster had fled the scene that the workers discovered their bargain socks had no feet!

I wanted to show the jury that the front fee scam for which Weinberg had been arrested before his conversion to FBI operative bore an uncanny resemblance to the Abscam operation. Using the respectable-sounding London Investors as a front, Weinberg had separated dozens of desperate businessmen from hundreds of thousands of dollars on the promise of arranging financing for their ventures. Weinberg had used a number of accoutrements to gussy up the London Investors fraud—posh offices, forged bank documents, a classy British secretary, and a variety of stories about compliant/corrupt bank officers. But there was nothing to compete with the cover the FBI had given him—a legitimate banker at Chase who would verify the sheikh's bank balance of hundreds of millions.

Not only had Weinberg walked scot-free on the London Investors scam, he had simply incorporated its elements into promising tens of millions in financing for legitimate deals to his Abscam targets. The idea of a wealthy Arab investor had come from Weinberg, down to the very names for the sheikh and his associates used in the scam.

The focus of my cross-examination was to prove that despite the FBI's denials, Weinberg had continued to use all the tools in his London Investors toolbox to create a performance that would appear to be an agreement to bribery by an elected official. This way Weinberg would please his new masters, complete his plea deal, and collect his salary and bonuses. And by extracting extra kickbacks on the side from his Abscam targets, Mel could make additional scores and satisfy his natural inclination to pull the wool over everyone's eyes.

I wanted the jury to appreciate the scope of Mel's criminal enterprise.

Q: In the London Investors scam, you had actually franchised the
   scam to con men all over the world.
A: That's correct.
Q: Right. You were like the McDonald's of con men?
A: That's correct.

In order to prove that the "coaching" defense applied to the Myers situation in the absence of tape-recorded proof, we started the cross-examination by playing the tape of Senator Williams being coached to "come on strong." The Williams coaching episode occurred weeks before the Myers meeting. On cross, Weinberg denied any conversations about coaching Myers and denied telling Errichetti or Criden that the congressmen would never be asked to do anything in the future. It now came down to whether we could prove that Weinberg's denials were lies—by showing he would lie about everything else.

For example, Errichetti claimed that he had kicked back to Weinberg some of the cash proceeds from his cut for bringing in congressmen. Weinberg denied it. Similarly, one of the middlemen in the Williams case claimed Weinberg had solicited three Piaget watches worth upward of $5,000 each from him. Weinberg denied asking for the watches, claiming they were an unexpected gift. Errichetti claimed Weinberg had asked him for three television sets, an expensive stereo system, and a microwave oven. Weinberg denied receiving any of it. Errichetti produced receipts and a nephew who testified to helping the mayor deliver the gifts to Weinberg.

Judge Pratt, in his post-trial opinion, found the evidence about the gifts to Weinberg "inconclusive." Specifically, he ruled that Errichetti's nephew had lied about the microwave and found the other evidence regarding the kickbacks and gifts to be "unpersuasive."

However, a Senate select committee, which took testimony from Weinberg and the FBI agents "supervising" him, came to the opposite conclusion. The committee found that Weinberg had indeed solicited and received all these items, and more. The committee concluded that Weinberg failed to report receipt of these items contemporaneously, and then lied to his government handlers when they later confronted him. The committee received sworn statements from Weinberg's wife and son detailing how Mel had removed the serial number plate from the microwave oven and had attempted to hide other items he had solicited from his Abscam marks. The committee concluded that there were "strong indications that Weinberg gave perjurious testimony in the criminal proceedings and before the Select Committee." If the select committee could obtain the evidence to support their conclusion, why couldn't the FBI?

Indeed, Judge Pratt's finding on the gifts was essentially mocked by Weinberg himself. In a book written by *Newsday* editor Robert Greene, with Weinberg's cooperation, Weinberg admitted he solicited the Piaget wristwatches and casually asked, "So what if I scammed the mayor for a T.V.?" To Weinberg, this was in keeping with his role as a corrupt employee of the sheikh. The FBI simply didn't understand that he needed to take kickbacks to establish his undercover persona.

The missing tape recordings were another important area for our attack on Weinberg's denial that he schooled Criden and Errichetti to have the congressmen merely put on a show. Weinberg denied destroying any of the audiotapes he had recorded. Instead, he claimed that a half dozen or so of the cassettes were stolen from his garment bag on a flight from Florida to New York. Additionally, he denied recording over previously recorded conversations, explaining that any anomalies on the tapes were likely the result of his having dropped the recording device on occasion.

Mel's "stolen" audiotapes explanation was preposterous on its face. Why would a thief remove only audiocassettes from his luggage? When it came time to present the defense case, I called Mark Weiss, one of the tape experts selected jointly by the White House and special prosecutor's office during Watergate to examine the famous 18½-minute gap on the Nixon tapes. Weiss testified unequivocally that his examination of the Abscam tapes in question demonstrated that they had been deliberately recorded over and that dropping the recorder could not have explained the overrecording.

Judge Pratt found, without further comment, that "once when [Weinberg] was flying to New York from Florida, a number of tapes—less than ten, were stolen from his flight bag." In all, Pratt dismissed the missing tapes issue as essentially irrelevant.

The select committee reached a different conclusion. After questioning Weinberg under oath and comparing the different and contradictory versions of the stolen tapes incident Mel had given at different times, the committee found that Weinberg had provided "an astounding plethora of self-contradictory" statements and had clearly lied under oath. Additionally, the committee concluded that Weinberg had "deliberately ensured that particular conversations would not be recorded or otherwise preserved." The committee not only found "strong indications that Weinberg gave perjurious testimony in the criminal proceedings," it also concluded that it could not rely on Weinberg's uncorroborated statements "for the truth *of any issue.*"

Judge Pratt, on the other hand, looked upon Weinberg as a heroic figure, worthy of praise for devoting three years of his life to the investigation and sacrificing his "career" as a con man due to the publicity over Abscam. Personal sacrifices? Career as a con man? What about working off his three-year sentence?

An episode that we learned about only later underscored the FBI's ineffective supervision as well as Weinberg's penchant for making a buck when the opportunity presented itself. Margot Dennedy was an FBI agent assigned to the Abscam investigation in an undercover capacity, playing the role of an attractive personal secretary to the sheikh. During the investigation, Dennedy had responded to an urgent call and participated in the arrest of a would-be hijacker at JFK airport. The next day, Agent Dennedy's photograph appeared on the front page of many newspapers, including New York's *Newsday* and the *Philadelphia Inquirer.* A few days later, the intrepid Weinberg telephoned his FBI contact to report that he had received calls from Errichetti and two other middlemen who claimed to have identified Dennedy in the photograph. Mel told the FBI agent he had succeeded in convincing each of them that they were mistaken. Despite the agent's fears that attending a previously scheduled meeting with Errichetti posed an unacceptable risk of physical danger, Weinberg courageously insisted on going through with the meeting. Following that meeting, Weinberg's supervisors requested approval from headquarters of a

$15,000 award for Weinberg for "having reinstated the credibility of Abscam . . . at tremendous personal sacrifice."

The only problem was that the calls from Errichetti and the others identifying Dennedy never happened. As the select committee concluded, Weinberg fabricated the incident in order to profit financially by defrauding the FBI. And when confronted by the committee with the evidence, Mel simply denied ever having reported the receipt of the calls. Who was lying—the FBI agent who had recommended a bonus or Mel?

It was clear that by constantly arguing throughout the trial that there were significant defects in the way the Abscam investigation was run, I was trying Judge Pratt's patience. Often a judge will try to bully a lawyer into dropping an argument or a line of questioning. Here the defense lawyer must be careful to weigh the consequences of persistence. I continued to press my argument.

Then came some sensational news. Unbeknownst to me, the United States attorney for New Jersey and two of his Newark-based assistants assigned to the Abscam investigation had complained loudly to their superiors at the Department of Justice about the unfairness of the unfolding investigation. In particular, the trio pointed to Puccio's inability to control Weinberg. They had taken the drastic step of writing a memo outlining their concerns. Instead of heeding those concerns, the DOJ had simply cut the New Jersey prosecutors out of further involvement in the investigation. It was apparent that a high-level decision had been made at Justice that the Newark memo had to be turned over to the defense, albeit belatedly, while the trial was still ongoing.

Judge Pratt called the lawyers into chambers for a conference. It now became clear that at least part of his displeasure with me was grounded in his belief that someone had leaked the memo to me before it was officially disclosed. How else would I have been able to make the same arguments based on due process of law and fundamental fairness that the Newark prosecutors had made a year earlier? As if someone needed to be a Harvard Law professor to see the glaring warning signs after the coaching of Senator Williams.

I argued passionately to Judge Pratt that my seven years of experience as a federal prosecutor gave me a sufficient basis to understand proper FBI and DOJ procedure as well as more than a passing acquaintance with constitutional notions of due process of law and fundamental fairness. Finally, the judge seemed to accept the argument that I had come to my views about the fairness issues independently. He shook his head and said, "Mr. Ben-Veniste, you are the Jack Nicklaus of defense lawyers."

"Hold on," I replied, trying to inject a bit of levity into a tense situation, "I don't know too much about golf, but that seems to be in the nature of a compliment, Judge."

With only the hint of a smile, the judge replied, "Anyone who is compared in his profession to Jack Nicklaus can only regard it as real praise. But Jack Nicklaus does it differently from any other golfer. Mr. Ben-Veniste, you do it differently than anyone else."

Despite the fact that I didn't understand what the hell he was talking about, I took the judge's analogy as a compliment and continued to press the fairness argument.

The memo provided little that we hadn't already discovered ourselves, but it served to confirm our resolve. Edward Plaza and Robert Weir were the assistant U.S. attorneys under U.S. Attorney Robert Del Tufo who wrote the memo. Plaza later testified eloquently before a House congressional subcommittee investigating Abscam: "Abscam represents the selective use of technology to create an illusion of criminality. It is and was tantamount to prosecuting the actors in a play for following a script . . . Abscam is a perversion of the truth."

What we didn't know at the time of trial, and what would have helped in making our argument to the jury, was that Plaza and Weir had confronted Weinberg and the FBI team after the coaching of Senator Williams. Weinberg retorted that "if he didn't put words in the subjects' mouths, the government would never be able to make cases."

We succeeded in convincing Judge Pratt to instruct the jury that if it believed that Myers was only "playacting" when he made promises for future action and took cash from the make-believe sheikh's representatives, then it should acquit all defendants. In other words, if Myers, Errichetti, Criden, and Johanson had conspired "merely" to swindle the sheikh, then the crime of bribery had not been committed. This alone was a major victory, although it was to be short-lived.

After two days of deliberation, the jury convicted all four defendants of conspiring to commit bribery.

––––––––––

THIS WAS MY FIRST loss in a criminal defense case and it did not go down easily. Despite preparing intellectually for a bad verdict, I had felt empathy for Howard Criden and the tough road he faced ahead, and for the consequences for his two sons and his elderly uncle who was by his side throughout the trial. My more experienced colleagues were more sanguine, particularly Ray Brown and John Duffy. We had put up a terrific fight in the face of extraordinary odds against us. And we had developed a strong record for the upcoming appeal. The crassness of the conduct displayed on videotape overwhelmed our nuanced appeal to sensibilities. *Candid Camera* this was not. This was a United States congressman who took money in a hotel room from an Arab businessman. Our defense might have worked for a lesser personage defrauding a crooked oil-rich sheikh seeking to buy influence, but not for a congressman. In fact, after all the Abscam trials were concluded, all of the public officials who took money were convicted. Seven different juries who heard the cases reached the same result: guilty.

But there was a difference in the way the judges who presided over these trials looked upon the government's conduct. Judge Fullam conducted a post-trial review after the convictions of Philadelphia city councilman Harry Jannotti and council chairman George Schwartz. He noted that Weinberg and the undercover agents "made it clear that their sole aim was to please their Arab employer by being able to tell him truthfully that which he was interested in hearing, namely, that money had been paid to high officials. The agents did not require any commitment that the public official would actually be influenced by the payments; they were interested only in appearances. Fullam criticized the FBI for never chastising Weinberg for his coaching technique, and went out of his way to lambaste Puccio for failing to report the Williams coaching episode to his superiors at the Department of Justice.

Judge Fullam was right on the money, recounting how Criden and Johanson were drawn in by promises of financing for a "perfectly legitimate" casino project, and how Criden and Errichetti were schooled by Weinberg into believing that money was to be made "by merely arranging introductions of officials who would present themselves as corruptible, irrespective of their genuine inclinations, . . . and without asking for or receiving any quid pro quo." Judge Fullam concluded that the government's conduct was so outrageous and overreaching as to amount to a violation of due process of law. Although he expressed "great reluctance" at overturning the convictions and ordering a judgment of acquittal, noting that no one who has viewed the videotapes "could avoid feelings of distaste and disgust at the crass behavior" revealed, he did so in the interest of protecting more important freedoms. "In the long run, the rights of citizens not to be led into criminal activity by governmental overreaching will remain secure only so long as the courts stand ready to vindicate those rights in every case."

Would that Judge Fullam had been assigned to the Myers case. Nor was Judge Fullam alone in his conclusions. Judge William Bryant, for many years the distinguished chief judge of the Federal District Court in the District of Columbia, presided over the trial of Representative Richard Kelly, the only Republican snared in the Abscam investigation. Like Fullam, Judge Bryant was unwilling to accept at face value the representations made by the government. "Although the Department of Justice and the FBI disavow any purpose of testing the virtue of members of Congress, that, in fact, appears to have been the sole object of the operation." Judge Bryant used as the litmus test to determine the legitimacy of a sting operation its approximation of real-life circumstances. Finding Abscam to be unlike any sting operation previously known to him in his vast experience as lawyer and judge, Bryant expressed his visceral reaction to the "unwholesome spectacle" of government agents "hard about the business of corrupting public officials." He noted the potential for odious political mischief inconsistent with fundamental precepts of fairness when public officials are corrupted by governmental overreaching. Judge Bryant overturned Kelly's conviction and ordered the charges against him dismissed.

But Judge Pratt viewed his obligation differently. In a demonstration of consistently circular reasoning, he saw nothing of relevance beyond what had been captured on videotape. Nothing about the government's conduct rose to the level of fundamental unfairness. Weinberg's off-camera conduct was of little importance.

The FBI, preeminent in the world for its crime-solving capability, was unable to identify the government employees responsible for leaking the entire Abscam prosecution memo, tipping the media to the location of the undercover house in Washington, and allowing certain reporters a preview of the videotapes. Not that it would have mattered to Judge Pratt, who saw no prejudice to the defendants from the deliberate and massive leaks. Finally, in what was for me a seriously twisted coda to this opinion, Pratt attacked the motives of the New Jersey prosecutors for coming forward with their concerns about Weinberg putting words in the targets' mouths and about the fairness of the investigation and prosecution. To Pratt, Plaza and Weir had acted out of jealousy and embarrassment because Puccio and his minions, not the New Jersey prosecutors, had uncovered corruption by Jersey politicians. Judge Pratt went on to ridicule the concerns Plaza and Weir expressed for fundamental fairness: "They acted as if they had convinced themselves that the highest duties of a prosecutor were to manufacture arguments for defendants, to follow an ultra-cautious approach, and to be skeptical of all new investigative techniques."

Had George Pratt been familiar with the highest duties and responsibilities of federal prosecutors, he would have praised rather than reviled Plaza and Weir. Every man and woman who takes the oath to become a federal prosecutor is inculcated with the words of former Supreme Court justice George Sutherland:

> The United States Attorney is the representative . . . of a sovereignty whose obligation to govern impartially is as compelling as its obligation to govern at all, and whose interest, therefore, in a criminal prosecution is not that it shall win a case, but that justice shall be done. As such, he is in a peculiar and very definite sense the servant of the law, the twofold aim of which is that guilt shall not escape or innocence suffer. He may prosecute with earnestness and vigor— indeed, he should do so. But, while he may strike hard blows, he is not at liberty to strike foul ones. It is as much his duty to refrain from improper methods calculated to produce a wrongful conviction as it is to use every legitimate means to bring about a just one.

In a similar vein, U.S. attorney general and later Supreme Court justice Robert Jackson observed,

> The role of a prosecutor in a criminal case is not only to be a plaintiff, but also to represent the defendant. Only by exercising this dual responsibility can the government be an agent of justice. Justice is not upheld if the law is stained in order to obtain a conviction. Prosecutors who suborn perjury or withhold exculpatory evidence desecrate the law.

JUDGE PRATT SENTENCED HOWARD Criden to six years in prison. The court of appeals did not reverse any of the convictions in the Pratt trials; indeed, appellate courts considering Judges Fullam's and Bryant's decisions reversed them and reinstated the guilty verdicts against Jannotti, Schwartz, and Kelly. In the end, it was the words and actions captured on videotape, not the behind-the-scenes manipulations, that were the reality.

To be sure, I was disappointed in the result, but not so enthralled with the logic of my arguments that I could not appreciate another viewpoint. But I did take heart from the clarity and proportionality of the Fullam and Bryant decisions, as well as the dissent of appellate Judge Ruggero J. Aldisert (joined by Judge Joseph F. Weis Jr.), who recounted how the European immigrants who came to his western Pennsylvania community at the turn of the twentieth century told tales of the feared secret police and the agents provocateurs of their native countries. To Judge Aldisert, the combination of government overreaching and deliberate leaks to the press produced the unmistakable aroma of totalitarianism: "To the Department of Justice, its operation was a taste of honey; to me, it emanates a fetid odor whose putrescence threatens to spoil basic concepts of fairness and justice that I hold dear."

MONTHS AFTER THE CRIDEN trial, I bumped into a journalist who covered the Abscam trials for one of the New Jersey papers. He told me of an experience he had with Mel Weinberg that demonstrated the extent of the man's cunning.

The journalist—let's call him Al—had arranged to interview Mel in a diner in New Jersey. He opened with a question about how Mel could get the congressmen and other officials caught in the Abscam net to perform as they had on videotape.

"It's all about your preparation and how much effort you're willing to put into it," Mel replied, easing his portly frame into a booth. "For example, how would you like to see me get the waitress to buy us lunch?"

"What are you talking about?" asked Al, a bit too eagerly.

"Okay, just listen, you won't have to do anything."

A middle-aged woman with a name tag pinned to her waitress uniform came to the table, her pencil poised to take their orders.

"How're you guys doin' today?" she inquired brightly.

"Fabulous," was Mel's instant reply. "Betty, I never had a better day in my life."

"Well, what are you gonna have today, hon?" The waitress took the men's lunch orders. The order complete, Betty returned to the subject of Mel's demeanor, obviously intrigued.

"So what's got you so bright eyed and bushy tailed today?" Her face brightened, playing up to Mel's ebullience.

"Betty, you are not going to believe this, but this morning I looked at my lottery ticket and it matched what was in the paper. I won! I can't believe it myself, four point two million dollars!"

Al did his best to keep a straight face, amazed at the enormity of the lie. No matter, Betty was riveted 100 percent on the goateed con man.

"Come on, you're putting me on."

"I swear on my grandmother's grave. This is the luckiest day of my life. I feel so good, I'll tell you what I'm going to do. How long have you worked here, Betty?"

"Going on seven years, now," Betty replied.

"I'll tell you what I'm going to do," Mel repeated. "I am going to send you a mink coat. What size are you—about twelve?"

"Get outa here," exclaimed Betty, her cheeks reddening.

"I'm not gonna ask for your home address—you'd be foolish to give it out to a stranger, I know that. I'm going to send it to you right here at the diner, if you feel okay with that. I mean it, I feel so blessed, I have to share my good luck. I can tell you have a good soul. Do me a personal favor and write your full name down for me with the address of the diner."

By now, the waitress's face had turned a bright red. She moved away shaking her head. When she returned with their orders, Betty almost self-consciously looked into Mel's eyes. "You were kidding, right, about the lottery and all?"

"On my children's heads," Mel exclaimed, raising his right hand in the familiar posture of taking the oath. "Why would I put you on? This is the luckiest day of my life. If you don't want to write the information down it's up to you. But the mink coat is yours."

The interview progressed as Mel and Al chewed their food. "I can't believe you, Mel," said Al, returning to the gag with the waitress. "How do you expect anyone to believe anything so far out? And, anyway, even if she did, why would she pay for our lunch?"

"Weren't you watching her at all? She wants to believe. She's there. Just watch."

The waitress returned with the check and on the back of a blank green check from her pad she had written the information Mel had requested.

"Okay, Betty, you're in business!" Mel bounced up from the table, giving the matronly woman a hug and a pat on the back. "I can't believe my luck—what an incredible day."

At the same moment, Mel reached for his wallet in the inside pocket of his sport coat. And then quickly, he patted the back pocket of his trousers. "Omigod, what an idiot I am." Mel slapped his forehead with the heel of his palm. "In all the confusion, I left the house without my wallet!" Mel shook his head for emphasis.

Al sat, disbelieving, as Betty patted Mel on the arm and picked up the check. "Don't worry about it, doll, lunch is on me."

As the two men stood to leave, Mel confided, chuckling, "She wrote down her *home* address—I knew she would." The horrified journalist, now lamenting his role in Weinberg's little frolic, told me he surreptitiously reached in his pocket and left enough money on the table to cover the bill and a generous tip. "The man is an evil genius."

TWO YEARS AFTER THE Abscam trials, Judge Pratt was appointed by Ronald Reagan to the Court of Appeals for the Second Circuit, where he served for thirteen years before resigning to reenter private practice.

After the congressional oversight hearings on Abscam, the FBI and Department of Justice undertook measures to better ensure fair standards for launching sting operations and supervising undercover operatives. In the quarter of a century since Abscam, the nation has been able to function without a repetition of such techniques. Virtually everyone associated with Abscam was wrong or naïve or incompetent or corrupt or just plain greedy. It left a bad taste in my mouth that still lingers.

CHAPTER FOUR

Whitewater

I had met Bill Clinton only once prior to my engagement as counsel to the Democrats on the Senate Whitewater Committee. I was driving my family to a student car wash fund-raiser at Sidwell Friends Lower School, where my older daughter, Danielle, was a sixth grader. As we entered the campus on that late spring day in 1993, I had no idea the president was going to be there. At first, I assumed the ambulances and police cars were evidence of some terrible accident. When I saw the guys with suits and earphones, it clicked that Clinton must be on the grounds, as Chelsea had enrolled that year as a Sidwell student. "Oh, the president must be here," I announced. "The president of what?" asked my mother, along with us for the outing. Toby had recently moved to Washington from Florida, carrying her trademark feistiness along to the nation's capital. "President of the United States," I replied. "His daughter goes to Sidwell, too." "Good," she replied. "I'd like to give him a piece of my mind." "I'm sure you'll get the chance," I said.

Sure enough, there was Clinton, in khakis and a polo shirt, sitting in the sports field bleachers, sipping a Diet Coke. After a while I went over and introduced myself. Clinton seemed approachable, chatting with a smattering of fellow Sidwell parents. After a few moments of small talk, I mentioned that my mother had a question she would like to ask. This would be good. Clinton focused his famous gaze on the diminutive former Brooklynite.

The tough talker folded like a cheap suit. "I just wanted to say congratulations for winning the election," she stammered.

I was impressed. "You certainly gave him what for," I said with a smile. Uncharacteristically, she had no comeback.

Clinton's first months on the job were marred by a variety of missteps. His first two choices for attorney general, Zoë Baird and Kimba Wood, were withdrawn, casualties of having employed undocumented household workers, before his third pick, Janet Reno, was confirmed. The "don't ask, don't tell" compromise on the issue of gays in the military came at considerable political cost. The fertile subject of discord between the president and the first lady was inaugurated with a news account of an argument during which Hillary supposedly launched a White House lamp in the general direction of the president. Only four months into his term, the president was down to a 36 percent public approval rating.

Then there was the $200 haircut on Air Force One on the tarmac at the Los Angeles airport, delaying thousands of other travelers. The firing of seven employees of the White House travel office followed, evoking outcries about the seemingly heavy-handed way the matter had been handled.

But the July 1993 suicide of Vincent Foster, a childhood friend of Bill's who had been a law partner and close friend of Hillary's, was of a completely different character. Unlike the toughened hides of others who had felt the partisan slings and arrows directed at the covey of new political targets freshly arrived from Arkansas, Foster proved tragically vulnerable. The deputy White House counsel had been subjected to a vicious attack from the right-wing media for his role in the travel office imbroglio. Unable to cope with the profound changes from the more genteel lifestyle he enjoyed in Little Rock, and predisposed to depression, Foster internalized the criticism and tormented himself with doubt. Before his friends could fully appreciate what was going on, the despondent forty-eight-year-old lawyer drove his car down the scenic George Washington Parkway to Fort Marcy Park and shot himself in the head.

Emblematic of the way the Arkansans were treated by their critics, a number of conspiracy theories immediately circulated about Foster's death. Right-wing radio personality Rush Limbaugh breathlessly informed his legion of faithful "dittoheads" of the rumor he had heard that Foster had been murdered in an apartment owned by Hillary Clinton, his body then planted in Fort Marcy Park.

The first major news article mentioning Whitewater appeared in the *New York Times* on March 8, 1992, during the presidential race and was written by Jeff Gerth. It was titled, "The 1992 Campaign: Personal Finances: Clintons Joined S&L Operator in an Ozark Real Estate Venture." Gerth raised questions about the Clintons' investment in a rural Arkansas land development deal with their friends Jim and Susan McDougal. Gerth's story focused on whether the Clintons benefited improperly from the arrangement, whether then governor Clinton had wrongly interceded with Arkansas officials on the McDougals' behalf, and whether the Clintons' tax treatment of their investment was on the up-and-up.

The Clintons were complete novices when it came to investing and looked to Jim McDougal, who had enjoyed some minor success in previous real estate ventures, as their tutor. The price they were to pay for McDougal's tutelage was beyond estimation.

On August 2, 1978, the McDougals and Clintons purchased approximately 230 acres of undeveloped land in Flippin (I'm not making this up), Arkansas. The two couples paid $202,611 for the Whitewater property and financed the purchase with a $182,611 loan from the Citizens Bank and Trust of Flippin and a $20,000 loan from Union National Bank in Little Rock. The property was bounded on one side by Arkansas Route 101 and on the other side by the White River. McDougal envisioned the undeveloped property as a retirement and vacation destination. He named it Whitewater Estates.

In June 1979, the Clintons and McDougals incorporated the Whitewater Development Company and transferred the land into the corporation. Jim and Susan McDougal were the officers of the corporation—Jim as president and Susan as secretary. As every investigation into Whitewater ultimately concluded, the McDougals managed the corporation and the Clintons had no involvement in its day-to-day affairs. These investigations include the Lyons report prepared by Denver attorney James Lyons during the 1992 presidential campaign, the reports from the law firm Pillsbury Madison & Sutro (engaged by the Resolution Trust Corporation), the Senate Whitewater Committee, and the independent counsel.

One common and often repeated statement in media accounts about the Whitewater land deal was that the Clintons and McDougals were partners, leading many in the public to believe the deal was constructed as an equal partnership, and that each partner knew or was informed about the day-to-day operations of the investment. As the Pillsbury report stated: "The evidence suggests that the McDougals and not the Clintons managed Whitewater. The evidence does not suggest that the Clintons had managerial control over the enterprise, or received annual reports or regular financial summaries. Instead, and as the Clintons suggest, their main contact with Whitewater seems to have consisted of signing loan extensions or re-newals."

To say the least, Jim McDougal's vision of a thriving recreational development on the White River went unrealized. On May 4, 1985, the Whitewater Development Corporation sold off its remaining twenty-four Whitewater Estates lots to Ozark Air in exchange for a used airplane and assumption of $35,000 on the balance on the McDougals' and the Clintons' original Citizens Bank loan. As the Pillsbury report concluded, "May 1985 marked the end of Whitewater as a project. By the end of May, the land was gone; all that remained behind was debt and notes receivable that did not generate enough cash to service the debt. The Company would continue to exist but there was never again any prospect that it might turn a profit." The Whitewater investment was a failure. While the Clintons wound up putting about $40,500 into Whitewater, they never received any return on their investment.

What the Clintons perhaps took for Jim McDougal's energetic self-confidence may have been the manifestation of the manic side of his later diagnosed bipolar disorder. As McDougal's manic-depressive illness worsened, he became at the same time less attentive to business affairs and more convinced of his business acumen—a prescription for certain disaster.

After the *Times* story, the next major news article regarding Whitewater came out more than a year later, on October 31, 1993, in the *Washington Post*. The article stated the Resolution Trust Corporation (RTC), the agency established by Congress to clean up the 1980s savings and loan mess, had asked federal prosecutors to open a criminal investigation into a bank controlled by the McDougals, Madison Guaranty Savings and Loan. The basis of the article was the collection of criminal referrals the RTC sent to Paula Casey, the U.S. attorney in Little Rock, asserting that bank fraud had been committed. On November 8, Casey, a new Clinton appointee, recused herself from the investigation, which was then turned over to Donald Mackay, a career prosecutor in the Department of Justice's fraud section.

Over the next couple of months, Republicans began calling for a special prosecutor to be appointed to investigate the Whitewater and Madison allegations as well as the facts surrounding Vincent Foster's suicide. Attorney General Janet Reno resisted, explaining to reporters, "If I appoint a special prosecutor, it's still *my* prosecutor and there will still be questions about that person's independence." But the mounting clamor for an independent investigation proved overwhelming. Over the objection of his White House counsel, Bernard Nussbaum, President Clinton joined the chorus, requesting that Reno make the appointment.

On January 20, 1994, Janet Reno announced the selection of Robert B. Fiske Jr. to serve as special counsel to investigate Whitewater. Fiske wrote his own charter, which gave him broad authority to investigate criminal activity directly and indirectly related to Whitewater. In explaining the breadth of his authority, Fiske stated it "was drafted by me to give me the total authority to look into all appropriate matters relating to the events that bring us all here today."

Fiske, a Republican moderate, had a gold-plated résumé. In 1976, Gerald Ford appointed him U.S. attorney for the Southern District of New York. Fiske was so well respected that Democrat Jimmy Carter kept him in the job after assuming the presidency. But conservatives did not like Fiske because of his past chairmanship of the American Bar Association's committee that evaluated potential federal court nominees. They blamed Fiske for the ABA's weak support for Robert Bork, whose failed nomination to the Supreme Court became a major grievance of the right wing.

One of the most vocal Republicans calling for an independent investigation was Senator Alfonse D'Amato of New York. D'Amato expressed strong confidence in the appointment of his fellow New Yorker: "I would have every confidence in any investigation undertaken by Bob Fiske," whom D'Amato praised as "one of the most honorable and most skilled lawyers anywhere."

Fiske set about his task with trademark efficiency and professionalism. Within six months he had nearly concluded two essential parts of his investigation—Foster's death and Clinton administration contacts relating to the RTC referrals of Madison Guaranty.

The transformative moment in the drama underpinning the attack on the Clinton presidency involved the substitution of Kenneth Starr for Special Counsel Bob Fiske in the summer of 1994. The switcheroo—a highly competent, moderate Republican, former U.S. attorney was replaced by an archconservative former appellate judge with no prosecutorial experience—was breathtaking in its audacity. Utilizing the newly reenacted independent counsel law as its crowbar, a combination of right-wing journalists, Republican congressional leaders, and conservative judges succeeded in dislodging Fiske and inflicting Starr on the Clintons—a decision that was to plague the Clinton presidency for the better part of the next six years.

The independent counsel law had been allowed to expire in December 1992, following the seemingly interminable investigation of the Iran-Contra scandal by retired (Republican) judge Lawrence Walsh. The tension between having a credible and impartial investigation of the nation's highest political figures independent of the Department of Justice and having a prosecutor with a virtually unlimited budget focused on one subject was resolved in favor of letting the law lapse. The Republican congressional leadership, able to discount the obstructionism of the Reagan administration's key players in the Iran-Contra affair, railed against Walsh and the law under which he was appointed.

To my mind, the success or failure of an independent counsel or special prosecutor is almost entirely dependent on the character, experience, and integrity of the person appointed. Archie Cox and Leon Jaworski set the standard—fair, cautious about overreaching, and ultimately successful in fulfilling their mandate. Jacob Stein, who was appointed as independent counsel to investigate Reagan attorney general Edwin Meese, demonstrated the same diligence and judgment as Cox and Jaworski by concluding his investigation promptly with no leaks or hoopla. Within six months, Stein concluded that no charges were warranted against Meese. Bob Fiske had approached his task in the same efficient and professional manner.

The principled objections of the Republicans to what they claimed in 1992 was an unconstitutional violation of separation of powers inherent in the independent counsel law had somehow evaporated by 1994. A new law must be passed, they demanded. Fiske's early conclusion that Vince Foster committed suicide for reasons unrelated to Whitewater was unacceptable to the right wing. Fiske was subjected to unrelenting attacks by the usual subjects at the *Wall Street Journal,* the *Washington Times,* and the right-wing talk radio bloviators.

Passage of the new independent counsel law was step one. Under the law, an independent counsel was selected and supervised by a panel of three judges hand-picked by Chief Justice William Rehnquist. Rehnquist, named to the Supreme Court by Richard Nixon and elevated to chief justice by Ronald Reagan, chose David Sentelle, a conservative judge on the DC Circuit Court of Appeals, to head the panel.

Step two. Rather than appoint Fiske to continue his work begun as special counsel under the new independent counsel law, the Sentelle panel named Sentelle's former colleague on the federal Court of Appeals for the DC Circuit, Kenneth Starr, to replace Fiske. The supposed reason: to allay criticism that Fiske was not sufficiently independent—after all, he had been appointed by Attorney General Janet Reno. Never mind she had done so in capitulation to the demands of the same claque that supported Starr's substitution. In its August 1994 statement accompanying the decision, the panel wrote, "It is not our intent to impugn the integrity of the Attorney General's appointee, but rather to reflect the intent of the act that the actor be protected against perceptions of conflict."

The public may not appreciate that sitting judges don't necessarily relinquish their prior political relationships. Indeed, it was reported that Judge Sentelle had been spotted just before Starr's appointment having lunch with conservative Republican senators Jesse Helms and Lauch Faircloth. Sentelle responded in writing to a press inquiry, "To the best of my recollection, nothing in these discussions concerned independent counsel matters . . . Senators Faircloth and Helms are old friends of mine and I lunch with one or both of them from time to time."

Yet Faircloth, the junior senator from North Carolina, had been a persistent critic of Fiske. At about the same time as he was lunching with Sentelle, Faircloth was quoted as criticizing Fiske for lack of aggressiveness in pursuing his investigation: "I feel very strongly that he [Fiske] represents more the problem than the solution of clearing up the Whitewater problem." But Sentelle and Faircloth never discussed replacing Fiske with Starr.

Nevertheless, it was possible that Ken Starr was himself subject to "perceptions" of conflict of interest. Revelations on the heels of Starr's appointment showed that Starr had been retained by a conservative group earlier in the year to rebut Clinton's claim that he ought to be immune from suit in the Paula Jones sexual harassment case while he was in office. No matter. What was done, was done; Fiske was out and Starr was in. It would now be up to the Sentelle panel to supervise Starr's work to ensure it was fair and proper. No perception of conflict there, either.

Meanwhile, Republicans in the House and Senate kept up a steady drumbeat for parallel congressional inquiries into the same areas of investigation. Led by D'Amato and Faircloth and supported by Republican leader Robert Dole, the Senate acquiesced, voting in June 1994 to require the Senate Committee on Banking, Housing and Urban Affairs to conduct hearings into the following: (1) communications between officials of the White House and the Department of Treasury and the Resolution Trust Corporation relating to Whitewater and Madison Guaranty Savings and Loan; (2) the Park Service Police investigation into the death of White House deputy counsel Vincent Foster; and (3) the way White House officials handled documents in the office of Vince Foster at the time of his death.

During this investigation, the committee was chaired by Wisconsin Democrat Donald W. Riegle Jr.; the ranking member was Senator D'Amato. The Banking Committee heard thirty witnesses during six days and nights of public hearings from July 29 through August 5, 1994. The committee issued two separate reports following its investigation. The first dealt with the suicide of Vince Foster.

> *The Committee finds no evidence of "improper conduct" in the Park Police investigation, which accurately concluded that Mr. Foster committed suicide in Fort Marcy Park on July 20, 1993. There is no evidence that any variances from normal investigative procedures undermined the Park Police investigation. Furthermore, there is no evidence of any attempt by the Park Police to alter the findings or conclusions of their investigation.*

The Banking Committee's second report focused on the contacts among the White House, Treasury, and the RTC. The committee found no law or ethics standard that clearly prohibited the contacts that had occurred. The committee added that the new White House counsel, Lloyd Cutler, had made a new rule for the Clinton White House: "No contacts with respect to any particular law enforcement investigation could be initiated without the prior approval of the White House Counsel." On the final issue—the handling of documents in Foster's office the night of his death—the Banking Committee chose to postpone its investigation since the independent counsel's inquiry into this subject had not yet been concluded.

The 1994 midterm election gave control of the Senate to the Republicans. By May 1995, a resolution had passed creating a "special committee" made up essentially of the Senate Banking Committee plus a few other senators to conduct an investigation of the Whitewater Development Corporation "and related matters." Chairing the committee was Senator Alfonse D'Amato.

Al D'Amato's personal history of less than punctilious regard for the ethical strictures attendant to public office made him an unlikely choice to lead such an inquiry. He had grown up in the heyday of Republican-dominated Long Island political life, where a 1 percent kickback of salaries by Nassau County employees to the political machine was still the rule. Allegations of D'Amato's association with reputed mob figures dogged him for much of his career. In one instance, U.S. Attorney Rudy Giuliani claimed that D'Amato had telephoned him on behalf of two mobsters, one of whom was allegedly implicated in the sensational murder of mob boss

Paul "Big Paul" Castellano. D'Amato explained he was merely acting on behalf of a friend and didn't know the details of Rudy's investigation.

In the late 1980s, D'Amato found himself embroiled in several ethical controversies regarding grants and contracts from the Department of Housing and Urban Development. According to the *New York Times,* "He helped secure a $1 million H.U.D. grant for a swimming pool in his beachfront hometown of Island Park, L.I.; his cousin and other politically connected people were granted the opportunity to purchase 44 H.U.D.-subsidized homes in Island Park; all of those 44 homes went to white families although H.U.D.'s goal was to house 17 black families there, and several of Mr. D'Amato's fund-raisers and contributors received awards to build H.U.D.-subsidized housing."

In 1991, the Senate Select Committee on Ethics investigated sixteen allegations of ethical abuses relating to D'Amato's office. One of the main subjects was the actions of the senator's brother, Armand. Armand D'Amato had lobbied on behalf of Unisys (and its predecessor, Sperry) for navy contracts, sending letters to the Defense Department on his brother's Senate stationery bearing the senator's signature, for which Armand was paid the tidy sum of $120,500 by Unisys. Unisys was awarded $100 million in defense contracts. Alfonse told the Ethics Committee the letters were sent without his knowledge. A variety of different allegations of improper solicitation of campaign contributions from companies seeking government contracts rounded out the picture of a politician charting his own course where ethics were concerned. Although the committee found there was "no credible evidence" that the senator "engaged in any improper conduct," it nevertheless concluded that D'Amato "conducted the business of his office in an improper and inappropriate manner." D'Amato simply stonewalled persistent demands to release the transcripts of his extensive testimony over four days before the Senate Ethics Committee.

An example of the conflict posed by D'Amato's loose view of ethical strictures was his 1993 one-day stock-trading windfall of $37,125. This trade involved Computer Marketplace, Inc., a small California company whose shares were being sold in an initial public offering by Stratton Oakmont Inc., a Long Island securities company. Normally, such IPOs are available only to a broker's best and biggest customers. According to press reports, the trade was the senator's first with the firm. As the senior Republican on the Senate committee overseeing the securities industry, D'Amato might have been more circumspect. When Hillary Clinton's lucrative 1978 commodity futures trade surfaced, D'Amato found himself somewhat hamstrung by his Stratton Oakmont deal in launching a full-out attack.

Commenting on the anomaly of D'Amato charging the president with ethical lapses, political pundit Mark Shields observed, "The moral high ground is a place where Mr. D'Amato is subject to nosebleeds." The distraction from serious inquiry inherent in D'Amato's often clownish efforts to grab the media spotlight invited retorts like this from DNC chairman David Wilhelm: "Being attacked on ethics by Senator D'Amato is like being called ugly by a frog."

Yet D'Amato was determined to put the rumors and insinuations behind him and establish himself as a power in the Republican Party. He saw the Whitewater Committee chairmanship as his opportunity to grab the brass ring. The cocktail chatter from New York City was simple and unvarnished. "Al D'Amato says he's going to take Clinton down." That got my attention.

So when Senator Paul Sarbanes put out the word that the Democrats were looking to hire a new chief counsel, I expressed my interest. Sarbanes, the senior senator from Maryland, had distinguished himself as a member of the House of Representatives on Peter Rodino's Judiciary Committee during the Watergate impeachment hearings. While I didn't know him personally, Sarbanes had a reputation as an intellectual and highly ethical congressman and senator, dedicated to protection of the rights of the working men and women of America. Although he had started his career as a lawyer with a prominent Baltimore law firm, the call of public service soon lured him away. The trappings of wealth and position held no interest for Sarbanes. Among the hundred members of the exclusive club that is the United States Senate, Sarbanes invariably was dead last in the ranking of senators by accumulated wealth.

I learned that mine was a long name on a short list of applicants being considered for the job. I met Paul Sarbanes at his office in the Hart Senate Office Building, the most modern of the three buildings housing Senate offices. He wore his hair combed straight back. His drab suit and tie could easily have predated his swearing in as a congressman a quarter century earlier. There was not a whit of pretense or officiousness about Paul Sarbanes. I would be very comfortable working with him.

The son of Greek immigrants, Sarbanes had earned a scholarship to Princeton University, where his record of academic excellence and achievement in sports (basketball and baseball) earned him a prestigious Rhodes Scholarship to Oxford University, after which he went on to Harvard Law School. We talked about my career as a prosecutor and defense lawyer, and shared our perspectives on Watergate. Paul was candid in revealing that the Democratic members of the Whitewater Committee regarded their assignment with dread and apprehension, fearful that some new information about Clinton would drop from the trees and tarnish them for supporting the leader of their party.

Sarbanes too had heard the rumors about D'Amato's boast to "take down" the president. I told him that if I were to be selected as counsel to the Democrats, I would not shirk from exposing evidence of misconduct. But by the same token, if D'Amato and his allies were simply trying to damage the president by using the committee to hype up rumors and innuendo, then it would be up to the Democrats to provide a factual counterbalance. Sarbanes expressed his full agreement and told me he and the leadership would be making their decision soon. A day later, the senator called to say I had the job.

Meanwhile, Senator D'Amato had selected Michael Chertoff to be his chief counsel. Chertoff, about ten years younger than I, had also been an assistant U.S. attorney in the Southern District of New York, serving under my former colleague Rudy Giuliani. A native of New Jersey, Chertoff had gone on to be appointed U.S. attorney for New Jersey by President George H. W. Bush. Since neither Chertoff nor I wanted to leave our private law practices, a deal was brokered whereby the Senate Ethics Committee permitted us to be employed by the Senate on a part-time basis. That may have been the last thing the Republicans and Democrats on the Whitewater Committee agreed upon.

The seeds of our eventual success in exposing the overblown assertions of the Republican majority were sown by selection of an extraordinary staff. Because the rules provided the majority with an overwhelming advantage in the size of its staff and budget, the minority would have to outwork and outlawyer the majority. The core of our staff were my two deputies, Neal Kravitz and Lance Cole. Kravitz, curly haired and wiry, had a ready smile and the patient mien that often characterize a person of extraordinary intellect. In addition to his strong legal experience as a public defender, Neal was an accomplished musician, having served as a trombonist for the Boston Pops in the early 1980s. Neal had important experience with congressional investigations, including a stint with the Senate Select Committee on POW/MIA Affairs in 1991–1993, and with the Senate Banking Committee's 1994 investigation into the death of Vince Foster and other Whitewater-related matters. Having a deputy with fresh experience in the 1994 Whitewater investigation was extremely helpful.

Neal brought not only an impressive legal background and great experience but also our mascot, Oscar, his wheaten terrier. The staff was assigned to a dark and dank warren of connecting rooms in the basement labyrinth of the Russell Senate Office Building. During the many weekends when we were the only people working in the building aside from the security guards, Oscar provided welcome comic relief, bounding after a tennis ball down the deserted hallways.

Lance Cole, like Neal, was an honors graduate of Harvard Law. Lance joined the staff from the white-shoe law firm of Debevoise & Plimpton, where he had worked on several high-profile investigations of failed savings and loan associations, as well as a wide variety of complex corporate regulatory matters. His experience made him a good fit to work on the Whitewater land transactions and Madison Guaranty Savings and Loan pieces of the committee's investigation. Lance gave us an extra bonus in dealing with the many allegations that were centered in Arkansas. Lance had graduated from the University of Arkansas (first in his class), and had grown up in the small town of Yellville, the county seat of Marion County. Marion County, in rural northwest Arkansas, was the location of the Whitewater real estate project. Although he had been practicing law in Washington since the mid-1980s and had no personal or political ties to the Clintons, Lance's affable manner, together with his authentic Arkansas background, helped him establish an easy rapport with the many Arkansas witnesses called before the committee.

The only indispensable member of the staff (myself included) wasn't even a lawyer, although Tim Mitchell later went on to graduate from Catholic University Law School while working full-time at the Senate. Another holdover from the Senate Banking Committee and its 1994 investigation, Tim also had experience with the savings and loan industry and the RTC. Tim absorbed and organized the mountain of documents and testimony that flooded into the committee, working nearly 24/7 for the entire period of our existence. We depended on Tim's organizational skills and memory of arcane facts to locate documents and transcripts of testimony at a moment's notice.

Once the committee's work got under way, I developed a strong working relationship and personal affection for this talented young man. On many occasions during the hearings or depositions, he would be reaching for a document or page of previous testimony to illuminate a point I wanted to make, even before I asked for it. As he sat behind me while I questioned witnesses in public hearings, I needed only to reach my hand back in Tim's direction to know with confidence that the document I was thinking of would magically appear. I soon began to call him Radar, after the mind-reading Corporal Radar O'Reilly from *M*A*S*H*.

The Whitewater Committee's first day of public hearings was to center on Webster Hubbell, the hapless longtime friend of Bill and former law partner of Hillary. Hubbell had resigned his position in the Clinton Justice Department as associate attorney general in disgrace after it was revealed that he had improperly charged his former law firm and clients for some $384,000 in personal expenses. The Republicans had scheduled opening day to be an occasion for public humiliation for Hubbell and, by association, for the Clintons.

But first, the Republican majority had a nasty little gimmick in store for us. Shortly after the bright television lights went on, and Al D'Amato gaveled the maiden voyage of the Whitewater steamship to order, the junior senator from Alaska, Frank Murkowski, held aloft for the cameras the briefcase that had belonged to Vince Foster. Before Hubbell was sworn in as a witness, Murkowski used his opening statement to launch into a discussion of Foster's so-called suicide note. The torn-up page from a legal pad had been belatedly found by a White House lawyer in the bottom of the briefcase, three days after Foster's death. As dozens of cameras clicked and whirred wildly, the beefy Alaskan intoned,

> Mr. Chairman, I have the briefcase in question here. This briefcase is the property of Vincent Foster. It's from the Rose Law Firm Professional Association, Little Rock, Arkansas. Vincent Foster, Jr., Rose Law Firm, 120 East 4th Street, Little Rock, Arkansas with the phone number. As anyone can plainly see, it would be pretty difficult not to see 27 pieces of paper from a legal notebook.

Murkowski's point was that the delay in turning over the note was deliberate.

> Now, here's 27 pieces of paper in this briefcase. They represent, if you will, an 8½ by 11 sheet of paper. If one is looking in here, you're going to find 27 pieces of paper; we've already had testimony that other papers had been removed from the briefcase. So anyone looking in here—it's pretty hard not to observe that there's some pieces of paper in the briefcase in question.

Following this demonstration, Senator Sarbanes, surprised to learn that the briefcase was in the committee's possession, had the following exchange with Chairman D'Amato and Senator Murkowski:

SARBANES: Mr. Chairman, could I inquire of Senator Murkowski whether he got that briefcase from the Independent Counsel?

CHAIRMAN: Yes, the Independent Counsel did furnish us with—

MURKOWSKI: I made the request for the briefcase, Senator Sarbanes.

SARBANES: When was it furnished to us?

CHAIRMAN: Yesterday.

SARBANES: Thank you.

I whispered to Sarbanes that this was an ambush. We had never been advised that Starr had made the extraordinary decision to turn the briefcase over to the majority, much less the purpose they intended to make of it.

Paul continued:

SARBANES: Was this side advised of the furnishing of the briefcase?

CHAIRMAN: Yes. We had left word to the Minority Counsel, but I think there was a little problem in some communications. We had made some requests, but counsel did advise or attempted to advise Minority counsel that we had received this yesterday.

D'Amato noticed the muted stirrings of outrage from our staff. He continued, "If I might, just for purposes of clarification, there were at least a half dozen phone calls that were made yesterday by our counsel to Minority counsel to advise him of this and other matters, and during that period of time we were not able to make contact, so I just suggest this was not some sleight of hand."

This was classic D'Amato. His first instinct was to claim we were notified. This quickly morphed into "we attempted to advise" the minority staff the night before. Of course, we were in full preparation mode in the bat cave until late the previous evening. There had been numerous exchanges of calls between our staff and the majority. The claim that they were unsuccessful in giving us notice was complete bullshit, exactly the "sleight of hand" D'Amato protested it was not.

John Kerry was the only senator on the committee who had not attended the briefing I held for the minority the night before. The former prosecutor was known to be highly independent—even something of a loner—and had not been shy about criticizing President Clinton. It was the subject of some speculation as to how the junior senator from Massachusetts (and future presidential candidate) would respond to the challenges of service on the committee.

Any chance of wooing Kerry to their cause was blown by the D'Amato-Starr briefcase caper. The Republican committee members were treating Foster's briefcase as a shameless object of political theater. Kerry had arrived at the hearing just as Murkowski hefted the accordion-style leather briefcase for the cameras, declaring that no one looking in the briefcase could have missed the scraps of paper on the bottom.

Kerry saw red. He immediately put together the game Starr and D'Amato were playing and was outraged. He jumped right in:

> Mr. Chairman, a point of personal privilege before Senator Sarbanes begins, if I may. I've been sitting here, frankly, disturbed by the demonstration that took place here with the briefcase, which I believe runs counter to the spirit of these hearings for a number of reasons, Mr. Chairman. As a matter of personal privilege, I would just like to say, Senator Murkowski held up a briefcase which, for whatever reasons, we were not aware was going to be here and, for whatever reasons, was made available on very short notice. That briefcase was held up in a very dramatic fashion to suggest that, when held like this, these pieces of yellow paper were somehow visible to Mr. Nussbaum.
>
> Now, I just spent a moment looking back through the depositions, and there is nothing in the depositions that factually suggests that this is how the yellow paper was found or that this is how the briefcase was held or that this is the manner in which they might even have been visible.
>
> In point of fact, the briefcase was down on the floor within reaching distance of the chair [Nussbaum] was seated in, and he reached over and pulled out files. When those files were in there, you can't see in it, I can't see in it, nobody could see in it. For Senator Murkowski to sit here suggesting that was a facsimile of what happened is just false, calculated to have attracted every camera in the room that turned toward that briefcase . . .
>
> I think it is a calculated, inappropriate way to begin these hearings, and I think the record should show that.

Kerry then called for the clerk to bring the briefcase to him and promptly demonstrated how the torn-up note in the folds of its bottom could easily have eluded a quick search. The next day's newspapers showed dueling photographs of Murkowski and Kerry displaying Foster's briefcase and drawing opposite conclusions.

In truth, I could see no reason why the administration would deliberately delay making Foster's note public. But unfortunately, it fit into a preexisting pattern of late production of documents. Whether it was a draft suicide note, or just an attempt at putting on paper what had been bothering him, Foster's handwritten note was indisputably the work of a deeply disillusioned man:

I made mistakes from ignorance, inexperience and overwork

I did not knowingly violate any law or standard of conduct

No one in the White House, to my knowledge, violated any law or standard of conduct, including any action in the travel office. There was no intent to benefit any individual or specific group

The FBI lied in their report to the AG

The press is covering up the illegal benefits they received from the travel staff

The GOP has lied and misrepresented its knowledge and role and covered up a prior investigation

The Ushers Office plotted to have excessive costs incurred, taking advantage of [the Clintons' decorator] Kaki and HRC

The public will never believe the innocence of the Clintons and their loyal staff

The WSJ editors lie without consequence

I was not meant for the job or the spotlight of public life in Washington. Here ruining people is considered sport.

Foster's note was a chilling reminder that the rough-and-tumble Washington partisan warfare—where ruining people's lives and reputations is, indeed, considered part of the game of politics—produces real casualties.

Hubbell, a gentle giant of a man, sat stoically at the witness table through the Foster briefcase episode, waiting patiently for the Republicans to vent their spleen upon him. None of Hubbell's misdeeds had anything to do with his long association with the Clintons or his official duties during his brief stint at the Justice Department. No matter. Bill Clinton had appointed him and would share in Hubbell's public shaming.

The first hearing, featuring D'Amato's disingenuous denial of sandbagging us with Foster's briefcase, set the tone for the rest of the inquiry. While the Republicans may have reaped some short-term benefit with a blatantly political embarrassment of Webb Hubbell, their actions clearly exposed an intent focused on hyperbole rather than investigation. And they lost any chance of winning John Kerry's support.

In comparison to the bipartisan 9/11 Commission a decade later, the Whitewater Committee quickly devolved into one of the most politically partisan investigations in memory. As insignificant as was the subject matter that passed for "scandal" in the 1990s, the smoke and mirrors through which it was projected to the American public by a compliant news media set a new and dangerous standard for our entertainment-based culture. While journalism professors and historians may debate whether the media is on the whole pro-left or pro-right, Whitewater showed it to be wholeheartedly, and rather uncritically, pro-scandal.

In December 1994, Hubbell pleaded guilty to two felonies—mail fraud and tax evasion—admitting he defrauded his former law firm and clients out of at least $384,000. Independent counsel Robert Fiske concluded that Hubbell charged personal expenses to his personal credit cards and then had these expenses either paid by the client or written off as firm business expenses. These included credit card bills from a Victoria's Secret at Little Rock's Park Plaza Mall, an unidentified fur company, and clothing purchases in Dallas. It struck me as particularly dumbfounding that Hubbell had squandered the opportunity to repay his law firm for his personal expenditures before the matter escalated into a criminal case.

THE MAJORITY WAS IMPLACABLE in its hectoring of the White House officials who searched Foster's office for a suicide note in the aftermath of the deputy White House counsel's death. Christopher Dodd was one of the Democratic members of the committee who could always be counted on for an infusion of common sense into the proceedings. The silver-haired and silver-tongued senator from Connecticut made this observation:

> Mr. Chairman, . . . there are sort of three fact situations. You get a witness that says well, I don't recall. The immediate accusation is you're being disingenuous.

> If you have witnesses with conflicting testimony, the allega-
> tion is someone's lying. And if you have witnesses that have con-
> sistent statements, it's a conspiracy.
>
> This is getting ridiculous. So you're trapped no matter what
> you say. You're either disingenuous, lying or conspiring, and
> that's just foolishness.

One of my great advantages as counsel to the minority was the deep respect the Democratic members of the committee had for Paul Sarbanes. Paul's confidence in me soon transferred into their trust of me and our staff—a huge benefit in such an undertaking, where fractious backbiting and second-guessing is often the case. We began to operate as a team. The day before each public hearing, our staff would produce a thick briefing book providing the senators with background on the witnesses and how they fit into the overall picture. We would then meet together for an hour or so in the evening with the senators and one or two of their personal staff; I would explain what to expect at the hearing and how we would counter the majority's predictable mischaracterization of the facts and their significance. We would provide suggested areas of inquiry and spe-cific questions that the senators might wish to use at the hearing. No mat-ter how quick a study—and virtually all of them were—their other obligations left them little time to develop relevant and insightful ques-tions on their own. Lance Cole, in particular, did yeoman service in brief-ing the senators' personal staff on what was going on so that they could look sharp to their bosses.

In addition to Senators Sarbanes, Kerry, and Dodd, three of our sena-tors were women. The Republicans had none. I developed an immediate rapport with Barbara Boxer, the junior senator from California and ex-Brooklynite, who was later to play an important role in questioning the Republicans' star witness, Jean Lewis. Barbara could always be counted on to push D'Amato back whenever the chairman went too far over the top—a not infrequent occurrence. Carol Moseley Braun of Illinois, the only African American then in the Senate, had a great sense of humor and a smile that lit up the room. I was conferring with her in the middle of one of Lauch Faircloth's tirades. On her notepad she had sketched a stick drawing of Senator Foghorn, as she called him, complete with pointy KKK hat and robe. Patty Murray, the newly minted senator from Washington, rounded out our trio of women. Richard Bryan of Nevada and Paul Simon of Illinois provided an extra measure of moral heft to our side.

The clash between the hype the majority disseminated to its favored media outlets and the actual facts was beautifully illustrated during a hearing focused on whether James McDougal had received favorable treatment by an Arkansas state agency in return for hosting a political fund-raiser for Governor Clinton in April 1985. The Republicans had sold a story previewing the hearing based on the conclusion that a decision by the Arkansas Development and Finance Agency to lease space from McDougal's Madison Guaranty Bank was a quid pro quo, in which McDougal was rewarded for the fund-raiser. Not only did the facts brought out at the hearing show that the leasing decision had been made a full year *before* the fund-raiser, but the ADFA officials summoned before the committee to testify about their decision provided a reasoned basis for their action that refuted any notion of intercession by Governor Clinton. This was typical of the Whitewater dynamic—an ominous conclusion hyped to the press, followed by testimony refuting the hyped story. What set this hearing apart was the reaction to the testimony of the ADFA officials by Senator Frank Murkowski, who had lumbered into the hearing room just as the officials were explaining the decision they had made a decade earlier.

"Murky," as the staff fondly referred to him, consulted his briefing book, which contained the newspaper articles the majority had planted previewing the day's hearing. A puzzled frown crossed his face as he bellowed for a point of order, interrupting the testimony:

> Mr. Chairman, isn't the point here simply to draw a conclusion that [then governor Clinton] played a major role in the selection of this building?

This was new ground even within the Alfonse-in-Wonderland tenor of the hearings. Inconveniently, the evidence once again rebutted the preconceived conclusion, a point I made when I resumed questioning. What was so unusual was that a member of the majority took umbrage—with a point of order, no less—at still another departure from the hyped version of events.

As the hearings progressed, the Republican staff became more brazen in manipulating the press. David Bossie, a member of Senator Faircloth's staff, took to cozying up to reporters in the hearing room while hearings were going on, feeding them tidbits for the next day's news stories, even as testimony unfolding before them refuted the prior day's account.

Lauch (pronounced "Lock") Faircloth, the junior senator from Clinton, North Carolina, was a colorful Southern bookend to the committee's dyed-in-the wool New York chairman. A hog farmer by profession, Fair-cloth delighted in spicing up his attacks on the Clintons with creative analogies.

> Mr. Chairman, I want to dispel the notion that we keep hearing of White House cooperation. Anything we have gotten from the White House has been comparable to eating ice cream with a knitting needle.

He so enjoyed his own humor that he often repeated successful lines as building blocks for new ones.

> I said before in the first hearing, it was like eating ice cream with a knitting needle to get anything out of the White House. Well now, it's reached the point of skinning a hippopotamus with a letter opener, and we still aren't getting anything.

After it became clear that they were getting nowhere with the allegations against Bill Clinton, the majority began to focus more and more of their attention on the first lady and her law practice in Little Rock prior to her husband's election to the presidency. Faircloth kept up a steady drumbeat, threatening to haul Hillary Clinton before the committee.

Sarbanes and I discussed what our response should be. It required a certain suspension of reality to understand why a Senate committee would spend so much time and energy on the former law practice of a private citizen, totally unrelated to anything involving the president's conduct in office. Nevertheless, the recurring pattern of refusal to produce documents, followed by a grudging reversal and ultimate production, provided fodder for her critics' claims that Hillary Clinton was hiding something.

Sarbanes and I decided we would not protest but instead would call the majority's bluff. "Go ahead and call Hillary Clinton," we told D'Amato privately. We made it clear we would enjoy the matchup, watching Clinton eat D'Amato's lunch at a public hearing. D'Amato did not risk attempting to bring the first lady before the committee but instead continued to use the hearings to snipe at her.

Nothing epitomized the disconnect between form and substance as much as the tempest over Hillary Clinton's missing billing records. For months the majority sought copies of the Rose Law Firm's billing records as the Rosetta stone that would unlock the mysteries of her involvement in legal representation of Madison Guaranty Bank. Webb Hubbell, who along with Vince Foster was Hillary Clinton's partner at Rose, testified that he had ordered a printout of the computerized records when an issue arose during the 1992 campaign about possible contacts Mrs. Clinton may have had with the Arkansas Securities Department. Foster apparently had them in Washington, but after his death they could not be located. Because of the passage of time, they could not be reproduced by the law firm in Little Rock. Of course, the assumption proclaimed by the majority was that they had been spirited out of Foster's office by Clinton loyalists in the dead of night following his suicide. The first lady's statement that she had done little actual work for Madison, corroborated by other lawyers at the firm, was drowned out by the cacophony of cries that the damning evidence contained in the records must have been destroyed. Lost in the hue and cry over these "critical" billing records was any objective analysis of why the hell we were focusing on the first lady's law practice a decade before she came to Washington. But missing they were, and the Republicans and the media had a field day speculating on their obviously incriminating contents.

Until, in January 1996, they turned up in the "book room" on the third floor of the White House residence. A photocopy of the computer printout was found by Carolyn Huber, a longtime friend of the Clintons and sometime babysitter for Chelsea Clinton. Huber was in charge of the book room, used to store the Clintons' gifts, photographs, and personal items. She discovered the records in a box of photographs and other materials awaiting cataloging under a table in her office. Realizing these must be the long-sought-after billing records, Huber immediately called the lawyers, and the records were turned over to the committee and Ken Starr the next day.

The news of this amazing discovery dominated the front pages of newspapers throughout the land in boldfaced type that would be appropriate to announce a cure for cancer. Amid all the sturm und drang, a simple analysis of the records confirmed what Hillary Clinton had been saying all along: She and the law firm had done relatively little work for Madison.

BEFORE I GOT INVOLVED with the Whitewater investigation, I had no true appreciation of the dynamics of partisan congressional hearings. During Watergate I had enough to do to keep up with my responsibilities as a prosecutor without paying much attention to what was going on behind the scenes at Senator Ervin's Watergate Committee. Whitewater provided some serious on-the-job training.

For example, I was amazed at how much power was vested in the committee chairman as compared to the mere members. And nowhere was the phrase "majority rules" more subject to practical application. The Republican majority set the agenda and determined what witnesses would be called and when. Under the rules, we had no right to call witnesses, nor could we subpoena documents. The huge inequality in budget—the Republican majority had twice as much money as we—accounted for us being substantially outnumbered in staff and resources.

It was clear that to avoid being steamrolled by the majority, we would have to be in a constant mode of resourcefulness. But I was determined that we would operate according to the rules, without leaking confidential information or adopting the methods of the other side. I felt that in the long run if there were no facts to back up the hyperbole, the Republicans' case would fall of its own weight. We would need to keep our eye on the ball for the big picture and not allow ourselves to be distracted by petty skirmishes.

Very early in our proceedings, one of my staffers brought a disturbing piece of information to my attention. It seemed that one of Chertoff's staff-members had something of a history himself. According to the story, as a college student the staffer had been involved in secretly videotaping a classmate having sex with a coed. The video had been passed around campus and came to the attention of the administration, which took swift and appropriate action against the budding pornographer.

Chertoff's staffer had quickly established himself as a thoroughly irritating partisan, functioning as an intermediary between the D'Amato and Starr camps through his prior relationship with certain of Starr's assistants. It appeared that the ambitious young man had been given full authority to leak information to the press in advance of hearings. Moreover, the young Republican had been making up for his lack of actual trial experience with an air of officiousness and disdain toward the young lawyers on the Democratic staff, who had quickly branded him as the most unlikable of our counterparts. Ironically, the young videographer was later captured on C-SPAN's video of one of the committee's hearings in an übergross moment of personal hygiene (reminiscent of Paul Wolfowitz's later grooming faux pas), which earned him the nickname "Waxie."

I called our staff together for an impromptu meeting in the bat cave. I told them I had heard the story about Waxie that was making the rounds.

Toby and me, Brooklyn, 1945.

My dad in Belgium, January 1945.

At home in Laurelton, Queens, during my sophomore year at Stuyvesant High School.

Speaker of the House John W. McCormack holds forth in his Capitol office, January 1969. *(Charles H. Phillips/Time & Life Pictures/Getty Images)*

The Speaker's chief aide, Martin Sweig, July 22, 1971. *(Associated Press)*

The Speaker's "dear friend," convicted fixer Nathan Voloshen, April 7, 1970. *(Associated Press)*

Watergate Special Prosecutor Archibald Cox explains why he can't accept the "Stennis Compromise," at the Washington Press Club the morning of the Saturday Night Massacre, October 20, 1973. *(Associated Press)*

Together with the next Special Prosecutor, Leon Jaworski, and Carl Feldbaum and Jill Wine, January 15, 1974. *(Corbis)*

Rosemary Woods demonstrating how she might have accidentally erased part of the June 20, 1972, Nixon-Haldeman tape recording. Quite a stretch. *(White House photo)*

The cover-up trial team: me, Jill Wine, and Jim Neal entering the U.S. Courthouse, Washington, DC, November 8, 1974. *(Associated Press)*

My opening statement to the jury at the Watergate cover-up trial. Judge John J. Sirica, upper right; defendants H. R. Haldeman, lower left; and John Mitchell, lower right. October 14, 1974. *(Sketch by Freda Reiter for ABC News, courtesy of Corbis)*

Convicted con man turned Abscam undercover operative Mel Weinberg (holding cigar) and his federal agent escort leave U.S. District Court, Brooklyn, August 18, 1980.
(Associated Press)

Me with my client, Philadelphia lawyer Howard Criden, August 29, 1980.
(Associated Press)

Abscam prosecutor Thomas Puccio arrives at Brooklyn Federal Court, December 2, 1980. The videotapes trumped everything else.
(Associated Press)

Senator Paul Sarbanes looks on while I engage with Whitewater Committee Chairman Alfonse D'Amato and chief counsel Michael Chertoff, Hart Senate Hearing Room, July 19, 1995. (*Associated Press/Marcy Nighswander*)

Jean Lewis testifies before the Senate Whitewater Committee, November 29, 1995. (*Associated Press/Dennis Cook*)

Testifying before the House Judiciary Committee impeachment hearing. Lance Cole, left, and my wife, Donna, right, look on. December 8, 1998. (*Associated Press/J. Scott Applewhite*)

Our outstanding leaders: 9/11 Commission Chairman Thomas H. Kean and Vice Chairman Lee Hamilton, July 22, 2004. *(Courtesy of David Coleman)*

Condoleezza Rice finally appears before the 9/11 Commission on April 8, 2004. From top left: Commissioners Kerrey, Gorton, Gorelick, Kean, Hamilton, Fielding, and me. *(Corbis)*

"And I ask you whether you recall the title of the [August 6] PDB?"
(Associated Press/Charles Dharapak)

"I believe the title was 'Bin Laden Determined to Attack Within the United States.'" *(Corbis)*

During my appearance with John Lehman on *Meet the Press*, June 10, 2004, I stated, "Take it to the bank—there was no connection between al Qaeda and Iraq regarding 9/11." *(Alex Wong/Getty Images)*

The 9/11 family steering committee members Carol Ashley, left, and Mary Fetchet, right, with me and Commissioner Tim Roemer, December 8, 2008. *(Scott J. Ferrell/Congressional Quarterly/Getty Images)*

José Melendez-Perez, the U.S. Immigration Service Inspector who stopped potential twentieth hijacker Mohamed al Kahtani from entering the United States, testifies at the 9/11 Commission hearing, January 26, 2004. *(Courtesy of David Coleman)*

9/11 Commission executive director Philip Zelikow, January 26, 2004. *(Courtesy of David Coleman)*

There would be no repeating of this story, I cautioned, and God forbid it should be leaked to the press by someone on our team. The leaker would be fired on the spot. We were not going to play the game that way. End of story.

Except it wasn't. While the increasingly unpleasant Waxie's collegiate misconduct was never publicly revealed during the Whitewater Committee's lifetime, a later published book by a chastened right-wing insider contained a remarkable coda to the story. In his tell-all confession *Blinded by the Right*, David Brock revealed that a mini–power struggle had been fought behind the scenes between Waxie and David Bossie. Without the benefit of a law degree, Bossie had made his bones working for right-wing hit men in the anti-Clinton camp going back to the 1992 election. Bossie, the burly young Faircloth appointee, sported a buzz cut and lived in a suburban Maryland firehouse where he was a volunteer. He was such an unapologetic yahoo and eccentric figure, I found his lack of hypocrisy refreshing.

Unbeknownst to us at the time, Bossie had sought to leapfrog Waxie in the Republican staff pecking order, using whatever means might become available. According to Brock, then a darling of the anti-Clinton movement, Bossie approached him to see whether he could come up with any juicy tidbits that might undermine his rival. Brock sprang into action, calling upon his pal Ann Coulter to assist in the incipient hatchet job. Brock remembered that some years earlier, Waxie had unburdened himself to Brock and Coulter about his college past, seeking guidance as to how he might minimize the incident if it ever came to light in the context of applying for a political position that required Senate confirmation. Brock explained Bossie's request for ammunition against Waxie to Coulter but confessed he couldn't remember the details of Waxie's confession. Coulter was Johnny-on-the-spot, providing Brock with dates and details— even remembering how Waxie had lamented that the student newspaper had written a story about the scandal that could be found by accessing the paper's morgue. Brock passed the intel on to Bossie, who reported back that he was able to confirm the story. Armed with the scandalous details, the Republican investigator-cum-fireman had what he needed to undermine his rival.

With friends like Brock and Coulter and colleagues like Bossie, Waxie didn't need enemies. For Bossie's part, it was only a matter of time before his career as a paid congressional investigator would come to an abrupt halt. In 1998, he was caught having doctored audiotapes of a

Webb Hubbell jailhouse conversation to falsely suggest that Hillary Clinton was somehow involved in billing irregularities at her former law firm.

––––––––––

ALTHOUGH MY COURTROOM EXPERIENCE as a prosecutor and defense lawyer has always proved a great advantage in questioning witnesses, there is a huge difference between a trial and a congressional hearing. If a trial might be analogous to a chess match, a congressional hearing more resembles a knife fight. I am reminded of a scene in *Butch Cassidy and the Sundance Kid* when Butch finds himself face-to-face with Harvey Logan, a six-foot-nine-inch knife-wielding villain who sought to wrest control of the gang from Butch and Sundance through hand-to-hand combat. As Logan advances, Butch protests to the other gang members who circled the combatants, "No, no, not yet. Not until me and Harvey get the rules straightened out." "Rules in a knife fight?" asks the momentarily distracted giant, as Butch kicks him squarely in the cojones, ending the contest.

That is not to say there are no rules in a congressional hearing. But they are a lot different from court rules. For example, there is no rule against hearsay. In fact, there are no rules of evidence at all. The questioner may refer to a newspaper story or a rumor as part of the question. Or he or she might simply make a statement or observation and ask the witness no question at all. As counsel you can go forward, backward, or sideways without interruption by some pesky judge. You get to ask your questions while seated in a comfortable chair at a superior height in relation to the witness normally reserved for the judge in a courtroom setting. And you can have a cup of coffee or get up to stretch your legs any time you feel like it. A courtroom lawyer could get mighty spoiled.

Of course, there were limitations. Al D'Amato was gifted in seeing where I was going with a line of questioning, and interrupting my progress with some detour and frolic of the chairman's prerogative. Strangers complimented me on my patience in the face of these obvious attempts to sidetrack my questioning. Actually, I had no choice. D'Amato was a senator and the chairman. I was just a hired hand. Sometimes, after an interruption that took several minutes, I resumed by completing my sentence at the point of interruption.

D'Amato was sensitive about being targeted by journalists for a variety of idiosyncrasies, from his fractured syntax to his imperviousness to ethical norms. While the editors were willing to publish the breathless hype about the next scandal just around the corner that the right-wing machinery was pumping out through the committee's apparatchiks, they were not so quick to embrace the chairman, whose foibles were still good copy. D'Amato sought Paul Sarbanes's approval whenever he had a chance, to boost his stature by engaging in polite conversation with him on the dais in front of the cameras. We used this to our advantage from time to time.

Every once in a while, when I felt I really needed a stretch of uninterrupted interrogation time, I would ask Paul to engage D'Amato in conversation so that I could proceed without the usual speed bumps. Sarbanes would oblige by chatting up the chairman about some nasty remark by a columnist that was just *so* unfair to Al. Meanwhile, I would take care of whatever business was at hand, without interruption. Once, D'Amato was so engrossed in Paul's sympathetic patter that not even Chertoff tugging at this sleeve could bring him back to the proceeding.

On one memorable occasion, we had spent hour after hour with former state officials called to discuss the Arkansas Water and Sewer Authority, and whether former governor Clinton had pressured them more than a decade earlier to benefit the ubiquitous McDougal. The nonsense continued until late in the afternoon, the usual time for my inner gremlin to assert itself.

I began my questioning with the admission that prior to that day's hearing, I had been sadly ignorant of the history of the Arkansas Water and Sewer Authority in the early and mid-1980s. But with my newfound education came an appreciation, even a thirst, for more information about such a fascinating topic. But why should we limit ourselves to a mere dozen years ago, or even this century? I asked somewhat rhetorically. And why should the committee restrict itself to a narrow parochial interest in Arkansas? Why not expand our inquiry overseas? Why not the Paris sewer and water system as portrayed by Victor Hugo through the eyes of Jean Valjean in *Les Misérables*? The baffled witnesses blinked their eyes, wondering if my question called for a response. We moved on.

THE DENOUEMENT OF THE first phase of our hearings came in late November 1995 with the much-heralded testimony of L. Jean Lewis. Lewis had become the darling of the conservatives for her work as an RTC investigator, attempting to link the Clintons to check kiting and other questionable activities by James McDougal at his Madison Bank. Lewis claimed political interference by the Clinton administration in following up on her RTC referrals for criminal investigation of Madison, and asserted that she had been unfairly treated by her superiors because of her pursuit of legitimate investigative leads. Lewis and the right-wing Landmark Legal Foundation, a persistent critic of the Clintons funded in part by the Scaife Foundation, had found each other by the time Lewis first testified publicly before a House committee chaired by Representative Jim Leach (R-IA) in August 1995.

With the encouragement of the Republican majority, Lewis made a number of inflammatory claims in her testimony, which received front-page coverage. Lewis asserted her belief that Bill and Hillary Clinton had knowledge of McDougal's check kiting because some of the checks involved mortgage payments McDougal made on the Whitewater project. This was Lewis's sole justification for naming the Clintons as material witnesses in a September 1992 written referral she sent to the FBI and the U.S. attorney in Little Rock. Lewis told the House committee that she "suffered personally and professionally" for her actions, implying that she was the victim of unjustified retaliation for her conscientious efforts. Lewis produced a tape recording of a conversation between her and April Breslaw, an RTC lawyer who visited her Kansas City office, to buttress her assertion of improper pressure from above. Acknowledging that she did not inform Breslaw that she was being taped, Lewis made the astonishing claim that she had not intended to surreptitiously tape her visitor but that an old and malfunctioning cassette recorder had "turned itself on," unexpectedly capturing the conversation.

The House Democrats had done little to shake Lewis's testimony beyond charging she was in league with conservative partisans like Landmark, and that her assertions about the Clintons had no basis in fact. Our procedures on the Senate side were more favorable to an in-depth exploration of the facts and motives involved. For example, we would be able to take the witness's sworn deposition in advance of public testimony and, unlike the five-minute rule in the House, which limited questioning to a ridiculously short amount of time, I would have as much time as necessary to question witnesses—ceded to me by Senator Sarbanes out of the minority's allocated time. This would be as close to a real cross-examination as a congressional hearing allows.

We took Lewis's deposition four weeks before the public hearing. In addition to a personal attorney, Lewis showed up with a truculent lawyer from the Landmark Legal Foundation named Mark Levin who tried to insert himself into the proceedings from time to time. The majority was represented by Robert Giuffra, who did his best to interpose objections to my questions, giving Lewis a bit of a breather. I did what I needed to do to pin Lewis down under oath for later use at the public hearings.

Lewis's magical tape recorder explanation for her surreptitious recording of April Breslaw would be central to testing her credibility on other issues. Carefully, I had Lewis recite in detail the circumstances of her malfunctioning tape recorder, how it turned itself on and how she had thrown it away and bought a new recorder weeks after Breslaw's visit. I gave her all the rope she would need to hang herself.

It was one thing to ridicule Lewis's obviously bogus explanation. It would be quite another thing to *prove* it was false—particularly since the majority was unwilling to agree to subpoena the records we wanted.

So we wrote a letter to Lewis's lawyer and followed up by publicly calling for Lewis to produce the records we had requested, including documentation reflecting the purchase of the new recorder. Lewis's lawyer eventually responded with a letter attaching a bank statement. He circled an entry for a purchase two weeks *after* her meeting with Breslaw. We gave the assignment of verifying the purchase to two investigators Paul Sarbanes had wangled from the General Accounting Office. They contacted the store identified on the bank statement and reported that the check was for an expensive pen and other items, not a tape recorder. Then, through a combination of enterprise, legwork, and good luck, they were able to locate an office supply store near Lewis's office that had sold her the new portable recorder. The sales slip showed it was purchased by credit card in Lewis's name, days *before* Lewis's meeting with Breslaw. Our investigators told the store manager to hold on to the paperwork—he would be hearing back from us soon.

Lewis had told and retold her version of events under oath. A deliberate and surreptitious recording of a colleague was unlikely to be the subject of a mistake or hazy recollection. Combined with documentary evidence and sworn testimony of other witnesses refuting other important pieces of her testimony, her testimony about the tape recorder would be critical to assessing Lewis's overall credibility.

Jim Pittrizzi, one of our GAO investigators, delivered us an unexpected piece of evidence the night before the Lewis hearing. We had developed a fairly compelling picture of Lewis's motive of self-aggrandizement and her penchant for exaggeration and outright fabrication. Now came evidence of her personal feelings toward Bill Clinton. Lewis had produced a disk from her government computer in response to the committee's demand for documents. A cursory look revealed nothing of particular relevance.

Our investigators wanted a look at the original, so Tim Mitchell had made a request to the majority to see it. The process of searching computer files for deleted data had become standard operating procedure for investigators by this time. Jim called our attention to a long, rambling twenty-two-page letter Lewis had written to a friend a month before she began her review of Madison Guaranty Bank. In the course of unburdening herself about personal problems, Lewis gratuitously referred to then governor Bill Clinton as "a lying bastard." Although she had deleted the letter, Lewis had not "written over" this portion of the disk. Jim informed us it had been a simple matter of calling upon the computer's "undelete" function to restore the letter.

Now we were faced with a difficult decision. Even though the personal letter was on a government disk turned over by a witness pursuant to an official request, and therefore entirely within our legal right to use, was it acceptable to confront Lewis with her own words in a private letter? Sarbanes and I conferred. Our decision was that we would give Lewis every opportunity to acknowledge her preexisting opinion of Clinton, and then use the letter to "refresh her recollection" only if she denied having expressed a negative opinion.

The Republicans hoped the appearance of Jean Lewis would breathe new life in the Whitewater Committee's hearings. After four months, there was no fire to show for all the smoke signals the majority had sent up. On November 29, 1995, the media turned out in force, to see how Jean Lewis would fare. Lewis made a good appearance, looking professional in a tailored suit, attractively styled short hair, and owlish round eyeglasses. After Chairman D'Amato gaveled the hearing to order, Lewis read her prepared statement. In it she ranged far beyond her personal knowledge of facts, drawing conclusions about alleged misconduct by the Clinton administration and suggesting areas of inquiry for the committee to pursue, including that the committee invite the president and the first lady to testify before it. Rather than a witness statement, it was more of a proclamation that Jean Lewis would be the official spokesperson for the hardline opponents of the Clintons. She wound up her twenty-minute statement with a personal attack on me for having the effrontery to question her about whether she had sought to write a book about her exploits and other matters unrelated to Madison or Whitewater. She concluded, "Mr. Ben-Veniste also suggested the timing of the first criminal referral may have been politically motivated because the Clintons are named as possible witnesses and beneficiaries of criminal conduct and the referral was sent to the Justice Department during the Presidential campaign."

Perhaps Lewis and her team of supporters at Landmark and the majority staff thought the best defense would be an aggressive offense. We would see. But I was glad to have the central issue raised by the witness herself.

The majority decided to begin by playing Lewis's secret recording of April Breslaw. Amazingly, she had dictated a prologue onto a copy of the original and gave that altered copy to the committee. The notion of an investigator altering a tape recording in that way would have provided a field day for lawyers in a trial setting. But this was not a court of law and D'Amato ordered it played, advising me that he was not going to permit "nitpicking—I'm not going to permit it from either side." A fair and balanced ruling. I responded by noting that the circumstances under which Lewis made the tape would, in fact, be questioned by us.

The tape was played. Interestingly, Lewis's claim in her opening statement that Breslaw sought to pressure Lewis by conveying a message that "the people at the top would like to be able to say that Whitewater did not cause a loss at Madison" was shown to have omitted Breslaw's preceding phrase, "I think if they can say it honestly, the head people would like to be able to say . . ." Small beer, perhaps, but indicative of the larger misrepresentations to come.

Robert Giuffra was assigned responsibility of questioning Lewis for the majority. Obligingly, he had her reiterate the strange tale of the eight-year-old tape recorder's prior history of "popping on" by itself.

> It had a history of not working some days, working other days. On that particular day, because of a project that I had due to Mr. Iorio [her boss], my desk was very full of files and other paraphernalia and although the recorder was laying where it usually was, by my calculator, I was shuffling a lot around and I suspect I may have knocked it and in so doing may have turned it on, but I was not aware it was on when the conversation initiated. I later became aware it was on and consciously chose to let it run.

Guiffra had Lewis recount that the timing of her September 2, 1992, written referral on Madison Guaranty Bank was apolitical and that not to have named the Clintons as witnesses would have been "imprudent . . . because they were part of Whitewater and could have easily had knowledge of what Mr. McDougal had been doing with those funds."

It was now my turn to ask some questions. The legendary law professor John Henry Wigmore described the art of cross-examination in his seminal work, *Wigmore on Evidence,* as follows:

It may be that in more than one sense [cross-examination] takes the place in our system which torture occupied in the medieval system of the civilians. Nevertheless, it is beyond any doubt the greatest legal engine ever invented for the discovery of truth. However difficult it may be for the layman, the scientist, or the foreign jurist to appreciate its wonderful power, . . . cross-examination, not trial by jury, is the great and permanent contribution of the Anglo-American system of law to improved methods of trial-procedure.

I began my examination of Lewis showing that among the troubled banks for which she was given responsibility, Madison was thirteenth in order of priority, with other bank losses approaching $1 billion in the late 1980s meltdown, dwarfing Madison's $60 million loss. Lewis grudgingly acknowledged that FBI agent Steven Irons repeatedly contacted her regarding the investigation of these other banks, which she had put aside to pursue Madison. Why had she set a different priority?

> BEN-VENISTE: Did you tell Special Agent Irons that you had given up an opportunity in Washington, DC, a job opportunity, just to be able to work on the Madison matter?
>
> LEWIS: No, sir, I don't recall saying that to Mr. Irons.
>
> BEN-VENISTE: Did you tell Special Agent Irons that, in order to work on the Madison referral, you not only gave up a job opportunity, but in order to work on it, you thought you or it, the Madison referral, could alter history? Do you recall telling him that?
>
> LEWIS: No sir. You raised that question in my deposition, and I've thought about it significantly since then, and I do not recall saying that.

Tradecraft 101 for the trial lawyer stipulates that you ought not ask a question on cross-examination for which you don't already know the answer. Steven Irons was a straight arrow. We had his testimony and contemporaneous notes about his dealings with Jean Lewis ready to go.

I put Irons's handwritten notes up on the large monitor in the hearing room. We were off to the races.

> BEN-VENISTE: Agent Irons' note says "JL called—Just about ready. She has a deadline of 8/31," August 31, 1992. "Gave up a job

opportunity in DC just to do referral. She or it could alter history. Very dramatic."

These are the contemporaneous notes of Special Agent Steven Irons, who will be here to testify this week and who has testified under oath before this committee in deposition.

Does that help refresh your recollection that in August 1992, you called Mr. Irons and you told him that you gave up a job in Washington just to work on the Madison referral, and you thought that you or it could alter the course of history?

LEWIS: Mr. Ben-Veniste, Mr. Irons' contemporaneous notes are not something I'm going to argue with because I have known Mr. Irons and worked with him extensively.

BEN-VENISTE: So you accept Agent Irons' notes, then, if I understand your testimony, of his conversation with you?

LEWIS: I will accept Agent Irons' notes, but if I made that comment, then knowing my sense of humor, it was probably made in much more of a sarcastic tone than a dramatic tone.

BEN-VENISTE: That you turned down the job offer and thought you might alter the course of history was a joke to you?

LEWIS: No, I don't believe I said that was a joke. I believe I said that my tone can sometimes become sarcastic, and if I made that comment, it was probably more in that vein than of drama.

Drama or sarcasm, Lewis had backed off her nonrecollection. Her motives were now coming into sharper relief. I turned to the question of whether Lewis had exaggerated her supervisor's timetable in trying to get the FBI to act immediately to open an investigation.

BEN-VENISTE: Who gave you a deadline of August 31, 1992, to finish the criminal referral on Madison?

LEWIS: That was a self-imposed deadline because I had begun the drafting process, had planned to leave for a vacation in mid-August to attend my 20th high school reunion, and hoped to have it completed shortly after I returned.

BEN-VENISTE: Did you tell Agent Irons that your bosses had imposed that deadline on you?

LEWIS: No, sir, I don't believe I ever told him they had imposed a deadline.

BEN-VENISTE: Now, with respect to any self-imposed or other deadline imposed—and we'll get Agent Irons' testimony on this later this week—it is true, is it not, that there was no particular reason for urgency in connection with the Madison referral?

LEWIS: That's true, there was no particular urgency.

BEN-VENISTE: Indeed, Mr. McDougal had already been prosecuted and had been acquitted, and he was the principal target of your referral: correct?

LEWIS: That's correct.

BEN-VENISTE: Mr. McDougal at the time that you were working on this referral, you learned, was impecunious; correct? He had no money?

CHAIRMAN: I'm glad you explained that one.

LEWIS: Thank you, Mr. Chairman.

CHAIRMAN: Any time.

LEWIS: My knowledge of his financial circumstances were such that he had no money, that's correct.

BEN-VENISTE: He had no ability, as far as you know, to repay anything in connection with the losses associated with Madison?

LEWIS: Correct.

BEN-VENISTE: He was living, you knew, in a borrowed mobile home; correct?

LEWIS: I had read that in an article, yes, sir.

BEN-VENISTE: You knew that he had been in poor health, had been hospitalized for a mental breakdown?

LEWIS: I knew he had health problems, yes, sir.

BEN-VENISTE: His wife had left him, you knew that?

LEWIS: Yes, sir.

Indeed, the mentally disturbed McDougal had already been indicted and acquitted of bank fraud. There was no question that McDougal had played fast and loose with his responsibilities as the bank's president. We were not about defending McDougal. But since he had already been acquitted of criminal charges and there was no prospect of collecting a civil judgment from him, why did Lewis put aside more substantial investigations to focus on Madison—if not to try to damage Clinton's chances weeks before the election by implicating the candidate in a fraud investigation?

BEN-VENISTE: Now, you recognized, did you not, at the time you were working on the Madison referral that any publicity about then-candidate Clinton being involved in an FBI or Grand Jury investigation, even as a witness, could have negatively affected his chances in the general election for President of the United States?

LEWIS: I accept that was a possibility, yes, sir.

I established from Lewis's direct supervisor, Richard Iorio, who sat next to Lewis at the hearing, that the normal time for the FBI to respond to an RTC criminal referral was ninety days, and that he had not directed her to make any inquiries of the FBI to follow up on the Madison referral.

I then put another of FBI agent Irons's notes up on the big screen.

BEN-VENISTE: It is dated 9/18/92. It is the typed note produced from the FBI file in Little Rock. It says:

"Jean Lewis of RTC was in the office today for [a] meeting . . . Prior to, she asked me what status of Madison was, told her not decided, but meeting scheduled. After her meeting she waited for me. She again asked for status and was told she would have to ask the U.S. Attorney. She advised her boss, Richard Iorio, kept asking her to try to find out what it was we were doing. I reminded her of the sensitivity and that, even if the U.S. Attorney decided to go forward, these cases took longer than a month to determine what was there. She advised everyone above her in RTC was aware of the referral."

Now, does that refresh your recollection, Ms. Lewis, about your conversation with special Agent Steven Irons?

MS. LEWIS: I remember attending that meeting that Mr. Irons references in Little Rock, and I do remember speaking with him before and after the meeting.

MR. BEN-VENISTE: That's a start.

At that point D'Amato jumped in. This was not going the way he planned. Had Giuffra briefed his boss on the downside of Lewis's testimony revealed in the deposition?

CHAIRMAN: It's a better start than that of a lot of witnesses I've heard heretofore. They couldn't even recall where they were.

BEN-VENISTE: We take one witness at a time, Mr. Chairman.

CHAIRMAN: I understand, but I thought it would be interesting to make an observation. I know witnesses who can't even remember what they wrote.

BEN-VENISTE: Thank you. Ms. Lewis?

LEWIS: Yes, sir.

BEN-VENISTE: Did you tell Agent Irons that your boss, Richard Iorio, kept asking you to try to find out what the FBI was doing with respect to your referral, after all it had been there all of 2 weeks already?

LEWIS: No, Mr. Ben-Veniste, I don't remember specifically posing that question to him.

BEN-VENISTE: Do you deny saying that to Agent Irons?

LEWIS: No, I'm not going to deny it. Obviously, Agent Irons remembers better than I, I guess. I don't recall.

Examples of Lewis's flexibility with the facts were mounting. More retreats from her sworn testimony were to come.

BEN-VENISTE: In your deposition, you claimed that you had not made any contact with Agent Irons from the time that you sent over the criminal referral until [after the presidential election] December 1992. Do you recall that testimony?

LEWIS: Yes, I do.

BEN-VENISTE: In addition to the references that I've provided to you . . . there are at least eight contacts which are recorded of you pressing the FBI and the U.S. Attorney's Office for information of a follow-up nature as to what was going on with your referral. Can you provide any explanation for that, Ms. Lewis?

MS. LEWIS: As Mr. Iorio has already said, Mr. Ben-Veniste, during that time frame, I was in frequent contact with the FBI [over] . . . an active and ongoing investigation. If, during any of those conversations, I posed the question about the Madison referral, I don't recall specifically doing so, but I'm certainly not going to deny that I may have asked.

I returned to Lewis's comment about altering history:

BEN-VENISTE: Ms. Lewis, how could it be that providing a criminal referral the target of which, Mr. McDougal, was an individual who had been prosecuted and acquitted, was completely broke, living in a borrowed mobile home, and who had suffered a mental breakdown, could alter the course of history?

LEWIS: Mr. Ben-Veniste, it's not my job to be the judge and jury on such matters. When I find evidence of criminality, I follow through on my procedures, I write my referrals, submit them to the appropriate authorities, and leave it to them to be the judge and jury on that.

BEN-VENISTE: What I'm referring to is your reference to Agent Irons in August 1992, before you even sent the criminal referral over, that you wanted to be a part of this event that could alter the course of history. Now, surely you couldn't have been talking about the event being sending in a criminal referral targeting Mr. McDougal, could you have been?

LEWIS: I don't remember making that comment, sir.

BEN-VENISTE: You just indicated to us that you had no argument with the fact that Agent Irons' contemporaneous note, where he characterized your statement as being very dramatic, was accurate?

LEWIS: I do not take exception to Mr. Irons' notes because, as I said, I worked with Mr. Irons for a long time. I have a great deal of respect and admiration for him, so I'm not going to argue with those notes. Knowing myself, I would characterize a comment like that something along the lines of oh, yeah, right, Steve, I'm going to be big in the middle of this because I'm sure it's really going to change the course of world history.

After this lamest possible explanation, I moved into the territory of her personal disdain for Bill Clinton.

BEN-VENISTE: Let me ask you this, Ms. Lewis: Did you, at the time that you first began your work in connection with Madison, have an opinion about then-candidate Bill Clinton?

LEWIS: No, sir. At that point, I knew very little about Mr. Clinton.

BEN-VENISTE: Did you express a view about Mr. Clinton to any friend or acquaintance of a derogatory nature?

LEWIS: Mr. Ben-Veniste, I think it's fairly well documented that I am a conservative, I am a Republican, and there may have been occasions upon which I may have made comments to my friend, but I don't think those are comments that are appropriate for a proceeding like this.

BEN-VENISTE: You don't think they are appropriate for a proceeding to inquire into whether you had a preconceived notion or bias against Mr. Clinton at the time you undertook this responsibility for providing a criminal referral? Let me ask you what you recall about expressing a negative view about Mr. Clinton.

D'Amato could see this was heading in a direction he didn't like. He jumped in to intercede.

CHAIRMAN: Mr. Ben-Veniste, we've gone well beyond, and I've permitted latitude. I will permit latitude to all of the members and to counsels, but when we start to get into the business of have you ever expressed an opinion politically to friends about X, Y, or Z, whether it's President Clinton, Governor Jim Guy Tucker, or whoever it is, I think we're going a little far.

If you want to say "did you ever tell any of your friends about the referrals," that's fine. Anything as it relates to her professional conduct—I've permitted that to come in—as it relates to her work or breach of fiduciary responsibility or the responsibility imposed upon her as an investigator, fine. But we're not going to get into whether or not you're a Democrat or Republican. Mr. Iorio, I didn't ask him whether he's a Democrat or Republican—

BEN-VENISTE: Nor did I ask Ms. Lewis.

CHAIRMAN: It doesn't matter. When we get into the business about whether or not you've expressed anything as it relates to somebody who is a candidate, well known for public office, people make expressions, and we're not going to get into whether she may have said he's too conservative, too liberal, too whatnot.

Why don't you proceed, but let's keep it on the line as it relates to her work and professional conduct. If you want to refer to conversations that she had with other people in connection with this, fine.

If we're going to get into the business of if you've ever expressed anything about Mr. Clinton, I have to tell you something, to my knowledge, I am not aware of her having leaked out any of this information or referrals or having given it in a manner that would have been detrimental. So, I think, if you want to look at that, if you have a suggestion that she may have done this, fine. Let's explore that and I'll restore whatever time—put an extra 3 minutes on and let's proceed.

LEWIS: Mr. Chairman, there is one part that I would like to clarify with regard to what Mr. Ben-Veniste just asked.

CHAIRMAN: All right.

LEWIS: I did, Mr. Ben-Veniste, and I will freely admit this, keep my politics at the forefront of my mind as I worked on that simply because, knowing my own conservative views and knowing those of Mr. Clinton, I held myself to a much higher standard going through the documentation that I was working at to ensure that there was very significant and substantial evidence before even proceeding with that.

Now Paul Sarbanes spoke up, correcting the chairman's mischaracterization of my question.

SARBANES: Mr. Chairman, let me just make this observation. First of all, no questions were asked by Mr. Ben-Veniste to Ms. Lewis whether she was a Republican or a Democrat or a conservative or a liberal. I think it's perfectly warranted to find out whether Ms. Lewis, as she went into this Madison matter in which she included the Clintons as witnesses in her referral, had a preexisting bias or strong attitude with respect to Mr. Clinton. It's a perfectly legitimate question.

She has just asserted that she made an effort to adopt a higher standard, but it's reasonable, then, to ask what were the preexisting biases that may have existed.

BEN-VENISTE: Let me first establish, it is correct, is it not, Ms. Lewis, that I never asked you what your political affiliation was, in your deposition or here today?

LEWIS: No, sir, that's correct, you did not ask.

BEN-VENISTE: You volunteered that just now.

LEWIS: That's correct.

BEN-VENISTE: My only question to you was whether you had a very strong view about Mr. Clinton personally, which you expressed to others, of a very negative nature, even prior to the time that you began your investigation in 1992.

CHAIRMAN: Don't answer that. We're going well beyond now. If you have something—

BEN-VENISTE: Yes, I do.

CHAIRMAN: Go ahead. Continue.

BEN-VENISTE: Is the ruling—

CHAIRMAN: Does it mean because somebody has had a negative opinion of someone in public life or office that it's relevant at this hearing?

SARBANES: Yes.

CHAIRMAN: I don't believe it is . . .

SARBANES: Yes.

CHAIRMAN: The witness does not have to answer. I think she went way beyond what she had to in terms of indicating that she was, in terms of her own political views, a conservative and differed with Mr. Clinton. As it relates to what she may or may not have indicated to people has no bearing here at this time . . .

This is still America, and people have a right to express their opinions about what they think of various candidates.

SARBANES: Mr. Chairman, if that's a stipulation that Ms. Lewis, in fact, made such disparaging comments—

CHAIRMAN: I didn't stipulate to that. I'm saying that it's irrelevant.

SARBANES: I don't know that she needs to answer the question, but, otherwise, if it's not a stipulation, I think it's perfectly relevant to find out how much bias or preexisting prejudice she may have had as she went into this examination of the Madison matter.

I stood by as Lauch Faircloth tried to claim the floor and Barbara Boxer skirmished with him, asking the chairman to limit interruption of my questioning. Order was momentarily restored until a new wave of disputation arose.

CHAIRMAN: Let us continue. Mr. Ben-Veniste, you can continue to examine.

BEN-VENISTE: But I may not inquire as to the issues of personal bias?

CHAIRMAN: I didn't say that. If you want to say personal bias, let me tell you something, let's look at what the witness said. She said she bent over backwards because she did have a difference of opinion and she kept that foremost so she would attempt to be fair. That's how I read that . . .

Let's accept it in terms of the question of bias, she answered quite clearly that was not the case and she went out of her way.

BEN-VENISTE: But now I'm asking about whether she had expressed a personal bias against Mr. Clinton on a very personal level, and if the ruling is that I may not ask that question, I will go on.

CHAIRMAN: Did you have a personal bias toward any of the people that you were—

SARBANES: That's not the question.

CHAIRMAN: Toward Mr. Clinton, did you have a personal bias?

SARBANES: Did she express a personal bias?

CHAIRMAN: Now, if we're going to start saying that she may have indicated to somebody politically what her feelings were—

SARBANES: Not politically. Strike politically.

CHAIRMAN: How do we get in and differentiate? I would suggest that Ms. Lewis can indicate whether or not she had a personal bias. That certainly is well within the realm of a proper question, whether she did have a personal bias.

BEN-VENISTE: Ms. Lewis, did you express a personal bias about Mr. Clinton in 1992?

D'Amato was moved to break into rhyme.

CHAIRMAN: Oh, my God. As the tension mounts and fills the air of whether or not a personal bias was there.

BOXER: Mr. Chairman, motivation is important and I don't think it's funny either.

CHAIRMAN: Motivation? How about looking at the facts in the record?

BEN-VENISTE: I got as far as asking a question.

SARBANES: We've been trying very hard to bring out the facts, and we've had this question before us now for about 10 minutes, and Ms. Lewis is constantly prevented from answering by interruptions from the other side:

CHAIRMAN: Let me say this: The Chair is going to make a ruling. As it relates to the question of personal bias, certainly, I think you're well within the right of people to ascertain were you personally biased and did that interfere with any of your actions.

Now, that's a complete and thorough question. Did you have a personal bias and did that bias interfere with your actions? Did you take unwarranted actions as a result of that, as distinguished by whether or not you had a political bias or political views, did you have a personal bias that influenced your actions?

BEN-VENISTE: Mr. Chairman, am I still asking questions here? I don't understand.

CHAIRMAN: I'm telling you if you're going to ask a fair question, the question comes down to was there any personal bias that interfered with the performance of her duties or affected the performance of her duties, that is a proper question.

SARBANES: No, because, the proper question is whether there was any personal bias. Then we need to evaluate on the basis of the answer to that question—

CHAIRMAN: You can answer.

SARBANES:—Ms. Lewis's conduct.

CHAIRMAN: Now we're getting into—Ms. Lewis, go ahead.

LEWIS: Thank you. I'm going to take the silence as a shot this time. As to any kind of a personal bias, I had no personal bias against Mr. Clinton, didn't know Mr. Clinton. As far as my potential political bias, as I have already stated, I kept my conservative views and potential bias versus very liberal views at the forefront of my mind to make sure that I stayed with a higher standard of care in documenting the evidence and the allegations I was about to make because they were very serious.

Lewis had provided the opening for me to confront her with the specific words she used.

BEN-VENISTE: Did you express to a friend of yours in 1992 your view that Mr. Clinton was "a lying bastard"?

LEWIS: Mr. Ben-Veniste, I cannot recall ever having made a statement like that.

BEN-VENISTE: I'll help you recall because we have, from the disk that you provided to this Committee, a letter, and I'm not going to show the rest of the letter to anyone, but I will show you the reference and ask whether it refreshes you recollection that you so referred to then-candidate Clinton in February 1992?

Showing a witness a document to refresh her recollection is standard procedure. There would be no need to make the letter public if she simply acknowledged having made the statement.

> LEWIS: I confess, I'm curious where you got this letter.
> BEN-VENISTE: We got it from you.
> LEWIS: I don't think this was on a disk I gave you, Counsel.
> BEN-VENISTE: Apparently you didn't think it was on the disk, but it was. That's the funny thing about these disks. I don't understand how they do it, but they can find the stuff on the disk that nobody thinks is there. I hate it when that happens, but here it is, Ms. Lewis.

The ball was in Lewis's court.

> LEWIS: Obviously, Mr. Ben-Veniste, I will claim authorship of this document, and yes, sir. I did make that comment.
> BEN-VENISTE: Thank you. Now, with respect to—
> CHAIRMAN: Mr. Ben-Veniste, could you furnish us a copy of this document?
> FAIRCLOTH: Mr. Chairman, is the statement not true?
> BEN-VENISTE: If I may continue, Mr. Chairman. I've asked one question. I had 10 minutes. My red light is on.
> CHAIRMAN: Go ahead, continue. I would suggest this. I would like to see the document.
> FAIRCLOTH: Is it the truth, Ms. Lewis?
> LEWIS: Senator Faircloth, you're not tripping me up on that one again.
> BEN-VENISTE: If I could have 10 minutes, I'd like to explore the surreptitious taping of Ms. Breslaw.

Having Lewis acknowledge that she made the remark, I was eager to move on. There was no need to intrude into any part of her personal letter. Faircloth interjected, calling for the whole letter to be made available.

> BEN-VENISTE: Ms. Lewis, do you want to get into the rest of this letter? I'm prepared to respect your privacy with respect to the rest of it.
> LEWIS: Thank you, Mr. Ben-Veniste, I do appreciate that.

But Al would not let it rest.

CHAIRMAN: Isn't it a somewhat humorous comment at the end as
it relates to your son, if you take a look at that, or someone
else?

Lewis then explained that the comment about Clinton was made as a
gratuitous reference in the context of explaining that one of her former
stepsons was having serious emotional problems at the time.
Sarbanes again put the matter in context.

SARBANES: I think that makes it more relevant, Mr. Chairman,
with respect to the question of bias because the letter, as Ms.
Lewis has said, dealt with family members but her aside, which
dealt with this particular politician, went on and made this
judgment about him.

So I think it's very relevant to the bias condition . . . because
it demonstrates a certain frame of mind and point of reference
with respect to then-Governor Clinton. That's all. We have it,
you have it, and we'll evaluate it accordingly.

I resumed questioning, laying the foundation for the new evidence we
had discovered about Lewis's tape recording of Breslaw.

BEN-VENISTE: Now, I want to focus on your claim that, magically,
the tape recorder began to record of its own volition and the
various versions of this story that you have told under oath up
to this point.

In the first instance, you testified, did you not, that this
tape recorder was eight years old and would go on and off. It
would record on its own for a period of time prior to the time
that Ms. Breslaw came to your office, right?

LEWIS: I believe what I testified was that in the December [depo-
sition] proceeding the recorder began to hiccup, I think was
the way I put it. Some days it would record when I wanted it to,
some days it would not record when I wanted it to.

BEN-VENISTE: Did you say it recorded on its own prior to the time
that it recorded Ms. Breslaw?

LEWIS: Yes.

BEN-VENISTE: So the recorder managed to capture the entire conversation that you had with Ms. Breslaw, which is about 35 or 40 minutes; right?

LEWIS: That's correct.

BEN-VENISTE: There was a 1-hour cassette in that recorder so it was fortuitous that there was enough tape on there to tape the whole conversation; right?

LEWIS: Yes.

BEN-VENISTE: The magical tape recorder, and I'm holding up the tape recorder which you subsequently purchased after Ms. Breslaw's taping. The tape recorder that you used, you say you threw away shortly after Ms. Breslaw was taped surreptitiously by you, correct?

LEWIS: I disposed of the recorder. I don't recall exactly when.

BEN-VENISTE: You said it never worked again after Ms. Breslaw was taped with it, right?

LEWIS: No, sir, I don't think that's accurately how I testified.

BEN-VENISTE: What do you recall about whether the tape recorder ever worked again?

LEWIS: I seem to recall that I tried it a few more times, and it finally died. At that point, I replaced it with the one, I believe, you're holding in your hand.

BEN-VENISTE: "Finally" being a week or so later?

LEWIS: Within a matter of days, I believe, yes, sir.

BEN-VENISTE: It's true, is it not, that just before Ms. Breslaw visited your office, you purchased a supply of micro cassettes for your tape recorder?

LEWIS: I believe I purchased a group of microcassettes, or a box, sometime between December and February.

BEN-VENISTE: Sometime prior, according to your testimony—I can read it back to you—in the *days* prior to Ms. Breslaw's visit, you said?

LEWIS: Yes, sir, I recall that.

BEN-VENISTE: OK. Now, you had the tapes on hand, you had the recorder on hand. Our issue is—and we can resume with this in a little while after lunch because we won't have time to fully develop it—the issue is whether, in fact, you tape-recorded Ms. Breslaw with the old tape recorder which malfunctioned and magically came on to record her conversation or whether, in fact, you deliberately recorded her conversation with the new tape recorder?

LEWIS: Mr. Chairman, may I respond to that?

CHAIRMAN: Absolutely.

LEWIS: Thank you. Mr. Ben-Veniste, I purchased that new recorder well after I had that conversation with Ms. Breslaw. As I have previously testified, the old one worked sometimes, didn't work sometimes, it was eight years old, it was used on a regular basis, and I did throw it away when it ceased to function. I did not deliberately set out, which I believe is your inference, to trap Ms. Breslaw in any way.

BEN-VENISTE: We will explore that when we come back, with the Chairman's permission, of course.

The table was set. Lewis knew we were going to challenge her story. She had over the lunch break to think whether, without being able to issue a subpoena, we had somehow gotten the evidence of when she purchased the new tape recorder.

After we resumed, the majority set out to show that Lewis's work had resulted in investigative leads that were used by independent counsel Kenneth Starr to indict Jim and Susan McDougal and Jim Guy Tucker, then the governor of Arkansas, who had been involved in transactions with McDougal wholly unrelated to the Clintons. Reindicting McDougal was like shooting fish in a barrel. The only reason a Senate committee was pursuing this was Lewis's exaggerated claims about the Clintons' involvement, and her claim that she was improperly thwarted in her investigative efforts.

Before concluding the magical tape recorder story, we used our next turn at bat to illuminate the extraordinary professionalism displayed by U.S. Attorney Charles Banks and the FBI agents in the Little Rock field office in dealing with Jean Lewis's 1992 referral.

BEN-VENISTE: I'd like to ask you who the U.S. Attorney was in August and September 1992, when you submitted your criminal referral?

LEWIS: Charles Banks.

BEN-VENISTE: Mr. Banks was a Republican appointee of President Bush, was he not?

LEWIS: Yes, sir.

BEN-VENISTE: Mr. Banks was the person who was responsible for determining whether your criminal referral had any merit and should be pursued, isn't that so?

LEWIS: He should have been the final authority, yes, sir.

BEN-VENISTE: Let's put up FBI Exhibit 1000 and provide a copy of that to Ms. Lewis, please. FBI 1000 is a letter dated October 16, 1992, by Mr. Banks to Mr. Don Pettus, who was the special agent in charge of the FBI office in Little Rock, is that correct?

LEWIS: Yes, sir, to my knowledge.

BEN-VENISTE: All right. If you turn to page 2 . . .

[KIT] BOND: Mr. Chairman, I think this comes from the talking points from the White House that, according to *Dateline*, were prepared to use in attacking Ms. Lewis, and I have some excerpts from the White House talking points, page 3 of the White House talking points, but I'd like to see the full letter.

Kit Bond of Missouri was another of the more partisan Republicans on the committee, but he lacked the humor of D'Amato and Faircloth. Senator Bond repeatedly tried to insinuate that our examination of Lewis had been scripted by the White House. Psychologists refer to this type of behavior as projection. Bond assumed, incorrectly, that we were doing what he might do under similar circumstances—take marching orders from the White House. In fact, we never did so, in part because we wanted to avoid just such a claim but, mostly, because we were much more focused and capable of doing the job on our own, without outside help.

BEN-VENISTE: Excuse me, Mr. Chairman. This is a document that we received from the FBI in response to our request many months ago, Senator, and it has been testified to by Mr. Banks and by Mr. Pettus.

CHAIRMAN: OK. So noted.

BEN-VENISTE: May I continue, Mr. Chairman?

CHAIRMAN: Yes.

The critical portion of Banks's letter to the head of the FBI office in Little Rock demonstrated that he viewed the timing of Lewis's referral and her persistent calls to follow up on it as an attempt by her to interfere in the political process. I read the letter aloud.

"Neither I, personally, nor this office, will participate in any phase of such an investigation regarding the above referral prior to November 3, 1992. You may communicate this orally to officials of the FBI or you should feel free to make this part of your report.

"While I do not intend to denigrate the work of RTC, I must opine that after such a lapse of time the insistence of urgency in this case appears to suggest an intentional or unintentional attempt to intervene into the political process of the upcoming presidential election. You and I know in investigations of this type, the first steps, such as issuance of grand jury subpoenas for records, will lead to media and public inquiries of matters that are subject to absolute privacy. Even media questions about such an investigation in today's modern political climate all too often publicly purport to 'legitimize what can't be proven.'

"For me personally to participate in an investigation that I know will, or could easily, lead to the above scenario and to the possible denial of rights due to the targets, subjects, witnesses or defendants, is inappropriate. I believe it amounts to prosecutorial misconduct and violates the most basic fundamental rule of Department of Justice policy. I cannot be a party to such actions and believe that such would be detrimental to the Department of Justice, FBI, this office and to the President of the United States [referring to President Bush]."

This was the strongest possible rebuke, made even more forceful since it came from a Republican appointee. D'Amato's antennae went up, as the chairman sought to defuse the import of Banks's reaction to Lewis's ploy, and an incipient attempt by the Bush Department of Justice to push the FBI into action before the election.

CHAIRMAN: Fine. Who is this letter written to?
BEN-VENISTE: It was written to the special agent in charge of the Little Rock FBI office.
CHAIRMAN: Fine.
BEN-VENISTE: Now—
SARBANES: On October 16th.
CHAIRMAN: On October 16th. Again, Mr. Ben-Veniste, the point is that there was no leaking of information from Ms. Lewis. This letter was not directed to her, it was directed to an FBI agent and I fail to understand how it is that this would impact

on the testimony of Ms. Lewis, but go ahead. It's your time. Restore the time.

BEN-VENISTE: I can answer that for you, Mr. Chairman. The reason—

CHAIRMAN: You'll do it on your time.

SARBANES: All right. We're on our time.

BEN-VENISTE: I'll be pleased to do it. The reason why it is relevant is because there was pressure being put on the FBI office and then the U.S. Attorney to do something.

CHAIRMAN: Not by Ms. Lewis.

BEN-VENISTE: Ms. Lewis contacted the FBI and the U.S. Attorney's Office by our count, according to records in the possession of this Committee, on eight separate occasions between August 31st and December 1992, notwithstanding Ms. Lewis' sworn denial of having done so.

I then took advantage of the absence of strict rules of evidence in congressional hearings and used other witness statements and documents to nail down how the law enforcement professionals had evaluated Lewis's referral.

BEN-VENISTE: Ms. Lewis, with respect to the certain assumptions and presumptions that you made regarding Mr. or Mrs. Clinton's knowledge, is it correct to say that you acknowledge that there was no evidence that Mr. Clinton or Mrs. Clinton knew that Mr. McDougal was involved in this check kiting among his different companies? Isn't that so?

LEWIS: That's correct, Mr. Ben-Veniste, I never stated there was evidence to that effect.

BEN-VENISTE: Indeed, when the referral was evaluated by Mr. Banks, he testified that the referral did not cite to a tangible document or witness, to anyone that says that these people have knowingly participated in a criminal fraud on this institution . . .

Mac Dodson, who was the deputy and a career prosecutor in the Little Rock office, serving under Mr. Banks, stated, "I don't think there was anything in the referral that indicated any wrongdoing by any of the witnesses." . . .

Special Agent Steven Irons testified, "Ms. Lewis had listed on her referral and stated what she thought the involvement of the Clintons was, and I've said that, based on my review, I don't agree with the characterization that they were necessarily aware of the check kiting activity." . . .

Fletcher Jackson, a career prosecutor in the U.S. Attorney's Office in Little Rock, testified, "Basically, all it was was McDougal was overextended on debt. He was doing his debt-carry by doing all of these maneuvers and manipulations. No more. No less." . . .

Special Agent in Charge of the Little Rock office Pettus testified under oath, "There was no reason to believe based on the referral or the evidence cited in the referral that Bill Clinton knew of any alleged wrongdoing regarding check kiting or campaign contributions."

Mr. Johnson, another career prosecutor in Little Rock, testified, "It amazed me" that Ms. Lewis would conclude that forgery had occurred based solely on her own observation. He testified that he thought that Ms. Lewis was "reckless" for doing so.

The unanimous repudiation of Lewis's motives and assertions by six nonpartisan law enforcement professionals who reviewed her referral refuted any notion that she had been the victim of political interference.

Barbara Boxer, who had become totally engaged in prepping for Lewis's appearance before the committee, took her turn questioning Lewis. We had discovered some interesting evidence about Lewis's private entrepreneurial efforts related to the Clintons. Boxer honed in on Lewis like a laser, questioning her about a November 1993 letter she had written to a T-shirt manufacturer hawking her idea for a line of "shirts, bumper stickers, coffee mugs, etc." with the acronym BITCH, standing for "Bill [or Bubba] I'm Taking Charge Here." Lewis suggested that the "political climate" was ripe for her concept.

I appreciated Lewis's feistiness and dark sense of humor, but she shouldn't have used her RTC computer and work phone to promote her side business, or compromised what should have been an objective investigation. Boxer nailed her on both counts.

Kit Bond interrupted, seeking a ruling from the chairman to declare Boxer's inquiry irrelevant. A perplexed D'Amato suspended the clock while he read the letter.

Senator Boxer defended her question, pointing out that a witness's attempt to profit from an ongoing investigation was certainly relevant. D'Amato was boxed.

Boxer continued, forcing Lewis to admit her profit motive. As to whether the meaning of her acronym was pejorative, Lewis pronounced that it wasn't—she was only referring to the fact that the first lady was "a very strong, assertive woman," and that Lewis herself had been characterized as a strong, assertive woman, and "I have no objections—and forgive me gentlemen [she told Barbara], as to someone calling me a bitch—that's fine."

As the Republicans returned to their theme that McDougal and Tucker were subsequently prosecuted for fraud, I got ready to deliver the coup de grâce on the magical tape recorder. Senator Sarbanes went first, finishing off the professional evaluation of Lewis's 1992 referral with the evaluation by career Department of Justice attorney Jerry McDowell that "the referral had come in half-baked . . . it looked like a junky case, that if it had any merit, the RTC should have fleshed it out, or go on to more productive things."

Jean Lewis stared ahead without speaking. Suddenly, she slumped in her chair. David Bossie, the volunteer fireman, ran to her side to provide assistance. As Lewis was helped from the hearing room, her lawyer informed us that she was experiencing chest pains. D'Amato quickly adjourned the hearing until the next day, pending Lewis's ability to continue. Outside, Lewis was wheeled on a gurney to an ambulance, which sped away with lights flashing and siren blaring.

Jean Lewis never reappeared to conclude her testimony. We were informed that she spent the night under observation for elevated blood pressure at a local hospital but was in no danger. To my knowledge, she was never called again as a witness in any forum on the subject of Whitewater.

Whether suspicion that we had gotten proof to refute her cock-and-bull story on the tape recording of April Breslaw contributed to her collapse, we may never know. Later, after we had pressured the majority to issue a subpoena for the documentation we knew was being held by the store manager in Kansas City, I delivered a public status report concluding the saga of Lewis's tape recorder.

BEN-VENISTE: Mr. Chairman, I wanted to give you a status report with respect to the request for information that had been submitted regarding Ms. Lewis. We were trying to ascertain when, in fact, she purchased the second tape recorder to determine whether her explanation of the old tape recorder coming on by itself really was a credible explanation for how she tape-recorded Ms. Breslaw.

Obviously, it was important to us to learn whether she had purchased the tape recorder prior to the Breslaw meeting or, as she had contended, whether she purchased it afterwards. In response to our request, we received a letter of November 7, 1995, from her counsel, identifying a purchase made on February 17, 1994, which would have been then some two weeks after her meeting with Ms. Breslaw.

When our staff contacted the store in question, it was learned that the item which was identified in that letter and the accompanying bank statement did not, in fact, refer to the purchase of the tape recorder, but referred to the purchase of a pen and some other items.

So yesterday, we issued subpoenas and we received from Office Depot a receipt which reflects that on January 17, 1994, an Olympus Pearl Quarter Model S-924 was purchased by Ms. Lewis at the Office Depot store in question for $49.99, that the account number reflects the identical number of Ms. Lewis' work number which we have in other material, and that, in fact, the so-called new tape recorder was purchased in advance of her meeting with Ms. Breslaw, which would then call into question why, if she had a new tape recorder, would the Breslaw conversation be taped by an old tape recorder.

Obviously, we have additional information to obtain in connection with this. This is an interim report. We have the new tape recorder because we requested that Ms. Lewis provide that to this Committee. The Independent Counsel's Office has the original tape made on that tape recorder. I believe that it might be advisable for us to send the new tape recorder to the Independent Counsel's office because tape experts will be able to compare the original tape to the new tape recorder and determine whether it was made on that tape recorder, and obviously, that would be of significant interest.

CHAIRMAN: I will ask our attorneys to pursue this matter as we have initially and as we will continue to do and offer, obviously, Ms. Breslaw the opportunity through her attorneys—

BEN-VENISTE: Ms. Lewis.

CHAIRMAN:—to respond accordingly—excuse me, Ms. Lewis; I am so interrelated with the two of them now—but Ms. Lewis to respond through her attorneys.

I knew from my Watergate tapes experience with the 18½-minute gap that technology existed capable of identifying the unique "fingerprint" made by a tape recorder when in Record mode. That was why I had insisted that Lewis's new tape recorder be subpoenaed and kept in the committee's custody. Clearly, had Kenneth Starr wished to investigate a perjury charge against Lewis, he could have had tests done matching the original cassette with the new recorder, corroborating the evidence that Lewis had misstated under oath the circumstances of the surreptitious recording of Breslaw. But Starr obviously had more pressing matters on his agenda. We never heard whether tests were performed, and Lewis was never charged.

In the immediate aftermath of the hearing, we received the welcome news of Lewis's prompt recovery. I confessed to Sarbanes that I was relieved that Lewis's collapse had come during his questioning rather than mine. Our staff began referring to the reserved and überpolite senator as a terrifying cross-examiner, while his longtime friend and administrative assistant, Peter Marudas proclaimed Sarbanes to be "the Johnnie Cochran of Baltimore."

Of course, I caught hell from the majority, particularly from Kit Bond, for questioning Lewis about the "lying bastard" phrase in her letter. In the months that followed, Bond repeatedly demanded that I disclose how I was able to restore the letter Lewis had deleted. To think that I had figured out how to restore the letter was ludicrous, since my colleagues were well aware of my total lack of technical sophistication. But I was not about to give up our GAO investigator, who might have been subjected to political retaliation. So every time Bond brought the subject up at a hearing I simply sat stoically, not responding. Chairman D'Amato, who, unlike Bond, had authority to make such an inquiry, wanted no more of Jean Lewis and never echoed Bond's demand.

The Landmark Legal Foundation, whose rising star was left with her credibility in tatters, went bonkers. Mark Levin wrote a long diatribe to the Senate Ethics Committee demanding that it take action against Senator Sarbanes and me for violating Lewis's privacy rights. Of course, the same procedure for restoring deleted computer data had long been employed by investigators and, indeed, was then being used by Ken Starr's minions—in far more costly and technically challenging fashion—to restore deleted White House e-mails. Unsurprisingly, the Ethics Committee, chaired by Republican Mitch McConnell, summarily rejected Levin's complaint, provoking a hissy fit press release from the right-wing lawyer, blasting the committee.

Nevertheless, in hindsight I wish D'Amato had stipulated to Lewis's bias, or had stuck to his original ruling, excluding the evidence. Notwithstanding Lewis's protestations to the contrary, there was abundant evidence of her personal bias without the "lying bastard" reference, and the furor it caused was an unnecessary distraction.

The status report closed the book on Jean Lewis. A three-month hiatus was to follow, as the Republicans fought to push the hearings further into the 1996 election cycle, still hoping that something would turn up that would stick to Bill Clinton.

———————

THE SENATE RESOLUTION ESTABLISHING the Whitewater Committee included a provision requiring the committee to provide a progress report to the full Senate by January 15, 1996, and to make recommendations as to whether additional time was required for the investigation. Unsurprisingly, the majority and minority came to different conclusions as to whether additional time was needed. D'Amato proposed to have the committee's investigation continue indefinitely beyond the original end date of February 29, 1996, and asked for an additional $600,000 in funding. D'Amato said the committee needed the additional time because the White House had impeded the investigation by failing to turn over documents, and that the committee was unable to question certain witnesses due to Ken Starr's prosecution of the McDougals and Tucker in Arkansas. In August 1995, Starr had brought charges against Jim Guy Tucker, along with Jim and Susan McDougal, for fraud, conspiracy, and making false statements to obtain federally backed loans (totally unrelated to Whitewater) in the 1980s. Democrats rejected the D'Amato proposal and responded with a resolution that would extend the life of the special committee for five more weeks and a final report to be issued by May 10.

With no new resolution in place by February 29, the committee no longer had authority to investigate. The stalemate continued into April. On April 17, the Senate came to an agreement and approved a resolution providing an additional $450,000 along with authority for the committee to continue until June 17, just five months before the election.

The break in the hearings gave me some breathing room to catch up on my neglected private law practice and to spend some quality time with my family. My younger daughter, Olivia, then three years old, had grown accustomed to seeing me on television, as Donna tuned in to the hearings at home. Paul Sarbanes had been a guest at our home and we had visited with Paul and Christine at their home in Baltimore. So it was only mildly

surprising that Olivia picked Sarbanes out of a handful of senators surrounding minority leader Tom Daschle at a news conference. "There's
Senator Sarbanes—he's a good guy!" Olivia exclaimed, pointing to the
television screen. "That's right," Donna replied, reflecting on the fact that
Olivia seemed as conversant with national political figures as with *Ses-
ame Street* characters. But Olivia's next comment—"Where's D'Amato?"—
floored us. "Where's D'Amato?" became a code phrase at our house for
Olivia's early introduction to politics in the nation's capital.

TO JUSTIFY THEIR BLATANTLY partisan strategy for extending the committee's life span well into the campaign season, the Republicans had to
look busy, which meant scheduling hearings on more and more arcane
subjects. On one memorable occasion, Alfonse fell victim to his own strategy of "more is better."

One afternoon, D'Amato confided to me that he was having some difficulty in his personal life. Seeming more agitated than usual, Al explained that it was his birthday, ordinarily a happy occasion. His pals
from New York were coming to Washington to help him celebrate. But
his girlfriend at the time, *New York Post* gossip columnist Claudia Cohen,
wasn't the least bit interested in hanging with D'Amato's posse. Claudia
wanted a more intimate dinner so that they could "work on their relationship." The colorful chairman emphasized the strangeness of the
"relationship" explanation by visually providing the quotation marks,
wiggling two fingers in each hand next to his head. "So now I got to have
two birthday dinners tonight to keep them apart."

Apparently, he had not clued Chertoff in on the evening's taxing social
schedule, as Mike droned on with a witness into the late afternoon, once
again going right for the capillary on another of Clinton's supposed Arkansas peccadilloes. "Okay. This is going to take me another half hour
to straighten out," I whispered to Sarbanes. "Why are you telling me
this?" Paul wanted to know. "I'm talking to Al," I answered. Sure enough,
D'Amato's extraordinary auditory powers had swept up my comment.

I began my examination by sending a document down for the clerk to
mark for identification and hand to the witness. As the witness studied
the document, D'Amato scooted his chair behind Sarbanes and motioned
to me to meet him. The chairs on the dais were equipped with casters allowing for mobility without having to stand up. I scooted over. The chairman grabbed my forearm in a claw hold. "Richard, it's five o'clock—you're
fucking torturing me here." "I can't help it. Michael just raised a whole

new issue." "Can't you shorten it? It's my birthday, for crissakes!" "I can do it in ten minutes—unless Michael starts up again. Then I make no promises." D'Amato scooted his chair over to Chertoff, who was busy consulting his notes. "Mikey, shut the fuck up!" the chairman implored. There were no further questions from the majority.

IT NEVER CEASED TO amaze me how many people were watching the hearings on C-SPAN. Between the televised hearings and the frequent interviews I gave on the Sunday network news programs on NBC, ABC, CBS, and CNN, the *MacNei/Lehrer NewsHour* on PBS, Charlie Rose, Larry King, *Hardball* (but no shows with screeching harridans or thuggish wing nuts, thank you), it was possible to counter some of the distorted spin put out daily by the right wing's well-oiled machinery.

But there was some unintentional collateral damage. A case in point involved my nephew, Trevor. Donna's brother and sister-in-law frequently tuned in from their home in Northern California to keep track of what was going on in our lives in the nation's capital. The hearings were rebroadcast by C-SPAN at odd and seemingly unpredictable hours. Late one evening, Dale and Janet returned home from an outing and reflexively turned on the TV, which had been tuned to C-SPAN. Six-year-old Trevor, already out of sorts from a long car ride, recoiled from the screen in horror. "Not the Uncle Richard show!" he wailed.

On the positive (and still collateral) side, one frigid winter afternoon as the hearing droned on, I took advantage of the microphone to make a direct plea to the mayor of Washington, the colorful and controversial Marion Barry, to plow my street in Northwest DC. Whether or not there was any causal relation, our street was plowed the next day, while surrounding streets remained unplowed for several more days. I became a minor hero on our block, taking full credit for the rare appearance of the snowplow.

One of the most appealing aspects of my Whitewater assignment was the opportunity to work closely with Paul Sarbanes, one of the finest public servants I have ever known. Sarbanes's parents came from Laconia (from which the adjective "laconic" is derived), and true to his heritage, Paul could be defined by a certain economy of movement and speech. But when Sarbanes spoke, his peers in the Senate listened. He was also known as one of the Senate's best thinkers. Indeed, from time to time when I would raise some point or other, Paul would say, "Let me think about that." He would then proceed to think quietly while I stood by, waiting for the thinking portion of our interaction to segue back to actual conversation. For me, this was a new experience. As a trial lawyer, I was accustomed to thinking on my feet and making quick decisions. Paul was just the opposite.

One evening, our legal team was in the bat cave reviewing the transcript of a particular witness's testimony. There was a difference of opinion as to whether the stenographic transcript had omitted something important the witness had said. Since all of the hearings were televised by C-SPAN, we were able to verify whether the transcript was accurate. As we fast-forwarded the videotape, looking for the point in the testimony at issue, we laughed at how goofy everyone looked with their eyes blinking madly and hands moving in herky-jerky fashion. Except Senator Sarbanes, who looked about the same as when we viewed the proceedings at normal speed.

I had occasion to mention this phenomenon to Paul, as I implored him to take immediate action to counter one of the many gambits D'Amato and company had come up with. I argued that unless we acted quickly, the window of opportunity to put forward a counterpoint would slam shut. Unconvinced, the famously deliberate member of the nation's greatest deliberative body drew upon his vast storehouse of classical literature to respond. "Richard, in the fable of the tortoise and the hare, whom did you identify with?"

––––––––

THE LAST HURRAH FOR the majority in the extended, and equally unrevealing, last phase of the committee's work was to be the appearance of David Hale.

David Hale was another eccentric Arkansas character who was destined to have his fifteen minutes of fame as part of the anti-Clinton cabal. A disgraced former Little Rock municipal judge, Hale had been investigated for a number of financial swindles, big and small, that culminated in an FBI search of his office in 1993. In an effort to add a political dimension to his plea-bargaining strategy, Hale had turned to Clinton's political archenemies for help. Hale's interrelationship with the McDougals provided the backdrop for a claim that Governor Clinton had pressured Hale to make a $300,000 loan to a company controlled by Susan McDougal, which in turn was used by the McDougals to pay down a portion of their debt on the Whitewater investment. Hale and his allies tried to enhance his bargaining position with federal authorities in Little Rock by feeding his claim of Clinton involvement to the *New York Times* and other media outlets. In the course of doing so, Hale embellished his claim with details, later proved false, such as his supposed close political relationship with Clinton. After Kenneth Starr took over the federal investigation, Hale was able to reach a plea deal to plead to two felony counts in return for his promise to testify as a prosecution witness under complete immunity for any other violations of federal law Hale may have committed.

Thus, David Hale stood as the only person in the entire Whitewater saga who had ever claimed direct dealings demonstrating wrongdoing by Bill Clinton. As such, it was inevitable that Hale would be called before the Whitewater Committee to repeat his sensational charges in front of a televised audience of tens of millions. Al D'Amato was salivating at the prospect of being master of ceremonies for Hale's delivery of a damaging blow to the Clinton presidency.

From my perspective, David Hale would be a dream witness to cross-examine. I had begun to build a dossier on Hale's misdeeds, character, and anti-Clinton relationships from day one of my engagement as counsel for the minority. Our staff had collected an impressive amount of ammunition reflecting on Hale's misconduct and lack of credibility.

Among my favorite tidbits involved Hale's paranoia and penchant for overdramatization. At the same time as Hale was operating a number of businesses as a one-man financial crime wave (the head of the Small Business Administration later testified that Hale's operation was "one of the most blatant cases of fraud against the [SBA] program I have ever seen"), he was sitting two or three days a week as a municipal judge hearing traffic and hot-check misdemeanor cases. At considerable taxpayer expense, Hale had installed a bulletproof screen in front of the bench and a metal detector at the entrance to his courtroom. Hale had once claimed to be the subject of a plot by a group of current and former courthouse employees to murder him and had ordered special security precautions, including armed escort by the sheriff's department to and from the courthouse. The basis for the claim turned out to be an overheard comment by the girlfriend of one of the alleged plotters at a birthday party that "if Hale died, I wouldn't cry."

A glimpse into Hale's character was provided by his dealings with a secretary who had confided that her family was having trouble meeting mortgage payments on the family farm. Hale suggested that the family deed the farm to a company he controlled, which would allow the land to be developed while the creditors would be kept at bay. In the end, no development took place and the bank foreclosed on the farm—but not before Hale had helped himself to 133 acres. In a subsequent civil action, the secretary's family won a $500,000 judgment against Judge Hale.

The differing versions of Hale's account of Clinton's alleged pressure on him to lend money to Susan McDougal's company would provide fertile ground for cross-examination. Hale's early interviews with the FBI, and outtakes of television reporters' interviews with him, were at odds with Hale's later claim that Clinton pressured him to make the SBA-backed loan. Moreover, Hale's decision to align himself with some of Arkansas's most virulent anti-Clinton characters was shown to precede the newly minted claim of Clinton pressure. Records showed that Hale made more than forty telephone calls to Jim Johnson, a retired Arkansas Supreme Court justice, segregationist, and ardent Clinton hater, in the aftermath of the FBI's search of Hale's office. Under Johnson's tutelage, Hale was soon in touch with Floyd Brown of Citizen's United—creator of the infamously racist Willie Horton television ads when Michael Dukakis was running for president—and the committee's own David Bossie, who was then a young Citizen's United operative. Indeed, statements of an NBC cameraman who filmed a November 1993 interview of Hale revealed Bossie's role in orchestrating the interview and coaching Hale throughout.

Cross-examination is 90 percent preparation and 10 percent inspiration. We wanted to be fully prepared for the day Hale appeared before the committee. So as early as November 1995, we began pressing the majority to issue subpoenas for Hale's documents and to schedule his sworn deposition. For the next five months we continued to urge that Hale be subjected to prehearing questioning under oath. But it was not to be. The majority stonewalled our efforts. Instead, Hale's debut as a witness would be reserved for the trial of Jim Guy Tucker and the McDougals in Little Rock. There was no way that Ken Starr would allow Hale to be subjected to a real cross-examination before his appearance at trial. For his part, Chairman D'Amato was content to allow Starr to take the lead, using the upcoming trial in May as grounds to extend the hearings four months beyond the original date for concluding the committee's work.

Despite a disorganized case put forward by Starr's deputies (Starr, an accomplished appellate lawyer with no discernible trial experience, wisely stayed away from the courtroom), Jim McDougal was able to snatch defeat from the jaws of victory. Displaying the full measure of his mercurial, if not pathological, personality, McDougal rejected his lawyer's pleas not to testify and took the stand as a witness in his own defense. This was an unmitigated gift to the prosecution. Not only did it give them a chance to regroup and to use McDougal's cross-examination as a vehicle to re-present their case, it allowed the jury to experience McDougal's arrogant and dismissive demeanor. McDougal succeeded in engineering his own conviction and was likely responsible for dragging his ex-wife, Susan, and former governor Tucker down with him.

As it turned out, David Hale's appearance as a witness in the Tucker/McDougal trial was, by all accounts, a complete bust. Hale testified to his supposed contact with Clinton, while President Clinton's videotaped testimony denying any conversation with Hale about the Susan McDougal loan was played to the jury. Although it found sufficient evidence to convict the defendants, the jury's informal verdict on Hale's credibility was damning. In postverdict comments to the press, one juror stated that the jurors considered Hale "an unmitigated liar [who] perjured himself; David Hale invoked the President's name for one reason: to save his butt." Another juror agreed, adding, "I didn't believe a thing Hale said." Indeed, Starr's lead prosecutor, Ray Jahn, who presented Hale's plea-bargained testimony to the jury, felt the need to distance the prosecution's case from the media-hyped version of events Hale had promoted. In his closing argument, Jahn told the jury that there wasn't any evidence that Clinton had pressured Hale to make the loan to Susan McDougal, nor did the prosecution claim that Clinton was involved in wrongdoing.

Once the Tucker/McDougal trial was over, the onus was on D'Amato finally to conclude the committee's work. A seemingly endless year of investigation had produced virtually nothing of substance.

Would the Republicans risk another black eye by putting David Hale front and center to parrot his now publicly discredited claim about Clinton's alleged pressure? In a heartbeat! The lure of the long-awaited Hale and the attendant publicity obviously overwhelmed any concern about the validity of his accusation. So be it—we were locked and loaded. The long-shelved subpoena was finally served on Hale's new lawyer, Theodore Olson, a close social and political friend of Kenneth Starr (and later George W. Bush's solicitor general).

But a funny thing happened on Hale's way to the forum. Olson announced to D'Amato—he would not deign to communicate with the minority—that unless the committee conferred complete immunity on his client, Hale would assert his Fifth Amendment privilege and refuse to testify. Yet Hale had already testified under oath—protected by his plea bargain with Starr—and had undergone days of cross-examination during the Tucker/McDougal trial. And he had already been sentenced to twenty-eight months in prison, half of what he might have received without Starr's recommendation of leniency. Why was he balking now that his big moment to appear before the cameras had finally arrived?

One reason was the pending criminal investigation targeting Hale that, try as they might, neither Hale nor Kenneth Starr could derail. At the heart of the investigation, led by plucky Arkansas state prosecutor Mark

Stodola, was a brazen scam perpetrated by Hale involving scores of poor, mostly African American residents of Pine Bluff, who had purchased burial insurance from Hale's National Savings Life. For a premium as little as $1 per month, National committed to pay for a casket and funeral service when the policyholder died. When a state review showed that National was insolvent, Hale was directed to deposit $150,000 into National to cure the deficiency. Yet a later surprise audit revealed that the same day in July 1993 that Hale deposited the $150,000 into National, the identical sum was transferred *out* to another company controlled by Hale. In September, state insurance regulators seized National as insolvent, and the insurance commissioner referred the matter to the Pulaski County prosecutor, Mark Stodola, for investigation.

While he was leading the federal inquiry, Robert Fiske had adopted a hands-off policy regarding the state investigation of insurance fraud, which was unrelated to Hale's fraud involving federally insured loans. But Starr reversed course, attempting to muscle Stodola into dropping the insurance fraud investigation. Stodola, however, wouldn't back down and wrote to Starr of his determination to prosecute Hale.

This was the context in which Olson's demand for immunity was presented. Not surprisingly, Kenneth Starr chimed in with a letter to the committee stating that he was not opposed to congressional immunity for Hale. Because conferring such immunity could compromise the burial insurance case, a concern validated by an opinion provided by the non-partisan Senate legal counsel, the Democrats on the committee refused to reward Hale with an "immunity bath" in return for his appearance. In a straight party line vote, the Republicans voted unanimously to confer immunity, the Democrats against. "We should get David Hale's testimony," I told the *New York Times*, "but without giving him a get-out-of-jail-free card." The night before the vote, I had asked the staff to prepare a blow-up of the Monopoly card depicting the mustachioed, top-hatted icon flying out of jail on little angel wings, as a visual aid to help make our point.

The next morning, they brought a three-by-four-foot blowup to the hearing room. I took Paul Sarbanes aside to show him our handiwork. Paul smiled wanly and rolled his eyes. "A little too over-the-top?" I asked rhetorically. The Monopoly card never saw the light of day. It was beautiful, though.

The Senate rules require a two-thirds committee vote to confer immunity. John Kerry summed up the minority position, emphasizing that this ought not to be an immunity-or-nothing decision. "Hale has already spent nine days in a court of this country testifying under oath. He had been subjected to cross-examination. That testimony is in our record. There is no great mystery about what he is going to say except what he might say if he had a blanket use immunity, for which he can say anything."

But it may have been that Hale and his allies had used the immunity demand, which they had reason to know the Democrats would reject, to cloak a far more sensitive concern about being questioned by us. Two years after our hearings were concluded, a series of startling facts were unearthed about the anti-Clinton machine, including allegations of secret cash payments to David Hale.

The central player in the new revelations was the archconservative billionaire Richard Mellon Scaife, the reclusive scion of the Mellon banking fortune. According to later published reports, Scaife had poured millions into something called the Arkansas Project, a hydra-headed effort from 1993 to 1997 to discredit Bill Clinton. Using a foundation set up by the conservative *American Spectator* magazine as its cover, money was funneled to a variety of lawyers and surrogates to peddle gossip about the Clintons— the more outlandish the better. The Arkansas Project's connection to David Hale was revealed when Caryn Mann, an Arkansas funeral home employee, blew the whistle on her former boyfriend, one Parker Dozhier, whom she claimed delivered cash in varying amounts to Hale, which Dozhier had, in turn, received from the *Spectator*'s Arkansas Project account. Dozhier, proprietor of a bait shop and "lakeside resort" in Hot Springs, was a longtime friend of Hale's. The bait shop provided a point of rendezvous between a variety of "Star Wars bar" characters in the anti-Clinton orbit, *American Spectator* writers, and various representatives of the national press who passed by to feed on the chum dispensed at Dozhier's bait shop.

In the aftermath of his outing by Mann, Dozhier told the Associated Press he was on the Arkansas Project payroll for $1,000 a month to clip local newspapers items about Clinton. Mann's eyewitness account of cash passed from Dozhier to Hale was corroborated by her seventeen-year-old son, Joshua Rand. Beyond denying the allegation of cash payments to the Starr witness, the bait shop–cum–clipping service impresario reportedly added menacingly that young Joshua was "destined to become a chalk outline somewhere."

No one could make this stuff up. In the ensuing investigation, the meetings among Hale and the *Spectator* executives and lawyers at Dozhier's establishment were confirmed. Moreover, Ted Olson, Hale's lawyer before the committee, was reportedly introduced to his client through the same *Spectator* folk who were meeting with Hale and Dozhier. Olson, a nationally prominent appellate lawyer and activist in conservative Republican circles, denied knowledge of the Arkansas project or any improper payments to Hale, whom he reportedly represented without a fee. And at the end of the day, when Kenneth Starr announced in 1999 that he was resigning as Whitewater special counsel, it was to accept a Scaife-subsidized chair at Pepperdine University.

It's possible, with all this hidden Arkansas Project baggage in the background, that Hale and his lawyers were not too thrilled about our having a go at Hale in deposition before he would testify in public. Perhaps they were just as happy to use Hale's Fifth Amendment privilege to duck testifying before the committee and call it a day. While I was somewhat disappointed at having to shelve all our Hale artillery, D'Amato was livid. His closing act was gone and the Whitewater tank was finally empty. Certain that Starr had double-crossed him by not delivering Hale, he reportedly cussed Starr up and down.

And so the hearings ended. Not with a bang, but with the whimper of Hale's nonappearance and each side writing its version of the Whitewater investigation in a final report of more than six hundred pages. It was a huge undertaking for our staff, and Paul Sarbanes reviewed every page in draft before it was completed. We pulled no punches in the minority report, assailing the majority for its "superheated and untenable" conclusions. In short, there was no "there" there. We answered the central question of whether Bill Clinton misused the powers of the presidency with a clear and unequivocal no. And with respect to whether Bill Clinton, prior to his election to the presidency, misused his gubernatorial position to favor the McDougals, our conclusion was that Governor Clinton did not abuse his office. And as to Hillary Clinton, our conclusion was equally clear: No credible evidence had been presented to show that she engaged in improper, much less illegal, conduct.

Yet dozens of hardworking and idealistic young men and women had been dragged before the committee—some of them for repeated depositions and public testimony. The costs could not be measured only in their onerous legal bills, or even in the public expense of carrying on a wide-ranging and overlong inquiry—millions of dollars in direct expenses, not to mention the loss of services of those individuals sorely distracted by being caught up in the process. Unless one has lived through such an investigation, it is difficult to appreciate the psychological and emotional toll. Vince Foster was but the most tragic example.

Together with the original Senate Whitewater inquiry chaired by Senator Riegle, the investigation lasted nearly two years. The D'Amato phase alone encompassed fifty-one days of public hearings involving testimony from 159 witnesses, as well as an additional eight days of public meetings. Private depositions of some 245 individuals resulted in thirty-five thousand pages of transcripts.

Only the hard-core wing nuts continued to flog the Whitewater story as anything of substance after the committee published its final report on June 17, 1996. And although Ken Starr prolonged his investigation for years thereafter as a roving trawler with nets deployed to gather whatever flotsam and jetsam might come his way, he never claimed that there was credible evidence that Clinton had broken the law in any of the permutations that comprised Whitewater.

To the extent the 1996 presidential election could be seen as a referendum on the significance of the Whitewater pseudoscandal, it was a clear defeat for the Republicans. Clinton cruised to victory. He was now free to use his prodigious talents to advance the political agenda endorsed by the electorate.

Although I had had no prior interaction with Bill or Hillary Clinton, after the 1996 election, Donna and I received a number of invitations to attend social functions at the White House—dinners, movies, and the like—where we chatted with the Clintons on a wide variety of subjects. The highlight was a weekend at Camp David to watch the Super Bowl. I found the president to be insatiably curious and well informed on virtually any topic that came up in conversation—from sports to history to show business, you name it, Bill Clinton knew about it. And he loved to talk. With a perpetually replenished Diet Coke in hand, the president would hang out with his guests well after dinner swapping anecdotes and regaling us with his encyclopedic knowledge of politics. Hillary Clinton was warm and caring, with a ready wit and great sense of humor—quite the opposite of the portrait painted by her detractors.

But any hope that Bill Clinton could wrench himself free of the personal scandals that dogged his first term was dashed by two intersecting developments: the Supreme Court's loopy decision allowing the Paula Jones sexual harassment case to go forward on the theory that it wouldn't interfere with the president's official duties, and the titanic disaster of the Lewinsky affair. Whatever we had accomplished by putting the Whitewater allegations into proper perspective was effectively undone by Clinton's immensely stupid and narcissistic dalliance with the aggressively flirtatious young intern. I was tremendously let down—first by the news of the affair, and second by the fact that Clinton had stumbled into a perjury trap when questioned about his relationship with Lewinsky during his sworn deposition in the Paula Jones case. The latter showed the dark side of Clinton's vaunted self-confidence, dramatically exacerbating his situation, as he tried to parse his way out of making a politically damaging admission. Clinton had moved from commander in chief to enabler in chief, providing Ken Starr as well as the nationwide network of Clinton detractors with what two years of Whitewater investigations failed to deliver—evidence of impropriety.

As the facts swirling around the Lewinsky affair began to unfold, the wagons started to circle the White House in an all too familiar pattern. Stories were floated to the press about how Monica Lewinsky was some kind of stalker with a history of going after married men and had made untrue statements about a relationship with the president. I called Paul Begala at the White House to pass along some pointed, albeit unsolicited, advice. "It's looking a lot like some people over there are preparing to make this all about a deranged intern making up a pack of lies about the president. Paul, given the number of private visits a young, attractive intern reportedly made to the office of the president of the United States, I don't believe for a minute that nothing was going on." Paul mumbled something that sounded like agreement.

The calmer, less theatrical member of the James Carville–Paul Begala political-consulting partnership had become a friend. We had chatted by phone over the previous couple of years, with Paul seeking my advice or opinion on a variety of subjects. I had always been happy to oblige. For the first time, I had taken the initiative. Paul was one of Clinton's most trusted political advisers, and he spoke to the president every day.

"The first thing you should know, Paul," I continued, "is that if the strategy of attacking Monica goes forward, I'm off the bus. I could no longer support the president. Such a strategy would not only be wrong and immoral—in my view it could lead to his impeachment and removal from office, with millions of his supporters abandoning him. Instead, he needs to face up to this honestly and apologize to his family and the public for his selfish and hurtful conduct. The American people are the most forgiving in the world—we are a nation built on second chances. If he apologizes quickly and sincerely, they will forgive him."

I don't know if Begala passed along my advice to the president—I never asked him. The revelation that Lewinsky had kept a blue dress stained with Clinton's semen closed the door to further consideration of the "deranged stalker" defense of the indefensible. To my mind, the blue dress actually saved the Clinton presidency.

Bill Clinton's first try at an apology on national television fell far short of the mark. He seemed more angry than contrite. I telephoned Begala from a family scuba-diving vacation to express my disappointment in the president's performance. "I know, I know," Paul began, "the day before the speech he had it down. He just couldn't bring himself to do it when the time came."

The public generally agreed. In the ensuing weeks Clinton got better at apologizing. But no amount of sincerity or abasement short of resignation would satisfy Clinton's political enemies or Kenneth Starr.

Despite my disappointment in Bill Clinton's behavior, it struck me as a perversion of the constitutional remedy of impeachment to attempt to remove the twice-elected president of the United States for what amounted to a refusal to admit under oath to a consensual extramarital affair. The stunning hypocrisy of those in Congress who led the charge for impeachment, Newt Gingrich and Speaker Dennis Hastert in the House—who were guilty of far more egregious infidelities than Clinton—was only par for the course in Washington. Here hubris and hypocrisy have operated as Scylla and Charybdis on the Potomac, waiting to devour the politically powerful since the seat of government was moved here in 1800.

No doubt the right wing thought they had nailed Bill Clinton's hide to the wall. I listened with a mixture of interest and revulsion as William Kristol smugly assured the small group in the greenroom before our appearance on ABC's *This Week* Sunday program that Clinton would succumb to the pressure and resign in a week or two. Clinton was able to show them that wishing would not make it so. He had climbed the steps to the scaffold and put his head in the noose, but he was unwilling to pull the lever for the trapdoor himself.

The most dangerous threat to the Clinton presidency, apart from Clinton's own self-destructive tendencies, was independent counsel Kenneth Starr. It appeared to me that this brilliant, moralistic, and unctuously polite former appellate judge had convinced himself before he took the prosecutor's job that Bill Clinton was morally unfit to be president. Armed with near religious certainty, Starr took it upon himself to rid the nation of the Svengali who had beguiled its electorate into twice choosing him as president. I did not subscribe to the theory of some Starr critics that he saw his role as independent counsel as a stepping-stone to a coveted berth on the Supreme Court. To the contrary, I believe Starr knew that involving himself in such high-stakes controversy would make it politically impossible for him to be confirmed, were he ever to be nominated to the highest court. But that did not diminish, in my eyes, the threat Starr posed to the proper application of constitutional balance.

I disliked Starr's methods. The constant leaking of confidential information from his office was a prime example. He was on occasion raked over the coals by the chief judge of the DC federal court for "serious and repetitive leaks" emanating from his office. I disliked his unwillingness or inability to distinguish between misuse of presidential power or outright criminality on the one hand, and the moral failings of a flawed human being on the other. Despite his protestations to the contrary, Starr had been on the hunt to find evidence of Clinton's rumored extramarital escapades well before the Lewinsky affair was disclosed. Indeed, Starr had sent his FBI investigators to Arkansas as early as the spring of 1997 to dig up information about Clinton's sex life. When Bob Woodward broke the story of Starr's prurient interest, the independent counsel lamely sought to justify the FBI interviews on grounds that perhaps Clinton had engaged in pillow talk about his Whitewater investment during the alleged dalliances. Who knew if this moral crusader actually believed such nonsense?

The combination of moral certitude and lack of prosecutorial experience resulted in heavy-handed tactics with any number of witnesses. Many former prosecutors, regardless of party affiliation, voiced their concerns as evidence of departures from recognized limitations on appropriate prosecutorial behavior began to mount.

Perhaps, at its core, my objection to Ken Starr was that he wasn't Archie Cox or Leon Jaworski. There had been significant precedent on how to handle investigative responsibilities, so significant that the future of the highest elected official in the land could be affected. Cox and Jaworski were cautious and studiously nonpartisan. Starr acted as drum major for the rush to impeachment. Instead of an objective report of the facts uncovered by his investigation, he authored a polemical screed filled with salacious sexual detail, urging Congress to impeach.

While I felt disheartened and even betrayed by Clinton's reckless conduct in engaging in his relationship with Lewinsky and then grossly exacerbating the situation by his disingenuous testimony when confronted, I was unwilling to see him railroaded out of office for conduct that did not approach the "high crimes and misdemeanors" standard specified by the Framers of the Constitution. So I wrote editorials for the *New York Times* and *Washington Post,* and appeared frequently on television to denounce the attempt to remove Clinton from office. My point was simple: The punishment sought was vastly disproportionate to Clinton's improper conduct. And the actions of Kenneth Starr, who pursued Clinton with the zeal of a modern-day Captain Ahab, contravened the proper boundaries of an independent counsel.

This was not to say that Clinton's personal conduct and clumsy attempt to avoid telling the truth about it did not warrant some sanction. I made that point in my public statements and in testimony I gave before the House Judiciary Committee during its hearings on impeachment. I was asked by Republican congressman Edward Pease to elaborate on my thinking.

> I mean to make the distinction between the meaning of high crimes and misdemeanors in the category of treason and bribery versus the conduct with which you are now struggling. And it seems to me entirely proportionate, reasonable, and in the greatest interest of this country to apply a common sense and moderate approach to the conduct in question and the kind of remedy with which you will deal with that conduct. And in my view, a reprimand, be it a censure, be it a rebuke, some formal declaration of disapproval of the conduct is the appropriate remedy . . . All of that conduct, if I may, flows from his personal deposition in a civil matter. He appeared in his personal capacity before a grand jury. And I think that's the distinction. Were he to have lied about the misuse of power, say he had someone on this committee—Mr. Barr, for example—audited by the IRS, or had his phone bugged by a plumbers unit, or broke into his psychiatrist's office with the purpose of obtaining records . . .
>
> [EDWARD] PEARSE: I think I understand. I understand your—
>
> BEN-VENISTE: . . . all of those things would, indeed, rise to a level of scrutiny.
>
> [ED] BRYANT: And I appreciate—thank you.
>
> BEN-VENISTE: Thank you, sir.

The hypothetical I concocted was analogous to Nixon's plumbers' operation to disparage Daniel Ellsberg in advance of his criminal trial for the unauthorized disclosure of the Pentagon Papers. Breaking into Ellsberg's psychiatrist's office, Nixon's operatives sought damaging personal information they could use to smear Ellsberg. Representative Bob Barr, Republican of Georgia and a member of the Judiciary Committee, was one of Clinton's most relentless pursuers. I had once debated him at Georgetown Law School and found him way over the top on the zealousness meter. Hypothesizing a bag job on an imaginary Barr psychiatrist was my way of having a little fun.

The Republicans had done their research on me in advance of my testimony. It is always effective cross-examination to use a witness's prior statements to contradict his present testimony. It fell to Representative Robert Goodlatte of Virginia to attempt to hit me with my own bat.

> Mr. Ben-Veniste, you actually set this story straight a long time ago, long before you ever heard of Paula Jones or Monica Lewinsky, long before Bill Clinton was ever on the national scene. You wrote a book back in 1977 called *Stonewall: The Real Story of the Watergate Prosecution,* by Richard Ben-Veniste and George Frampton Jr. and in that, in the closing, you wrote about the Watergate proceeding, "Did the system work? True, the nationally televised debate and vote on articles of impeachment was a shining hour for the House Judiciary Committee. But all in all, the total course of the committee's investigation exposed the extreme political nature of impeachment." This is about the Watergate proceeding. "The cumbersomeness of the process, its politicization, and the unwillingness of so many in Congress to recognize objectively the stark facts of criminal wrongdoing that were put in front of them make the Nixon impeachment case an unpromising precedent."
>
> And here's where I think you are so farsighted, more farsighted than anybody who's been before the committee today: "Next time, might it not be a potent defense for a president charged with wrongdoing to argue that his conduct, however improper, fell short of the spectacularly widespread abuse of the Nixon administration? If Watergate or more is what it takes to galvanize the impeachment mechanism, can we really rely on it to protect us in the future against gross executive wrongdoing?"
>
> Now let me ask you about the title of the book, Mr. Ben-Veniste, *Stonewalling* [*sic*]. That is an effort to obstruct justice, to keep the process from moving forward, from discovering the truth. Is that not an accurate definition of that?

Indeed, I wrote those words marveling at how the Republicans had put up such a furious fight in the face of Nixon's own tape-recorded incriminating statements—irrefutable evidence of the president's involvement in obstruction of justice and subornation of perjury. The collapse of Nixon's congressional support was in large measure a reaction to the

barefaced lies he told to senior leaders of his party as well as a response to
Nixon's underlying criminal conduct.

> BEN-VENISTE: The title of the book came from Mr. Nixon's in-
> junction to his subordinates to stonewall, to deny everything,
> to blame everything on the lower-level individuals, so that the
> higher-ups would not be detected. And—
> GOODLATTE: Let me ask you this: Do you believe that President
> Clinton has engaged in stonewalling in this matter?
> BEN-VENISTE: I believe that President Clinton had tried to obfus-
> cate at the very beginning a very inappropriate relationship of
> a private nature about which he was, I'm sure, and should be,
> ashamed.

Goodlatte then gave me the opening I needed to hammer home the
distinction between personal misconduct and misusing the powers of the
presidency, by asking whether I saw Clinton's intransigence and obfusca-
tion as comparable to Nixon's stonewalling.

> BEN-VENISTE: The stonewalling devices that were involved in
> Watergate involved individuals denying such things as the mis-
> use of the FBI, the misuse of the CIA, the misuse of the Internal
> Revenue Service to inflict pain and embarrassment upon ene-
> mies of the President of the United States.

Under questioning by Democrat Melvin Watt of North Carolina, I
tied the question of whether Clinton's misconduct warranted impeachment to what I saw as the excessive and inappropriate zeal of Ken Starr's
investigation:

> The subject matter here, which we all know is about the pres-
> ident's unwillingness to 'fess up to an inappropriate relation-
> ship that he had with a young intern, is the core of everything
> that we are talking about. It is the core of what he walked
> into when his deposition was taken [in the Paula Jones civil
> case].
>   The Jones lawyers were armed with the information that
> Linda Tripp had surreptitiously tape recorded from Monica
> Lewinsky. So they knew they had something the president
> didn't know they had, and the president gave testimony as art-

fully as he could, I think, to try to evade answering the questions about Ms. Lewinsky. He should not have done that.

That's an understatement.

The question is whether everything that springs from that—Mr. Starr criminalizing that conduct by opening an investigation—which, in my view, no other federal prosecutor in this country would go after, at least no one of any reputable stature in this country—and then try to draw from that the concept of an obstruction of justice, putting him before the grand jury, asking questions about where he touched Ms. Lewinsky, where Ms. Lewinsky touched him, on what day of the week in what place in the White House, in what month of the year. How in the world can we be discussing removing a twice-elected president of the United States on the basis of this kind of conduct? That is the question that I raise. And that is, I think, the issue of proportionality and common sense that the American public has grappled with and has come to some conclusion, I think, expressing their great common sense. As a trial lawyer, I see people from all walks of life in a courtroom, and I have great respect for their collective common sense.

Nevertheless, the Republicans were determined to press forward with impeachment in what was a terrible misapplication of what the Framers had in mind in providing a process for removing a president from office. Whether they were motivated by revenge for Nixon's disgrace or true outrage over Clinton's conduct, they had the votes in the House to force a trial in the Senate, in which Clinton was easily acquitted, the votes falling short of a simple majority, much less the two-thirds required for conviction. Historians and constitutional scholars will puzzle over the meaning of the Clinton impeachment. Perhaps they will see it as the last paroxysm of our nation's puritanical heritage.

———————

DAVID HALE WAS EVENTUALLY convicted of lying to insurance regulators regarding his burial insurance scam. However, he avoided any more jail time when Republican governor Mike Huckabee commuted Hale's sentence because of Hale's medical condition (bad heart).

Al D'Amato had the misfortune to run for reelection in 1998. Instead of catapulting himself to a leadership role in national politics, D'Amato's Whitewater misadventure dragged him down to defeat at the polls. But the resourceful New Yorker dusted himself off and set up shop as a consultant, raking in big bucks from a variety of clients with government problems. D'Amato sought to bury the hatchet with his former political adversaries, and in 2002 the Suffolk County, Long Island, federal courthouse was named after him by a bipartisan vote in the U.S. Congress. Is this a great country, or what?

Kenneth Starr became dean of Pepperdine Law School in 2004. He was later quoted as saying that, in retrospect, he regretted being assigned responsibility for investigating the Lewinsky matter, notwithstanding that it was Starr himself who sought to expand his jurisdiction to cover Clinton's testimony about Lewinsky. In 2007, Starr was quoted extensively in *Her Way: The Hopes and Ambitions of Hillary Rodham Clinton* by Jeff Gerth and Don Van Natta Jr., with respect to Hillary Clinton's grand jury testimony about the billing records. In a full-page opinion piece in the *Legal Times of Washington,* Starr was lustily criticized for violating the sacrosanct federal rules imposing an obligation of secrecy on prosecutors regarding grand jury testimony. Scott Horton, law professor and board member of the National Institute of Military Justice, saw Starr's actions as a precursor to Bush II administration attorneys general John Ashcroft and Alberto Gonzales's use of prosecutorial power as a political tool.

In 2002, Jean Lewis was appointed to the $118,000-a-year position of chief of staff to the Department of Defense inspector general's office. The Pentagon's inspector general, with a staff of 1,240 employees and a budget of $160 million, is the largest IG's office in government. It is mandated to investigate fraud and audit Pentagon contracts. If there were any overcharging or misconduct in connection with the billions of dollars awarded to Halliburton and other companies for operations in Iraq, it would be up to the Pentagon's IG to root it out. In 2005, Lewis's boss resigned under bipartisan criticism for shielding Bush administration political appointees from investigation and misleading Congress.

CHAPTER FIVE

The 9/11 Commission

The assignment to sit on the 9/11 Commission was different from anything I had undertaken before. We had suffered a national catastrophe of unprecedented dimension. The public, Congress, and the president needed to understand what went wrong—how it was that nineteen foreigners, half of whom couldn't speak English, were able to elude our defenses and strike a blow that shook the very foundations of our security. What were the facts, and how credibly could we assess what went wrong and what steps were needed to correct our vulnerabilities?

Why had President Bush and the congressional leaders of his party opposed the creation of such a commission? Only Senator John McCain and a handful of Republicans in Congress had joined the Democrats in support of an investigative commission.

The families of the 9/11 victims proved to be the decisive element in the battle over whether a commission would become a reality. Totally committed to a full investigation of the facts, the 9/11 families established themselves in the halls of Congress and in the media as a force to be reckoned with. Unschooled in the ways of Washington, the families compensated with unmatched perseverance and focus on the goal of achieving an investigation that would put integrity above politics.

Years later, on the day the commission's final report was published, Carol Ashley, one of the dozens of stalwart family representatives, greeted me at a reception at the Woodrow Wilson Center. Reflecting on what had been accomplished since the families first attempted to see a bipartisan commission appointed, she observed, "Who could have thought when we started out that we could have come this far?"

"That's because you didn't realize what you were trying to do was impossible," I replied.

"WHAT DO YOU THINK of Kissinger being appointed to chair the 9/11 Commission?" I had known Tim Russert, the host of *Meet the Press,* for some years, having been a guest on his Sunday morning program from time to time. We spoke briefly in the aisle of the USAir shuttle to New York as the other passengers settled into their seats awaiting takeoff. I responded by rolling my eyes. Nothing quotable.

"I think they should put you on the commission," he announced.

"Interesting," I said as I took my seat.

Russert, one of the most respected journalists in the nation, had been prescient. Only days before, Tom Daschle, the Senate minority leader, had phoned, asking whether I would serve as one of the five Democrats to be appointed to the nascent commission. I knew Daschle from our occasional meetings during the time I served as chief counsel to the Senate Democrats on the Whitewater Committee. I held him in high regard as one of the most credible and honest leaders in American politics. Daschle's call had not come out of the blue. I had discussed the possibility of serving on the commission with my good friend Paul Sarbanes and with Senator Hillary Clinton. Both had urged me to consider serving and said they would recommend my selection to their Senate colleagues. Apparently, George Mitchell, the former Senate majority leader from Maine, whom Daschle had tapped to serve as the commission's vice chair, had told Daschle that he wanted me on the commission. Tom told me that President Bush's decision to name Henry Kissinger to chair the commission would create extra difficulties in getting to the truth. No kidding. Throughout the Nixon presidency, Kissinger—national security adviser and later secretary of state—had expertly managed the press, keeping the nasty secrets quiet while doling out tidbits of gossip to skewer his adversaries inside and outside the administration.

"Richard, we need you to ask the tough questions and find out what went wrong. I don't have to tell you how important this commission will be."

I told Senator Daschle that I would be honored to serve. He said that he and Dick Gephardt, the House minority leader, had agreed on four of the five appointments the Democrats would make.

The president and Republican leaders of the Senate and House would name the commission chair and four other members. In addition to Senator Mitchell and me, Daschle and Gephardt would name Senator Max Cleland, the Vietnam War triple amputee who had been defeated in the 2002 Georgia senatorial race, and Tim Roemer, a six-term Indiana congressman who had decided not to stand for reelection in 2004. Roemer had been a member of the House Intelligence Committee and had served on its bipartisan joint inquiry to investigate 9/11, whose attempt to obtain testimony and documents relating to 9/11 had been blocked by the White House in important respects. Roemer had been a strong advocate for creating a commission to conclude the work started by the joint inquiry committee, and had developed an excellent rapport with the victims' family groups. Tom told me that he and Gephardt had not yet settled on the fifth appointment. As Daschle mentioned those under consideration, I hoped to hear the name of my friend and former law partner, Richard Davis. Rich and I had been colleagues at the U.S. attorney's office and were both assistant Watergate prosecutors, and I knew he was interested in being selected. Instead, Daschle asked me about Jamie Gorelick, the former Clinton administration deputy attorney general and general counsel at the Pentagon whom Dick Gephardt wanted for the final slot. I told him that I had heard only very positive things about Jamie and would be pleased to serve with her.

Although the law creating the commission specified that the commissioners would be serving on a part-time basis (so as not to add the burden of finding qualified people willing to give up their regular jobs in the private sector), it was clear this would require a commitment of time and effort beyond normal pro bono work. I had recently made the switch to a new law firm, Mayer Brown, in February 2002. How would the firm's leadership and my new partners react to such a significant commitment of time? I need not have been concerned. Ty Fahner, the firm's chairman, a former Illinois attorney general (and dedicated Republican), could not have been more supportive.

But what about the Kissinger issue? I was to be only one of ten commission members. For more than twenty-five years, since Watergate, I had been captain of the ship in every case I had undertaken. How would it be to work under Kissinger's chairmanship? No question, Kissinger was a world-class figure whose name alone would assure that attention would be paid. But his detractors, of whom there was no shortage, pointed to many episodes of questionable and secret activities to which Kissinger was directly linked: the 1973 assassination of President Salvador Allende in Chile, the secret bombing of Cambodia during the Vietnam War, and the wiretapping of journalists during the Nixon years, to name just a few. How would Kissinger's support for a dominant executive branch and penchant for secrecy square with leading a commission whose job would be to uncover and report to the nation the unvarnished truth of what led to the 9/11 catastrophe? Indeed, it was only years later that it became known through Bob Woodward's reporting that Kissinger had been a regular, albeit secret, visitor to Bush at the Whitehouse, providing advice validating the conduct of the president's foreign policy. The task of providing a credible accounting of what went wrong would face a daunting Kissingerian hurdle from the outset.

The Kissinger issue soon resolved itself. All commissioners were obliged to file extensive reports with the Senate Ethics Committee identifying business clients for the past three years. Within seventeen days of the announcement of his appointment, Kissinger resigned rather than disclose a list of all clients who had paid his company at least $5,000 in any year for his consulting business. Two days earlier, George Mitchell resigned as vice chair for essentially the same reason.

It was a stroke of unparalleled fortune that Bush turned to Thomas Kean, the former two-term governor of New Jersey, to replace Henry Kissinger. While it was not apparent to me at first, Tom Kean proved to be the best second choice in recent political history.

Tom Daschle and Dick Gephardt turned to former Democratic congressman Lee Hamilton to replace Senator Mitchell as the commission's vice chair. Hamilton, the former chairman of the House Permanent Select Committee on Intelligence and the Committee on International Relations, had impeccable credentials as an expert in international relations and in finding bipartisan consensus in Congress. After thirty-four years representing the people of his Indiana district, Hamilton was now serving as president of the Woodrow Wilson Center in Washington.

The Republican leadership soon announced their four additional selections: former senator Slade Gorton of Washington, former Reagan administration navy secretary John Lehman, former four-term governor of Illinois James Thompson, and former Reagan White House counsel Fred Fielding. I didn't know Slade Gorton, who had been defeated in the 2000 election, but what I had heard was not reassuring. That's the thing about hearsay—it often proves to be unreliable. Slade turned out to be one of the finest, most reliable, and most levelheaded members of the commission.

John Lehman, perhaps the most conservative of the Republican appointees, cut a dapper figure in well-tailored double-breasted suits and a youthful hairstyle. The influential Senator John McCain had recommended Lehman, a New York investment banker, after the White House had supposedly nixed his first choice, former New Hampshire senator Warren Rudman. The word was that McCain's choice would be committed to supporting any subpoena that might be proposed to compel the administration to produce relevant documents. As it happened, the opposite was closer to the truth.

I knew Fred Fielding from the time he was John Dean's deputy in the Nixon White House. Dean had kept Fielding away from the toxic fallout of the Watergate cover-up, and Fred went on to establish a highly successful law practice in Washington, serving as Ronald Reagan's White House counsel along the way. A consummate Republican insider, Fred had been actively involved in providing advice to the Bush transition team as it assumed the reins of power after the 2000 election. Fielding's connection to the White House resumed in 2007, when Bush tapped him to replace Harriet Miers as his White House counsel.

Of all the appointees, I knew Jim Thompson best. Jim and his close friend Joel Flaum had been my professors during the year I spent on a Ford Foundation fellowship in postgraduate legal studies at Northwestern University Law School. Their glowing recommendation had facilitated my hiring by Bob Morgenthau. "Big Jim" Thompson, who rose to prominence as U.S. attorney in Chicago, earned the nickname "governor for life" for his four terms as Illinois's governor. Joel Flaum had been appointed to the federal bench in Chicago by Ronald Reagan and later elevated to the Seventh Circuit Court of Appeals by George H. W. Bush, where he became chief judge. I had maintained a friendship with Jim and Joel over the years despite our geographic distance.

The legislation passed by the Republican-controlled Congress gave the commission only eighteen months to complete its task (the Republicans had first proposed a one-year limit) on a miserly budget of $3 million. Because 9/11 occurred on President Bush's watch, the Republican leadership didn't want a report that might be critical of the Bush administration's inability to detect or prevent the attack released too close to the 2004 election. The paltry $3 million budget would inhibit our chances of digging very deeply in the time allotted. It was clear that we would have to get cracking, wasting no time hiring a staff and getting up to speed on what had already been uncovered by the joint inquiry, which had spent eleven months investigating 9/11. It seemed to me a no-brainer to get the JI's work product and make up for the time lost during the Kissinger/Mitchell false start.

Such was not to be. I learned from Lee Hamilton that, inexplicably, instead of immediately convening an initial meeting of commissioners, Governor Kean would be taking a ten-day vacation on the Caribbean island of Anguilla. Hamilton explained that Kean simply told him his family went there every year—it was a tradition. Hamilton raised a second point. It appeared that Kean, who had served as president of Drew University in Madison, New Jersey, since 1990, was not exactly au courant on the Washington scene. According to Lee, Kean was unaware that Louis Freeh was no longer director of the FBI or that Robert Mueller had replaced him more than a year earlier. Kean was frank to admit he didn't know the GAO from the GSA. My early concerns about the Kissinger chairmanship were replaced by a new sinking feeling about the direction of the commission.

There were a million and one things that needed to get done: hire a staff and a staff director, as well as a deputy director and general counsel; find office space, including a secure SCIF (sensitive compartmented information facility) in which classified documents would be stored and reviewed; secure computers, office equipment, and supplies; get commissioners and staff who did not already have security clearances cleared on an expedited basis. All of this would chew up precious time.

The president had signed the bill into law on November 22, 2002, and by law, the commission would go out of business in May 2004. The clock was ticking.

Fortunately for me, I already had a code word (above top secret) security clearance due to my continuing pro bono service on a commission to which President Clinton had appointed me in 1998 to declassify documents relating to individuals complicit in World War II war crimes. Because U.S. government departments and agencies such as the CIA, the army, and the FBI still maintained these records in secret, I was cleared to review these materials in order to advocate for their release. It was a simple matter for my security clearance to be expanded to higher levels of code-word compartmented access for the commission work at hand.

Although the Democratic appointees caucused by phone and met informally in December, there was to be no meeting of the commission as a whole until January 19, after Tom Kean returned from his Caribbean holiday. Meanwhile, we received word that Kean had sought guidance from the White House on selection of a staff director and chief counsel to the commission. Reportedly, the White House had declined to make a recommendation but wished to preserve the right to veto candidates for these critical positions. On the other hand, Lee had a cordial one-on-one meeting with Kean in December and reported agreement on a number of issues directed at fostering a bipartisan atmosphere. Most important, Lee told me that he liked the former New Jersey governor and thought he could trust him. Although I had never worked with Lee before, I had enormous respect for his record of achievement and mastery of foreign relations. Not insignificantly, his tall bearing, steel gray buzz cut, and robust speaking voice reminded me very much of Archie Cox.

In mid-December, Tom Daschle had arranged for the Democratic appointees to meet with a small delegation of family members of 9/11 victims, the "families" as we all referred to them, in one of the ornate meeting rooms on the Senate side of the Capitol. Up to then, I had busied myself with the nuts and bolts of serving on the commission—filling out the ethics forms, clearing my litigation calendar of all but the most essential matters, and trying to get up to speed on what was already known about the 9/11 plot. It had been a while since I had dealt with the cauldron of emotions I had felt on 9/11 and the days and weeks that followed the tragedy. There in front of me was a small sample of the lives that had been so deeply affected by the murder of their loved ones: Kristen Breitweiser, Laurie Van Auken, Mindy Kleinberg, and Patty Casazza, who became well known as the "Jersey girls"—all New Jersey residents whose husbands had been killed at the World Trade Center. Steven Push's wife, Lisa Raines, was a passenger on the plane that crashed into the Pentagon. Sally Regenhard, whose son, Christian, was killed; Bill Harvey, whose wife of one month, Sara Manley, died; Carol Ashley, who lost her twenty-five-year-old daughter, Janice; Robin Wiener, whose brother Jeffrey, thirty-three, perished—all at the World Trade Center. Each of them spoke briefly of his or her individual loss and of what they all expected of the commission. They expressed dissatisfaction with the secrecy and shortcomings of the congressional joint inquiry's work—why wasn't the JI provided full access to necessary documents or allowed to interview high-level members of the Bush administration? They wanted answers, a full and credible investigation, accountability—not partisan bickering or finger-pointing.

How could communications between fire and police at the World Trade Center have been so inadequate?

Where was our vaunted NORAD air defense on 9/11?

Why weren't pre-9/11 leads and clues followed up by CIA and FBI officials?

Why were the hijackers allowed to enter and travel freely in the United States?

What was the role of Saudi Arabia?

What were the defects in our system of granting visas to Saudis?

Why had the FAA security failed?

How were the hijackers financed?

Why were our intelligence and law enforcement agencies unable or unwilling to share the information they had and work together to protect us?

What was the role of our foreign policy leading up to 9/11?

Why was access to the roofs of the twin towers locked, and why were the buildings unprepared for evacuation?

Were we prepared to use the subpoena power we had been granted to get *all* the documents and witnesses needed to investigate fully?

What changes did we need to make so that future attacks could be prevented and the lives of others preserved?

The cumulative message was clear: Put aside political partisanship and get to work. Get to the truth of how the wealthiest and most powerful nation on earth could be subjected to such a devastating attack. Then report that truth to us and the American people. These brave and determined Americans whose lives had been shattered deserved answers. Could we fulfill their expectations?

The five of us introduced ourselves. When my turn came, I spoke of my background as a native New Yorker and named some of the trials and investigations I had conducted. I told them that I knew how to ask questions, listen, and follow up. I assured them that I had no hidden agenda or political aspirations. I pledged to do the best I could to find the truth, and that I would not hesitate to use any and all means at our disposal to do so. Finally, I told them, tongue-in-cheek, that in pursuing evidence from the administration I would follow Ronald Reagan's sage advice in dealing with the Soviets—"trust but verify."

The families remained a constant source of inspiration when the going got rough (and it did) and a vivid reminder that we were not conducting a mere intellectual exercise. These same individuals, together with others including Carie Lemack, who lost her mother, Judy Larocque; Mary Fetchet, whose twenty-four-year-old son, Bradley, was killed; Beverly Eckert, whose husband, Sean Rooney, perished; and Monica Gabrielle, whose husband, Richard, also did not survive the attack on the World Trade Center were present at every hearing and public event to support and encourage us in our work.

As I thought about what I had signed on to, I saw no clear path for success. Given the president's objection to creation of the commission, the paltry budget allocated by the Republican-controlled Congress, the initial appointment of Henry Kissinger, and the arbitrary deadline for completing our work, the task ahead was daunting. Others appointed by the Democratic leadership had vast experience in foreign policy, national security, and overseeing the intelligence agencies. I knew how to ask questions and persist until I got answers. And I didn't like being lied to.

THE FIRST MEETING OF the commission was scheduled for late January 2003, two months after the statute creating it was signed into law. We would be playing catch-up for the remaining life of the commission. As we approached our first meeting, I wrote as simplified an agenda for our communal task as I could describe:

1. What were the facts?

2. What were the systemic defects?

3. What changes have already been put in place, and are they working?

4. Recommendations for further change

Lawyers are big on precedent. The two most relevant precedents of the twentieth century were the investigation of the attack on Pearl Harbor and the investigation of the assassination of John F. Kennedy. How could the 9/11 Commission avoid the mistakes of these two earlier investigative commissions, whose findings evoked pointed criticism and skepticism for decades afterward?

I set about researching the history of the Roberts Commission, created by President Franklin Delano Roosevelt to investigate how and why the United States was caught by surprise on December 7, 1941, when the Japanese attacked Pearl Harbor, and whether any derelictions of duty or

errors of judgment on the part of U.S. Army or Navy personnel contributed to the success of the attack. The commission was led by Supreme
Court Justice Owen J. Roberts and four high-ranking military officers
(three retired and one active duty). The inquiry was begun eleven days after the attack; the commissioners questioned 127 witnesses behind closed
doors and delivered its report to President Roosevelt on January 24, 1942.
The president released it to the public the next day.

The Roberts Commission put the blame squarely on the shoulders of
the two chief military commanders at Pearl Harbor: Admiral Husband E.
Kimmel, commander in chief of the Pacific fleet, and General Walter C.
Short, commanding general of the U.S. Army Hawaiian Department,
finding them guilty of "dereliction of duty" and "errors of judgment" for
not conferring sufficiently regarding warnings from Washington, and for
not putting adequate defense measures into place.

I found an eerie parallel to the 9/11 attacks. The Roberts Commission
concluded that the failure of Kimmel and Short to cooperate "resulted
largely from a sense of security due to the opinion prevalent in the diplomatic, military and naval circles, and in the public press that any immediate attack by Japan would be in the Far East." Nevertheless, the
commission found that "the existence of such a view, however prevalent,
did not relieve the commanders of the responsibility for the security of
the Pacific fleet."

But while the Roberts Commission had reviewed a large number of
documents, it had not examined the "Magic" intercepts—the name given
to the secret breaking of the Japanese diplomatic code. Largely as the result of this omission, rather than ending the debate over culpability, no
fewer than seven more investigations of Pearl Harbor were authorized by
Congress and the military services. Blame was apportioned beyond Kimmel and Short to the War Department, the chief of naval operations, and
other Washington officials for failing to timely transmit the Magic intercepts and other information to Hawaii. I found the history of the Roberts
Commission so instructive that I asked a colleague at Mayer Brown, Mar-
cia Tavares Maack, to prepare a memo summarizing that history, which I
sent to each of my fellow commissioners in early January, before our first
meeting.

The failure of the Warren Commission's investigation of the Kennedy
assassination to satisfy the suspicions of a large number of Americans
was close enough in memory that all of my new colleagues were well ac-
quainted with the variety of conspiracy theories that still thrived forty
years later.

Both the Roberts and Warren commissions operated behind closed doors and were compromised by a failure to obtain and examine critical evidence. The first lesson for me was that we needed to demand and get access to all relevant information relating to the 9/11 attack. Second, in order to satisfy the public that we were, in fact, conducting a robust and credible investigation, we would need to hold open hearings and be as transparent as possible about what we learned. But the highly partisan manner in which the commissioners had been selected by the president and political leaders of Congress in the aftermath of a battle over whether there was to be a commission at all were strong factors presaging failure for the new commission. I did not handicap the odds for success as good.

On January 13, 2003, the five Democratic appointees met with Lee Hamilton in his office at the Wilson Center. We talked about nuts-and-bolts issues regarding possible office space, staff appointments, and budget. Would office space, estimated to cost $1 million, be contributed by one of the agencies, or would we have to spend a third of our meager budget just to house our staff in a secure environment? Max Cleland had toured one of the prospective office locations to evaluate its wheelchair access. I was impressed by the courage it took for this man simply to get out of bed, get dressed, and get to work every day. He had been defeated for reelection in a close race where the voters in Georgia were bombarded with TV ads and literature questioning Max's patriotism and commitment to the defense of a country to which he had given three of his limbs in service. He had no savings to speak of and needed to find a job that would sustain him while he served on the commission. Although Lee reported that he and Kean had determined that none of the commissioners would have a personal staff, we committed to Max that he would have a dedicated staffer to help him with logistics and other staffing needs. As time went on, Max's growing depression became cause for concern.

The authority to hire staff was given by the statute creating the commission to the "Chair, in consultation with the Vice-Chair, in accordance with rules agreed upon by the Commission." If we needed to have formal rules agreed upon we might never get going. Lee reported that Governor Kean told him he had a favorable impression of Philip Zelikow, a candidate for staff director who was then director of the prestigious Miller Center at the University of Virginia. Lee shared that view and would call Zelikow promptly to discuss the position. Jamie Gorelick knew Zelikow to be "deeply knowledgeable" but close to the president's national security adviser, Condoleezza Rice. Tim Roemer added that Rice had refused to testify or even be interviewed by the joint inquiry on which he had served. I had no idea who Zelikow was, but if Lee Hamilton was for him I would support that decision. Despite Jamie's observation, none of the commissioners raised an objection to Zelikow. Lee next brought up the name of Chris Kojm for the deputy staff director position. Lee and Chris had a long-standing relationship, and Lee gave him his highest recommendation.

Jamie and I proposed James Hamilton (no relation to Lee) for chief counsel to the committee. Jim's résumé showed a long and distinguished career as a public servant and trial lawyer going back to Watergate, when he served as a deputy to Sam Ervin on the Senate Watergate Committee. Lee met with Jim and was impressed. He told us he was prepared to put Chris Kojm and Jim Hamilton forward to provide balance to Kean's proposed selection of Phil Zelikow. Lee told us that Tom Kean had agreed to such a balance. Tim Roemer mentioned a number of former staffers from the joint inquiry who were well versed in the facts and already had security clearances. We needed to be able to hit the ground running. That was taken somewhat tongue in cheek, given the fact that we were not going to have our first meeting as a commission until two months after our start date. I proposed we hire Lance Cole, an outstanding lawyer on our staff during the Whitewater investigation who had since become a professor at Dickenson Law School, and Rajesh De, a young lawyer recently at the Department of Justice whose former professor at Harvard Law, Philip Heyman, had given him his highest recommendation.

Lee and Tom had also agreed that there should be a staffer who would act as liaison with the families. Indeed, Kristen Breitweiser, a lawyer who had lost her husband, Ronald, in the WTC attack, was discussed as a possible hire. Kristen had been one of the more outspoken advocates for the creation of the commission and a critic of the administration's foot-dragging. Ostensibly, because the families would not be united behind appointment of Kristen or any single representative, Tom had determined that no member of the families' advocacy groups would be hired.

We discussed how the staff might be organized along teams dealing with the extensive scope of our investigative mandate: the extent of preparedness for and immediate response after the attacks; commercial aviation warnings, oversight, and response; passenger screening; FAA and NORAD preparation and coordination; CIA, DIA (Defense Intelligence Agency), NSA, and INR (Bureau of Intelligence and Research at the State Department) foreign intelligence warnings; FBI, Department of Justice, and state and local law enforcement preparedness and warnings; customs and INS border security; State Department visa process; intelligence assistance from foreign governments; Treasury Department money transfer, banking, and money laundering; congressional oversight and reform needed. And this was only the short list. Clearly, there was no shortage of experts to talk to from various government agencies and private think tanks. Our first order of business would be to assimilate the information developed by the joint inquiry. But there was a problem: The Republican leadership of the JI had not yet allowed the members of the new commission to review its classified report. Tick, tick, tick.

Finally, two months after the commission was created, the ten commissioners met together for the first time for an informal dinner hosted by Lee at the Wilson Center on Super Bowl Sunday. It was a good opportunity to size each other up before we got down to business at our first official meeting, scheduled for the next day. My initial skepticism about Tom Kean's commitment and competence began to dissipate. Tall and plainly dressed, Tom had a ready smile and an open, honest countenance. He was a political anomaly—a Republican governor of a substantially Democratic state who had been reelected with a record majority and had retained his popularity through and beyond his second term in office. His patrician accent was nothing like anything I had heard before emanating from the state of New Jersey. His "aw shucks" style belied a family fortune. Tom had a *Mr. Smith Goes to Washington* air of naïveté about him, yet he had grown up in DC's posh Kalorama neighborhood of embassies and mansions, attending St. Albans, one of the city's premier private schools. Here was a true study in contrasts.

As the evening drew to an early close (we were to learn that Lee was a devout practitioner of a Midwestern early to bed early to rise regimen), I offered Tom a ride to his hotel in Georgetown. One-on-one, the governor was charming and funny. And he was serious about the very personal effect 9/11 had on him—many friends who worked at the World Trade Center, and hundreds more residents of New Jersey, commuters to lower Manhattan, were lost. The fact that scores of children in a number of local New Jersey schools were left fatherless had affected him profoundly. As I headed home after saying our good nights, I thought that maybe Tom Kean was a man I could work with. I slept better that night.

The next day, we sat around the conference table in Lee Hamilton's executive suite at the Wilson Center. Kean led off with a trademark self-deprecating statement. He was very pleased with the selection of his fellow commissioners, each one more qualified than the chair. Tom expressed his delight to be working with a co-chair as enormously well respected as Lee Hamilton. The governor made it a point to refer to Lee as his co-chair rather than the vice chair, his actual title, reinforcing the perception that we would be bipartisan in our work. Ours would be an opportunity to provide extraordinary service to our country. Tom's initial message was clear—we faced many dangers, "potholes," he called them, in a very politicized town. As we began our work in the run-up to a presidential election, we would have to work hard to become an integrated, unified group. Tom closed with the observation that we had neither enough time nor money, yet we were expected to produce a report in the end that would withstand scrutiny. The expectation our chairman referred to was largely our own. Few in the Washington corps of pundits, the "nattering nabobs of negativism," as Spiro Agnew famously called them (courtesy of Bill Safire's speechwriting), believed our commission could succeed. But the pundits underestimated the determination of a group of ten type A personalities to succeed, aware that our individual reputations were on the line. We knew what we needed to do and what the cost of failure would be for the nation.

Lee Hamilton spoke next, praising the backgrounds of his new colleagues. "If we do the job right, we can help make the country safer. No more important commission has ever been created." Lee returned Tom's compliment: "The president chose wisely in naming Tom Kean." It was now official: We were an outstanding group, if we did say so ourselves.

Lee wasted no time in getting into specifics about the need to organize our staff into eight to ten substantive task forces. I had advocated making a distinction between those conducting the fact investigation and those who would be making policy recommendations. Lee seemed to support such an approach. He concluded by echoing Tom's call for cohesion: "A solid report, supported by all commissioners, is our goal."

We went around the table with each commissioner having a chance to speak. Fred Fielding assured us that he had no preconceptions as to ultimate findings. He noted the cynical view then prevalent—the commission would devolve into partisan bickering that would be our undoing. "No commission will ever satisfy everyone," Fred predicted, "but everyone should be satisfied by the way in which we operate."

Max Cleland spoke of the need for transparency in order to bring the pubic along. Max was particularly interested in our delving into the psychological effects of terrorism. Jim Thompson, alluding to the obvious influence of the families, stated that the commission should be "no one's captive" and must maintain its own balance.

I pointed to the need for an "open, credible investigation" of the facts leading up to 9/11 upon which any recommendations for change must be based. Opponents of the commission were ready to pounce, and the best way to enable them would be for there to be a leak from the commission of some piece of classified information. (I am pleased to say that no such leak ever took place.)

Slade Gorton, our oldest member, traveling from his home in Seattle, had the most arduous commute to attend our meetings, yet I don't remember him missing one or ever being late. He spoke of the great challenge of Islamist terror and urged us to focus on priorities rather than delving into the trivia of "answering 150 questions."

Jamie Gorelick, the only woman on the commission, proved herself to be a tireless contributor from the get-go. Jamie had significant experience in the Clinton administration. She combined her A+ work ethic with a gracious yet persistent manner. We needed to develop a strong, "tied-down" factual record. Because we were already behind the curve, we would need to buy ourselves time to demonstrate our credibility.

John Lehman quickly demonstrated his penchant for contrarian thinking. Taking issue with Fielding's earlier statement, the former navy secretary announced that he held a definite preconception—that the "intelligence establishment is deeply dysfunctional and will fail more dramatically if we don't do something about it." Moreover, both the Clinton and George W. Bush administrations were responsible for that failure.

Tim Roemer, as a former member of the joint inquiry, was intimately familiar with many of the hurdles we would face in obtaining access to essential documents and witnesses, which the administration had refused to provide the JI. The former congressman representing the South Bend, Indiana, district that included the University of Notre Dame injected some humor into Tom and Lee's opening praise for their highly qualified colleagues. Roemer cited Harry Truman's observation that the future president had spent "the first six months in Congress wondering how I got elected, and the next six months figuring out how the rest of you got elected." Happy to leave behind the "degrading discourse" in Congress, Tim expressed belief that staffing and initial decisions would account for 60 percent of our success.

Roemer's remarks provided a segue to Tom and Lee's introduction of their choice for staff director, Philip Zelikow, the most controversial hire the commission was to make. Zelikow took a seat at the table and explained that he had given some considerable thought to the task that faced us. Working backward from a proposed end result, the fifty-year-old historian/lawyer suggested that we publish our final report in book form to be made available to the public. He laid out his concept of the major themes we would cover, substantially weighted to policy, and proposed hiring a nonpartisan staff. Philip, with black hair and a pale complexion, was earnest and formal in his manner and highly deferential to the commissioners. Zelikow did not volunteer a discussion of his prior relationship with President Bush's national security adviser, Condoleezza Rice, or his role in the Bush transition operation. Before excusing Zelikow, Tom stated that no staffer would be hired without the agreement of Lee, Phil Zelikow, and himself. This was an eye-opener. It appeared that our new staff director had negotiated an agreement for a personal veto over any new hires. Tom's deference to Phil Zelikow would become a source of anxiety for me and others on the commission as time went by. The tension between Zelikow's powerful intellect and growing mastery of the facts on the one hand and his autocratic tendencies on the other stimulated a sense of uncomfortable watchfulness.

Following Zelikow's presentation, we discussed selection of our chief counsel. Kean candidly reported that the White House had voiced its opposition to offering Jim Hamilton the job. Surprisingly, it was Slade Gorton who immediately voiced the view that it would be unacceptable for the White House to have a veto over staff hiring. The other Republican commissioners were more muted. John Lehman allowed as he would be satisfied with whatever recommendation was made by Tom and Lee on hiring. Lee reported that his choice for deputy staff director, Chris Kojm, had agreed to accept the offer and would be joining us soon.

Kojm had served in a variety of positions as a key staff assistant to Lee Hamilton for some fifteen years as Hamilton made his way up the ladder of seniority on the House International Relations Committee. For the past five years, Chris had served as a high-ranking official in the State Department, focusing on intelligence policy and coordination. Soft-spoken, bespectacled, and slim, Chris was the prototype of the devoted congressional staffer. His deferential manner belied a healthy measure of steel in his backbone when the situation called for it. Chris proved to be a calming influence over the roiling waters periodically caused by Zelikow's abrupt and dismissive attitude toward the staff.

The dynamic of this newly formed group began to develop. I was concerned that the White House felt bold enough to reach in at this early stage to block a very capable and experienced lawyer from being appointed counsel—and that Tom Kean would accede. What would this mean about his independence later?

I was not alone. Jamie and I met with Phil Zelikow a few days later to discuss organization of the task forces and suggestions for new hires. I pushed for hiring lawyers experienced in questioning witnesses and digging for facts. There were a variety of present and former prosecutors who had expressed an interest in signing on. Phil was on a charm offensive, agreeing in principle to all our suggestions. We again raised the issue of hiring Jim Hamilton as counsel. Zelikow's answer was that Tom Kean had told him flat-out that he wouldn't hire Jim. No point in discussing the subject with Phil, his hands were tied.

Jamie and I took our concerns to Lee in a call the following day. We told him that we thought we had been sandbagged—that Lee had earlier confirmed to us that Zelikow's connection to the Bush administration would be balanced by a strong and experienced counsel picked by Lee. Yet when Lee had put Hamilton's name forward, after an extensive interview, he got a red light from Tom. Lee simply confirmed that "the White House and some outside people Tom had spoken to have hardened their view about Jim Hamilton." It became clear not only that Zelikow had been given substantial discretion on hiring staff, but that as a sharp-elbowed bureaucratic in-fighter he seemed determined to prevent hiring any strong counterpoint to his position.

Tim Roemer dialed in from a soccer game where one of his brood of four young kids was playing. As the commission's youngest member at forty-eight, Tim had a full schedule of extracurricular coaching and kids' events to soak up any "spare" time. Tim reported on a long meeting he had with Zelikow during which Phil had told him that Jim Hamilton's résumé showed a high level of partisan politics. In fact, Hamilton's "political" experience was very close to what we knew about Zelikow's. The lack of appreciation for equality of treatment was disturbing. The White House complaint centered on Hamilton's service on the Clinton transition team and as a member of the President's Foreign Intelligence Advisory Board. The symmetry between Zelikow's and Hamilton's professional experience was close to exact. So why was Hamilton "too partisan" but Zelikow acceptable?

As we moved forward with figuring out our organizational structure and staff, the inability to fill the position of counsel dragged on as more than an irritant. We had procured a floor of office space, complete with an approved SCIF, in a government-controlled building a short walk from my law office. To say that the building was nondescript would be a considerable compliment to its architect. The name on the building seemed an obvious CIA front, while the well-guarded lobby provided a telltale clue, despite the building's seemingly innocuous tenant roster. By and large, we were able to keep the location of our main office secret for the duration of our tenancy, allowing commissioners, staff, and visitors valued privacy. Eventually, we were able to cram more than half of our staff into the single-floor suite, with the balance of staff in a downtown DC office and a small office in Manhattan. We held our second commission meeting on Lincoln's birthday in the conference room of our new office. Commissioners, being part-time, did not need offices of our own. When we weren't meeting as a group, we used the conference room as our reading room for classified documents or scrounged a temporary desk in one of the staff offices.

It did not take long for the areas of my greatest concern to come into sharp focus. I wanted this to be a bipartisan commission in word, deed, and appearance. This would be essential to its credibility. That meant a counterbalance to Zelikow, who had attracted immediate criticism for his ties to the Bush 41 administration and his close relationship with Bush 43 national security adviser Condoleezza Rice. I pushed early and continuously throughout the life of the commission for the most vigorous and independent examination of the facts and circumstances leading up to 9/11. I had no quarrel with those who were more interested in policy considerations and recommendations. But I felt those recommendations would have to flow from a robust and credible investigation of the facts in order to be accepted by Congress and the public. And I believed we should operate in as open a manner as possible. I was therefore taken aback by the proposal voiced by our chairman at the February meeting that the minutes of our meetings reflect only decisions made by the commission and not include the comments of individual commissioners or record the way we might vote individually on issues before us. Eventually, after a few meetings, I was to prevail in my repeated request for more "fulsome" minutes that reflected what we talked about and how we voted. And, when we were finishing our final report, I proposed that we include the minutes of our meetings in an appendix to the report. My proposal was soundly rejected; the minutes were not to be publicly available until July 2009, five years from when we issued our final report.

I believed the commission would have a necessary role to play in protecting Americans' civil liberties and privacy rights from those who saw the 9/11 attacks as a means to promote an agenda of consolidating and accreting presidential power and providing ever more intrusive authority to law enforcement and intelligence agencies, whose appetite for such power is near insatiable. This was to be a major theme of my opening remarks at our first public hearing.

It was fitting that our public debut took place in New York. A tour of Ground Zero was arranged for us, without fanfare or publicity. The gaping hole where once stood a brash and broad-shouldered monument to our nation's wealth and world leadership in commerce was a metaphor for the transient nature of all that is worldly. And a stark reminder not only of what had been lost, but also that the work in front of us would have real consequences.

One thing that we could all agree on was that the $3 million that Congress had allocated would be grossly insufficient to carry out our mission. We discussed the most efficient way to press for adequate funding. Again, the families were to be our most dependable asset in arguing for the funds we needed. We needed to stop the foot-dragging in getting every commissioner the security clearance needed to begin reviewing classified documents. And, inexplicably, even those of us who had clearances were still being denied access to the congressional joint inquiry report. Tim Roemer found himself in the Alice-in-Wonderland position of being denied access to the very report he helped write while a member of Congress. It almost seemed like some powerful folks in Washington would be happy if we never got started.

I pressed to have a public hearing as soon as humanly possible. We needed to shine some light on the speed bumps that were delaying us. Not surprisingly, the mere announcement that we would hold a public hearing on March 31 had a galvanizing effect on the Republican leadership's objections to our budget request and on commission access to the joint inquiry report. Suddenly, the White House was in competition with Congress to provide an additional $10 million in funding. And the week before the hearing, commissioners with security clearances were finally allowed access to the JI report. I spent a full day reading the report in a secure room on Capitol Hill—only four months after the official start of the commission's work. Yet security clearances for half the commissioners, including our chairman, were still being held up by red tape.

We were making no progress on selecting a strong candidate for the chief counsel position. Jamie passed along an alarming comment from an acquaintance of Zelikow's who told her that "based on what he knew of Zelikow's intentions," Jamie "should resign to protect her reputation." Despite the obvious parallel experience between Jim Hamilton and Phil

Zelikow, it was clear that Jim Hamilton had no chance. Jamie put it bluntly: "We've been rolled." There was to be no consensus in the selection process. Jamie and I interviewed and sent along a half dozen potential candidates for Lee's consideration, including my former Watergate colleague George Frampton, only to see them rejected out of hand by our chairman for supposedly being too partisan. Rich Davis faired better, but after meeting with Zelikow declined to pursue the opportunity to serve as counsel. It seemed clear to me that the White House—perhaps together with Zelikow—was being given veto power. I stopped recommending candidates—my endorsement was the kiss of death. Lee's desire to find common ground with the Republicans trumped any concern over counterbalancing Zelikow.

Was this worth resigning over, or escalating what had been a private matter into a public imbroglio? Despite my concerns, I decided not to dig my heels in over the issue of counsel. Were I to do so, I would be giving the opponents of the commission the partisan fight they were hoping for. I would see how things played out. Eventually, Tom and Lee settled on hiring Daniel Marcus, a retired partner at the prestigious Wilmer Cutler Washington law firm and a former assistant attorney general for the Civil Division in the Clinton administration. Dan proved to be a hardworking and insightful counsel, known for his patient, low-key manner. But he proved no match for Zelikow's domineering personality.

––––––––––

THE FIRST PUBLIC HEARING, held at the old Federal Customs House in lower Manhattan, was more sparsely attended than we had expected. The commissioners sat on a long dais on the elevated stage of the auditorium. We were interspersed evenly so no Democrat appointee would sit next to another Democrat and vice versa for the Republicans. This practice was to continue for the duration, projecting to the public that we would be bipartisan.

We were to hear from selected survivors of the attack, perhaps most movingly from New York Port Authority police officer David Lim, who tearfully told of his incredible survival despite being trapped in the collapsing North Tower. (His K-9 partner, a yellow lab named Sirius, was not as lucky.) But first, each of the commissioners was called on by Tom Kean to make a brief personal statement. Tom began by emphasizing the diversity of the innocent victims of the murderous attack and the central question facing the commission: "how such a dastardly attack could occur and succeed in a nation as strong as ours, militarily, economically, and technologically." What evidence was available in advance of the attack? What if people had acted differently? What could have been done to avert the attack?

When it came my turn to speak, I reviewed the problems caused by delays in making the joint inquiry report available, delays in providing security clearances for commissioners and staff, and the stinginess of our initial funding. All three issues were resolved promptly after calling public attention to them. This was a valuable lesson: Although I would not change my practice of refusing to leak information to the media, I would speak out publicly and for attribution when I thought we were not getting the cooperation we deserved. The White House quickly learned it could count on me using the megaphone provided by open hearings to do just that.

I used the remaining few minutes allotted to raise an issue that had received insufficient public attention in post-9/11 America—the need for balance between protecting against future terror attacks and the need to protect our civil rights and liberties. "This balancing will be no easy task," I continued, "but it is imperative that we get it right." I quoted from an opinion of Supreme Court Justice Thurgood Marshall: "History teaches us that grave threats to liberty often come in times of urgency, when Constitutional rights seem too extravagant to endure," and from Sandra Day O'Connor, who cautioned, "It can never be too often stated that the greatest threats to our Constitutional freedoms come in times of crises." I expressed the hope that the commission would reflect the importance of the need to respect and maintain that balance when it came time to make our recommendations.

I felt then—before revelations of torture, illegal wiretapping, and unwarranted surveillance of antiwar protestors came to light—that the grant of additional authority to combat the terrorist threat must be both measured and subject to careful oversight. Congress proved too willing to provide a knee-jerk response to a laundry list of measures for which there were no adequate safeguards. How many fledgling democracies have seen the embers of freedom stamped out by ruthless demagogues who exploited public fear to concentrate police and military power in their own hands? The demagoguery of the Bush administration, as it sought to conflate launching the invasion of Iraq with responding to al Qaeda's 9/11 attack, was only beginning to reach its full-throated potential.

It was amusing to see myself depicted as a "liberal Democrat" by critics from the right. In fact, I have always regarded myself as a moderate, supporting the death penalty, opposing late-term abortion (except in cases of danger to the mother's life), and favoring rapid immersion of non-English-speaking immigrants into English-language proficiency, to name a few issues where I depart from liberal dogma. The proficiency of the right wing and its media cohorts in pigeonholing opponents into pejorative generic categories proves to be one of its most enduring political strengths—and one of the significant challenges to those who support a pluralistic society.

The commission's first hearing included appearances by New York mayor Michael Bloomberg, who not unpredictably used the occasion to berate the federal government for short-changing the city's request for financial assistance, as well as two panels of experts who discussed various aspects of the terrorist threat. The reaction to the hearing was less than enthusiastic—and for good reason. Nothing "new" had been uncovered. The 9/11 survivors and victims' families had been heard from before, experts were a staple on cable television, and the mayor of New York complaining about mistreatment by the feds was hardly newsworthy. Even though they had been provided a public forum, the families were agitated at the prospect of another lackluster review of 9/11.

My relationship with Tom Kean was to take a major step forward. I invited Tom to dinner the next time he was to be in Washington. I wanted to explain my objectives directly to him, rather than have myself defined by others who might have his ear. I was delighted by his ready acceptance of a one-on-one dinner. As we sat across the table in a well-worn booth at the Washington Palm, Tom surprised me by taking the initiative in explaining *his* reasons for accepting the chairmanship. He reiterated in detail the personal loss he had suffered and his determination to find and report the facts in a way that would be both open and credible. He discussed his upbringing in Washington with true affection for the town John Kennedy called a combination of "southern efficiency and northern charm." Of course, things had changed quite a bit since then. The capital had become more urbane with better restaurants and cultural outlets. But the personal relationships among members of Congress that had once flourished across the political aisle were largely gone, replaced by mistrust and personal attacks. We discussed the reasons for this, including the corrosive effect of raising ever-increasing amounts of money in a never-ending campaign fund-raising cycle. This, in turn, required members to travel outside of Washington with much greater frequency, leaving few opportunities for the kind of nonpartisan social interactions common in the past.

The fewer number of truly contested elections in the House had led to more extreme positions, both on the left and the right, as candidates positioned themselves to be most attractive to their base in winning primaries. Kean lamented the fact that moderate Rockefeller Republicans like himself were facing near extinction on the national level. He then mentioned his friendship with Bill Clinton dating back to when they both served as governors. Both Clinton and George W. Bush had signaled that opportunities for cabinet positions were open for the former New Jersey governor, but he could not be lured to Washington.

I finally got the chance to explain my appreciation of the importance of our shared assignment and my commitment to get the facts, no matter whose political ox might be gored. We owed as much to the American people. Tom assured me that he shared that commitment and would not be cowed or manipulated by the White House. We told a few war stories and shared some laughs before we parted that evening.

I felt reassured by Kean's openness and candor. Tom exuded the self-confidence of someone very comfortable with who he was. While we might disagree on individual issues, I never doubted his integrity or commitment.

That commitment was soon put to the test, as the commission faced its first crossroads since the appointment of Henry Kissinger.

The question of whether to hold open, fact-based investigative hearings was put to a vote. To my thinking, the need for robust hearings was the closest thing to a no-brainer. In order to establish credibility with the public and with Congress we would have to get on their radar screen, show that we were willing to ask probing questions and demand answers of the civilian and military leaders responsible for protecting our nation—from the president of the United States on down. To suggest that we were going to have policy recommendations adopted, much less our fact-finding conclusions accepted, on the basis of a closed-door inquiry and our pretty résumés was delusional. Too many well-intentioned and superbly staffed commissions had seen their reports and recommendations on fixing holes in our national security ignored and gathering dust in the National Archives. But we had the chance to make a difference if we seized the opportunity and showed the nation our determination to get the facts.

Yet there was another viewpoint. Public hearings would sap precious time from the staff, who would be obliged to prepare the way for such hearings, taking them away from other responsibilities. Lee Hamilton spoke up: We don't really learn that much new from public hearings; the real work is done by the staff through interviews and review of documents. I was stunned. This was a true holy shit moment. Didn't Lee get it? In order to assure compliance and candor in the interviews and document production there would have to be consequences for failure—and the most effective would be the specter of being taken to task in public. If we gave that up, we could kiss our collective ass good-bye. There was no question that the other Democrats—Gorelick, Cleland, and Roemer—wanted open hearings, but if we were outvoted six to four, the commission would be strangled in its crib.

Then Tom Kean spoke up. He favored open hearings and "bringing the public along" as we sought answers to why our intelligence and law enforcement agencies were taken by surprise. Were we headed for a five–five impasse? Fred Fielding, Jim Thompson, and John Lehman joined Hamilton in opposing hearings. But Slade Gorton broke ranks and cast the deciding vote in favor of open hearings, making the final tally six–four in favor.

We had survived a near-death experience, and I give Tom Kean and Slade Gorton all the credit for thwarting a move that would have delighted a White House reluctant to provide a full account of the run-up to 9/11. I never truly figured out Lee Hamilton's vote. I have enormous respect for Lee's intellect and ability. Clearly, his primary focus was in making policy recommendations. Perhaps his bad experience with Colonel Oliver North in the Iran-Contra hearings over which he presided as chairman of the House Intelligence Committee—where North's media-savvy performance seemed to wrest control of the hearings from his congressional interrogators—had a scarring effect on Lee. But when we were all done, Lee acknowledged that his vote against open hearings was a mistake and that the hearings were key to our ultimate success.

Phil Zelikow's penchant for control was epitomized by an early memo he circulated to all staff members warning them that they should not respond to individual commissioners' questions to them but should refer all questions to him. This was hardly the kind of relationship I had envisioned with the staff, and I expressed my view to Tom and Lee in strong terms. I also objected to Phil's edict to the staff that there should be no discussion between members of different task forces as to the substance of what they were learning in their investigations. Such restrictions would serve to imitate the very "stovepiping" that had badly served the nation in pre-9/11 interrelationships among the member agencies of our intelligence community. Although Tom Kean rebuked Zelikow for his "inappropriate" staff memo, Tom and Lee left Phil to more or less his own devices when it came to staff administration. From time to time, Chris Kojm would step in to quell minirevolts by the staff against Zelikow's authoritarian style, using his soft-spoken diplomatic training to soothe ruffled feathers. In the end, I felt we had lost the opportunity for encouraging more synergistic thinking, which would have been the product of more open collaboration by our highly talented staff members.

The combination of the process for selection of our chief counsel and Zelikow's autocratic approach to controlling the staff had a demoralizing effect on me. In late March, Senate minority leader Tom Daschle called me to offer his appreciation for "hanging in despite a very frustrating period." Tom expressed his continued confidence in me "to ensure that the commission's work gets done." I welcomed Daschle's "attaboy." With our first investigative hearing on the horizon, the dynamic was about to change—very much for the better.

Our May 22–23 hearing proved among the most trenchant in getting to the truth on the state of America's civil and military air defenses on 9/11 and what actually happened that day in the skies above New York, Washington, and Pennsylvania. For the first time, the beribboned leaders of NORAD, the North American Defense Command, publicly described the shortcomings of our preparedness on 9/11. We pulled no punches in our questioning. Quickly contradicted was the assertion by Condoleezza Rice in the immediate aftermath of 9/11 that "no one could have anticipated that [terrorists] would use planes as weapons." The air force brass confirmed what our staff investigators had documented: There were a dozen examples of plots known to the intelligence agencies where planes would be crashed into buildings. Indeed, as recently as the May 2001 summit meeting of the G8 leaders in Genoa, attended by President Bush, an air cap had been established above the meeting place to enforce a no-fly zone protecting against just such a contingency! Moreover, tabletop and actual air force exercises premised multiple coordinated attacks in the United States by suicide pilots, including NORAD's Amalgam Virgo 02 exercise, which was scheduled for June 2002 and would simulate simultaneous hijackings of civilian commercial aircraft in the United States and Canada. According to the Amalgam Virgo scenario, which was in late stages of planning by September 2001, FBI agents were to play the role of passengers, and Royal Canadian Mounted Police and other FBI agents would pose as the hijackers. The plan called for military fighter planes to respond by either forcing the hijacked planes to land or shooting them down.

Yet, as Major General Craig McKinley admitted under my questioning, NORAD was still in a cold war posture on 9/11, positioning its resources to protect against a nonexistent threat from a defunct Soviet Union. Despite knowing the aspirations of our terrorist enemies, NORAD had not adapted to meet the threat.

Twice I asked General McKinley, commander of the First Air Force and the Continental United States NORAD Region on 9/11, to define NORAD's core mission.

> BEN-VENISTE: I asked you about your responsibilities, sir, and I ask you again, whether it was not your responsibility at NORAD to protect the United States and its citizens against air attack.
>
> MCKINLEY: It is, and it was, and I would just caveat your comment by saying that our mission was at that time not designed to take internal FAA radar data to track or to identify tracks originating within our borders. It was to look outward, as a Cold War vestige, primarily developed during the Cold War, to protect against Soviet long-range bomber penetration of our intercept zone.
>
> BEN-VENISTE: Well, I think, sir, that you have used a good term, not good for the United States, but accurate, in terms of the vestigial mandate operationally to look outward toward the borders rather than inward. And as vestigial you mean, I am sure, as a result of our decades of confrontation with the former Soviet Union.

Simply put, on 9/11 NORAD was looking only one way, and as it turned out, the wrong way.

It was clear that communications between the FAA—the guardian of civil commercial aviation—and NORAD were abysmal on 9/11. Questions were raised but not adequately answered about who gave orders to shoot down commercial airliners on 9/11 and whether the strict chain of command had been followed. Had President Bush been in charge, as the White House maintained, or was his role as commander in chief usurped by Vice President Cheney? We would need to probe more deeply.

Even though the staff had complained that they didn't have enough time to adequately prepare for the hearing, an important milestone had been reached. The press and public saw that our commission was united in its determination to require accountability. The tough questioning drew praise from the families and other supporters of the commission's creation. And it began to give hope to the skeptics. But the real shocker of our first venture into a fact-based investigative hearing was to come a year later, when it was shown in our final public hearing that the account of 9/11 given by air force NORAD commanders had been a false concoction in material respects, contrived to make it appear that NORAD was better prepared to deal with the suicide hijackers of 9/11 than the facts would bear out.

———————

WHEN JAKE STEIN, DEAN of Washington's trial lawyers, was appointed independent counsel to investigate allegations swirling about Reagan attorney general Edwin Meese, a reporter asked Jake for a comment on the transition from his regular practice as a defense lawyer to his new role as investigator/prosecutor. "At a time in life when most faculties are in decline," Jake responded, "it's nice to get subpoena power." Getting authority to subpoena documents was an essential piece of the legislation creating the 9/11 Commission—one the proponents of a vigorous investigation fought hard to include. It was again surprising to see the commission members debate whether or not to use our subpoena power to collect the documents we needed from each relevant agency. Given the shortness of time, Jamie Gorelick and I proposed sending subpoenas to the CIA, DOD, FBI, and other agencies to make clear that our requests for relevant documents had the force of law. Indeed, it was not at all unusual for these agencies to respond to subpoenas in connection to various judicial and legislative hearings. Nevertheless, it was the consensus of the others that issuing subpoenas would be "too confrontational" and "punitive," without first giving the agencies the opportunity to respond "voluntarily" to our written requests. Punitive? For Jamie and me, a subpoena was an everyday occurrence, kind of like a formal "hello" in a legal context. We were handily outvoted.

Our staff team investigating the FAA/NORAD response on 9/11 was sent out into the field to conduct interviews at certain NORAD bases. They found a trove of recordings from September 11 that had not been produced to the commission in response to our specific written demands. The subsequent decision by the commission to authorize subpoenaing these documents and others the Department of Defense had withheld (on an identical six–four vote as the vote on whether to hold fact hearings) was greeted with headlines reporting the "stain" on the administration for requiring us to resort to subpoenas. Okay, punitive it would be. In the altered reality of the commission's investigation, the various administration agencies now had a reason to fear being subjected to a subpoena—a badge of dishonor for failure to cooperate with our requests.

The FBI was slow off the mark in making its records available. FBI director Robert Mueller quickly became personally involved, ensuring that the FBI became a model of cooperation. Of course, the stakes were extremely high for the FBI. On the one hand, the bureau is perhaps the most impenetrably hidebound and change-averse bureaucracy in Washington. On the other hand, it was clear that unless significant changes were made to the way the FBI collects, disseminates, and shares terrorist information, its many critics might succeed in wresting control of its intelligence-gathering function by giving it to a newly created domestic intelligence agency along the lines of Great Britain's MI5.

There were numerous missed opportunities by the FBI to at least interrupt the 9/11 plot, if not arrest the conspirators before they struck. Without recounting that history in detail here, the failure to follow up on the warnings of diligent FBI field agents about foreign-born Muslims attending U.S. flight schools; the failure to intercept two al Qaeda members known to be in the United States, Nawaf al Hazmi and Khalid al Mihdhar, before their participation in the 9/11 hijackings; and the failure to discern the importance of Zacarias Moussaoui to unraveling the 9/11 plot or at least pressing for robust defensive measures to enhance airline security, were individually and in combination a shocking blow to the FBI's reputation as the world's preeminent law enforcement agency. I had worked with many very capable and dedicated FBI agents during my years as a prosecutor and had dealt with an equal number as defense counsel in criminal cases where the FBI had an investigative role. But the leadership and upper management of the FBI had a history of resistance to change that was unparalleled in Washington—be it race or sex discrimination in hiring, or its shockingly slow transformation into the computer age.

Bob Mueller understood that unless he could convince the 9/11 Commission that the FBI was willing to make the changes necessary to meet a new environment where jihadist terrorist acts within our borders were a reality, we might well recommend that the nation create an entirely new agency to do the job. In the end, the commission's recommendation that a modified FBI was preferable to an American version of MI5 was in no small part a testament to the commission's assessment of Mueller's sincerity and integrity. But could one person, no matter how dedicated and well-meaning, counter decades of a culture so resistant to change?

I thought it best to do some research on MI5. Was it the model we ought to be emulating? Fortuitously, a high official of MI5 posted to Washington was a particular friend of the British embassy's military attaché, John Keeling, who with his wife, Sue, had become friends of ours through their daughter's friendship with ours at our local public grade school. A short, roundish, and thoroughly likable fellow, he looked far more like a university classics professor than a James Bond cloak-and-dagger type. The success of MI5, I learned, although not unblemished, owed a great deal to its extensive history of cooperation with the Special Branch—Britain's national police force based in Scotland Yard. This relationship, developed over generations, allowed MI5 to focus on providing intelligence, which the Special Branch could use to initiate arrests or other overt police actions, if the evidence so warranted. Elizabeth Manningham-Buller, then head of MI5, visited us in the commission's office. We had a very lively interchange in which Manningham-Buller candidly expressed her view that the MI5 model was not particularly suited to the United States. Listening to the MI5 chief, I was reminded of the Texan who asked his British host about his secret for maintaining the extraordinary manicured grounds of his country estate. "Simple, really," answered the Brit, "you plant the best grass seed, roll the grounds well, wait four or five hundred years, and there it is . . . no problem."

Bob Mueller expressed a willingness to accept the concept of "a service within a service"—creating a corps of analysts recruited and specially trained with a mission different from the prototypical law enforcement special agents of the FBI portrayed in the media. Mueller agreed with my suggestion that these new analysts might look more like the actor Wally Cox, made famous in the role of the timid milquetoast hero of the 1950s TV sitcom, *Mr. Peepers,* or Agatha Christie's Miss Marple than the square-jawed Efrem Zimbalist types, and more likely would be mathematicians, English lit majors, or computer geeks than former military police or college jocks. In discussing the advantages of broadening the FBI's mission rather than create a new domestic surveillance agency, Mueller emphasized the fact that the FBI was indoctrinated in and sworn to uphold constitutional restraints on police powers. Although instances of the FBI deviating from those principles are hardly rare—the unlawful surveillance and worse relating to the civil rights and anti–Vietnam War activists are two egregious examples—Mueller's point was persuasive. Who knew what the Bush White House might come up with if it were authorized to create a new domestic intelligence-gathering agency? Given its penchant for secrecy, its attempts to expand executive powers, and its steadfast belief that it was untethered by constitutional restraints in fulfilling its other responsibilities, there was no telling what Frankenstein monster might be stitched together in the bowels of the White House. A Bush-created secret intelligence police force would be a specter too frightening to unleash on the American people.

Throughout our history, great and wise leaders have recoiled from emulating our European cousins' police operations. Harlan Fiske Stone, attorney general under Calvin Coolidge (and later chief justice of the Supreme Court), did much to guide the FBI on a proper path. "A secret police may become a menace to free government and free institutions because it carries with it the possibility of abuses of power that are not always quickly appreciated or understood," he warned. Stone instructed the fledgling leader of the new Federal Bureau of Investigation, J. Edgar Hoover, to focus on *conduct* that violated the law, not on the *opinions* of individuals, political or otherwise, no matter how unpopular. Robert H. Jackson, former attorney general under FDR, Supreme Court justice, and chief prosecutor at the Nuremberg war crimes tribunal, made the point succinctly: "I can say with great confidence that the United States cannot become totalitarian without a centralized national police."

So despite its shortcomings and the skepticism expressed in our internal deliberations about the FBI's ability to adapt to the challenges of a post-9/11 world, we did not recommend creation of a new MI5-type organization.

AS IF THE SLOW start and limited time for completion of our report didn't put enough pressure on us, the White House exacerbated the situation by imposing annoying and unnecessary restrictions on our access to documents and witnesses. Despite the fact that we had our own secure SCIF in our K Street office, White House counsel Alberto Gonzales insisted that we trek over to the Eisenhower Executive Office Building on 17th Street at Pennsylvania Avenue to review White House documents. Moreover, a minder was required to sit in the secure room with us while we read, and any notes we took were held and reviewed for classification purposes—returnable to us by appointment. (By contrast, the FBI allowed our staff real-time access to its computer system.) Further, the White House imposed restrictions on interviews of executive office personnel by requiring an administration monitor to be present. Although we protested, there was no forum other than public opinion to appeal these annoying and potentially chilling restrictions. The evidence of White House obstructionism was beginning to accumulate. While Gonzales and company won the early rounds, their victories were not cost free—as the later battles over access to the President's Daily Briefs (PDBs), and the commission's demands to interview President Bush and Vice President Cheney, and to obtain public testimony from Condoleezza Rice were to demonstrate.

One of the most fascinating days I spent in the secure room at the Eisenhower Building was listening to the tape recording of the air threat conference that took place on September 11, 2001, for eight hours starting at 9:34 A.M. I was tremendously impressed by the cool professionalism of Captain Charles Leidig and the military staff at the National Military Command Center (NMCC) at the Pentagon in dealing with the chaos unfolding in the skies over the northeastern United States. The NMCC's mission was to coordinate and establish the chain of command between the National Command Authority (the president and the secretary of defense) and the military command that must carry out their orders. Incredibly, despite numerous attempts to patch in key officials of the Federal Aviation Authority at the air traffic control center, they were never able to bring them onto the line. The glaring deficits in communications capability were exacerbated by Secretary of Defense Donald Rumsfeld's absence from his command and control responsibilities, as he chose instead to assist the rescue party that had formed at the site of impact at the Pentagon. The lines of authority for military command ran directly from the president as commander in chief to the secretary of defense. To add to the confusion, and contrary to protocol, a White House videoconference was initiated, seemingly in competition with the NMCC's significant event air threat telephone conference that Leidig initiated at 9:39 A.M.

While senior military personnel tried frantically to locate Rumsfeld, Vice President Cheney assumed control from his chair at the conference table inside the PEOC (Presidential Emergency Operations Center) deep beneath Pennsylvania Avenue. Filling the leadership vacuum while President Bush was airborne and Rumsfeld was missing, Cheney had issued orders to military commanders to shoot down nonresponding commercial airliners approaching Washington, DC—a decision that raised the supersensitive issue of whether Dick Cheney had preempted the president's authority.

When Secretary Rumsfeld finally entered the air threat conference at 10:39 from NMCC headquarters—roughly an hour after the teleconference had begun—he was greeted with the startling news that about twenty minutes earlier Cheney had issued a shoot-down order:

CHENEY: There's been at least three instances here where we've had reports of aircraft approaching Washington—a couple were confirmed hijack. And pursuant to the President's instructions I gave authorization for them to be taken out. [*There was a brief pause as Rumsfeld processed this information.*]

RUMSFELD: Yes, I understand. Who did you give that direction to?

CHENEY: It was passed through the [operations] center at the White House from the PEOC.

RUMSFELD: OK, let me ask the question here—has that directive been transmitted to the aircraft?

CHENEY: Yes, it has.

RUMSFELD: So we've got a couple of aircraft up there that have those instructions at this present time?

CHENEY: That is correct. And it's my understanding they've already taken a couple of aircraft out.

RUMSFELD: We can't confirm that. We're told that one aircraft is down but we do not have a pilot report that did it.

As the secretary of defense immediately realized, without providing the fighter pilots with explicit instructions on the rules of engagement for the destruction of passenger aircraft, an enormously dicey and potentially disastrous situation had been created. In fact, no planes had been shot down. As it turned out, Cheney's order had never been communicated to the fighter pilots flying under NORAD's control. This proved fortunate, as the last of the hijacked planes, United 93, one of the planes Cheney mistakenly reported to have been "taken out," had crashed in a Pennsylvania field at 10:03 A.M., at least ten minutes before Cheney had issued the shoot-down order. As I listened to the drama unfold, I was struck by the calm efficiency in the voices of the military participants, and later Rumsfeld, in comparison to the emotional and excited Cheney.

Although President Bush and Secretary Rumsfeld each told us that they had spoken by telephone earlier that morning at about 10 A.M., neither could remember anything that was said. And when I heard President Bush finally join the air threat teleconference from Air Force One, I got the distinct impression that this was the first time the two men had spoken since learning of the terrorist attack. Indeed, I found Bush's greeting to his secretary of defense jarringly out of proportion to the gravity of the disaster, as the president alluded to Rumsfeld's long-ago combat experience in what might be more appropriate to a locker room conversation.

My puzzlement over the tone of this interaction was increased by the fact that in the first version of the transcript of the air threat conference provided to me by the White House, Bush's exchange with Rumsfeld was not included.

To say the least, the White House was highly sensitive to the suggestion that Vice President Cheney had overstepped his proper bounds on 9/11 and intruded into the president's domain. Our staff did a painstaking investigation of the time line of Cheney's and Bush's contacts that morning, as well as reviewing the notes of the staff aides, including Lewis "Scooter" Libby and Cheney's wife, Lynne, who were in the PEOC with the vice president. There were inconsistencies in the vice president's version of events that could not be squared with his claim that he had received shoot-down authorization from the president prior to his communication of such an order to a military aide between 10:12 and 10:18. None of the notes taken by his aides reflected that he had told them of receiving such a momentous and chilling authorization from the president to shoot down an unarmed commercial airliner filled with innocent passengers. Indeed, Cheney's reference to having received such authorization from Bush in this 10:39 interchange with Rumsfeld was the first recorded mention. In our final report we simply set out the facts to allow the public to draw its own conclusions.

A related issue was the claim that a specific threat against Air Force One had been received by the White House from an anonymous caller. The caller had supposedly used the secret code name for the president's airplane, claiming that "Angel" would be the next target of attack. This in turn was used by the vice president and Condoleezza Rice to buttress their advice to President Bush that he should not return to Washington from Florida (as he had reportedly planned to do), but should divert to a military base.

Chief White House spinmeister Karl Rove immediately sprang into action to protect Bush's macho image. Rove turned to reliable administration supporter William Safire of the *New York Times*, who breathlessly wrote on September 13, 2001:

> A threatening message received by the Secret Service was relayed to the agents with the President that "Air Force One is next." According to a high [White House] official, American code words were used showing a knowledge of procedures that made the threat credible.
>
> (I have a second, on-the-record source about that: Karl Rove,

the president's senior adviser, tells me: "When the President said 'I don't want some tinhorn terrorists keeping me out of Washington,' the Secret Service informed him that the threat contained language that was evidence that the terrorists had knowledge of his procedures and whereabouts. In light of the specific and credible threat, it was decided to get airborne with a fighter escort."

Safire expanded on his "scoop," wondering how the terrorists would have gotten "code-word information and transponder know-how." The conclusion: "The terrorists may have a mole in the White House." The prescription: "The first thing our war on terror needs is an Angleton-type counterspy." (Safire's reference was to the CIA's famously obsessive mole hunter, James Jesus Angleton.)

Rove's efforts to enlist Safire on the Air Force One threat scenario were of a piece with White House spokesman Ari Fleischer's. Fleischer stated in a news conference on September 12 that there was "real and credible information that came into the White House and that is the reason why the White House, Air Force One, took the actions that it took." Two days after the attack, President Bush refused to provide answers at a press conference relating to the threat to Air Force One.

Fleischer was pressed to provide more information at his own press briefing. A reporter asked, "The President, when he was asked today about the threat to Air Force One, said, 'I will not discuss the intelligence that our country has gathered.' And yet, you and other senior administration officials have discussed the intelligence. Does he have a problem with that?"

Fleischer responded with the need to protect "sources and methods." The intrepid reporter pressed on, noting that no law enforcement agency— the FBI, Secret Service, or the military—had claimed that Air Force One had been a target, and he questioned the credibility of the supposed threat. Fleischer's response: "Well, I think that people understand it's credible."

But as Rove and Fleischer knew or should have known by September 13, the "credible threat" against Air Force One was a bunch of hokum. No White House switchboard operator was ever produced confirming receipt of any threat against the president's plane. Indeed, immediate attempts by the Secret Service to track down the provenance of an anonymous "warning" phoned in to the White House showed that there never was a call that used the code name for Air Force One. The confusion, which was quickly identified, supposedly came from either a Secret Service agent or a military aide referring to Air Force One by the code name "Angel." But both the Secret Service and the military watch command denied involvement, and no one ever acknowledged having passed such a message to Cheney. What was immediately clear was that the president's plane had never been identified by any 9/11 anonymous caller. And despite all the hoopla over the terrorist possession of the secret code name for Air Force One, "Angel" was not a secret name at all and had been used for at least twenty-five years as a shorthand radio designation for the president's plane, appearing in print as such. But for the White House spinners, the obvious dangers of returning to Washington from Florida, where the president had been engaged in a photo op reading the now famous *The Pet Goat* to a class of second graders at Emma E. Booker Elementary School in the midst of the day's mayhem and confusion, was not good enough. There had to be a "credible" threat to the president's person involving a breach of security, a mole reporting to al Qaeda, or some such fantasy. Only then could the macho president be persuaded by Secret Service agents to seek a more secure location before returning to the capital.

Yet there was no clarification of the facts forthcoming from the White House. Rove, Fleischer, and company were content to leave the story out there. Over initial White House objections, the commission got access to press interviews of the president and his top advisers regarding national security matters on the theory that at a minimum, a commission charged with investigating 9/11 ought to have *at least* as much information as journalists given special access to the nation's decision makers. The White House found it impossible to argue that its transcripts of interviews about 9/11 were protected by privilege or national security concerns.

On October 24, Condoleezza Rice gave an interview to Bob Woodward, on condition of "deep background," for a book Woodward was writing on Bush's first year in office. Describing the events of 9/11 in regard to the decision for the president to delay his return to Washington, Rice acknowledged that it was "probably somebody in the communications channel that had actually used the code name, not whoever had called in. So, it's not now clear whether there really ever was a threat against Air Force One."

What intrigued me was that Rice, only a week after her Woodward interview, was back flogging the "credible threat" story to Evan Thomas, a senior editor at *Newsweek*. Rice described how she and Cheney discussed whether the president should return to Washington. Upon her entry into the PEOC around 10 A.M., Cheney told Rice he was firmly against it but that the president was still insisting on returning immediately to Washington. At that point, according to Rice, a "communicator," one of the military officers on duty at the White House, informed her that "there has been a named threat against Air Force One. They say there is an attack pending on—that the next attack is against—and then he called a code name for Air Force One . . . The Vice-President was right next to me. So if there was ever at that point any thought that the President might come back, it was now gone, because we knew we didn't want him to land at Andrews."

When Thomas asked whether the call was now resolved to have been a crank, Rice replied, "I don't know if it was a crank call or a real threat . . . I don't think we're going to ever know. Thomas: "I mean, how did they know about the code name?" Rice: "That's why we still continue to suspect it wasn't a crank call. But who would have even known the code name is still beyond . . ."

Rice's vacillation was disturbing, but even more so was the speculation that the whole thing had been embellished and seized upon by the vice president, seeking to convince the president to stay away so that Cheney could run the immediate response from the PEOC.

THE ISSUE OF WHY we were caught by a surprise attack in which hijacked airliners were converted into flying bombs by suicidal al Qaeda pilots was central to our mission. In reconstructing what was known and what warnings were communicated by our intelligence agencies to the president and cabinet secretaries, it was critical to see the relevant documentary records. Among the most intriguing were the PDBs prepared each day by the CIA for the president's eyes. President Clinton, a voracious reader, devoured these reports and the backup materials supplementing them. President Bush preferred an oral briefing, often personally delivered by CIA director George Tenet.

The contents of the PDBs would provide a reliable indication of what the president was told in real time about the potential for a domestic attack, and would also track the best intelligence the CIA had to present to the commander in chief. Obviously, we needed access to the PDBs. Yet the suggestion that the commission should have the temerity to ask for such highly classified material sent the Bush White House into full stonewall mode.

The administration's initial strategy was to slow-walk our document requests. The logical step before conducting interviews was for the staff to review the available written record. Yet responses to our document requests by the relevant agencies were only trickling in. It was clear that unless we got a little starch in our collective spine, the administration was going to succeed in running the clock on us. The supporters of subpoenaing the records had lost the initial internal battle; I expressed my serious concern over the consequences to our end product if we didn't do something to disrupt the status quo. How about issuing an "interim report," where we would publicly express our view regarding compliance with our document requests? After all, there was a provision for issuing interim reports in the law creating the commission. But my suggestion was tabled in favor of giving the administration more time to comply and not appearing confrontational. On June 26, 2003, after another month of delays and obfuscations, we voted again. This time the consensus favored expressing our displeasure and concern over the pace of cooperation in an interim report that would be made public. Of course, there was considerable gnashing of teeth and drafting and redrafting of the language in the interim report. For me, the language was less important than the overall message that the commission would not passively accept an administration timetable for compliance that fell far short of our needs.

Tom and Lee decided that they would present the interim report together at a press conference held at the auditorium of the Wilson Center on July 8. I wanted to see firsthand how our chair and co-chair would handle questions from the national media.

Tom and Lee were surprised at the turnout—full coverage by television and print journalists as well as family members. I took a seat in the front row as an unsubtle reminder of my dissatisfaction with the administration's responsiveness and the various speed bumps it had erected in our path.

The written statement, carefully crafted to avoid characterizing the administration's poor performance in so many words, was read aloud by Tom and Lee alternating—again emphasizing the commission's bipartisanship. Governor Kean's closing made clear that we expected the White House to live up to its professed determination to provide full cooperation to the commission. He alluded to future interim reports that would report on progress.

The press corps wasted no time in cutting to the chase. Was the commission seeking to pressure a "recalcitrant" Bush administration? Would the commission push to obtain the PDBs? Would we seek to interview President Bush? Did we object to minders being present at interviews? Would we need more time to complete our inquiry? Despite the co-chairs' attempts to respond diplomatically, the bottom line was unambiguous: The commission would not passively accept only such crumbs of evidence the administration might deign to hand out.

The interim report proved to be just what the doctor ordered to deliver a robust message to the White House. The networks led their nightly news with coverage of the press conference, while the story of the impediment to our inquiry resulting from administration delays captured the front pages of the major newspapers. I hung back after the news conference to have a word with our chairman. My wide smile and outstretched hand telegraphed my feelings. Tom flashed a gap-toothed smile and shook my hand. "You done good, boss," I told him.

There was a sea change in agency cooperation following the press conference. The documents gushed in faster than our staff could review them. For the first time, the families seemed truly pleased, while the press began to take notice of the commission as a force with which the administration would have to reckon.

As the staff began to sift feverishly through the new information and conduct interviews of lower-level government employees, the commission continued to hold a number of policy-based public hearings through the summer and fall of 2003, featuring a variety of high-level officials from prior administrations, academics, and other experts. This produced a collective yawn from the media, which had previously heard most of what these witnesses had to say. The families again grew impatient. When were we going to question the officials of the Clinton and Bush 43 administrations? Where was the accountability?

The eight-hundred-pound gorilla in the room through all of this was the U.S. invasion of Iraq. No member of the commission was more agitated or vocal than Max Cleland. The specter of America following a course so similar to our disastrous experience in Vietnam was too much for Max to bear quietly, notwithstanding the fact that the commission's charter gave us no authority over the decision to invade Iraq or the strategy that followed. Max was determined to speak out regularly, including at commission hearings, to voice his opposition to the war—to the particular consternation and hand-wringing of the Republican commission members.

My belief was that the Iraq invasion was at best premature, if not altogether unwarranted. We had not secured our objectives in Afghanistan— the Taliban was on the run but still alive. Osama bin Laden remained at large. Had we not learned from the Soviets' experience in Afghanistan about the challenges and costs of trying to occupy a Muslim country?

With our mission there becoming increasingly muddled, why were we diverting precious military resources to occupy Iraq, a country that posed no immediate threat to the United States? Indeed, it seemed to me that we invaded Iraq for exactly the opposite reason from the one given. Rather than posing a threat, Iraq's military was degraded far below what it had been when we last attacked and prevailed during the 1991 Gulf War. I discussed my concerns with Paul Sarbanes, who expressed similar views. I had seen how the authorization to use force had escalated beyond reason in Vietnam. Once U.S. troops are committed to the battlefield, the political dynamic swiftly changes from any rational discussion of the merits and objectives of the use of military power to "support the troops" or be branded defeatist or disloyal. The critical point for Congress to check the president's action is *before* troops are committed. Sarbanes's vote against the use of force resolution gave me some sense of representation (since as a DC resident I have no voting representation in Congress).

One of the key justifications given for the Iraq invasion was a supposed connection between Saddam Hussein and al Qaeda. Throughout 2003, the administration, particularly through Vice President Cheney, continued to flog an al Qaeda–Saddam connection and, by extension, a 9/11-Saddam nexus, to drum up support for the Iraq war. Although we had no authority to investigate the other false or exaggerated claims regarding WMD and the like, one of the primary issues the commission *was* charged with investigating was identifying who sponsored the 9/11 attack. Thus we were obliged to determine whether any evidence supported the administration's claim of an Iraq–al Qaeda connection. Former CIA deputy director for intelligence Douglas MacEachin, heading our al Qaeda team, took the lead in running down all available information. Doug proved to be an outstanding addition to our staff. Stocky and nearly bald, MacEachin could often be spotted in his signature beat-up brown leather jacket, cadging a smoke on the sidewalk outside our headquarters. Doug's craggy face would light up with a wry smile when he discussed the penetrating research he had conducted that left no wiggle room for administration revisionists. In addition, another highly experienced CIA hand, Michael Hurley, a superstar young academic, Alexis Albion, and Warren Bass, a brilliant thirty-three-year-old historian with a wry sense of humor were totally dependable resources for cutting to the chase.

The Republicans on the commission, particularly John Lehman, were open to providing the maximum opportunity for the administration to prove its case. Lehman pushed for inclusion of Laurie Mylroie, a highly credentialed academic (Harvard faculty, Naval War College, Washington

Institute for Near East Policy) with a symbiotic relationship with Bush administration neocons Paul Wolfowitz, John Bolton, and Scooter Libby. Not only did Mylroie proclaim the existence of an Iraq–al Qaeda connection relating to the 9/11 attack, she found an Iraqi hand in virtually every attack against U.S. interests since the 1993 bombing of the World Trade Center, including the bombing of the Murrah Federal Building in Oklahoma City, for which Timothy McVeigh was convicted.

Even the most ardent supporters of the Iraq policy were taken aback by Mylroie's extraordinary claim that not only was Iraq involved with al Qaeda's operations, but 9/11 "mastermind" Khalid Sheikh Mohammed (the infamous KSM), as well as other top al Qaeda leaders, were in fact Iraqi intelligence agents. I found that the best way of dealing with Mylroie's bizarre assertion of Saddam Hussein's ubiquitous role in international terrorism was to let her go on at some length to describe her convoluted theories. I elicited the fact that virtually no other Middle East expert shared her interpretation of Saddam's role. This point was hammered home by other experts such as Judith Yaphe of the National Defense University, whose testimony followed Mylroie's in the same hearing. Indeed, while they were desperate to find someone to give credence to an Iraqi nexus to 9/11, no one from the administration was willing to echo Mylroie's bizarre theories. At the end of the day, John Lehman admitted to me that Mylroie's testimony was an embarrassment.

Importantly, after an exhaustive review of the available data, MacEachin and the commission staff concluded there was no evidence of a connection between Iraq and the 9/11 attack. Moreover, while there was contact between Iraqi intelligence agents and al Qaeda members over the years— it was expected that the Iraqis would want to keep tabs on bin Laden— there was no *operational* connection. Indeed, the available evidence pointed to a palpable enmity between Saddam and bin Laden. This was logical, as Saddam had built his brutal dictatorship on a solidly secular foundation, while bin Laden supported overthrow of secular leaders in favor of return to the caliphate and Islamist theocratic rule.

I found the administration's attempt to conflate the 9/11 attacks with the invasion of Iraq, packaged as "the war on terror," to be as mendacious a piece of business as the Bush presidency produced. Various polls showed that a substantial majority of the American public, as many as 70 percent at one point, held the belief that Saddam's Iraq was behind the al Qaeda attack. Future historians and political scientists will study how public opinion was manipulated well after the facts debunking any such connection had surfaced.

There was little doubt in my mind that the 9/11 attack was immediately identified as a potential pretext for a president and his coterie predisposed to take down Saddam and his regime. Within hours of the attack, Secretary of Defense Rumsfeld ordered a review of plans for an invasion of Iraq. By the next weekend at meetings of top cabinet officials and the president at Camp David, a group composed of the vice president and his aides and Secretary Rumsfeld and his deputy, Paul Wolfowitz, tested the waters on responding to the World Trade Center and Pentagon attacks with an invasion of Iraq. "Not yet," was the president's response.

I had the opportunity to question former secretary of state Colin Powell in advance of his formal appearance before the commission. "Was there any evidence put forward by the proponents of invading Iraq at those Camp David meetings linking Saddam to the attacks?" I asked. Powell responded that there was not. "Did you conclude that an attempt was being made to use the 9/11 attacks as a pretext to invade Iraq?" Powell looked me in the eye, smiled, and responded, "Richard, I have answered your question."

On June 16, 2004, our staff report refuting the notion of an Iraq–al Qaeda connection to the 9/11 attacks was released as part of a public hearing on the 9/11 plot. Perhaps because of its focus on the way we portrayed the shoot-down order and whether the vice president had usurped presidential authority in another portion of the same report, the White House raised no advance objection to our conclusion that Iraq played no role in the attack. The report went on to state that on the basis of exhaustive examination of the facts, there was no credible evidence of any collaborative or operational relationship between al Qaeda and Iraq against the United States.

For obvious reasons, our conclusion made front-page headlines. The New York Times proclaimed, "Panel Finds No Qaeda-Iraq Tie." But Bush and Cheney were not willing to let go of their cherished campaign of disinformation. The next day Bush was questioned by the press about the commission's report. "The reason I keep insisting that there was a relationship between Iraq and al Qaeda is because there was a relationship between Iraq and al Qaeda," Bush replied.

Vice President Cheney chose a less tautological response, touting a claim that Mohamed Atta, ringleader of the 9/11 suicide bombers, had met in Prague with an Iraqi intelligence officer on April 9, 2001, only five months before the attack. The problem with Cheney's assertion was that it was based on a single-source Czech informant, later contradicted by the Czech intelligence service and ultimately refuted by the Iraqi diplomat who had been identified as the person who supposedly met with Atta. More important, the Cheney statement was contradicted by painstaking work performed by the FBI in reconstructing Atta's whereabouts before the attack. Atta had been captured on an April 4 Virginia Beach bank surveillance video; thereafter, calls seeking lodging were placed on Atta's cell phone from cell sites in Florida to various hotels and apartments. On April 11, Atta leased an apartment in Coral Springs. All the other bits of circumstantial evidence further eroded the assertion that Atta was in Prague on April 9.

Yet Cheney would not let go of the Iraq–al Qaeda connection. On June 20, John Lehman and I appeared on *Meet the Press*. As always, Tim Russert was well prepared. He played a clip of Cheney being interviewed on his program two years after 9/11. Pointing to a *Washington Post* public opinion poll that found a whopping 69 percent of Americans believed Saddam Hussein was involved in the 9/11 plot, Russert asked Cheney for his reaction. Cheney responded somberly that he was not surprised, given the growing body of intelligence information supporting a connection between Iraqi intelligence and al Qaeda operatives. Once again, without specifically endorsing the idea of a Saddam role in the attacks, the vice president fanned the flames of such misinformed opinion.

Russert turned to me for reaction. Trying my best to be diplomatic, I said that I did not know how Americans had come to such a conclusion, but that on the basis of the commission's exhaustive collection and review of evidence, the American people could "take it to the bank—there was no connection between al Qaeda and Iraq regarding 9/11."

In an interview following our hearing, Cheney had stated that he had information to which the commission was not privy that supported his contention that there was a connection. Again, Russert turned to me for my reaction. I stated that I had no knowledge of any secret information on the subject that we hadn't reviewed. I pointed to the fact that our staff report had been reviewed by the White House office without comment, but if the vice president had any additional evidence, he should make it available to us promptly. Tom and Lee publicly called upon Cheney to produce any new evidence. None was forthcoming. There was no secret evidence.

Our review of the Atta bank surveillance video produced one of the more lighthearted moments in the midst of a particularly tense period. As we gathered around the conference table, a large still photograph was illuminated on the projection screen. The image of Mohamed Atta approaching the teller's window was unmistakable. But the next customer, visible over Atta's right shoulder, also appeared recognizable. An older man with a steel gray buzz cut and wearing a military fatigue jacket bore a striking resemblance to our own Lee Hamilton! Was this another example of a missed opportunity to nab a terrorist, as ringleader Atta slipped through Vice Chairman-to-be Hamilton's fingers? Or was there a more sinister explanation for this seeming coincidence, one even the most whacked-out conspirators had never considered? Lee laughed heartily, and then somewhat uncomfortably, as the speculation continued around the table. But when it came time to show the surveillance photo at a public hearing, Atta's image was enlarged to the point of obscuring the customer behind him.

ALTHOUGH THERE WERE MANY smaller skirmishes, three principal areas of conflict over access to important evidence developed: review of the President's Daily Briefs, questioning of President Bush and Vice President Cheney, and public testimony by Condoleezza Rice.

White House Counsel Alberto Gonzales was the point of contact between the commission and the White House when issues of access could not be resolved at the staff level. Tom and Lee would shuttle between our office and the White House, reporting on the status of negotiations with "the Judge," as Gonzales liked to be called, a reference to his two-year stint on the Texas Supreme Court as an appointee of then governor Bush. The president, on the other hand, enjoyed referring to his Texas protégé by the nickname "Fredo" (perhaps after the hapless middle son of Godfather don Vito Corlenone).

It was the consensus of the commission members that whatever legal skills Gonzales might have, he had a tin ear politically. Without going into his reversals of position on hard-line denials of access that have not become public, the White House about-face on each of the three major issues proved the point. Because we had to use the equivalent of a blowtorch and pliers to extract critical evidence, the White House lost the opportunity to get credit for cooperation with the commission's search for the truth. And because Bush had publicly pledged his support for the commission in signing the bill creating the commission (trying to salvage some PR benefit despite his prior opposition), the hypocrisy of fighting our requests for evidence was obvious.

As I had been in the forefront of advocating a vigorous and unimpeded review of all relevant evidence in order to fulfill our promise to the American people as well as provide credibility for our ultimate recommendations for reform, I was the natural hard-liner in the negotiations. It was my view that to the greatest extent feasible we should resist White House attempts to limit our investigation of the facts. The White House had on its side the potential for assertion of executive privilege, the approaching due date for our report, and a compliant Republican-controlled Congress. We had the families, vocal Democrats in the House and Senate, as well as a growing segment of the public on ours. I was convinced that the only way to force access to the evidence was to blow up the White House strategy of secrecy and bring our disagreements into the bright light of public scrutiny. So long as we steered clear of revealing national security secrets we were entitled to fight openly for what we needed.

I told my colleagues that I would not sit quietly while the president denied access to critical evidence and ran the clock on us. I made clear that I would not leak information, but I would speak openly and for attribution. And I did. This caused some hand-wringing and tut-tutting from Tom and Lee about negative reaction from Gonzales and others in the White House, making negotiations more difficult.

At the same time, Lee complained that Gonzales had known our fallback positions during negotiations. It was solemnly agreed that this was counterproductive to our interests and whoever was informing the White House of our internal strategy discussions should stop. This was the strange reality of our circumstance, and I accepted it as such. The White House knew all about our internal deliberations. At commission meetings I often sat next to the affable Fred Fielding. I found it convenient to mention my views to Fred with the expectation they would be communicated to the White House—kind of like having a kids' tin can phone on a string from K Street to Pennsylvania Avenue.

In hindsight, I have no doubt that without injecting the disinfecting properties of sunlight into the dispute, and exerting maximum pressure on the White House, we would not have prevailed over the administration's attempt to restrict our access to information.

By the fall of 2003, the PDB issue was front and center in our negotiations with the White House. What better source than the information the CIA and the rest of the intelligence community had collected about Islamist terrorism prior to 9/11 that was communicated to the president in his morning briefing? Were there important lapses in what Presidents Clinton and Bush had been provided? Had they failed to take appropriate action based on what they were told? The PDBs might hold the key to unlock the answers to these questions.

The congressional joint inquiry had already tried and failed to persuade the White House to make relevant PDBs available for their review. This would be used as an argument by the White House to deny the commission access. Since we were a creature of congressional legislation, how could a mere commission trump the denial of Congress's access? Instead, the White House offered a compromise. We would be briefed on the contents of the PDBs but would not get to review the documents ourselves. This smelled to me too much like the Stennis compromise offered by President Nixon, offering a White House summary of the president's secret tapes instead of the actual tapes we had subpoenaed. Watergate special prosecutor Archie Cox had properly rejected such a "compromise." I expressed my view that the PDBs were of such central importance to the integrity of our investigation that we should accept nothing short of our own review.

Tom and Lee urged that we accept the offer for a briefing, but we made it clear that by doing so we were not agreeing to forgo our own review of the documents. With great fanfare, the administration assembled a gaggle of lawyers from the CIA, the NSA, and the White House to give the commissioners a PowerPoint presentation in the secure Executive Office Building SCIF. Our briefers ponderously provided statistics on how many PDBs dealt with terrorism during the Clinton administration, how many during Bush, who in each administration had access to the PDBs—everything we might want to know about the PDBs except what was in them! It was mid-October, only seven months left until our report was due.

The White House strategy backfired. Commissioners who had patiently watched months of negotiations go by were antagonized by the bogus briefing. Finally, Tom Kean had enough and gave an on-the-record interview to the *New York Times* expressing frustration at the White House foot-dragging and stating that we would use all the tools at our disposal to get access to the PDBs. Since we had only one actual tool in our toolbox, Philip Shenon of the *Times* figured out Tom was referring to our subpoena power without Tom actually having to utter the dreaded S-word.

The White House began to cave. They now offered Tom and Lee limited access to the PDBs. At a meeting to discuss the offer, I stated my opposition to any proposal that allowed the White House to choose which commissioners would have direct access. I supported Tim Roemer's motion to authorize a subpoena for Clinton and Bush administration PDBs, which failed six–four with Lee voting with the Republicans. I was prepared to accept a compromise where representatives of the commission selected by us would have direct access to the PDBs and then report back to the full commission on their contents. Time was against us if we became involved in full-scale litigation to enforce a subpoena. Even if we were successful, such a process would chew up our remaining time. The court of public opinion was again working in our favor, and the president had already blinked. If we could propose a review team that served our purpose, we could offer a compromise that would allow us to move forward in the investigation.

We voted for Jamie Gorelick and Phil Zelikow to constitute a two-person subcommittee of a committee of four—adding Tom and Lee—to review the PDBs and cull out those documents that had a direct bearing on our investigation. Tom and Lee would then review the core documents and, with Gorelick and Zelikow, report to the full commission on content. This was an excellent resolution, as Jamie was familiar with PDBs from her service as deputy attorney general in the Clinton administration.

The White House agreement to this compromise did not end the dispute; Gonzales and his staff found various ways to make the subcommittee's job even more onerous. There were restrictions about what notes could be taken, where the notes were stored, whether titles of PDBs could be reported, to name just a few. But in the end, after putting in hundreds of hours of arduous work, Jamie and Phil were able to provide virtually verbatim notes of the most important PDBs, and especially the August 6, 2001, briefing. In fact, it seemed to me later that almost all of the effort the White House put into its attempt to deny us access to the PDBs boiled down to trying to protect against disclosing that one briefing, a little over a month before 9/11.

In early December, Max Cleland announced that he would be leaving the commission. Still suffering the psychological effects of losing his Senate seat amid the scurrilous claims that he was insufficiently patriotic, Max found himself with no full-time job or financial cushion to provide for his support. This was a bad mix, and Max showed signs of falling into serious depression. At that point, Tom Daschle nominated Cleland to serve on the Export-Import Bank board, a full-time paid position that would require presidential approval and Senate confirmation. But Max had been bashing Bush on the Iraq war at every opportunity—and he had found many opportunities, including public commission hearings. Finally, the president gave his consent to Max's appointment, which also meant that as a government employee Max would be ineligible to continue serving on the commission. As we said our good-byes, I congratulated Max for the most unusual job-seeking strategy I had every witnessed—a full frontal attack on his chief executive. Max gave out with one of his signature guffaws and wished me Godspeed.

Tom Daschle phoned to ask me about a handful of possible replacements he was considering. At the top of his list was former Nebraska senator Bob Kerrey. What did I think? About all I knew about Kerrey in addition to his Senate career was that he had also been governor of Nebraska and had received the Congressional Medal of Honor for a mission he had commanded as a Navy SEAL in Vietnam in which he had lost the lower portion of his right leg. I also knew that he had dated actress Debra Winger. When reporters had pressed him on his relationship with Winger, Kerrey had famously replied, "She swept me off my foot." That was enough for me right there. "A senator for a senator seems like a good move to me," I replied.

Bob Kerrey turned out to be an excellent choice. As president of The New School in New York (we now had two serving university presidents, three former governors, two former senators, and two retired congressmen), Kerrey was a kind of Renaissance character, quick of wit, candidly outspoken, and very entertaining.

As we approached the meat-and-potatoes portion of our fact hearings, our chairman delivered a Christmas surprise. He had spent the better part of a day with a film crew from *60 Minutes*, walking around the campus of Drew University and being interviewed for the program. Apparently, Tom's musings about the commission's findings to date, which included observations that there were human failures along the way and that the 9/11 attacks were not "something that had to happen," were considered "hard news" by the folks at CBS, who led the evening news with Tom's comments, under a headline that "the attacks were preventable." CBS editorially juxtaposed Condoleezza Rice's comment in the immediate aftermath of 9/11 that no one could have imagined planes being used as weapons. Republican leaders went wild. I could only imagine what would have happened if I had been the one who made such obvious and indisputable remarks.

The January hearing dealt with border and aviation security. Among the high muckety-muck assistant secretaries and commissioners who testified was José Melendez-Perez, a line INS inspector working at Orlando International Airport. I had the chance to interview the unassuming, soft-spoken first-generation Mexican American in advance of our public hearing when staffer Janice Kephart brought him over to my office. Melendez-Perez's role in the 9/11 saga provided one of the most positive moments in our investigation. It showed how one man, conscientiously doing his job on August 4, 2001, was able to have a significant impact on the events that followed.

The Orlando airport was the disembarkation point for substantial numbers of Saudi visitors eager to enjoy Disney World and the many theme parks and attractions in the area. Customs and Immigration made clear that the Saudis were to be processed and admitted with a minimum of hassle, in keeping with the primary importance of tourism to the economy of the area.

But Melendez-Perez smelled something fishy about Mohamed al Kahtani from the moment he set eyes on him. The young Saudi impressed Melendez-Perez as being in excellent physical condition, someone who had undergone rigorous training—seemingly inconsistent with Kahtani's stated occupation as a car salesman. Further arousing the inspector's curiosity was the fact that unlike most Saudi visitors, Kahtani had traveled alone, without any family members and without a return ticket. Melendez-Perez decided that further questioning was in order, so he pulled Kahtani out of line for "secondary screening" and brought in an interpreter. The young Saudi gave inconsistent answers about how he was going to pay for his ticket home and whom he was going to meet and depend on to get around in Orlando, since he spoke no English. Most of all, it was Kahtani's demeanor that set off the inspector's alarm bells. Arrogant and disdainful, Kahtani seemed more like a hit man than a Disney World tourist. Risking going against the grain of the existing bureaucratic imperative, José Melendez-Perez took the initiative to deny Kahtani admission to the United States. He was put on the next plane back to Saudi Arabia.

As it turned out, Kahtani was to be the final "muscle" hijacker to join the 9/11 plot. Waiting for him in the airport parking lot was Mohamed Atta.

The implications of Melendez-Perez's actions were dramatic. All three hijack teams that achieved their objectives of crashing their planes into the designated targets of the World Trade Center and the Pentagon were composed of a pilot and *four* "muscle" hijackers. United 93 was the only team of four—a pilot and three "muscle" hijackers. Armed with information from cell phone communications that two planes had already crashed into the World Trade Center, the passengers on United 93 decided to fight the hijackers for control of the aircraft. Despite the fact that the hijackers had already used knives to murder a flight attendant and at least one passenger, a group of passengers armed with only the makeshift weapons of boiling water and a fire extinguisher battled valiantly to breach the cockpit. After furiously maneuvering the plane in an unsuccessful attempt to dislodge the counterattackers from their forward progress, the pilot and his henchmen conferred. Realizing that in only a matter of minutes the vigilante committee would achieve its objective of breaking into the cockpit, the hijackers abandoned their target of the U.S. Capitol building and deliberately flew the plane into the ground in a field in rural Pennsylvania.

If there had been five instead of four hijackers on United 93, might they have been able to barricade the cockpit for another fifteen or twenty minutes to allow pilot Ziad Jarrah to reach Washington? In culminating my questioning of José Melendez-Perez at our public hearing, I raised that possibility: "It is entirely plausible to suggest that your actions in doing your job efficiently and competently may well have contributed to saving the Capitol from being included in the catastrophe of 9/11, and for that we all owe you a debt of thanks and gratitude." The hearing room erupted in applause, long overdue recognition for Melendez-Perez who, up to that point two and a half years after 9/11, had received neither commendation nor promotion from his superiors at INS. John Lehman followed with the observation that "if everyone up and down the chain had been as professional as you, the attacks would not have happened."

In December 2001, Mohamed al Kahtani was captured on the battlefield near Tora Bora, Afghanistan. Kahtani was held for seven months at Guantánamo before his fingerprints were matched with the man Melendez-Perez had refused entry to the United States. He was turned over to an FBI interrogation team led by Ali Soufan, one of only eight FBI agents fluent in Arabic at the time. Soufan, using tried-and-true methods of patient interrogation, building a bond of trust with his subject, was reportedly making good progress, establishing Kahtani's connection to the 9/11 plot and identifying Kahtani's cousin in a Chicago sleeper cell, when Washington intervened. According to an account by prize-winning journalist Jane Mayer in *The Dark Side,* there was concern that Kahtani's interrogation was not progressing fast enough and that the young Saudi might be holding back critical information about impending terrorist attacks. Kahtani's interrogation was turned over to a Defense Intelligence Agency civilian who employed harsh and humiliating techniques against detainees, reportedly under Defense Secretary Rumsfeld's direct orders. Kahtani shut down. A fierce bureaucratic tug-of-war ensued among Defense, the CIA, and the FBI. Kahtani was subjected to several weeks of unrelenting and ever more abusive and humiliating torment. No new information was produced, but the extreme measures of the DIA interrogation caused the Pentagon to announce in May 2008 that it was dismissing all charges against Kahtani. Thus, at the same time our reputation as a nation committed to justice and humanity was being undermined, our ability to put a criminal directly involved in the 9/11 conspiracy on trial for his complicity in the plot that caused the greatest loss of life in our nation's history was destroyed.

THE DELAYS IN GETTING started and obtaining documents had predictable results. It put enormous pressure on our staff, which faced the dual assignments of preparing for rigorous fact-based hearings and integrating the fruits of our investigation into a draft final report. Under "normal" circumstances, these objectives would be complementary, not inconsistent. But with a May date for completion of our report, something had to give.

It was clear that we needed extra time. The only question was how much. Objectively, six months would be a reasonable amount of time for an extension. But six months would put us right at the November presidential election. There was no way that was going to fly, but it would provide a good basis to start negotiations. What was the absolute minimum amount of time we needed to accomplish both objectives? Assuming the staff worked like dogs day and night from January forward, we would need two additional months.

Of course, the White House was well aware of our dilemma—and our internal discussions. Informal inquiries to the White House about an extension were met with an absolute no. We were already behind the curve and needed to act immediately to get public opinion and our congressional allies lined up to introduce legislation to extend our deadline. Lee pointed out that seeking an extension was not without risk. If we were unsuccessful, people would criticize us for doing an incomplete job. So be it. If we didn't get the extension our product would be less than the public had a right to expect.

At the conclusion of our January hearing, we again used the bully pulpit to publicly express our concern. Tom Kean read a statement that summarized the back-and-forth of our discussions, concluding, "We have decided that the right course is simply this: put aside the politics and just ask for the time we really need. The Commission therefore requests that the Congress amend our statute to extend the time for completing our report by at least 60 days."

Public support was immediate. Senators John McCain and Joe Lieberman introduced a bill for a six-month extension. The White House realized that the optics of overtly opposing our request would be horrendous. Grudgingly, they agreed not to oppose a sixty-day extension for filing our report. But a new impediment arose in the person of House Speaker Dennis Hastert. As legislation in the Senate moved forward, Hastert stated that the House leadership would block any move to extend our time. Was Hastert the cat's-paw for the president, doing what Bush was politically precluded from doing himself? Hastert remained adamant as public pressure from the media grew—with many commissioners, including Tom and Lee, going on television to state our need for more time. There was simply no viable rationale the Republicans could fashion for opposing our request. Finally, after some hardball maneuvering by our Senate supporters, Hastert caved and agreed to give us a sixty-day extension. It was March 1 and we now had less than five months to finish our work.

THE TENSION BETWEEN OUR ability to get the facts and the government's ongoing effort to combat the jihadists came into sharpest focus in connection with our request to interview key al Qaeda members who had been captured since 9/11. Our staff had identified more than one hundred detainees whose interrogation reports were of interest. We were getting slow-walked on these requests, particularly by the Defense Department. Understandably, while the focus of the interrogations was directed at developing intelligence useful against future terrorist operations, our mandate was to collect and understand what was known about the 9/11 attack. Our staff effort was led by Dieter Snell, an experienced prosecutor from my alma mater, the Southern District of New York, who had led the prosecution of Ramzi Yousef, the ringleader of the 1993 bombing of the World Trade Center. Dieter had definite ideas regarding areas of interrogation that had not been adequately covered, at least according to the reports that were trickling in. And he wanted direct access to the detainees themselves, to gauge their demeanor as they responded to questions. I could understand Dieter's reasons—any trial lawyer wants to get an unfiltered shot at the witness. I estimated the chances of the administration acceding to such a request somewhere between slim and none.

CIA director George Tenet quickly shot down the proposal for direct access. Among the reasons he put forward was that the highest-value detainees were being held in remote and secret locations to maintain absolute security. We proposed that our staff could be transported to these places, blindfolded, if necessary, to maintain security. Tenet argued that the injection of new faces and personalities would interrupt the flow and rapport the CIA interrogators had painstakingly established with the detainees. This argument resonated with me from what I had read about techniques established by the military to break down resistance of POWs. Let them know the war was over for them—there was no way they would return to the battlefield. Establish trust—gradually win their confidence. But couldn't we feed our questions to the interrogators and observe the detainees, say, through a one-way mirror or some such device? No way. Tenet was having none of it. The best the commission could get, after drawn-out meetings involving Tenet, Rumsfeld, and Gonzales, was that the CIA would designate a point person to convey our questions and provide follow-up after the answers came back. We were in a take-it-or-leave-it situation. We had no legal recourse; in my view, no court would enforce a commission subpoena of the detainees. The administration had the better argument, and even if a district court ruled our way, the White House would appeal to a higher court, running out the clock. Should we make an appeal to public opinion? The White House begged Tom and Lee not to publicize the dispute on grounds of national security. My view was that we should not risk our credibility on this issue. Suboptimal though this detainee access process was, we took the deal.

Never, ever did I imagine that American interrogators were subjecting detainees to water boarding and other forms of physical torture, or that they were subcontracting out the dirty job to foreign governments more practiced in these methods. If Dieter Snell suspected that this was the reason behind the Bush administration's intransigence on granting us direct access to the detainees, he never confided in me. No one raised such a possibility at a commission meeting. In hindsight, we were snookered.

Years later, when the stories about detainee abuse at Guantánamo and Abu Ghraib were published, I was sickened by what had been perpetrated in the name of my country. In a stroke, we had surrendered a portion of the high ground that differentiates us from our brutal and lawless enemy. For moral as well as practical reasons (based on decades of studies that showed such seemingly expedient methods are actually ineffective in obtaining valuable intelligence), I felt betrayed. We are America; we are better than this.

———————

THE CULMINATION OF OUR investigation into the Clinton and Bush administrations' pre-9/11 response to the threat posed by al Qaeda was set for two days of public hearings in late March 2004. Designated "Counterterrorism Policy," it was to be our eighth public hearing but far and away the most dramatic from the standpoint of assessing political accountability for our nation's failure to prevent 9/11. Predictably, the finger-pointing between the Democrats and Republicans in the run-up to the 2004 presidential election had reached a level of high intensity. Our agenda included the two former secretaries of state—Madeleine Albright and Colin Powell; two secretaries of defense—William Cohen and Donald Rumsfeld; CIA director George Tenet, who had served in both the Clinton and Bush administrations; Richard Clarke, the counterterrorism "czar" who had served in both administrations, and the national security advisers to Clinton and Bush, Samuel Berger and Condoleezza Rice, respectively.

All would be present and accounted for except Condoleezza Rice. Three days after the commission sent the formal invitation requesting Rice's presence in public and, like the other witnesses, under oath, Alberto Gonzales responded that the White House refused to make Rice available, citing claims of executive privilege.

After much negotiating, we were given the opportunity to question Rice in private on February 7. Unlike other witnesses, the White House conditioned our access to Rice on the stipulation that she would not be placed under oath, no verbatim transcript of the interview would be made, and we would not seek to have her testify in public. In accepting two of these terms, we made it clear that we would not give up the option to request that Rice testify under oath and in public. Tom, Lee, John Lehman, Tim Roemer, and I sat across the conference table from Rice and three White House aides in the surprisingly cramped White House Situation Room. Unlike Hollywood's depiction of the president's crisis management center in films such as *Dr. Strangelove,* with huge video display screens and a gigantic conference table, the Situation Room is actually a small, unpretentious room in the subbasement of the White House that could barely accommodate the thirteen people in attendance. Sitting behind us on straight-backed chairs were four of our staff who had worked up background materials for the questioning. Chris Kojm had principal note-taking responsibility, while our counsel, Dan Marcus, and Mike Hurley also participated in the questioning. Phil Zelikow had successfully lobbied Tom and Lee to attend, although he was recused from directly participating in Rice's questioning by reason of his longtime professional relationship with her, inside and outside government. Our executive director's connections to the Bush national security adviser had provided continuing grounds for concern expressed by the families and the media. For his part, Zelikow proved to be less than meticulous about managing the optics and of distancing himself from Rice.

Condoleezza Rice's personal story is an extraordinary reaffirmation of the unique greatness of America as the land of opportunity. Born in the rural deep South and raised by her aunts, Rice was only three generations distant from the cruel bonds of slavery that gripped her ancestors since their arrival on these shores. Yet, through incredible determination, brains, and talent, she had risen from her humble beginnings to distinction, first in academia and then in government, as one of America's most prominent individuals, regardless of race or sex. In addition, Rice was an accomplished pianist and an outstanding athlete. Indeed, it was said that her ability to talk sports with, the president helped cement a strong personal bond between the two.

It was my first meeting with Condoleezza Rice. A ready smile and warm, gracious demeanor accompanied her articulate and self-assured recitation of the facts.

For four hours we went through a wide variety of subjects, from the transition of Bush taking office after the tumult of the 2000 election through the nine months prior to the attacks of 9/11. Although the Bush administration was soon to go on full-throated attack against its former counterterrorism czar, Dick Clarke, Rice was unfailingly complimentary about Clarke's dedication and competence. "Dick did a terrific job for me," she repeated. Her answers did not contradict the factual assertions Clarke had laid out in more than fifteen hours of interviews with commissioners and staff, but rather were interpreted by her in a way far less damaging to the Bush administration than what we were hearing from Clarke. We covered key issues of Bush's prioritization of efforts against al Qaeda, response to the October 2000 al Qaeda attack on the USS *Cole* in Yemen, the development and use of the Predator drone aircraft to hunt for Osama bin Laden in Afghanistan, the use of the Northern Alliance tribal leaders—particularly the charismatic warlord Ahmed Massoud to capture or kill bin Laden—and her role and that of President

Bush during the "summer of threat" leading up to 9/11. Clearly, Rice had a different interpretation of the role of national security adviser than her predecessor, Sandy Berger, as it related to protecting against terrorist attacks within the United States. Whereas Berger was intimately involved in coordinating the efforts of the FBI and Department of Justice and other federal agencies charged with domestic security during the heightened millennium threat environment, Rice did not believe her portfolio included coordinating the efforts of these agencies. Yet the high-level meetings of the NSC Principals Committee during the Clinton administration was credited with facilitating the sharing of information among the law enforcement and intelligence agencies that led to full exploitation of intelligence and leads from the thwarted plot to bomb Los Angeles International Airport. The Principals Committee was the senior interagency forum for consideration of national security matters. The secretaries of state, defense, and treasury were permanent members.

One of the principal questions I thought needed to be answered was why the United States had not responded to the suicide attack on the USS *Cole*. The more I learned about that subject, the more mystified I became about why Bush had not retaliated once it was determined that al Qaeda was responsible. Rice stated that no formal decision was ever made to put off an answer to the *Cole* but that Bush did not want to launch a "tit-for-tat" response against al Qaeda for the *Cole*.

She did not share Richard Clarke's view of his role in the Bush administration as a demotion from the counterterrorism role he had played for Clinton, nor did she recall that Clarke had made an urgent request to brief the new president directly on terrorism and the al Qaeda threat. Rice acknowledged that she had disagreed with Clarke's strong recommendation to fully fund Ahmed Massoud in an effort to kill or capture bin Laden. And she disagreed with Clarke's interpretation on the government dragging its feet on utilizing Predator drone surveillance to coordinate a missile attack on bin Laden and his lieutenants, and on arming the Predator with missile capability to launch an immediate attack if the drone spotted bin Laden.

Rice acknowledged that she had "misspoken" in regard to her famous statement in the immediate aftermath of 9/11 that "no one could have imagined" planes being used as missiles. Indeed, since Italian authorities concerned about planes being used as missiles in the airspace around Genoa had installed antiaircraft batteries during the G8 conference in the summer of 2001—an event with which Rice was intimately familiar—why had she not drawn the connection? She simply hadn't made the "leap of imagination," she said. Faced with an abundance of evidence that suicide attacks had not only been contemplated, but had been the subject of exercises coordinated by the military for years before 9/11, Rice stated that she should have said that "*I*" couldn't have imagined such a tactic. Yet neither Rice nor anyone in the administration had publicly made such a clarification.

I was particularly interested in the state of Rice's interest in and awareness of the potential for a domestic terrorist attack. She stated that she did not know what basis Dick Clarke had for believing that al Qaeda had sleeper cells in the United States but acknowledged that she knew the FBI had been actively seeking out al Qaeda members before 9/11. The administration had nothing other than "a pretty vague sense that al Qaeda might strike at home." Although we had not yet seen the August 6, 2001, PDB, we asked Rice about it. The issue of President Bush's knowledge of and personal involvement in dealing with the potential for a domestic terrorist attack was key to our investigation. Rice told us that Bush was very engaged and "interactive" during his CIA briefing sessions. On one occasion, during the period of intense reporting about al Qaeda in the gulf, the president asked "what al Qaeda could do in the United States." That led, according to Rice, to the August 6 PDB, "which was not current information in any way." The PDB made "a general mention of hijackings," she added.

We covered a substantial number of other subjects during our four hours with Rice. As one of the last items, dealing with events on 9/11 itself, we asked her about the alleged threat to Air Force One given as a reason to convince Bush not to return directly to Washington. Rice told us that in the days after 9/11 she learned "the threat might have been a garble," although she never heard "definitively." This was remarkable, given the fact that the phantom threat to the president's plane had been investigated and dismissed within twenty-four hours of the attack.

Clearly, there was a wide gulf between Dick Clarke's and Condoleezza Rice's interpretations of events during the seven months before the 9/11 attacks. I felt the American public ought to hear both versions in public sworn testimony—and that the commission had an obligation to make it happen. Clarke, who had resigned his position, had agreed to testify in public. After I reviewed Jamie Gorelick's verbatim notes of what was contained in the August 6 PDB, my resolve to fight for Rice's public testimony was dramatically heightened.

Meanwhile, another test of wills regarding commission access—this time to George Bush and Dick Cheney—was playing out. The president had offered to meet with Tom Kean and Lee Hamilton for fifteen minutes as a "courtesy" to the 9/11 Commission. It was absurd to think that the commission charged with investigating 9/11 could adequately perform its duties without an in-depth interview with the man responsible for safeguarding the nation—and I said so. As time passed, the offer of a "meeting" (not an interview) with the president became more expansive with regard to the amount of time allowed, but the president was adamant that his audience would be limited to our chair and vice chair. Unlike the compromise I had supported with regard to a subcommittee reviewing the PDBs and reporting back to the other commissioners, I argued that it was critical to the integrity of the process that *all* commissioners be allowed to attend and ask questions. And while Tom and Lee seemed disposed to accept the White House proposal, the other commissioners didn't want to be left out. Of course, there was no question that I was the commissioner whom the president was least likely to want asking him questions. Former President Clinton and Vice President Gore had already accepted our invitation for interviews without restrictions as to time or transcription. I reasoned that once it became public knowledge that Clinton and Gore had agreed to unconditional interviews, the pressure on Bush to meet with all ten commissioners would increase substantially. Tom and Lee agreed to wait. I had no doubt that my analysis was conveyed back to the White House.

AS MARCH 23, 2004, the first day of the scheduled two-day hearing, approached, I felt confident that we were prepared to provide the transparency that became a hallmark of the 9/11 Commission's legacy. In what other country in the world would its highest and most powerful officials be called upon in public to account for their actions while in office? This would be a dramatic demonstration of the strength of our democracy. Americans and others throughout the world would be able to judge the credibility of sworn answers to pointed questions—unfiltered by news media, if they chose to watch the live or recorded coverage—and make up their minds as to what had gone wrong and who, if anyone, bore responsibility.

Then came the report that Dick Clarke, certain to be the most explosive and controversial witness, had moved up the publication date of a book to coincide with his appearance before the committee. I had sat in on two of the three day-long interviews the staff had conducted of Clarke earlier in the year. White haired and somewhat taciturn, Clarke was a fount of information. He impressed me as being all business, with extraordinary recall of facts spanning decades of service in Republican and Democratic administrations as a counterterrorism expert since the Reagan presidency. His face set in what appeared to be a perpetual grimace, as though it pained him to go through it all again, Clarke was no warm and fuzzy personality. He had the reputation of someone who didn't suffer fools, and as one who was prepared to "break a lot of china" to get what he wanted. He looked the part. Not only did Clarke's book, *Against All Enemies,* recount his criticism of the Bush administration—literally in chapter and verse—for being inattentive to the pre-9/11 threat posed by al Qaeda, Clarke went on to blast Bush for diverting precious resources from the post-9/11 battle to defeat al Qaeda by invading Iraq. Clarke's thesis was that not only had Bush failed to provide the type of leadership that might have prevented 9/11 but also that the invasion of Iraq was a blunder that would actually make us less safe in the long run.

Clarke gave an exclusive interview to *60 Minutes* the Sunday before our hearing, producing headlines here and around the world. The White House was incandescent with outrage.

Meanwhile, White House counsel Gonzales reasserted the administration's refusal to make Rice available for this hearing. Instead, he proposed that we allow Deputy Secretary of State Richard Armitage to testify in her place. This was preposterous. Armitage would already be available to answer questions on the first day of the hearing, as he was scheduled to accompany his boss, Colin Powell. Armitage's responsibilities and knowledge of events were altogether different from Rice's. The White House gambit would thwart us from giving additional time to Clarke on the second day to fill the void left by Rice's absence. Over objections from Roemer, Gorelick, and me, Tom and Lee granted the White House request to schedule Armitage.

Day one started calmly enough, with former Clinton secretary of state Madeleine Albright testifying that the Clinton administration did not shirk from pursuing Osama bin Laden to the full extent possible, given the paucity of CIA intelligence on his whereabouts. Powell, accompanied by Armitage, followed Albright. I have always liked Powell. Like many Americans, I believe that Bush took advantage of Powell's loyalty and badly used this dedicated public servant to supply credibility for his grossly flawed Iraq policy. Powell suffered Bush's misuse of him without public complaint or recrimination. While Powell's service did much to bolster Bush politically, could anyone imagine Powell selecting Bush for a cabinet position if Powell were president instead of Bush?

True to form, Powell was solid and unwavering in his defense of the

Bush administration's actions in combating al Qaeda. He was also unsparing in his praise for Madeleine Albright and the briefing and continued support the outgoing secretary of state had provided on the issue of terrorism.

When it became my turn to question, I chose to direct my first comments to Richard Armitage, previewing my disagreement with the White House idea that he would provide an adequate substitute for Condoleezza Rice.

> Secretary Armitage, the administration has asked that you be allowed to testify tomorrow in place of Condoleezza Rice. No one could suggest that her role is not central to our inquiry and that her knowledge is different from yours, as she was a direct liaison between the president and the CIA and the FBI on issues directly relevant to our inquiry. That is why the commission unanimously requested that Dr. Rice appear.
>
> The only reason the administration has advanced for refusing to make Dr. Rice available is a separation-of-powers argument: that presidential advisers ought not have to appear before the Congress. I would call to your attention a report by the Congressional Research Service dated April 5th, 2002, well before the controversy arose about Dr. Rice's appearance. In that report, there are many precedents involving presidential advisers. Lloyd Cutler, counsel to President Carter, testified, came up to Congress to answer questions. Zbigniew Brzezinski, assistant to the president for national security affairs, appeared in 1980. Sandy Berger appeared as a deputy assistant to the president for national security in May of 1994 and again in his function as national security adviser in September of 1997. John Podesta, chief of staff to President Clinton, and several others in the Clinton administration have appeared before congressional committees.
>
> So I would ask, Mr. Armitage, without any disparagement of your service or of your knowledge, that when you leave here today you advise the administration of this report. I've got an extra copy for you to take with you. [Laughter] And we ask again, in all seriousness, that Dr. Rice appear. [Applause]

There was no question for the affable deputy secretary of state to answer, just another public shot across the bow to the White House.

I had only ten minutes allocated to me for questions (and answers). The math was daunting. In addition to the witness's opening statement, which we asked to be limited to ten minutes, allowing each commissioner one round of ten minutes added up to 110 minutes. We agreed that there would be "lead" commissioners for each witness, who would get an additional five minutes. During the hearing we could ask our chairman for leave to ask a follow-up question or two after all commissioners had their turn. Usually, Tom was obliging. We made no real effort to coordinate the subject matter of our questioning. It was not the most efficient system, but it seemed to work well enough.

I chose to question Colin Powell on the move by Rumsfeld and Wolfowitz to use 9/11 as a pretext to invade Iraq in the immediate aftermath of the attack. Utilizing our earlier interview of the secretary, I asked Powell a highly leading question:

> BEN-VENISTE: On January 21, you advised us of a full-day meeting on Saturday, September 15th, in which the issue of striking Iraq was discussed. You advised us that the Deputy Secretary of Defense [Wolfowitz] advanced the argument that Iraq was the source of the problem, and that the United States should launch an attack on Iraq forthwith. You advised us that Secretary Wolfowitz was unable to justify that position.
>
> Have I accurately described your recollection of what occurred?
>
> POWELL: There was a meeting of the National Security Council that Mr. Wolfowitz also attended on that day at Camp David, as you describe. There was a full day of discussions on the situation we found ourselves in, and who was responsible for it. And as part of that full day of discussion, Iraq was discussed, and Secretary Wolfowitz raised the issue of whether or not Iraq should be considered for action during this time. And after fully discussing all sides of the issue, as I think it is appropriate for such a group to do, the president made a tentative decision that afternoon . . . that we ought to focus on Afghanistan, because it was clear to us at that point that al Qaeda was responsible, the Taliban was harboring al Qaeda, and that that should be the objective of any action we were to take.

Powell went on to say that it was appropriate for the president to hear from all his advisers before making a decision. Nothing about Powell's personal opinion was included in his answer. So I tried again.

BEN-VENISTE: Is it not the case that Deputy Secretary Wolfowitz advocated for an attack on Iraq?

POWELL: He presented the case for Iraq, and whether or not it should be considered along with Afghanistan at this time. I can't recall whether he said instead of Afghanistan. We all knew that Afghanistan was where al Qaeda was.

BEN-VENISTE: But was there any concrete basis upon which that recommendation was founded in your view—to attack Iraq for 9/11?

POWELL: Secretary Wolfowitz was deeply concerned about Iraq being a source of terrorist activity. You will have a chance to talk to him directly about—

BEN-VENISTE: I've asked for your view, with all due respect, Secretary Powell.

POWELL: With all due respect, I don't think I should characterize what Mr. Wolfowitz's views were.

BEN-VENISTE: No, I asked for your view. In your view ... was there a basis?

POWELL: My view was that we listen to all the arguments at Camp David that day. And Mr. Wolfowitz felt that Iraq should be considered as part of this problem having to do with program [sic], and he considered—he wanted us to consider whether or not it should be part of any military action that we were getting ready to take. We all heard the argument fully. We asked questions back and forth. And where the president came down was that Afghanistan was the place that we had to attack, because the world and the American people would not understand if we didn't go after the source of the 9/11 terrorists.

I was out of time. I had pressed Powell as far as I could and this was as far as he would go. He sidestepped expressing his personal views on Wolfowitz conflating the al Qaeda attack of 9/11 with Iraq. On the other hand, the facts were out there as to what Wolfowitz was up to at Camp David. The determination to strike Saddam was a decision that was simply seeking a justification. "Not yet," ruled the decider in chief.

I used my time with Secretary of Defense Donald Rumsfeld to explore the notion that suicide hijacking of commercial planes was some sort of surprise tactic that our intelligence community could not have envisioned prior to 9/11. Rumsfeld had provided an opening by echoing Rice's post-9/11 remark, stating that he knew of no intelligence in the period leading up to 9/11 that indicated terrorists would hijack commercial airliners and use them as missiles to fly into the Pentagon or the World Trade Center. I ran through a litany of plots dating back to 1994 by Algerian terrorists to fly a plane into the Eiffel Tower, al Qaeda's 1995 Bojinka plot, which included flying an explosive-laden plane into CIA headquarters, and a variety of other plots, including one to fly a plane into the World Trade Center. I concluded with a challenge to justify his statement: "It seems to me that a statement that we could not conceive of such a thing happening really does not reflect the state of our intelligence community as of 2001, sir." All the while I questioned his boss, Deputy Secretary Paul Wolfowitz, who sat next to Rumsfeld at the witness table, stared at me with a look of hatred in his eyes.

After some back-and-forth, in which he proclaimed my questions good but better directed to others with law enforcement responsibilities, Rumsfeld fell back on the same reasoning as Rice: "Well, I didn't say 'we' didn't know, I said 'I' didn't know."

I had come a long way in my personal journey to find the truth of why the terrorists succeeded on 9/11. In the aftermath of 9/11, I was, like most Americans, prepared to accept the "no one could have imagined" explanation. Now I knew differently. Indeed, beyond the plots I had ticked off to Rumsfeld, there were detailed memoranda produced by various government employees over the years who specifically contemplated a scenario much like the one that had occurred on 9/11. As the heads of the various cabinet departments and agencies pointed fingers at everyone but themselves, it occurred to me that anyone flipping through channels on late-night television would see Japanese kamikaze pilots slamming planes into U.S. naval vessels in the Pacific. For years, the ongoing Palestinian intifada showed the terrorist weapon of suicide bombers employed with deadly regularity against Israeli civilians. During the 1996 Olympics, Dick Clarke had stitched together a plan to protect against suicide air attack in Atlanta, putting the Secret Service in the lead. The same "Atlanta Rules" were apparently invoked in January 1997 to protect the Clinton inauguration ceremonies, in August 2000 to protect the Democratic and Republican conventions in New York and Philadelphia, and in January 2001 to protect the Bush inauguration. For God's sake, a small plane had crash-landed on the White House lawn in 1994! And, as George Bush and the American contingent to the G-8 summit well knew, the Italians had taken extraordinary precautions just months before 9/11 to protect Genoa against just such an attack from the air.

Added to the general awareness of such a terror tactic was the information during the late spring and summer of 2001 from all intelligence sources that al Qaeda was planning a spectacular attack. The CIA and FBI knew that at least two al Qaeda operatives were in the United States; the FBI knew in July 2001 from its alarmed Phoenix field office that an unusual number of foreign Muslim men were involved in commercial airliner training; the FBI and CIA knew in August that Zacarias Moussaoui, identified as a radical Muslim with jihadist ties, was apprehended in Minneapolis; the FBI agent who arrested Moussaoui had postulated a plot to fly a plane into the World Trade Center; the CIA, reporting to its director and top officials on the Moussaoui arrest, titled its briefing "Islamic Extremist Learns to Fly."

No one could have imagined? Well screw Paul Wolfowitz, his dirty looks, and the horse he rode in on.

Next up was George Tenet, whose tenure included four years as CIA director in the Clinton administration and three years (up to that point) under Bush. Tenet had neither come up through the ranks at CIA nor pursued a career in the military. Instead, he had been a longtime aide to David Boren, who had served as chairman of the Senate Select Committee on Intelligence. I first met George Tenet in connection with my service on the war crimes declassification project where the DCI had pledged the CIA's complete cooperation. I found Tenet extremely personable. He had an easygoing, informal manner that belied the constant pressures under which he worked. A six-footer with a stocky build, I usually found him at meetings at CIA headquarters in shirtsleeves with his tie loosened and top shirt button undone, chewing on a large, unlit cigar. The only other CIA director I had known was Richard Helms, whom I had occasion to meet during the Watergate investigation. Helms was slim and urbane, always immaculately dressed, his hair combed straight back à la Fred Astaire. For all their differences in style, the two shared a tendency to be economical with the facts when it came to answering questions about their boss, the president.

Jamie Gorelick took the lead with Tenet, quickly drawing the distinction between the way the Clinton administration had brought together the heads of all relevant departments and agencies during the period of the millennium threat and the Bush administration's laissez-faire pre-9/11 approach. Clinton ordered daily meetings and knocked heads to ensure first that the FBI and the other agencies knew what they had, and second that they all shared the information. Was this merely a difference in style, or were there tangible consequences? Stephen Hadley, Rice's deputy, told us he was surprised to learn of the daily meetings during the millennium. Perhaps if there had been an effort to "pulse" the FBI special agents in charge of its regional offices for suspicious information during the 2001 summer of threat, the dots from Phoenix and Minneapolis would have been connected with the search for Hazmi and Mihdhar.

Bob Kerrey followed Jamie, wondering again why, in August 2001, there was no effort to aggregate everything the FBI had collected to determine whether the attack everyone was anticipating might come in the United States. Kerrey brought up the subject of the August 6 PDB.

> KERREY: The President was worried enough that he asked you, according to our staff, about the possibility of domestic attack, and that produced the famous presidential daily brief of the 6th of August, 2001. And—you look confused . . .
>
> TENET: (off mike [conferring with his aides])
>
> KERREY: Pardon me.
>
> TENET: I don't think that's how it happened, but go ahead, sir. It doesn't—please. I didn't mean to interrupt.
>
> KERREY: Go ahead and correct me if it happened differently.
>
> TENET: I don't know if I can, but go ahead.

In fact, Kerrey's preface was based on staff notes of the earlier Rice interview, which he had not attended, rather than an interview of Tenet. The whole issue of the level of Bush's personal engagement on the issue of terrorism in his seven months in office before 9/11 was a key part of the entire puzzle. Was Bush at least concerned enough about the possibility of a terrorist attack in the United States to have posed a question to his director of Central Intelligence? It seemed clear to me that another piece of revisionism about our famously incurious president was unfolding. Tenet's puzzlement was understandable.

I was next at bat and followed up immediately on the August 6 PDB. I read from a memorandum provided us by CIA: " 'The author of [the August 6 PDB] and others familiar with it, say they have no information to suggest that this piece was written in response to a question from the President.' " I noted that it went on to say that the PDB was prompted by an idea from the CIA. Tenet's antennae were up. Was the agency getting into a dispute with the White House? Tenet said he "wanted to go back and look at this."

In my private meetings with Tenet, I had pressed the DCI for information regarding his briefings of the president while Bush was on a six-week vacation in Texas, starting in late July. The whole idea of a president taking a six-week vacation after only six months in office and in the midst of the highest terrorist threat reporting the nation had ever seen seemed incredible. But Bush claimed to be staying in touch while at his ranch in Crawford. What was the subject matter of their conversations between August 6 and September 11? Although I had not yet seen the document, I knew that the August 6 briefing dealt with potential terrorist threats within the United States. What was the follow-up? Moreover, Tenet had been briefed by his senior staff on the FBI's arrest of Zacarias Moussaoui. What had he done with that information? That was an FBI case, "not my table" was the essence of his response. Had he told Bush that a potential terrorist had been arrested trying to learn how to maneuver a 747? Tenet sat at a spacious conference table on the top floor of the Langley building that housed the executive suite. Flanked by aides, Tenet had a huge loose-leaf binder in front of him. He pleaded a failure of specific recollection and had lacked the time, he said, to go through these materials to respond to my question. He asked for more time. There was no question Tenet had his hands full, dealing with issues of immediate concern to the nation's security. It was also clear that I was getting the runaround.

I moved to the topic of the Clinton administration's efforts to combat al Qaeda. Tenet had already made it clear that Clinton had given the CIA every authority it had asked for. Controversy surrounded the Clinton "memorandum of notification" that authorized the CIA to use its proxies among the anti-Taliban tribals in Afghanistan to capture bin Laden, or to kill him, if capture was not feasible. This finding was so closely held at the CIA that some middle-level officers doubted its existence. Further, Republicans attacked the Clinton record in pursuing Osama bin Laden as being insufficiently robust. On the evidence I had seen, there was room for fair argument that more could have been done, and the capture-or-kill order could have been clearer.

On the other hand, the Republicans had scorned Clinton's unleashing of cruise missile attacks on bin Laden and the al Qaeda leadership as a "wag the dog" effort to deflect attention from the Clinton sex scandals that were consuming the media at the time. Wag the dog was a reference to the film of the same name, in which a U.S. president stages a fictitious invasion of Albania to deflect attention from domestic political troubles. Without getting into Clinton's various peccadilloes, it seemed to me that the president had displayed an extraordinary ability to compartmentalize his tabloid problems and focus on striking at al Qaeda.

Rumsfeld had denigrated the value of cruise missile attacks on al Qaeda positions as "bouncing the rubble." I asked whether Tenet believed that the August 1998 attack in which forty cruise missiles were unleashed, narrowly missing bin Laden and killing a number of his entourage, was "bouncing the rubble." No, Tenet saw the '98 attack as being predicated on specific intelligence that made it a worthwhile effort. Yet it was the absence of "actionable" intelligence that was responsible for the inability to nail bin Laden. Repeatedly, we heard that the lack of human intelligence, or "humint" in spookspeak, rather than a lack of will was responsible for our inability to locate and kill bin Laden.

I turned to an issue that spanned several administrations—the failure of the CIA to keep track of the mujahideen America had supported in the Afghan war against Soviet occupation in the 1980s. "What has continued to puzzle and trouble me, George, is this: Didn't the CIA, knowing the proclivities and the extreme xenophobia of these jihadists, whom the CIA had helped to arm and train—why didn't the CIA seek to penetrate these organizations and keep close track of them in the years that followed the disbanding of the effort in Afghanistan?"

Tenet acknowledged that after "we drove the Russians out," essentially the United States left Afghanistan. He noted that Afghans who had been supported by the CIA in the Soviet campaign were on both sides of the current war. But that didn't answer the question about tracking the foreign jihadists, including bin Laden, who had fought the Russians, so I tried again.

"Given the fact that these were people trained in lethal modalities who hated the idea of foreign troops in Muslim countries, which was the basis of their attempt to throw the Russians out, don't you think you could have been more effective following up on some of these people, including Osama bin Laden?" Tenet acknowledged that the CIA did not keep track of those jihadists, many of whom showed up in other conflicts around the world. As to bin Laden, Tenet's answer was, "We didn't train him."

The prelude to the main event, Clarke, was Sandy Berger, Clinton's national security adviser. He echoed Tenet's testimony that Clinton gave the CIA the authority it needed to kill bin Laden. Berger provided a solid defense of the Clinton administration's attention to the looming threat of al Qaeda.

As far as I could tell, Berger performed admirably during his four years in the Clinton administration. That made it all the more astonishing when it was revealed that he had purloined and then destroyed copies of classified documents maintained by the National Archives. Apparently, Berger had snuck the documents out of the archives by hiding them in his clothing in the course of his review in preparation for testimony before the commission. Even more bizarre, he had destroyed at least some of them, even though they were copies. We were assured that no originals were destroyed and that we had access to all of the documents Berger had reviewed. We were told by Alberto Gonzales that because Berger was under active investigation by the FBI, we should not publicly disclose what we knew. Ultimately, Berger was disgraced by pleading to a misdemeanor, paying a $50,000 fine, and being disbarred from the practice of law. A brilliant career had self-destructed—and for what? Copies of documents that were unremarkable.

The spotlight turned to the much-anticipated testimony of Richard Clarke. He began with the shortest opening statement by any of the major witnesses. It was also the most powerful. Clarke stunned the packed hearing room in the Senate Hart Office Building with an abject apology.

> I welcome these hearings because of the opportunity that they provide to the American people to better understand why the tragedy of 9/11 happened, and what we must do to prevent a reoccurrence. I also welcome the hearings because it is finally a forum where I can apologize to the loved ones of the victims of 9/11. To them who are here in the room, to those who are watching on television, your government failed you; those entrusted with protecting you failed you, and I failed you. We tried hard, but that doesn't matter because we failed. And for that failure, I would ask, once all the facts are out, for your understanding and for your forgiveness.
>
> With that, Mr. Chairman, I'll be glad to take your questions.

The audience burst into spontaneous applause, led by the family representatives. Two and a half years had gone by since the tragedy of 9/11. Amid all the finger-pointing and recriminations, not a single government official, past or present, had stepped forward with an apology. Clarke's sincerity and courage resonated with hard-bitten journalists and ordinary Americans alike. I was pretty damn impressed.

Tim Roemer took the lead in questioning Clarke, homing in on the change in focus after the Bush team took over. Clarke had made a written plea to Rice, his new boss, to immediately convene a meeting of the NSC Principals Committee to review al Qaeda, to increase aid to the Northern Alliance of anti-Taliban tribal leaders, to increase the budget to fight al Qaeda, and to retaliate for the attack on the *Cole* by bombing the Taliban's infrastructure.

The response to Clarke's proposal was to demote him, and to have his counterterrorism security group report to the Deputies Committee rather than to the principals. The Deputies Committee lacked the authority to green-light Clarke's plan, and so it languished until September 2001. Clarke was blunt in describing the "Alphonse and Gaston" routine engaged in by the CIA and Department of Defense regarding who would pay for the newly developed Predator reconnaissance drone if one or more were shot down, and who would "pull the trigger" if an armed version was deployed. Clarke found this dithering unconscionable and potentially costing us the opportunity to nail bin Laden. He recounted three occasions when the unarmed Predator relayed real-time photographs of bin Laden, yet there was no coordination of the Predator with cruise missiles to take advantage of this "actionable intelligence." Clarke saw delays in arming the Predator with Hellfire missiles and squabbling between the CIA and DOD causing further delays because neither agency wanted the responsibility for firing missiles from the armed drone. Clarke's urgent request to brief Bush directly on counterterrorism became mired in bureaucratic red tape.

"My view was that this Administration, while it listened to me, either didn't believe me that there was an urgent problem or was unprepared to act as though there was an urgent problem," Clarke testified. Finally, in frustration, Clarke asked to be relieved of his counterterrorism responsibilities. On September 4, 2001, a week before the attacks, he wrote to Rice summarizing his frustrations. He urged policy makers to imagine a day after a terrorist attack, "with hundreds of Americans dead at home and abroad, and ask what might they have done earlier." Would that it had been hundreds instead of thousands.

When my turn came, I expressed my appreciation for Clarke's public apology, noting that he was the only official to have done so. Again, the audience gave him a well-deserved round of applause. I wanted to explore the question of why so little attention was paid to the possibility that the unprecedented threat level leading to the anticipated "spectacular" attack—so worrisome that Tenet was described as having his "hair on fire" during the summer—might be directed to the U.S. homeland. The World Trade Center had been bombed before by Muslim extremists; a plot by an al Qaeda operative to detonate a bomb at Los Angeles International Airport had been thwarted, leading to the roll up of al Qaeda sleeper cells in Brooklyn and Boston. Why wasn't more thought given to the possibility that the attack "might well take place in the United States"?

Incredibly, Clarke had not been informed by the FBI that two al Qaeda operatives who had been identified as having attended a planning meeting in Kuala Lumpur were in the United States. This despite Clarke's admonition that all unusual activities be reported to him. "For them to have this information somewhere in the FBI and not told me I still find absolutely incomprehensible." Clarke testified that had he received such information, he would have had their pictures in newspapers and on television programs like *America's Most Wanted*. This struck me as one of the most commonsense of the missed opportunities. The likelihood was good that someone would have reported seeing Hazmi and al Mihdhar, who were using their own names. Given what we knew about al Qaeda's aversion to risk in carrying out its terror attacks, the mere publication of the hunt for these men might have delayed the 9/11 attack, giving our law enforcement and intelligence agencies further time to utilize the clues they already had collected.

Following this line, I asked Clarke whether he had been informed of the arrest of Zacarias Moussaoui in Minneapolis. Again, Clarke was kept in the dark.

It had become more and more clear to me that had the president and his national security adviser forced the agencies—particularly the CIA and FBI—to sit down together in the same way Clinton's team had done well ahead of time during the millennium crisis to make contingency plans, they might have been able to connect the dots. Acting on Jordanian intelligence in late 1999 that a series of terrorist actions against the United States had been planned, high-level meetings were held almost daily, and the FBI and CIA were pushed to share information. Yet during August 2001, President Bush was busy clearing brush at his ranch in Crawford (just let brush try to attack the homeland), and had no direct contact with his attorney general or FBI director. Why wasn't the millennium model used by Bush to exert equivalent pressure on the FBI and CIA in the summer of 2001 to sit at the same table and share information?

Meanwhile, Clarke was about to feel the ire of three Republican commission members. First was Jim Thompson, a former Chicago prosecutor who was no slouch in cross-examining witnesses. At six six, even while seated "Big Jim" could be intimidating. Rupert Murdoch's Fox News, the unabashed cheerleader for America's right wing, had obligingly released the transcript of a "backgrounder" Clarke had given in August 2002. Such anonymous high-level administration source press briefings are common in Washington as a way for an administration to feed information to the media. By agreement, the identity of the briefer is kept confidential. Clearly, Clarke had emphasized the positive and minimized the negative as a loyal member of the Bush administration in that press briefing. This would be red meat for any trial lawyer worth his salt. Thompson began succinctly.

"Mr. Clarke, as we sit here this afternoon, we have your book and we have your press briefing of August 2002. Which is true?"

Clarke didn't flinch. He explained that he had been asked by the senior poobahs in the administration to try to counter the criticism in a recent *Time* magazine feature on the approaching first anniversary of 9/11. He had obliged. Thompson stopped short of calling Clarke a liar, but just barely.

John Lehman adopted a different approach. He started out by recalling his service with Clarke some twenty-eight years before and confiding that he had been a "fan" of Clarke's ever since. He complimented Clarke on his marketing skills, professing himself envious of seeing no less a luminary than Jim Thompson holding his book up in front of the two dozen clicking cameras and live television. He then zeroed in, accusing Clarke of a "real credibility problem" that Lehman hoped Clarke would clarify as being the product of an overzealous book publisher rather than the poor judgment of his old and admired friend. While Thompson had chosen the battle-ax, Lehman had selected the stiletto as his weapon of choice.

Clarke proved entirely capable of defending himself. He began by thanking his old friend for his admiration, noting that he had worked in three Republican administrations and was a registered Republican voter. He then shot down the accusation put forward by the White House that he was auditioning for a cabinet position, if the Democrats took the White House in the upcoming election, by proclaiming that he would not accept any such position were it offered. And, going to the heart of the criticism for his alleged flip-flopping, Clarke explained, "The reason I am strident in my criticism of the President of the United States is because by invading Iraq—something I was not asked about by the Commission, but something I chose to write about a lot in the book—by invading Iraq, the President of the United States has greatly undermined the war on terrorism."

The usually spontaneous Lehman had no retort.

The last of the three amigos was Fred Fielding, the amiable spear-carrier for the administration. Fielding focused on Clarke's testimony before the joint inquiry of Congress, asking why he hadn't expressed his deep concerns about "the lack of ability and urgency within the Bush administration." Clarke pointed out that he had provided a factual account entirely consistent with his later testimony—but, as still a member of the administration, he chose not to characterize the implication of those facts. It was true. There was no inconsistency in Clarke's recitation of the facts. But freed of the bonds of membership in the administration, and incensed by the implications of the Iraq invasion, Clarke was now drawing conclusions from those facts. The normally articulate Fielding seemed to fumble his parting shot: "I understand that, but I also understand, you know, the integrity with which you have to take your job."

We had time for a second round of questioning. Tim Roemer went through a number of issues, praising Clarke's candor and cooperation with the joint inquiry, of which Tim had been a member. When it came around to my turn, I noted that I had not seen any substantial differences in what Clarke said in his book and what was contained in his sworn testimony. I then offered to "cede my remaining time to Congressman Roemer if he'll give me his time with Condoleezza Rice," provoking a big laugh from the audience.

Slade Gorton, as usual, played it straight. He asked Clarke whether there was any basis for Clarke to recommend a military response to any provocation during the period from January to September when George W. Bush held the reins of power. Clarke returned to the *Cole* bombing, noting that the CIA had identified it as an al Qaeda operation by January. He had urged that we retaliate for the *Cole* by bombing the hell out of bin Laden's Taliban protectors in Kabul.

It seemed to me that this might have sent Mullah Omar and the Taliban leadership the message that their continued support and succor for al Qaeda would have some nasty consequences. Might a punishing cruise missile attack on the Taliban have resulted in their leadership telling bin Laden to forgo further attacks on U.S. interests? Might this have caused him to pull the plug on the 9/11 plot? Clarke's response was to have a significant impact on my assessment. "Unfortunately, there was no interest, no acceptance of that proposition, and I was told on a couple of occasions that, you know, that [the *Cole*] happened on the Clinton Administration's watch. I didn't think it made any difference. I thought the Bush Administration, now that it had the CIA saying it was al Qaeda, should have responded."

From my perspective, there was nothing developed in these examinations that detracted from the facts testified to by Richard Clarke. Indeed, the pro-administration witnesses credited Clarke's account of the facts. And the attack launched against Clarke's character—for providing his candid appraisal of what went wrong, and why he believed President Bush and his cabinet secretaries were insufficiently motivated to take the al Qaeda threat as seriously as he did—clearly backfired.

The evening of Clarke's testimony, reports circulated that the White House had fed questions to Jim Thompson and Fred Fielding in order to impugn Dick Clarke's credibility. To my knowledge, Jim and Fred never denied this. Critics assailed what appeared to be a coordinated effort among Fox News, the White House, and two Republican commissioners. But I expressed no criticism. Indeed, my public statements reflected my view that these witnesses should be subject to tough questioning to make sure that the truth came out. If the White House wanted to send its questions in this fashion, it was fine with me. Let it all hang out. Clarke had maintained his composure throughout. While the interjection of Clarke's criticism of the Iraq war policy was a tangent from the commission's focus on 9/11, Clarke's recitation of the facts fully supported his interpretation of the missed opportunities pre-9/11. And history will show that he was also spot-on regarding Iraq.

The most anticlimactic moment in all the hearings came with Richard Armitage's appearance following Clarke. The White House was on the horns of a dilemma of its own making. On the one hand, Bush's heels were dug in on his refusal to permit Rice's testimony, while on the other, the White House did not want its critics to utilize the vacuum created by Rice's "empty chair" by affording Clarke the opportunity to continue through the end of the day. So it filled the vacuum with Armitage, even though the deputy secretary of state had just appeared the day before alongside Colin Powell. That Tom and Lee accommodated the White House ploy was of a piece with their never-ending efforts to appear evenhanded.

At the same time that the White House was refusing to allow us to question Rice publicly, she was writing editorials and appearing on all manner of television programs to defend the Bush administration against the mounting criticism stimulated by Clarke's testimony.

I was the first to question Richard Armitage. He had the reputation of being a genial straight shooter, intensely loyal to his boss and best friend, Colin Powell. Armitage was also a good 250 pounds of muscle, devoted to a regimen of weight lifting.

I began by thanking Armitage for his service to the country and made clear that the comments I was about to make were not meant as any personal criticism. I may be brash, but I'm not entirely stupid.

"You are here because the Administration asked you to come here," I began. "We asked for Dr. Rice. The State Department was one of several line agencies that the White House staff coordinated. The NSC is the lead on coordinating and implementing counter-terrorism. The State Department was a spoke in the wheel. The NSC and Dr. Rice were the hub."

"In some respects," I continued, "I think you are in the position of Admiral Stockdale, who in 1992 said 'why am I here?'" The reference to the opening remarks of the seemingly puzzled vice presidential running mate of third-party candidate Ross Perot was not lost on the politically savvy Washington audience, or on Rich Armitage. I was starting to have a little fun.

Armitage responded, "The 13th Amendment applies to me as well as it does to all my colleagues. And I'm under no force to be here. They did request me." The wheels turning in my head were so pronounced they were probably visible. His colleagues? Rice? Whose ancestors were in fact the direct beneficiaries of the Thirteenth Amendment, abolishing slavery? I wouldn't go near this with a ten-foot pole.

Enough banter. I would home in on why substituting Armitage for Rice would not fly. In a series of staccato questions, I established that Armitage was not even cleared for classified briefings on counterintelligence until three months into the new administration; that he was unable to answer why Rice did not discuss the issue of al Qaeda sleeper cells in the United States with Dick Clarke, why she stated that no one could have predicted that hijacked airplanes might be used as missiles, or what information she had received prior to 9/11 to "suggest that the United States [homeland] might be a target in this period of extraordinarily heightened threat during the summer of 2001." Armitage was obliged to answer no to all of these. I began referring to Armitage as Rice's doppelgänger and directed my questions to "Armitage/Rice." I wasn't finished.

I asked whether Armitage had taken note of what Rice had said in at least some of her television appearances in the prior week. When he replied that he had not, I inquired whether he owned a television set.

Indeed, Rice had been sent out to do all the Sunday morning programs, among other televised appearances, to counter Clarke's assertions. The willingness of the president's national security adviser to comment publicly on the very issues that we were exploring yet refuse to testify before the commission under oath played very poorly in the court of public opinion.

I commented later that Condoleezza Rice had appeared everywhere but at my local Starbucks. My observation made the point succinctly and was widely quoted. A Starbucks rep even sent me a certificate for a free cup of coffee.

Earlier during the hearing, I had asked staffer Raj De to do some research on the president's pubic statements about cooperating with the commission. I ended with the observation that given the precedent of other NSC advisers giving public testimony before Congress, the seriousness of our inquiry, and the commission's unanimous vote that Rice appear, it seemed inconsistent with the president's oft-stated commitment to "cooperate fully" with the commission for him to refuse to allow Rice to come before us.

That Phil Zelikow had a blind spot when it came to any criticism of Condoleezza Rice was fairly obvious. I learned after Rich Armitage's appearance just how petty our staff director could be. Lance Cole told me that Zelikow had confronted Raj De after he noticed Raj responding to my inquiry during the hearing. "You are not working for the DNC," Zelikow hissed at the young lawyer. Raj kept his cool, explaining what I had requested him to find for me and telling the overbearing staff director to take it up directly with me if he had a problem. I never heard another word about the incident.

The March hearing firmly established our credibility as a commission willing to put top officials under oath and ask penetrating questions. The pieces of the puzzle of what might have been done to prevent the 9/11 plot from reaching its deadly culmination were falling into place. Still missing were Condoleezza Rice and George W. Bush.

Following the hearing, the drumbeat for producing Rice increased steadily. Alberto Gonzales led the White House counterattack, disputing the precedents I had cited in the Congressional Research Service paper regarding NSC advisers giving public testimony. He offered another private meeting with Rice under the same limited conditions as before. No dice—we were standing firm.

I believed the White House was again overlawyering a situation that should have been resolved through common sense. Instead of making Rice available to testify along with the other top-level administration officials in a national inquiry of great importance in which her testimony would be key, the White House continued to refuse. This reinforced the justifiable impression that the administration had something important to hide and exposed the hypocrisy of Bush's claim of full cooperation with the commission.

I had seen Jamie Gorelick's verbatim notes of the August 6 PDB before the March hearing. Since the document, its contents, and specifically its title were classified above top secret, there was no way I or others on the commission could properly reveal its contents while questioning other witnesses. Now that I knew what was in the document, I was incensed that the warning it contained was far more direct and contemporary than Rice's characterization of it as some historical relic in her interview with us and in subsequent public statements. We could not fulfill our responsibilities without bringing this memo to the public's attention and exploring its implications. Something would have to give.

On March 30, a week after Clarke's testimony, the White House threw in the towel. Not only would Rice appear before the commission in a public hearing on April 8, but Bush and Cheney would meet with all ten commissioners at the White House to answer our questions. It was as near to a complete victory as we could have hoped.

As the most vocal and persistent advocate for Rice's public testimony, I surprised my colleagues on the commission two days after the White House capitulation with an e-mail: "I will not be able to attend the Rice hearing, as I am scheduled to be in a trial and the judge will not permit me to be absent." Everyone knew how much I was looking forward to being the lead questioner for Rice's testimony. But, as the commissioners and staff also knew, I had been shuttling back and forth between Philadelphia and Washington for several weeks in connection with a case I was then trying for Starwood Hotels. I could only imagine how quickly the news was transmitted to the folks at the White House and the reaction it might have provoked. An hour later, I sent another e-mail: "April Fool!"

———

I HAD ACCUMULATED A thick notebook of materials in preparation for questioning Condoleezza Rice. Perhaps it was a coincidence that the White House had offered her testimony for the morning of the same day that we were scheduled to question President Clinton. Perhaps pigs would fly. Because we had agreed to conduct the Clinton interview at 1 P.M. at a General Services Administration (GSA) secure location across town, we would be obliged to leave the Hart building not later than noon—thus ensuring that our opportunity to question Rice would be shoehorned into an artificially constricted two-hour window. Cute.

Since I had only fifteen minutes allocated for my questions and there was no possibility of a second round, I had to prioritize a dozen areas I would have liked to ask her about down to two or, at most, three. At a commission meeting the day before the hearing, Fred Fielding asked me what I was going to cover with Rice, "so that we wouldn't duplicate our efforts." Fred had never made such a request in all our prior hearings. I told him not to be too concerned about overlap, and that the August 6 PDB would probably come up.

John Lehman offered a helpful reminder of the old adage to be careful what you wish for because you just might get it. It was true, Condoleezza Rice was without question the most articulate and impressive advocate for the administration's case that the White House could have put forward. Which is why it made no political sense for Bush to have fought tooth and nail against it.

Because of the hullabaloo over getting Rice to appear, the media was in full-out frenzy on the day of the hearing. The networks were covering her testimony live. There were more photographers and correspondents in the hearing room than I had seen at any time before, including John Dean's Senate testimony in Watergate. Rice arrived with an entourage of a dozen aides, lawyers, and security trailing her. I preferred a show of power to Rice appearing by herself to face the big, bad ten-member commission that had pressed so relentlessly for her testimony. That night, the brilliant satirist Jon Stewart devoted his television program to Rice's testimony. Stewart scored the tape of Rice and company striding through the Senate corridor and entering the hearing room with the theme music from *Star Wars, dun, dun, dun, dun da dun, dun da dun.*

Condoleezza Rice raised her right hand to the unique sound of scores of cameras whirring and clicking away. Smartly dressed in a beige suit, she sat at the witness table alone, her minions filling the reserved row behind her. Almost all witnesses submit a prepared written statement that they then summarize in the ten minutes allotted for an opening statement. Rice, however, went on and on for what seemed like an eternity. Ordinarily, the chairman of a congressional committee asks a witness to wind up after straying beyond the red light that signals time is up. In Jon Stewart's send-up that night, he interrupted Rice's statement at the point she mentioned the sinking of the *Lusitania* in 1915 to interject, "That's when she brought out the diorama." Tom and Lee waited patiently for her to conclude. It occurred to me that the former university professor was fully capable of lecturing for the entire two hours without answering a single question. Finally, she finished reading her prepared statement. Although Tom and Lee rarely questioned the witnesses at our prior hearings, they made an exception in Rice's case.

Our chairman's first question was premised on the briefings Rice had received from the outgoing national security adviser, Sandy Berger, and Dick Clarke, the counterterrorism czar, to the effect that al Qaeda should be her number-one priority and that she would be spending more time on terrorism than anything else. Kean asked Rice about these briefings and whether she discussed them with her boss. Rice spoke for several minutes, but she never provided an answer as to whether she discussed the briefings with Bush. Tom then asked her whether prior to 9/11 she had seen or heard any mention of terrorists using planes as flying bombs. Rice acknowledged that while the intelligence community certainly had such reports, she personally had received no such briefing. For the first time in public, Rice amended her earlier statement that "*no one* could have imagined" planes being used, to "*I* could not have imagined." Interestingly, she acknowledged that within two days of making her statement, people came to her stating that the intelligence community had in fact looked at such information prior to 9/11. She did not explain why she had waited more than two years to correct her misstatement. Rice went on to volunteer that the August 6 PDB did not provide such a warning. This was the second reference to the still classified brief. In her opening remarks she had alluded to the August 6 PDB as being the product of President Bush's curiosity over whether the homeland was vulnerable to an al Qaeda attack. Obviously, the president was sensitive to the assertion that he had demonstrated little, if any, initiative or leadership in addressing the pre-9/11 threat.

Next, Tom Kean ventured into the very minefield Lee had so long cautioned us to avoid—Iraq. Calling Rice's attention to the Camp David meetings on the weekend after 9/11, Kean asked where "the Administration placed Iraq in the strategy for responding to the attack?"

Rice acknowledged that although Rumsfeld raised and Wolfowitz pressed the idea of attacking Iraq, none of the president's "principal advisors" advocated attacking Iraq immediately. But, Rice continued, contingency plans were ordered "should Iraq act against our interests" or "in case we find they were behind 9/11." An interesting answer, given the later justifications for the invasion.

Kean ended with a softball, asking whether Bush had pushed Clarke to twist the facts to find a link between Iraq and 9/11, or "was he just puzzled by what was behind this attack." Rice assured us that the president would never push anyone to twist the facts.

As Lee Hamilton took over the questioning, I reflected that this was a somewhat different Condoleezza Rice from the one we had seen in our private interview. Before, she had been straightforward in her responses. Now they seemed embellished and far more wordy.

Combined with her expansive opening statement, her long answers to Tom and now to Lee, it was obvious that Rice had been coached to chew up the clock. Her next answers to Lee's questions confirmed her strategy. John Lehman, sitting to my left, leaned back in his chair. I leaned forward to catch the eye of Tim Roemer who was sitting next to John. Before I could say anything, Tim said, "She's filibustering." The White House knew we could not go over the time allotted and keep President Clinton waiting.

It was clear that the only way to get my questions answered was to take control. Most important in my mind was to correct the misstatement made repeatedly by Rice that the August 6 PDB was simply a historical recitation of bin Laden's interest in inflicting damage upon the United States. My reading of the document was that a prescient CIA analyst was attempting to get the president's attention by coupling the history of bin Laden's attempts to reach into the United States with terror plots with an *up-to-the-minute* account of potential al Qaeda sleeper cell activity consistent with preparing for a commercial airline hijacking. But how was I going to put the facts forward while the document was still classified?

To lead into the August 6 PDB, I recited the back-and-forth with George Tenet and his staff over the origin of the idea for a memo dealing with a possible attack on the homeland. I recited Clarke's testimony that from May to August during the elevated threat period there were repeated discussions of the possibility of a terrorist attack occurring at home. Then I referred to her acknowledgment in our prior interview that Clarke told her that there were al Qaeda cells in the United States.

> BEN-VENISTE: Did you tell the President at any time prior to August 6 of the existence of al Qaeda cells in the United States?

It seemed reasonable to know, since Clarke had been blocked from meeting face-to-face with the president, whether the national security adviser discussed with her boss the information she had learned from her counterterrorism guru.

She began with a signal for a long answer.

> RICE: First let me make certain—
> BEN-VENISTE: If you could just answer that question—
> RICE: Well, first—

BEN-VENISTE:—because I only have a very limited—

RICE: I understand, Commissioner, but it's important—

BEN-VENISTE: Did you tell the President?

Applause from the audience signaled that we weren't the only ones on to her game of running the clock. I looked over to Tom Kean. No help would be forthcoming from the chairman to keep the witness on track. I was on my own. Rice persisted, stating it was also important that she address the predicate statement I had made.

I pressed again. "Well, my only question to you is whether you told the President." Rice was undeterred. It took four paragraphs before she finally answered my first question. "I really don't remember, Commissioner, whether I discussed this with the President."

The wheels were turning in my mind about how I was going to deal with Rice's strategy. On the one hand, I had a lot of ground I wanted to cover. It seemed obvious to me that Rice had been coached to filibuster. With no judge or arbiter to limit her answers to the question asked, would it be perceived as rude for me to try to impose any limitation? If we had not been constrained to one round of questioning by squeezing Rice's testimony into the morning before the Clinton interview, I could have afforded to be more relaxed about the clock. I was pissed off enough about the continued mischaracterization of the still secret August 6 PDB as being strictly historical in nature to say to myself, "What the hell, go for it and take the consequences."

I thanked Rice for her answer. Incredibly, she took that as an invitation to continue talking.

RICE: I remember very well that the President was aware that there were issues inside the United States. He talked to people about this. But, I don't remember the al Qaeda cells as being something we were told we needed to do something about.

I could hardly believe my ears. The president, on a six-week vacation during the highest terrorist threat alert in modern history, knows there are al Qaeda cells operating in the United States and *needs to be told* that maybe presidential attention is warranted? No more Mr. Nice Guy for me.

BEN-VENISTE: Isn't it a fact, Dr. Rice, that the August 6 PDB warned against possible attacks in this country? And I ask you whether you recall the title of that PDB?

I was precluded from revealing the title. It seemed that all the fuss over the ground rules the White House had laid down that specified no disclosure of the titles of the PDBs was directed to this one explosive document. Rice could answer literally: yes, she recalled it; no, she didn't recall. A short, literal answer was not her style. She could refuse to touch the question, relying on the fact that the document was classified. This was the response I anticipated. Or she could reveal the title—a long shot.

> RICE: I believe the title was "Bin Laden Determined to Attack In-
>   side the United States." Now the PDB—
> BEN-VENISTE: Thank you.

Rice felt compelled to continue her answer.

> RICE: No, Mr. Ben-Veniste, you—
> BEN-VENISTE: I will get into the—
> RICE: I would like to finish my point here.
> BEN-VENISTE: I didn't know there was a point.

Was this over the top, rude? In hindsight, I should have restrained myself from making that comment.

> RICE: Given that you asked me whether or not it warned of at-
>   tacks—
> BEN-VENISTE: I asked you what the title was.

Both of us were right. But Rice ignored the word "possible" in my question and chose to respond as though I was suggesting the PDB warned of *specific* attacks.

> RICE: You said did it not warn of attacks? It did not warn of at-
>   tacks inside the United States. It was historical information
>   based on old reporting. There was no new threat information,
>   and it did not, in fact, warn of any coming attacks within the
>   United States.

I found Rice's answer only partially true and, for that reason, disingenuous. While the body of the one-and-a-quarter-page report dealt mostly with historical information about bin Laden's intentions to conduct terrorist attacks here, its intent was clearly to focus attention on *cur-

rent reporting consistent with an *imminent* attack within our borders. The last two paragraphs of the PDB, which I had in front of me as I questioned Rice, were critical to that conclusion.

> *FBI information since that time [1988 reports of bin Laden's intent to hijack a plane to force the release of Omar Abdul Rahman, the "blind sheikh"] indicates patterns of suspicious activity in this country consistent with preparations for hijackings or other types of attacks, including recent surveillance of federal buildings in New York.*
>
> *The FBI is conducting approximately 70 full field investigations throughout the U.S. that it considers bin Laden related. CIA and FBI are investigating a call to our embassy in the UAE in May saying a group of bin Laden supporters was in the U.S. planning attacks with explosives.*

Unfortunately, the CIA analysts who prepared the August 6 PDB had no information about the FBI's hunt for al Qaeda operatives (and eventual 9/11 hijackers) Hazmi and Mihdhar, then known to be in the United States. Nor was the FBI warning about flight schools known to the CIA analysts. Finally, the arrest of Zacarias Moussaoui was not to occur until the week after the PDB was delivered. But had President Bush convened his cabinet and required that the attorney general ensure that *all* suspicious activity consistent with a potential domestic hijacking be reported up the chain and shared, would not the prospect for interrupting the plot have been enhanced?

Yet, I could not read those classified paragraphs into the record. Instead, I recited for Rice the fact that by August 2001 the role of al Qaeda in the first bombing of the World Trade Center was known; that the plot to bomb Los Angeles International Airport was thwarted, resulting in the roll up of al Qaeda cells in Boston and Brooklyn; that a network of al Qaeda supporters was still active here and that a pattern of suspicious activity was noted, consistent with preparation for hijackings. Again, without revealing the contents of the PDB, I asked Rice whether she knew of such information as of August 6, 2001.

Clearly frustrated with the slippery slope she was on, Rice answered testily.

RICE: You have other questions that you want me to answer in—
as part of this sequence?

BEN-VENISTE: Well, did you not—you have indicated here that this was some historical document. And I am asking you whether it is not the case that you learned in the PDB memo of August 6th that the FBI was saying that it had information suggesting that preparations—not historically, but ongoing, along with these numerous full field investigations against al Qaeda cells—that preparations were being made consistent with hijackings within the United States?

RICE: What the August 6 PDB said—and perhaps I should read it to you—

Bingo! This was as good as it was going to get.

BEN-VENISTE: We would be happy to have it declassified in full at this time.

The reaction from the audience was immediate—Rice recognized that she had fallen into a trap.

But it was too late. Stating that the commission had had access to the PDB, Rice began to argue her position. But I kept my focus on the issue of classification. I pointed out that up until her testimony we were precluded from revealing even the title. I stated that if the administration were to declassify the document, "then others can make up their minds" about its meaning. With the disclosure of the title of the PDB, our camel's nose was firmly inside the tent. It was only a matter of time before the rest of the camel followed.

I then turned to the reaction the PDB evoked. I asked Rice if she would agree that there was nothing reassuring contained in the PDB.

"Certainly not," she responded. "There was nothing reassuring." She went on to say that there were no specifics relating to a time or date of an attack on New York or Washington contained in the PDB. Well, duh. If the specifics of the 9/11 attack were foretold and ignored, we would be dealing with something a little more robust than an investigating commission, like say, an impeachment inquiry. But I held my tongue.

I agreed that there were no specifics about the 9/11 attack. I then asked if it was correct that she was not with President Bush, who was vacationing at his ranch in Texas, when he received the PDB on August 6.

"That's correct," Rice replied, for the first time answering a question directly and succinctly.

I continued.

BEN-VENISTE: Now was the President alarmed in any way or motivated to take any action, such as meeting with the director of
the FBI, or meeting with the attorney general, as a result of
receiving the information contained in the PDB?

Rice began to stumble.

RICE: I want to repeat that when this document was presented, it
was presented as, yes, there were some *frightening* things—
and by the way I was not at Crawford, but the President and I
were in contact . . . The President was told this is historical
information—I'm told he was told this is historical information.

Without answering my question, Rice had said a lot. Moving beyond
the acknowledgment that there was nothing "reassuring" in the PDB,
Rice had characterized its contents as "frightening." And while she didn't
respond to the question of whether Bush was galvanized into some kind
of action, the simple truth was that he did not meet with the FBI or the
attorney general between August 6 and September 11. In fact, as we were
later to discover, Attorney General Ashcroft had told the acting director
of the FBI he was tired of hearing about terrorism.

What I didn't learn until 2006, when Pulitzer Prize–winning author
Ron Suskind published *The One Percent Doctrine*, was President Bush's
dismissive comment to the CIA officer who briefed him at his Crawford
Ranch on the possibility of an al Qaeda attack within the United States:
"All right, you've covered your ass now."

I finished my questioning of Rice with a summary of what had not
been done to connect the dots, asking whether in her opinion, with the
benefit of hindsight, if the president had asserted leadership to ensure the
CIA and FBI "pulsed" their agencies—"shaken the trees" as Richard Clarke
had put it—to make sure all relevant information reached the top, might
the plot have been interrupted? Rice was clear. "I do not believe it is a
good analysis to go back and assume that somehow maybe we would have
gotten lucky by, quote, shaking the trees."

Not even a teeny chance presidential leadership could have improved
our chances? Al Qaeda was lucky that none of its mistakes were exploited.
We were unlucky that our president felt it more important to clear brush
in Texas than give us a chance to get lucky by taking charge. "Not my table" was elevated to management policy of the nation.

As the other commissioners took their turns questioning Rice, I left my chair and began lobbying Tom and Lee and the others for the commission to take a public stand demanding that the president declassify the August 6 PDB and end the charade. Quite clearly, there was nothing in it that required continued secrecy, no clandestine methods of obtaining information or confidential sources.

Meanwhile, Fred Fielding had spent his fifteen minutes going over issues relating to institutional changes. Not a single question on the facts.

Bob Kerrey began by telling Rice that he wasn't going to pass up the opportunity to give the national security adviser his views on the conduct of the war in Iraq, which he had supported. The former Navy SEAL and member of the Senate Intelligence Committee told her that the result of continuing the same military strategy would be civil war. Further, our efforts would result in enhancing al Qaeda's ability to recruit jihadists to attack us. Kerrey has been proved right on both counts.

With Iraq off his chest, Kerrey turned to Rice's relationship with Philip Zelikow. Noting that this question had been bothering him since he was appointed to the commission, Kerrey wanted a clear answer on the record. Zelikow's prior connections to Rice and the Bush administration had rankled the families, who were vocal in expressing their concerns. Rice acknowledged that over the years she and Philip had worked closely as academics, and that Zelikow had been tasked by her during the transition "to help us think about the structure of Dick Clarke's operations."

No wonder Clarke, stung by his demotion in the new administration, had no love for Zelikow. Indeed, when Clarke agreed to make the galleys of his book available to us before publication, it was on condition that Zelikow be excluded from getting an advance copy. The issue of whether Philip's loyalty was tempered by a continuing relationship with Rice was bothersome, but little could be done about it. We were too far along, and Tom and Lee were too supportive of Philip for there to have been any likelihood of change. Being warned of Zelikow's relationships, we would need to ensure there were sufficient checks and balances in our procedures to avoid having our investigation's results marred by a conflict-of-interest charge.

I continued to learn more about Zelikow's interrelationships with the Bush administration as our work progressed and even after we had published our final report. One of the more startling revelations for me was Philip's authorship of a thirty-one-page memorandum, reportedly undertaken at Condoleezza Rice's request, that justified the concept of preemptive war. It was released by President Bush in September 2002 (without any indication of Zelikow's paternity) as "The National Security

Strategy of the United States" and provided the intellectual underpinning for the invasion of Iraq. This was different by an order of magnitude from Zelikow's earlier collaboration with Rice on a 1995 book about the reunification of Germany, or of his service on President Bush's Foreign Intelligence Advisory Board. Zelikow's authorship of the preemptive war memorandum gave facial credibility to later attacks on the commission's bona fides, including *New York Times* journalist Phil Shenon's mistaken conclusion that Zelikow had distorted our final report in favor of the Bush administration, contained in his 2008 book *The Commission: The Uncensored History of the 9/11 Investigation*. On balance, had I known about the preemption memo when Zelikow was being considered for executive director, I would have strongly objected to his being hired.

Next, Kerrey turned to a phrase Rice had used repeatedly to describe Bush's state of mind in planning to deal with al Qaeda: He was "tired of swatting flies." Since Bush had launched not a single attack against al Qaeda during his eight months in office, Kerrey wanted to know what had tuckered Bush out. "What fly had he swatted? How the hell could he be tired?" Kerrey definitely had a unique style. The Nebraskan focused on Bush's failure to retaliate for the *Cole* bombing, despite the muscular rhetoric of his campaign. "Why didn't we swat that fly?"

Rice launched into a long answer, making reference to a speech Kerrey had given years before, on her way to saying Bush was searching for a strategic answer rather than responding on a "tit-for-tat" basis. Bob Kerrey was getting more fired up. Was Rice suggesting they didn't respond to the *Cole* because of a speech Kerrey had made? The audience joined in the laughter. Kerrey noted the administration's refusal to admit it screwed up. "You obviously don't want to use the 'M' word here," an unsubtle reference to the Bush administration's refusal ever to admit mistakes. Rice shot back that she continued to believe that it would not have been a good thing to respond to the *Cole*.

As Kerrey pressed Rice on Richard Clarke's claim that he had presented Rice with a robust plan of action against al Qaeda that had languished in bureaucratic limbo, he lost patience with Rice's long answers. "Please don't filibuster me . . . It is not fair. I have been polite. I have been courteous. It is not fair to me."

Kerrey closed with the observation that everyone in Washington knew that the FBI and CIA didn't talk to each other. So given the fact that she knew al Qaeda cells were operating in the United States, why was there no follow-up to bring them together under White House leadership? Then, "in the spirit of further declassification," he read directly from the still classified August 6 PDB: "'The FBI indicates patterns of suspicious activity in the United States consistent with preparations for hijacking.'" The former senator was daring the president to come after him for publicly disclosing the content of a classified document—a felony. In addition to style, Kerrey had cojones.

Oddly, Rice's response focused on hardening aircraft cockpit doors against intrusion. "That would have made a difference. We weren't going to harden cockpits in the three months we had a threat spike." But, in fact, hardening cockpit doors was the first step taken in getting commercial airlines back into service after 9/11. Prohibiting carry-on knives and reconstituting a force of air marshals were other steps immediately taken. Pre-9/11, instituting these measures would have required executive leadership from a president engaged in understanding the potential threat and committed to action.

John Lehman used his time to take Condoleezza Rice through a number of things that were known by the intelligence community but that she acknowledged she didn't know. Lehman's point seemed to be that the Clinton administration was somehow responsible for not tutoring Rice adequately to get up to speed. This argument might have had some traction if the Bushies were not so disdainful about taking the Clinton officials up on their offers to spend time briefing the new crowd.

Tim Roemer had waited patiently for the opportunity to compare Dick Clarke's version of events with Rice's. Why wouldn't the president meet with Clarke? he asked. Rice began by praising Clarke as "a very, very fine counterintelligence expert" but claimed he never said he needed to brief the president. Wrong, said Roemer. According to Clarke, his request was denied. Rice couldn't remember such a request. Similarly, despite the "big, big threat," why didn't the cabinet officers convene as a Principals Committee? Roemer and Rice got into the August 6 PDB again, with Roemer asking whether the administration would simply declassify it so we could discuss its contents openly. Rice never answered that question, but pieces of the PDB were now being quoted in both questions and answers.

Rice's answer to Tim Roemer's question as to why nothing was done prior to August 6 was startling: "What we tried to do . . . was to have the domestic agencies and the FBI together to just *pulse* them and let them be on the alert."

Hang on. That was the very thing that was *not* done. In fact, only an hour earlier I had asked Rice why the president had not issued a directive to ensure that the FBI had "pulsed" the field offices to get all relevant information pushed up to the director. Now Rice was claiming that this is just what they did, even using the same term. But Roemer was on it, noting that no evidence of any such tasking existed.

Roemer too was put off by Rice's verbosity. "I'd appreciate it if you could be very concise here, so I can get to some more issues." Would Rice acknowledge any responsibility as national security adviser for the failure of the FBI and the domestic agencies to coordinate? Not a chance. No one had asked her for help. Again, "not my table."

Jim Thompson, the last commissioner to question Rice, could be relied upon to provide her with a soft landing. But her answer to Bob Kerrey's questions on the *Cole* did not sit well with Jim. At his invitation, Rice reiterated the reasons for not responding "tit for tat," this time adding a new reason: "We really thought the *Cole* incident was past." A moment of candor. The attack on the *Cole* had occurred on Clinton's watch, a month before the presidential election, a whole three months before Bush took the reins as the new commander in chief.

"What if, in March 2001, under your administration, al Qaeda had blown up another U.S. destroyer? What would you have done? And would that have been 'tit for tat'?" Thompson pressed.

Clearly taken aback, Rice admitted that she didn't know what they would have done. "Look, it can be debated whether or not one should have responded to the *Cole*," she added.

Despite the severe time limitation, we had at least touched on most of what I saw as the shortcomings of the Bush administration's pre-9/11 feckless attention to al Qaeda and the threat of a domestic terror attack. The public could make up its own mind. The warning more than a month before 9/11 of bin Laden's intention to attack us at home hung in the air. Before we concluded the hearing, Tom Kean made the public request I was seeking—that the White House declassify the PDB in full "because we feel it is important that the American people get a chance to see it."

We left quickly to keep our appointment with President Clinton. Clinton, with Sandy Berger at his side, put on a performance for which he was uniquely capable. He answered questions until there were no more. It seemed he would remain to put out the lights, if necessary. In the most riveting portion of his narrative, Clinton clarified how he came to give the order to the CIA for our tribal surrogates in Afghanistan to kill bin Laden after the missile attacks with the same purpose proved unsuccessful.

In what was news to me, Clinton told us that on at least three occasions he had used surrogates to warn the Taliban leaders that unless they heeded U.S. demands to expel bin Laden from Afghanistan, we would hold the Taliban responsible for any attack al Qaeda launched aainst U.S. interests. Why then had *he* not ordered an attack in response to the *Cole*? He would have, Clinton replied, but the CIA was unable to certify al Qaeda's responsibility for the *Cole* until after he had left office. The CIA had already confirmed that it had not reached such a conclusion until January 2001. I wished we had known about these warnings to the Taliban a few hours earlier, so we could have asked Condoleezza Rice about them. Might a missile attack on the Taliban in response to the *Cole*— consistent with Clinton's warning—have changed the equation for the Taliban's continued protection of bin Laden? Might they have ordered bin Laden to forgo further attacks against U.S. interests as a condition of remaining in Afghanistan? Now that President Bush had agreed to an interview, I resolved to ask him myself.

The reaction to Rice's disclosure of the August 6 PDB's title was nothing short of electrifying. The televised clip of that moment was shown repeatedly for days. The White House followed its usual MO regarding our request that they declassify the entire PDB. They refused. The stonewalling lasted all of two days before they caved in and made it public. Any doubts about the bona fides of the commission and its determination to get at the facts were erased, at least in most quarters of the country.

I knew I would catch hell from the right wing. It went from the ridiculous to the sublime. Of course, I was reviled by the usual suspects on talk radio for partisanship and grandstanding. A few nut jobs called my office with death threats. Perhaps the most ludicrous personal attacks focused on the suit I wore on the day of the hearing—a conservative charcoal gray, single breasted with a subtle chalk stripe. To the eyes of my critics, the pinstripes made me one of the crapshooters from *Guys and Dolls*. On the other hand, *Saturday Night Live* sent up a hilarious spoof of the questioning, complete with a very accurate reproduction of the hearing room.

The reaction from the White House was predictable outrage that I was "prosecutorial" in my approach. No mention of the filibuster strategy. Support from my colleagues on the commission varied along with the general theme, "Oh, that's just Richard being a courtroom lawyer. That's his style and he's good at it." Tom and Lee noted at our next meeting that the Clarke and Rice hearings had tested the commission's bipartisanship and that we needed to be sensitive to perceptions. I could live with that.

My confrontation with the White House over producing Rice as a witness and my questioning of her at the hearing put a further strain on my relationship with Philip Zelikow. The simmering pot would later come to a boil.

IT WAS A GREAT relief to get the Starwood trial behind me, particularly as it resulted in a complete victory for my client. As with any time I am actively engaged in a trial, all the other matters I have responsibility for in my law practice tend to pile up until the trial is over. But as I waded into the pile that inundated my in-box, it was clear that my first priority would be the mere three months we had left to complete our hearings and issue our final report. Our momentum was full on; our spirits were high. That's when a wall crashed into us.

In the week following Rice's appearance, we had two days of public hearings on law enforcement, counterterrorism, and intelligence collection within the United States prior to 9/11. My focus was on why the FBI had failed to effectively analyze and pursue the information it had collected pre-9/11 in a way that might have interrupted the plotters. It seemed to me that some personal accountability was in order for the connect-the-dots failures. The answer that there were institutional and systemic fault lines within the FBI took us only so far. Could these problems have been overcome through specific direction from the top?

A key witness was Thomas Pickard, a career FBI agent who was appointed acting director after Louis Freeh's resignation in June 2001. For better or worse, it was Pickard's lot to be in charge during the summer of threat up until a few days before 9/11 when Robert Mueller took over.

The FBI is a part of the Department of Justice and the FBI director's superior is the attorney general. During the long reign of J. Edgar Hoover, the FBI operated more or less independently of the DOJ (and everyone else). This had its benefits and drawbacks. On the one hand, the FBI was less vulnerable to outside manipulation; on the other, it was subject to Hoover's autocratic style and penchant for using investigative files for political horse trading, or worse. After Hoover's death, attorneys general began to exert more control over the bureau. It was important for the commission to know the interaction between the FBI and George Bush's attorney general, John Ashcroft, on the issue of counterterrorism.

Here our staff provided some truly eye-opening investigative leads. I was the last of the commission members to question Pickard in our public hearing on April 13, 2004.

Tall and lean, Pickard bore the mournful countenance of a man who had relived the run-up to 9/11 many times. First, I established that the acting FBI director had met some seven or eight tines with the attorney general during the summer of 2001. Pickard began each meeting with a discussion of either counterterrorism or counterintelligence, and reported at least twice that the CIA was concerned that there would be an attack by al Qaeda. Ashcroft's response? He didn't want to hear about terrorism anymore.

Tim Roemer had brought out Pickard's frustration that Ashcroft had refused to include terrorism as a top budget priority and had turned down a request for a $58 million increase for counterterrorism. Ashcroft's written denial of Pickard's appeal for more funding landed on Pickard's desk on *September 12, 2001.*

The sclerotic arteries of communication within the FBI kept important information from reaching its head. On 9/11, Pickard initiated a conference call with all of his SACs (field office special agents in charge). He asked whether anyone knew of information that might be connected to the suicide hijackings that had just occurred. Immediately, Pickard was told of the arrest of Zacarias Moussaoui, the hunt for Hazmi and Mihdhar, and the Phoenix memo—none of which had reached his desk. Had the president asked for up-to-the-minute information about a potential domestic attack, would Pickard have "pulsed" the field offices to ensure that all potentially relevant information was being sent to him? Pickard said he would have. And, finally, had either President Bush or Attorney General Ashcroft asked to meet with him between August 6 and September 11? Pickard responded that neither had made such a request.

A fairly clear picture of George W. Bush's pre-9/11 hands-off management style, as well as that of his national security adviser, had been developed. The sitting attorney general would be the next witness to be questioned under oath.

John Ashcroft had been state attorney general and then governor of Missouri prior to being elected to the United States Senate. He was appointed to be Bush's attorney general after losing his bid for reelection in 2000. His Democratic challenger, ex-governor Mel Carnahan, had died in a plane crash two weeks before the election. Under Missouri law, it was too late for the Democrats to substitute a candidate, so Ashcroft ran against a dead man—and lost. Carnahan's wife, Jean, was then appointed to the Senate seat.

As attorney general, Ashcroft was nothing if not controversial. His former Senate colleagues demonstrated their lack of bipartisan support in the 58–42 vote to confirm his appointment. Reflecting his ultra-conservative moral values, the bare-breasted statue *Spirit of Justice* in the Great Hall of the Department of Justice was draped with a curtain at taxpayer cost of $8,000.

Ashcroft's strategy to defend his pre-9/11 inaction was to mount a personal attack against Jamie Gorelick. "The single greatest structural cause of the September 11th problem," Ashcroft intoned gravely in his opening statement, "was the wall that segregated or separated criminal investigators and intelligence agents. Government erected this wall, government buttressed this wall, and before September 11th, government was blinded by this wall." He went on to describe a 1995 DOJ memorandum that spelled out "draconian barriers between the law enforcement and intelligence communities." The attorney general went to his windup; "Although you understand the debilitating impacts of the wall, I cannot imagine that the commission knew about this memorandum. So I have had it declassified for you and the public to review." And the pitch: "Full disclosure compels me to inform you that the author of this memorandum is a member of the commission."

So that was why Ashcroft failed to comply with the rule requiring submission of written statements at least a day in advance of open hearings. His aides had been observed literally sitting on a stack of copies of his prepared statement in the waiting room outside the ceremonial hearing room before Ashcroft was called to testify. All the better to spring his ambush on the unsuspecting commission. The document he had unilaterally declassified was a 1995 memo from Jamie Gorelick, then deputy attorney general under Janet Reno, to Mary Jo White, the U.S. attorney in Manhattan, spelling out procedures under which the prosecutors could utilize evidence gathered by intelligence agencies for the prosecution of the 1993 truck bombing of the World Trade Center. The implication of Ashcroft's dramatic presentation was that the Clinton administration had created the wall and that Jamie was its chief architect and stonemason.

Ashcroft's "gotcha" had the element of surprise—but not for long. There were a number of things wrong with the attorney general's blame-it-on-Gorelick's-wall attack. First, and most important, a correct application of the guidelines would not have prevented the sharing of information on Hazmi and Mihdhar's presence in the United States or the dissemination of the Phoenix memorandum. Nor should it have precluded the FBI from seeking a warrant to search Moussaoui's notebook and computer. It would have zero effect on information regarding Moussaoui's arrest being pushed up to the FBI director. As our staff investigators learned, prior to 9/11 the FBI and the Bush Justice Department were wary of the wrath of the chief judge in charge of the secret FISA (Foreign Intelligence and Surveillance Act) court, who had excoriated FBI agents and Justice Department lawyers alike for failing to comply with his instructions. This fear created a tendency to back off seeking a warrant in any area of uncertainty, such as in the case of Moussaoui's computer. Second, the guidelines restricting usage of intelligence were created during the Reagan administration in response to various court rulings and a law creating FISA, and were reiterated during the Bush I and Clinton administrations. Third, Jamie's memo was an attempt to clarify, not expand, the restrictions. Finally, and most demonstrative of the hypocrisy of the attorney general's attack, Ashcroft's own deputy had reaffirmed written guidelines for the wall only weeks before 9/11.

All of this would be brought out in short order. In the meantime, Ashcroft looked like the cat that swallowed the canary, while Jamie seemed stricken. Not only to suffer such an ambush at the hands of a sitting attorney general on national television, but to be blamed for the failures of 9/11—the calumny was monstrous. Our reaction as a group became a defining moment for the commission.

Jim Thompson was scheduled to question Ashcroft first. I would be next. During Jim's questioning, we hurriedly read the 1995 memo Ashcroft's minions had now handed out to the press simultaneously with showing it to us for the first time. We had spent hours interviewing Ashcroft privately. He had ample opportunity to bring Jamie's memo to our attention as part of that discussion. This was a breathtakingly cheap shot.

Slade Gorton, a former Washington State attorney general before his two terms in the Senate, had developed a strong collegial bond with Jamie. He and Tom Kean urged Jamie and the rest of us to let the Republican members of the commission take the lead in exposing Ashcroft's gambit for what it was.

So I stuck to my game plan in questioning Ashcroft. I brought out the fact that no one had told him in August 2001 that President Bush had supposedly requested a CIA briefing on the potential for a terrorist attack inside the United States. Wasn't it odd that the president, who surely understood that domestic counterterrorism was principally under the jurisdiction of the FBI and Department of Justice, wouldn't communicate his inquisitiveness to either the director of the FBI or the attorney general? Had the president made such a request of him, I asked, wouldn't he have "made sure that the president received a comprehensive report from the FBI"? Of course he would have, and it would have been darned comprehensive, too, Ashcroft answered. And in that process, I continued, "Were you to have pulsed the FBI and directed the FBI to push up any information that it might have had . . ." I was beginning to sound like a broken record. Enough already with the pulsing.

Under Jim Thompson's earlier questioning, Ashcroft had denied Pickard's claim that the AG told him he was tired of hearing about terrorism. Why in the world would the acting director of the FBI make up something like that? I had to believe that Pickard's recollection was more credible than Ashcroft's denial. Now Ashcroft was telling me that he had done plenty of pulsing without getting the information about the Phoenix memo, the hunt for Mihdhar and Hazmi, or the arrest of Moussaoui.

I began my next question with the premise that Ashcroft's "great experience" in the Senate and elsewhere prior to his appointment as attorney general must have given him some understanding of the FBI's traditional unwillingness to share information. Ashcroft interrupted me—what great experience in the Senate and elsewhere was I talking about? Ashcroft stated that he had spent his time prior to being named attorney general as governor of Missouri.

This was a totally weird remark. Hadn't Ashcroft served six years in the Senate, and wasn't he a former state attorney general who must have had experience with the FBI? Had I misremembered his résumé, or was Ashcroft having a *Twilight Zone* episode? I let it slide, accepting his claim that he was not well versed in the ways of Washington or the FBI's well-known distaste for sharing. I moved on to the fact that Ashcroft had removed counterterrorism from the statement of strategic goals of the DOJ. Moreover, the attorney general's denial of the FBI's plea for additional funding for counterterrorism, his lack of interaction with his president on domestic terrorism during the summer of threat and after the August 6 PDB, and Pickard's damning anecdote all stood in contrast to his claim that his number-one priority prior to 9/11 was to protect the American people against terrorism.

Slade Gorton followed me. I don't know what Slade had prepared prior to Ashcroft's preemptive strike against Jamie, but his filleting knife was out now, and it was honed to razor sharpness. He started with Ashcroft's claim in his opening statement that soon after taking office, he had decried the lack of clarity of Clinton's authorization to use lethal force against bin Laden. But had those authorizations been expanded in any way to the

Bush Administration in the months prior to 9/11? Gorton asked. Actually, not, Ashcroft was forced to concede.

Gorton moved to the wall, citing Ashcroft's claim of how the 1995 memo imposed draconian barriers on intelligence sharing.

> GORTON: I don't find that in the eight months before September 11, 2001, that you changed those guidelines. In fact, I have here a memorandum dated August 6 [some coincidence!] from [Ashcroft's deputy] Larry Thompson, the fifth line of which reads, "The 1995 procedures remain in effect today." If that wall was so disabling why was it not destroyed during the course of those eight months?

Slade had exposed a major hole in Ashcroft's logic. The AG's reaction was to keep digging. He took issue with the plain language Slade had just read, claiming that, in fact, the Thompson memo was "a step in the direction of disabling the wall."

> GORTON: But it was after August 6, 2001 that Moussaoui was picked up and the decision was made in the FBI that you couldn't get a warrant to search his computer. So those changes must not have been very significant.
> ASHCROFT: I missed your question, Commissioner.

Slade was happy to spell it out.

> GORTON: The warrant was rejected because FBI officials feared breaching the wall. Yet, that was after these changes that you say were significant.

Ashcroft's response was incomprehensible.

Slade had him on the ropes. He closed with a reference to a millennium after-action review conducted during the Clinton administration that made several recommendations geared toward disrupting the al Qaeda network. Did Ashcroft adopt any of those recommendations in the eight months before 9/11?

The attorney general harrumphed that this was a classified report and he hadn't seen it. But he added, "These are the very things we did following September 11."

GORTON: But the administration of which you're a part didn't take any of those actions *before* 9/11.
ASHCROFT: That's exactly correct.

Slade had done an extraordinary job of exposing Ashcroft's hypocrisy. Coming from a Republican and former Senate colleague, Gorton's performance was all the more devastating.

If John Ashcroft had thought at least one of the Republican commissioners would support his charges, it was wishful thinking. In fact, by the end of the hearing, Jamie had not even been identified by name as the author of the memo. And because she had properly recused herself from participating in any commission activity that involved her own participation in governmental action, Jamie asked Ashcroft no questions relating to the wall. Yet as we huddled in the greenroom after the hearing, Jamie was clearly distraught. The full scope of what Ashcroft had set in motion became apparent in the days that followed.

In the short term, Ashcroft's strategy proved successful, diverting attention from himself. Rather than focus on the FBI revelations of Ashcroft's tepid interest in terrorism, the lead story became Jamie's authorship of the 1995 memo and the attorney general's strident accusation. Immediately, the right-wing network of talk radio bloviators and columnists jumped on the bandwagon, broadening the ongoing personal attacks against me for the Rice questioning to include Jamie Gorelick and Tim Roemer. We were treated to a front-page editorial by Rupert Murdoch, the politically conservative owner of the *New York Post,* who branded the commissioners as "shills."

More disturbing, whether or not coordinated in advance with Ashcroft, the conservative Republican leadership in the House of Representatives let fly with a major offensive against the commission, using Jamie as the focal point of its attack. James Sensenbrenner of Wisconsin, chairman of the House Judiciary Committee, released a letter the following day calling on Jamie to resign from the commission, claiming that her Justice Department service created an insurmountable conflict of interest. Never mind that the statute Congress had passed creating the commission specified that the "individuals appointed to the commission should be prominent United States citizens with national recognition and significant depth of experience in such professions as government service, law enforcement, armed services, law, public administration, intelligence gathering, commerce and foreign affairs." Given those criteria, of course we would have individuals who were involved in some aspects of events the commission was looking into—that's why we adopted a recusal policy. The conservatives, who had always opposed creation of the commission, didn't like what we were finding and were even more displeased by our determination to share it promptly with the public. Perhaps this would be their last chance of upsetting the apple cart.

A number of other House Republicans followed Sensenbrenner's lead. Then the big dog, Majority Leader Tom DeLay, weighed in with a scathing letter to Tom Kean, calling for Jamie to resign and protesting that our open hearings presented a "dangerous distraction from the global war on terror. They undermine our national unity and insult the troops now in harm's way, to say nothing of those who have already given their lives to this conflict." It should have come as no surprise that the ethically challenged former exterminator from Texas would resort to such execrable tactics. It was of a piece with Vice President Cheney's prior statement that any serious probe of 9/11 foreknowledge would be "tantamount to giving aid and comfort to the enemy." Whenever our nation is about to flex its democratic principles, the right wing is on hand to denounce the effort as a threat to our troops in the field. You can set your watch by it.

Tom Kean and the Republican commissioners were determined to lead the public refutation of Ashcroft's charges and defense of Jamie's integrity. Slade Gorton appeared on several television programs and wrote an op-ed piece exposing the flaws in Ashcroft's argument. Tom and Lee held a joint press conference supporting Jamie against Ashcroft's unwarranted and factually untenable assertions. The normally sunny Kean let a bit of his irritation show by concluding his statement with the advice to Sensenbrenner that he ought to mind his own business.

The Clarke and Rice appearances had provided our critics the openings to claim that we were breaking down into partisan camps. But the hard questioning had produced a record where the public could see each of them respond openly and without the overlay of spinmeisters. The Ashcroft episode gave the commission the opportunity to close ranks and demonstrate nonpartisan solidarity.

Of course, it was a tremendous burden for Jamie to have to deal with the craziness that the coordinated right-wing attack inspired. Death threats and the most deplorable Internet postings were the predictable follow-on to the savaging she took on wing nut–dominated talk radio.

Although the attorney general had succeeded in diverting attention from his own record, the short-term gains were more than erased by the longer-term rejection of both the substance and the method of his ambush. Picking one of the most hardworking, capable, and popular commissioners as his target backfired big time. I was quoted at the time saying that a man ought to be better informed if he is going to attack a woman with nine brothers. At a dinner party attended by all commissioners following the issuance of our final report, I raised my glass in a toast "to John Ashcroft . . . who did more to unite the commission than any other individual."

THE PRESIDENT'S ANNOUNCEMENT THAT he would meet with the full commission on the condition that we interview him and the vice president together was still another public relations faux pas that provided the late-night television hosts with fresh material. What were they thinking over at the White House? From virtually day one, the inexperienced Bush was said to be overly reliant on the older Cheney. As time went by, the suggestion that Cheney was really the one making the decisions was reinforced by the vice president's long reach and ubiquitous presence. The requirement that Cheney be present for Bush's interview by the commission only enhanced such speculation and precipitated a new round of Bush being under "adult supervision" jokes.

April 29, 2004, the day of our long-anticipated meeting with President Bush and Vice President Cheney, had arrived. The logistical arrangements made by fiat in typical White House fashion were designed to minimize the visual impact of the commissioners trooping to the White House to interrogate its powerful occupant. Accordingly, rather than arriving on our own, in full view of the waiting press through one of the public entrances, the White House sent a minibus to collect us at our K Street office. The bus carried us directly through the gates to a side entrance. Reporters could see us disembark from a distance of about two hundred feet, as they peered through the bars of an iron gate—well out of question-shouting distance. What the press could see through telephoto lenses was the "wanding" of each commissioner by uniformed Secret Service officers. Had we entered through the ordinary visitor procedures, as I had done on many occasions in other administrations, we would have passed through ordinary airport-type magnetometers and our belongings run through the machine on a belt. Yet, on this magnificent spring day, eleven individuals (ten commissioners and Phil Zelikow) were wanded in the familiar pose of arms outstretched from our sides, despite the fact that each of us had security clearances high above top secret. Was this a not-so-subtle reminder of presidential power? The absurdity of the situation was highlighted by the fact that after the body wanding, no one asked to search the briefcase I was carrying.

We entered the West Wing and waited in the Roosevelt Room adjacent to the Oval Office. The room featured portraits of both Presidents Roosevelt, with a rousing painting depicting Teddy on horseback as a Rough Rider during the Spanish-American War over the fireplace mantel. Tom Kean and Lee Hamilton were asked to spend a few moments together with President Bush, Vice President Cheney, and Chief of Staff Andrew Card while the rest of us waited. It occurred to me that this room would be a perfect place to conduct our interview—it was spacious enough for all to have a seat at the large conference table and it would make note taking easier. However, a few minutes later, Tom and Lee returned and we were ushered into the Oval Office, greeted at the door by the president and vice president. We were invited to select seats on the sofas and straight-backed chairs arranged in a semicircle. The president and vice president sat next to each other in straight-back chairs, their backs to the ornate fireplace, above which hung a Rembrandt Peale portrait of George Washington. White House counsel Alberto Gonzales and two of his assistants joined Philip Zelikow in chairs against the wall. Bush wore a blue shirt, a blue patterned tie, and a blue pinstripe suit. The obligatory American flag pin was on display on the president's lapel, reminding us we were meeting with the president of the *United States*, not some other country's president.

Tom Kean chose a seat on the sofa to the left of the president; Lee Hamilton sat on the sofa opposite Kean, to Cheney's right. I chose a chair directly opposite the president, a large coffee table between us. Unlike Clinton and Gore, Bush and Cheney had refused to allow stenographic or tape-recorded transcript of the interview to be made. Zelikow, who would not participate in the questioning, would be our principal note taker. I scribbled my own notes as best I could in a binder on my lap.

Coffee and beverages were offered. I accepted coffee. The president seemed in good spirits—he greeted us warmly, expressed support for the commission, and thanked us for our "hard work." The irony of thanking us for hard work, which included getting him to agree to an interview he sought to avoid, before a commission whose existence he fought to prevent, fluttered gently through my mind. Still, it was gracious and politic of him to say so.

The president then told us that he was "extremely disappointed" in what had happened the day before at the Department of Justice. Without naming John Ashcroft, Bush was alluding to his combative attorney general's continuing offensive against Jamie Gorelick. Ashcroft had declassified more documents authored by Jamie while she was at DOJ and posted them on the DOJ Web site. The president wanted us to know the White House was not involved in the Justice Department's actions; indeed, he had "made his displeasure known." This was a felicitous beginning to our interview.

What I didn't learn until three years later was that a furious battle had erupted between the Justice Department and the White House only weeks earlier. As John Ashcroft lay in pain at George Washington Hospital following gallbladder surgery, he was visited by then White House counsel Alberto Gonzales and Bush chief of staff Andy Card, who tried to get the attorney general to override a veto by Ashcroft's deputy, James Comey. Comey had refused to approve portions of a domestic wiretapping program to be undertaken by the ultrasecret National Security Agency. Comey received word that Gonzales and Card were on their way, and rushed to the hospital, alerting FBI director Bob Mueller to join him there. At Comey's request, Mueller relayed orders to the AG's security detail to prevent Comey from being ejected from the hospital room. A confrontation ensued. The ailing AG refused to sign the authorization papers Gonzales and Card carried with them, and told them to deal with Comey, who had taken over the AG's responsibilities while he was incapacitated. The attorney general's wife was also present. As a gesture emphasizing her displeasure at the effrontery of the intrusion, Janet Ashcroft stuck her tongue out as Gonzales and Card retreated from her husband's hospital room.

In the following days, the White House decided to proceed with the program without authorization from Justice. Comey, Mueller, and a group of senior DOJ lawyers took the extraordinary step of threatening to resign if the order were not rescinded. Reportedly, the matter was resolved after Mueller met personally with Bush, and the surveillance directive at issue was modified.

Was it possible that the attack on Jamie had been an attempt by Ashcroft to show his fealty to the boss and make up for the showdown over the NSA surveillance program? If so, that backfired also. Bush's rebuke of his attorney general was made public by the White House immediately after our meeting with Bush. And on the heels of his reelection victory in November, Bush announced he was replacing Ashcroft with Gonzales as attorney general. Gonzales's alarmingly inept performance in that position made Ashcroft look good, if only by comparison.

But Bush's rebuke of Ashcroft was a nice way to begin our interview with the president. Bush finished his opening remarks by telling us he was eagerly awaiting our report, hoping that our recommendations would help address how we could best conduct the fight against terrorism.

With a big smile, Bush noted that as time was limited he would try to answer our questions "shortly"—a clear reference to Condoleezza Rice's attempt to run the clock. Later in the interview he repeated his promise not to filibuster. At any event, because of our persistence and unwillingness to break ranks (and the widely publicized fact that President Clinton had spent three and a half hours with us and answered all our questions), we had gone from a fifteen-minute "courtesy call" meeting with Kean and Hamilton to an interview by the full commission that would last more than three hours.

The president did not lose his good humor. Perhaps because of the ridicule that followed his insistence that he be interviewed in tandem with Cheney, he answered virtually all the questions himself. Indeed, almost all of our questions were directed to him personally. Later on I noted that Cheney rather than Bush was the beneficiary of the joint interview. We could easily have spent an equal amount of time asking the vice president questions, but our focus that day was on the president.

Bush displayed his much heralded charm. He had a little personal anecdote or comment for each of us. He was quick to laugh and did not bristle. I was struck by the man's likability quotient. Whatever might be said of his intellectual curiosity, his management style, or his pre-9/11 interest in terrorism as commander in chief, here was a formidable candidate in chief. There was no mistaking his appeal to voters.

After some pleasantries, Tom Kean started the questioning with the president's receipt of threat reports during the summer of 2001. Quickly, the subject turned to the August 6 PDB. Bush said he had received only one reference to domestic threats to that point—the result of his request to the CIA. Wow! That would mean that none of the discussions Clarke was having with Rice made it to the president's ears. He repeated the mantra that the August 6 report was "historical in nature."

Bush volunteered that there was *some* "operational" data from the FBI in the CIA's report. He found the fact that seventy FBI domestic terrorist investigations were reported to be under way was "heartening." That was interesting. Rice had just testified that the same report was not "reassuring," but in fact was "frightening." Bush went beyond what Rice had remembered, telling us that Rice had discussed the "Yemen threat" with him. This was a reference to a detention of two Yemeni nationals in downtown Manhattan that was included in the PDB. I made a note to follow up.

Under Kean's questioning, the president reported that he had received no information about either aircraft used as missiles or Islamic extremists learning to fly prior to 9/11. Next, Tom turned to the president's receipt of the news of the first and then the second plane hitting the Twin Towers. Why had he continued in the classroom with the children? Bush replied that he thought the first plane crash was an accident; after the second plane hit he stayed put, trying to gather his thoughts and project the image of a calm, unrattled president. Bush was an ardent believer in the interpretive value of body language. Indeed, he encouraged us to watch the body language between him and his vice president as a key to understanding their working relationship.

Once he was hustled out of the school by the Secret Service and onto Air Force One, he made calls to Cheney, Rice, and his wife, who was scheduled to visit Capitol Hill that morning. Both Cheney and Rice had advised him not to return to Washington. Bush said that an air force colonel—not Cheney or Rice—told him that Air Force One was a target. The information had come from a call to the Situation Room. I winced at not having had time to question Rice publicly about the phantom threat. Was it possible that Bush still believed it was true?

Tom turned to Vice President Cheney, trying to pin down his recollection of the time line of his conversation with Bush authorizing the shoot-down order. Cheney gave an extensive account of the extraordinary events of the morning when the Secret Service rushed him to the relative safety of the PEOC, grabbing him by the back of his belt to emphasize that his evacuation would not be the subject of negotiation. At that point, the second plane had hit the WTC and another hijacked plane was said to be a minute outside Washington. It turned out that this was American 77, which crashed into the Pentagon. In the underground tunnel leading to the PEOC he called the president on a wall phone and was patched through to Air Force One. He told Bush that Washington was under attack and "strongly recommended" that he stay away from the capital. Cheney made no mention of warning Bush about "Angel" being the next target. He spoke to Bush again after he arrived in the PEOC. Cheney recalled that he and Bush discussed the rules of engagement for the air force, at which time Bush gave him authorization to communicate a shoot-down order. Cheney claimed Rice overheard his end of the conversation—an account that Rice corroborated. But Lynne Cheney and the VP's ubiquitous aide,

Scooter Libby, who were both in the PEOC at that time and who were each taking notes of what they saw and heard, had no recollection of hearing about such an extraordinary order being given by the president, nor was there any description of it recorded in their notes.

The president endorsed Cheney's account. Perhaps the sensitivity over whether Cheney had acted first and got authorization later was behind the condition that we interview the two men in tandem. As best we could reconstruct events, at some point between 10:10 and 10:15, a report was given to Cheney by a military aide claiming (mistakenly) that a hijacked aircraft was eighty miles outside Washington and asking for authority to engage the aircraft. Cheney immediately gave the order authorizing fighter planes to shoot down the aircraft. Josh Bolten, deputy White House chief of staff, also seated at the PEOC conference table, suggested that the VP call the president to confirm the shoot-down order. Bolten had not heard any prior conversation about Bush having already given authorization to Cheney. Cheney called the president at 10:18 and spoke for two minutes. Meanwhile, on Air Force One, presidential press secretary Ari Fleischer recorded in notes he was making that at 10:20 Bush told him he had authorized a shoot down of aircraft, if necessary.

Apart from the discrepancy in the accounts of the shoot-down authorization, the "fog of war" confusion was still evident during our interview thirty months after the event. Tom Kean asked the president about the sequence of events leading to the scrambling of fighter planes out of Andrews Air Force Base under orders from the Secret Service, outside the military chain of command. Fighter planes from the 113th Wing of the District of Columbia National Guard based at Andrews had been launched at 10:38 under orders conveyed to General David Wherley from a Secret Service agent liaison who was speaking to another agent in the PEOC. General Wherley gave orders to defend the White House and the Capitol "weapons free," giving his pilots authority to shoot down hostile aircraft. The president asked Kean to repeat the question—he knew nothing about orders given by the Secret Service.

Lee Hamilton followed Tom. While the chairman's questions focused almost exclusively on the facts of 9/11, Lee was more interested in policy issues and the steps already taken to remedy the shortcomings revealed by 9/11. Bush's answers were animated and fulsome to the point of reminding himself of his promise not to filibuster.

Tim Roemer asked for some nuts-and-bolts answers on what was being done to implement the broad policies to combat terror. Bush spoke of working through Condoleezza Rice, his principal source of information and the lightning rod for his frustration over the time it took to coordinate military, diplomatic, and related policies. When Kean suggested to Tim that we didn't have time for the follow-up question he requested, Bush intervened. Grinning, he advised Tim to go ahead and ask his question—"It's my Oval Office." Roemer took the president up on his invitation, asking a few more questions, including why he had not responded to the attack on the *Cole*. Bush explained that attacking bin Laden with cruise missiles or bombers ran the risk of strengthening al Qaeda if we missed him—giving him a propaganda advantage by showing the world that American technology and military might were ineffective against bin Laden. But there was a different issue here that I would cover when my turn came.

Slade Gorton directed his questions to a number of 9/11 conspiracy theories. The president seemed well informed on this subject, saying he had seen things written in the German press that made the John Birch Society's stuff back in Midland, Texas, seem mild by comparison. What about the Saudi nationals who were in the United States on 9/11 and the high-level request to let them return home? Never heard about it until he read about it in the papers, said the president. The vice president murmured what sounded like agreement.

It was about 10:35 when I got my chance to ask questions. We had been going for a little over an hour. The atmosphere had been cordial. As usual, we had not divided up the questioning in advance—each commissioner was free to set his or her own priorities. While I was determined to get my questions answered, I would have to be especially careful to balance desire with diplomacy. I began by thanking the president and vice president for meeting with the full commission. I told them that I believed we were on the "same team" as far as getting to the truth of what occurred and in our goal to make the country safer.

I began with the summer of 2001, when the threat level exceeded anything the CIA had ever seen before. I told him that when we had met with George Tenet, Tenet seemed confused or unsure of how often he had met with the president during August. I then raised the now famous August 6 PDB, "Bin Laden Determined to Strike in U.S." Had he received information *prior* to August 6 on the "potential for an attack within the United States"? I asked.

"None," the president replied. Not only had no one discussed the potential for an attack on our homeland by al Qaeda, no one had told him there were al Qaeda cells in the United States.

How was this possible? Richard Clarke had provided this information to Condoleezza Rice, and he had put it in writing. When I had asked Rice whether she had passed information about terrorist cells along to the president she said she couldn't remember. But how could the president not be aware by September 2001 of the al Qaeda connection to the first bombing of the World Trade Center in 1993? Was he unaware of the bridges and tunnels plot in New York? Had no one discussed with him the planned millennium bombing of LAX?

President Bush went on to say that the only PDB he ever received on the domestic threat was the August 6 memo—and it was he who had asked for it, although he could not remember when. Had I known about the CIA briefer's reported statement about Bush's "cover your ass" comment, I could have asked him how that squared with his claim that *he* had asked for such a report. If he had requested such a report, why would he have sarcastically dismissed the CIA briefer who delivered it?

I then asked whether Rice had been in Texas when the CIA presented the August 6 PDB to him. No, but he had talked to her about the PDB "at some point." One of the specific items of *ongoing* investigation referenced in the PDB was the arrest of two Yemeni nationals to which Bush had alluded in response to one of Tom's earlier questions. The Yemenis were taking pictures of 26 Federal Plaza, in New York City. A building of no particular architectural distinction, 26 Federal Plaza housed the FBI offices and high-profile terrorist hunter John O'Neill's counterterrorism unit. Yet the men had told authorities that these were tourist photos taken at the request of a coworker in Indianapolis. The president said that Rice had told him that the Yemenis were just tourists and the "Yemeni situation" had been cleared up.

I wanted to make sure I had heard correctly. "Dr. Rice told you this?" I asked. The president confirmed that was correct. I took this as an opportunity to tell the president what we had learned about the FBI's investigation. Rather than the matter having been cleared up, it appeared that the individual whom the two detained Yemenis identified as the sponsor of their photography excursion had fled Indianapolis, leaving an uncashed paycheck behind. More disturbing, the man was using an alias and forged identity documents; moreover, the FBI had never been able to find him or learn his true name despite an intensive two-year hunt directed by the two top FBI counterterrorism officials in New York. The missing man had asked the two Yemenis visiting New York to express mail the undeveloped film to him. Why not send some postcards of true New York landmarks instead of all this? It didn't add up.

"This is the first I've heard of this," the president acknowledged.

I asked President Bush why he hadn't met with the FBI director after receiving the August 6 PDB. He replied that there were concerns that existed before his administration about politicizing the FBI and interfering in pending cases. This was sad but true. Indeed, President Clinton and his FBI director, Louis Freeh, had an openly hostile relationship for the last years of the administration. But this was no pending case subject to claims of political interference, and what about his national security adviser? "Had you asked Dr. Rice to follow up with the FBI? Do you know if she followed up?"

The president could not recall. But he thought the mention of seventy pending FBI investigations was a good thing, helpful—the same information Rice described as frightening. The president pressed on. If Rice or Tenet came in and told him there was a terrorist cell, he would have ordered them "to destroy it." It never happened.

I reminded the president that important information uncovered by the FBI and CIA in the summer of 2001 apparently did not reach the president's ears. I listed the two known al Qaeda operatives, Mihdhar and Hazmi, whom the CIA and FBI knew had entered the United States, FBI agents' sensitivity to the number of Middle Eastern men enrolled in U.S. flight schools, and particularly, the arrest of Zacarias Moussaoui in mid-August. Had CIA director Tenet ever mentioned Moussaui, whose arrest had occurred only days after the August 6 PDB was delivered to Bush in Crawford? This was critical—Tenet had been briefed shortly after Moussaoui's arrest by the FBI. The CIA had described the Minneapolis flight school student to their chief in a memo titled "Islamic Extremist Learns to Fly." The FBI agent who arrested Moussaoui pegged him as a possible suicide hijacker.

The president's brow furrowed. He could not recall any mention of Moussaoui. He explained how his meetings with Tenet would go. "Mr. President, we have a serious threat," the CIA director would say, then proceed to describe it. Bush would ask, "What are we doing about it?" But no one ever told him there was a domestic problem. The threat was always overseas. The mystery over the substance of any contact between Tenet and Bush between August 6 and September 11 continued.

President Bush volunteered that if there had been "a serious concern" in August 2001, he would have known about it. Being on my best behavior, I didn't come out and ask him what he thought a briefing from the CIA titled "Bin Laden Determined to Strike in U.S." was, if not a serious concern.

Instead, I asked whether the president had discussed the August 6 PDB with either the attorney general or the secretary of the treasury, the two cabinet officers who oversaw the FBI and other federal agencies charged with domestic law enforcement. Had he discussed the PDB with Attorney General Ashcroft to ensure the FBI was doing everything necessary? The president said that he could not recall, nor could he say whether Rice had any such discussion with Ashcroft.

As John Lehman took his turn with the president, I silently reviewed the answers on the PDB. The summer of 2001 marked the most elevated threat level we had ever experienced, providing convincing evidence that a "spectacular" attack was about to occur. CIA analysts had written a report for the president's eyes to alert him to the possibility that bin Laden's words and actions, together with recent investigative clues, pointed to an attack by al Qaeda on the American homeland. Yet the president had done absolutely nothing to follow up.

John Lehman's focus was on the Saudis' ambivalent role in dealing with al Qaeda and the harm caused by their support of radical Islamic clerics and their madrassas (religious schools) throughout the world, a recurring theme the former navy secretary had spent considerable time researching. The president was candid in describing the difficulty every U.S. president has faced in dealing with the Saudis and emphasized continuing disagreements with the Saudis over U.S. policy toward Israel.

Bob Kerrey returned to the issue of the *Cole*. Again Bush went through the reasons why an attack against bin Laden would not have been possible without an invasion of Afghanistan, which, in turn, was not feasible before 9/11 for a variety of reasons, which the president enumerated. The same lack of actionable intelligence that precluded targeting bin Laden for a missile strike would also have doomed a Special Ops hunt for the al Qaeda leader.

Jim Thompson wanted the president's recollection of his interchange with Dick Clarke on September 12, which Clarke had characterized as an attempt to pressure him to find a connection between the 9/11 attack and Iraq. Bush took issue with various details of Clarke's account but basically didn't recall it happening—certainly not the way Clarke characterized it in his book. "I read that page [in Clarke's book]," Bush reported. It would have been logical for him to ask Clarke about Saddam, given the fact that he had paid money to suicide bombers, Bush continued. But intimidate Clarke? "I don't think so." Bush shrugged his shoulders. "Maybe I did, I don't remember. But not the way Clarke's book said," he added.

Jim Thompson asked about Bush's interaction with President Clinton during the transition on the issue of terrorism. Bush grew contemplative, thinking back. Clinton had invited him to the Oval Office. He remembered a lot being said about North Korea but didn't remember that much was said about al Qaeda. He remembered that Clinton was very upset with Yasir Arafat and the collapse of the peace process.

Jamie homed in on the shoot-down order time line, asking Cheney if he could clarify discrepancies between our staff's information and what the White House had. Bush interjected, "Look, he didn't give orders without my authorization." Well, that got to the heart of it. Al Gonzales jumped in to say that he could provide further detail. Jamie switched gears, asking the president whether upon taking office he believed the CIA had sufficient authority to kill bin Laden. Further rebuking Ashcroft, Bush said he never heard the CIA lacked such authority and was sure Tenet would have told him if there were any question about it. The president expanded on his relationship with Tenet: a "policy guy, a strategic thinker." They had a great relationship. Tenet had taken pains in his testimony to distinguish between policy and operations, insisting he was not involved in making policy.

In response to a question from Jamie about the regular morning CIA briefings and the threat of a domestic terror attack, the president stated that prior to 9/11, the job of reaching out to domestic agencies was his chief of staff's responsibility, not Rice's. This was news! Rice had never said so. Jamie made sure she heard correctly. She had. I was trying to process this new tidbit. We had agreed as a condition of the Rice testimony and Bush/Cheney interview that we would not seek to question any other White House official, and this would include chief of staff Andy Card. But in prior interviews with our staff, Card had never indicated he had such responsibility.

At this point, Hamilton and Kerrey announced that they had prior commitments that required them to take their leave. I was stunned. After all we had gone through to get the president to agree to an extended interview, two of the Democrats were bugging out early? Hamilton said he needed to introduce the prime minister of Canada who was speaking at the Wilson Center, while Kerrey had an appointment with a financial donor to The New School University. Brother!

Bush took this news cheerfully, chatting with Kerrey about advances in prosthetics for our wounded veterans as he walked the two to the door and resumed his seat. Jamie finished up, questioning whether the Bush team got enough help from the departing Clinton officials during the short transition period after the disputed 2000 election. Bush laughed and said it would have been better to win on Election Day, but, yes, the Clinton folks had been very helpful.

Fred Fielding, mentioning his experience as counsel to Ronald Reagan during the assassination attempt in which the president was seriously wounded, asked about contingent arrangements under the Twenty-fifth Amendment in the event the president were disabled. Bush said he didn't believe he had ever discussed this with Cheney, nor was it something Cheney wanted to talk to him about. Gonzales interrupted again, saying they had discussed it once. Bush allowed as how the lawyers had conversed about the subject, but there was no problem regarding continuity of his policies—he knew they were on the same page. Bush described his relationship with Cheney as unique—there was no political rivalry. "The Vice-President isn't interested in my job and I'm not interested in his," he reassured us. He reminisced about how Cheney had come out to see him while he was in a pasture at his ranch with the results of the vice presidential search committee that Cheney had chaired. "Dick, you're it," the president had told him.

Fred was the last commissioner to have a turn. Bush remained in good spirits; he called us all by our first names and the mood was relaxed and unforced. No one made a move to show us the door. Tim Roemer jumped in with a question about a meeting with his CIA director on August 17, 2001. Tenet had just been briefed by his staff about Moussaoui's arrest in Minneapolis. Had Bush ever heard about Moussaoui before 9/11? No, and he could not recall any briefing by Tenet either on the 17th or otherwise about a domestic threat.

Bush segued into praise for Condoleezza Rice's ability, despite her relative youth, to keep up with the "stars," "thoroughbreds" like Powell, Rumsfeld, and Tenet. Rice was "phenomenal," never intimidated, despite the self-confidence of people like Rumsfeld. I got the strong impression that Rice played a critical role in filtering information from the thoroughbreds in a way Bush could understand and trust.

Gorton and Lehman engaged both Bush and Cheney in further discussion on response to the *Cole* and use of Special Forces on the ground in Afghanistan. But no one had touched on the information Bill Clinton had provided about threatening the Taliban.

The president looked my way and observed, "Richard, you seem to be champing at the bit to ask a question." So much for my poker face. I laughed at my obvious eagerness and leaned forward on the edge of my chair. I didn't understand what seemed to be a discontinuity between the diplomatic efforts initiated in one administration and the lack of follow-up in the next. Why didn't we make good on the threat to hold the Taliban responsible for al Qaeda's attack on the *Cole*? I went into some detail about why our intelligence agencies were clear by January 2001 that the *Cole* bombing was the work of al Qaeda. What did it matter that "command and control" linking bin Laden personally to the operation had not yet been established? The president went into the same routine about the risk of bin Laden dodging million-dollar missiles and laughing in our face. But I wasn't talking about a strike against bin Laden. We had been trying to nail bin Laden with missiles since 1998, but his moves were faster than our intel capabilities to pinpoint his whereabouts and deliver a lethal blow. We didn't need any more provocation to try to kill bin Laden. I explained that I was talking about retaliating against the *Taliban,* not bin Laden. I described my understanding of the various warnings that Clinton had communicated to the Taliban leadership to kick al Qaeda out of Afghanistan or bear the consequences of harboring them if they struck against us. Bush looked puzzled. No doubt, the president's receptivity to informality had affected me. "Look, we told the Taliban that unless they coughed up that hairball [bin Laden] we would attack *them* if al Qaeda hit us. We knew where Mullah Omar lived in Kabul." Bush got my point but not the premise. "Richard, what you are saying is news to me. I never heard about any threat to retaliate against the Taliban."

I was stunned. How could the new president not know the warning the outgoing president had communicated through diplomatic sources to the Taliban? Bush continued, "*I* never said 'cough him up or I'll blast you.' If I had said that, well—in that case you've got to be ready to blast."

At this point Al Gonzales volunteered that we didn't strike the Taliban because it was unclear until later that bin Laden had personally ordered the *Cole* attack. But this was my original point: Why would it have mattered? Once it was clear that this was an al Qaeda operation, it should have triggered retaliation against the Taliban as the United States had reportedly warned. Given what we knew now—that there was dissension within the ranks of the Taliban leadership on the issue of continuing to provide safe harbor in Afghanistan for al Qaeda—might a missile attack against the Taliban infrastructure have created at least a warning to bin Laden by the Taliban to forgo attacks against U.S. interests? This would have been eight months before the 9/11 attack. Bin Laden's focus had been on disrupting the Saudi and other disfavored Middle Eastern regimes, anyway.

What were the odds that a retaliatory attack against the Taliban would have changed the course of the 9/11 attack, which was already in its late stages of planning? Pure speculation. Might Mullah Omar and the surviving Taliban leadership just as easily become more entrenched in their support of al Qaeda and their hatred for the United States? Who knew?

Bush shook me out of my thoughts. "Richard, you know more about the evidence in the *Cole* than I do, you knew more about the Yemenis. Let me ask you a question: have you ever lost an argument?"

"Mr. President, I have two daughters."

Bush laughed heartily at the parallel.

He stayed on the subject, reiterating that *he* did not issue the threat. Moreover, if they missed Mullah Omar in such a retaliatory attack, they might wind up inflaming the situation and making it worse. Bush said the Taliban wouldn't even talk to anyone who wasn't Muslim, and then when they did talk it was only to give them this—he showed me the international "fuck you" sign of one arm crossed against the other with the fist up. "Mr. President," I responded, "I'm from New York City. That's like saying good morning." Bush laughed and went back to his observation about public relations benefits to the enemy of showing their guerrilla tactics were superior to our high technology. No, in order to get the Taliban and eliminate al Qaeda, you had to launch a massive invasion with the necessary logistical and strategic components—aircraft carriers based in Diego Garcia, bases in Uzbekistan and the other "stans," overwhelming force, supply lines, etc.

I asked whether only 9/11 could have provided the basis to launch such an attack. After all, I thought, an exasperated Dick Clarke had written Rice a memo on September 4, 2001, bemoaning the failure to retaliate for the *Cole* and the delays in taking action against al Qaeda and its Taliban protectors. "You are left waiting for the big attack, with lots of casualties, after which some major U.S. retaliation will be in order."

Jamie joined in. Would the formulation of a national security presidential directive on terrorism—still in process on 9/11—have untied the president's hands? Bush surmised that without 9/11 he might have gone forward, but it would not have been easy.

At this point Fred Fielding pointed out that we had been going for three hours. Fred must have had his eye on his watch for some time. But the president laughed and said he wanted to go for at least three hours and five minutes, an unsubtle reference to our long meeting with Bill Clinton.

I still had more questions. What about Rice's statement that no one had imagined using planes as weapons? Bush said that no one had ever discussed the possibility with her, but interrupted himself to say he shouldn't be speaking for Rice. Bush questioned whether I was sure of my facts that such information was available. I responded that the intelligence community had documented a dozen examples of plots involving suicide planes. And in Genoa, at the G8 summit, there was a cap over the city and antiaircraft batteries visible in the streets. Bush responded that they close the airspace wherever he travels; that was no warning that planes might be used as weapons. I knew other air traffic was halted during Air Force One's landings and takeoffs, but closing airspace over the cities to which the president traveled for the duration of his visit? Had he heard that Egyptian president Hosni Mubarak had warned the Italians about possible suicide planes at the G8? No, he had never heard about that. Because the airspace had been closed over Genoa, should he be thinking about airplanes hitting buildings? The president shook his head dismissively.

Tom Kean thanked the president for "a very good discussion," adding that the questioning had been good. For his part, Bush said he hoped we had enjoyed the opportunity. He emphasized that this ought not be a "gotcha" exercise but one in which we could all learn. He expressed his view that it was good that he had met with the whole commission, and that it was good that we had gotten the opportunity to see how he and Cheney "interfaced" with each other. Bush reiterated his belief in the importance of visual cues, noting that despite the criticism he had taken for his comment about looking into Russian leader Vladimir Putin's eyes, he continued to value such opportunities. In closing, the president reminded us of the seriousness of our purpose—the country was still at war with enemies who wanted to kill us. He then mentioned the interplay of terrorism with election politics, President José María Aznar of Spain had lost his bid for reelection on the heels of the Atocha train bombing in Madrid not because of the attack but because of the way he had handled the attack. (Aznar had immediately placed blame on Basque separatists and had clung to this conclusion in the face of persuasive and mounting evidence that Islamist terrorists were responsible.) This was unfortunate, Bush concluded, and had placed us more at risk.

The day was truly extraordinary. Bush had told us what he knew and what he didn't know, as well as how he got his information. I left with no doubt about Bush's likability or his personal commitment to the policies he had espoused. As for 9/11, there was no question in my mind that had the president and his national security adviser been aggressively attentive to the potential for a domestic terrorist attack, some of the information already within the possession of our intelligence and law enforcement agencies might have been utilized to disrupt the plot.

THE CLOSEST THE COMMISSION came to getting its collective head handed to it was during the hearings held over two days in New York. The subject was New York City's preparedness for a major terror attack and its immediate response to 9/11. Despite the unimaginable heroism of firefighters and police on that awful day, the question remained whether enough had been done to plan for responding to such an attack, and whether lives had been lost due to insufficient training and preparation and inadequate equipment.

There was no doubt that the courageous efforts of police and firefighters saved the lives of countless civilians who were led, or in many cases physically carried, to safety through darkness, debris, and incredible chaos. Of an estimated 16,400–18,800 individuals who were in the two buildings at the time of the attack, an untold number of survivors owed their lives to the bravery of the first responders during the evacuation. Tragically, 343 firefighters lost their lives that day, along with 37 members of the Port Authority Police Department, and 23 NYPD officers.

Bob Kerrey, president of The New School University, played host to our hearing in the university's spacious auditorium. Located in Greenwich Village, The New School was only a few miles north of where the World Trade Center had once stood.

Once again, the mere fact that we were having a hearing in New York seemed to have a galvanizing effect on events. Despite the passage of more than two and a half years since 9/11, Mayor Michael Bloomberg had not yet promulgated a revised emergency response plan to address the deficiencies in planning and incident command that became painfully evident on that tragic day. Then, less than a week before our hearing in mid–May 2004, Bloomberg unveiled his plan.

My colleagues were harshly critical of the mayor's tardy effort. On the first day of the hearing, John Lehman let fly with the most vitriolic attack by any of the commissioners. Referring to his experience in the Reagan administration, Lehman described New York's disaster response plan as "not worthy of the Boy Scouts, let alone this great city." Bloomberg's plan "puts in concrete a clearly dysfunctional system," Lehman added. "I think the command and control and communications of this city's public service is a scandal." The failure of the plan to clearly demark which agency—

fire or police—would be in charge during a disaster drew fire from Lee Hamilton, who called the plan a "prescription for confusion."

Lehman's truculence carried into his questioning of former mayor Rudolf Giuliani's fire commissioner, Thomas Van Essen, who fought back, calling Lehman's remarks outrageous and disgraceful. The commission had not anticipated the fury with which the New York tabloids conflated the commissioners' criticism with an attack on the bravery and heroism of the first responders. "Insult" was the *New York Post*'s front-page headline. "The bravery and selflessness of firefighters have been lost on the mean-spirited commission of outsiders," accused the editorial. Our leaders had not bargained for the expression of outrage generated by Murdoch, who had opposed the commission from the beginning. In hindsight, the criticism over Bloomberg's inadequate proposal could have been communicated without Lehman's hyperbole.

The second day of the hearing provided the commission's most awkward moment. On the one hand, the families were out in force, demanding answers from the former city officials whom they felt had contributed to the loss of life on 9/11 by not preparing adequately for the megadisaster that claimed the lives of their loved ones. At the other extreme, right-wing Republicans exploited the outrage of parochial, go-it-alone New Yorkers, in a last-ditch effort to impugn and embarrass the commission before we issued our final report.

Rudy Giuliani was to be the star witness of the day's hearing, and I was designated to begin the questioning. My relationship with Rudy went back to the early days of my professional career when Rudy arrived as a rookie lawyer at the U.S. attorney's office. I knew Rudy well, as he eventually became a member of the special prosecutions/official corruption section that I led. While we were never best buddies, we socialized and shared the locker room camaraderie of practical jokes and black humor that thrived in an environment of working twelve-hour days and weekends. I knew Rudy to be hardworking, inherently talented as a courtroom lawyer, and nothing if not ambitious. He prized his relationship with federal district judge Lloyd F. MacMahon, for whom he had clerked and whose recommendation made him a shoe-in for admission to our tight-knit fraternity of public servants in the U.S. attorney's office. When I left to join the Watergate special prosecutor's office, Rudy took my place as head of special prosecutions and notched many important victories during his tenure as an assistant U.S. attorney. He was succeeded as chief of special prosecutions by a serious young lawyer named Michael Mukasey, who was destined to become chief judge of the federal district court in the Southern District and later was tapped by George W. Bush to follow Alberto Gonzales as attorney general after Gonzales was forced to resign.

Rudy read a long opening statement, movingly recounting the horrors and heroism he had witnessed on 9/11. Ever the good trial lawyer, he laid out his principal theme in opening and closing. "Our enemy is not each other," he began. "Catastrophic emergencies and attacks have acts of great heroism attached to them, and they have mistakes that happen . . . our anger should clearly be directed, and the blame should clearly be directed at one source and one source alone, the terrorists who killed our loved ones."

I believed Rudy had a duty to explain why the fire department lacked the ability to communicate effectively with the police, particularly since police helicopters' warning of the impending collapse of the North Tower had not been relayed to the scores of firefighters who perished when the building fell. Why had they not been equipped with powerful and interoperable radios that could function in a high-rise conflagration? And why were the 911 emergency phone operators overwhelmed and unable to provide accurate or useful information to the desperate callers from inside the Twin Towers that day? Civilians who might have evacuated the buildings were advised to stay in place by 911 operators who were never provided guidance by police or fire department officials.

But, by the same token, Giuliani had done a superb job that day and in the days that followed, providing New Yorkers and the rest of the world with desperately needed leadership and reaffirmation that we would survive and overcome.

I began with a heartfelt statement. I recounted that on Labor Day, September 3, 2001, I took my wife and younger daughter to see the Statue of Liberty and the Twin Towers. After September 11, I, like tens of thousands, maybe millions of others said, "There, but for the grace of God go I." And we are the lucky ones, I said, the survivors, who must do better in the future to protect our loved ones and our institutions.

I said to Rudy, "You and I became friends at the U.S. Attorney's office in the early seventies prosecuting organized crime, labor racketeering, official corruption cases. The world seemed a much simpler place then." I added that I had followed his career since then with admiration, and while I sometimes disagreed with his decisions, I never questioned his unwavering dedication to New York City. On September 11, 2001, the City of New York showed what it was made of. The heroism of the firemen and the police officers who risked and, in unimaginable numbers, gave their lives in the quest for saving the lives of others. I told Rudy, "Your leadership on that day and in the days following gave the rest of the nation, and indeed the world, an unvarnished view of the indomitable spirit and the humanity, of this great city, and for that I salute you."

I then turned to the issue of the radios. There is no question but that on that day, thousands of lives were saved by the heroic actions of the first responders in evacuating the towers and the surrounding areas. Among the most significant problems we had seen were ones that reflect barriers to effective communication between and among the first responders because of equipment that had not been standardized. The country had seen an analogy to this in connection with its armed forces, which into the 1980s did not have standardized communications equipment, ammunition, and other things, which made cooperation among the army, the navy, the air force, and the marines a challenge during times of emergency.

These services, I continued, were proud, individual, and important sectors of our armed forces. It took strong leadership to butt heads together to require standardization, to require that we be able to communicate between and among the services. And now I finally got to my question:

> Given the fact that you were no shrinking violet, and given the fact that the differences in the equipment that were used, in the radios and other communication technology over the years, made it obvious that there could not be easy interagency communication, what barrier was there that prevented you from ordering standardization?

Rudy answered that there were "no barriers." Conceding that despite inherent differences in police and fire department needs for communication, when "they are in the same emergency, they really have to get on the same frequency in order to be able to communicate with each other." He elaborated.

GIULIANI: We had purchased for the fire department radios, I believe the radios came in, in early 2001, I think it was early 2001. I don't remember the exact date, but the radios had come in well before September 11, 2001. We had purchased for them new radios, they had attempted to use them and found them too complicated to use and had withdrawn them and were training people in how to use the new radios. That has proved to be so complex and so difficult that until a few weeks ago they haven't been able to do it. So there are significant differences in the way in which the two of them communicate.

And the best answer is to create an interoperable system so that the police radio can be switched over and be used the same way, again simplifying it somewhat. Generally, a police radio and a fire radio should operate differently because 90 percent of the time, 95 percent of the time, they're doing different things. Police officers are chasing criminals, firefighters are dealing in mass emergencies. But they should have radios that are interoperable, so that in an emergency, both of them could be switched onto the same channel.

Those radios do not exist today.

BEN-VENISTE: In the interim, would you not suggest that there has to be in place some kind of a system where communications can be synthesized, that even if the radios are not interoperable, that there has to be a level of communication which was not in place on 9/11?

GIULIANI: Well, it was in place, there are, there were—

BEN-VENISTE: But it didn't operate effectively on 9/11?

GIULIANI: It may not have operated but they all had a radio system that would have allowed them to communicate with each other, but they decided that they couldn't use it, that it wasn't operable, that they weren't able to get through. And part of the problem that you'll face, even when you create an interoperable system is that if too many people are trying to communicate at the same time in any channel, they will begin to interfere with each other.

BEN-VENISTE: But at the very top there's got to be some coordination, that's my only point.

GIULIANI: Yes, absolutely.

Giuliani had responded with facts that were too deep in the weeds for me to evaluate. Were the new radios purchased for the fire department after 9/11 too complicated to operate? Were truly interoperable radios simply unavailable? I believed that the accuracy of Rudy's answers would be the subject of deeper inquiry by the press and others with the technical expertise to evaluate the former mayor's response.

Indeed, longtime Giuliani critic Wayne Barrett of the *Village Voice* later wrote that a U.S. Conference of Mayors' study refuted Rudy's claim that the technology for interoperative radios did not exist prior to 9/11. According to Barrett, 77 percent of the 192 cities participating in the study had radios that were interoperable across police and fire departments.

I turned to the failure of the 911 emergency system.

> BEN-VENISTE: Let me move to a second area which we think there's got to be some movement and change, and that is in the area of the 911 emergency response . . . Individuals who were trapped in the building called 911 searching for answers to their immediate distress, and we found that those operators were not in a position to do anything other than receive information. It wasn't an interactive loop which obviously was called for in circumstances of this kind of dire emergency. Had you considered, prior to 9/11, the possibility in a disaster of this kind where people could go for information and receive it?

Rudy acknowledged that the system had failed. Number one, they weren't trained that way; they should have been but they weren't. And number two, even if that had been their instinct, they were so overwhelmed that they weren't able to do it.

> BEN-VENISTE: Well, this is an area that we feel there can be, and there should be a solution.
> GIULIANI: Absolutely.

I was only mildly surprised that neither Tom nor Lee had any questions to put to Rudy. The fusillade of criticism from the prior day's remarks was daunting, and the desire of the families for accountability was calibrated to a level unlikely to be met. Later, Tom and Lee were to say that their failure to question Rudy personally was a mistake. If so, the mistake was surely exacerbated later in the day by letting Mayor Bloomberg depart after reading a thirty-minute statement without answering any questions from the commissioners. Thus, Bloomberg was spared answering questions based on the issues raised by Lehman the previous day about the city's new plan.

With the exception of Bob Kerrey, none of the other commissioners asked Giuliani probing questions. Kerrey took issue with Rudy's plea for assigning blame only to the terrorists. "I don't believe its an either/or choice between being angry at those who did this and feeling anger toward those in government with responsibility."

The audience, with large numbers of family representatives, first grew restless and then abusively vocal. "Stop kissing ass, 3,000 people are dead," cried one. "My son was murdered because of your incompetence," shouted another. "Talk about the radios," cried the sister of a firefighter who died on 9/11. Kean was obliged to gavel for order and police removed anti-Giuliani demonstrators.

Clearly, this had been our worst outing as a commission. We limped out of town happy that New York City's pre-9/11 preparation and response to the attack on the World Trade Center was not as central to our mission as was the federal government's.

The commission regained its composure with its final hearing. We returned to the subject of pre-9/11 preparedness by the FAA and NORAD and the time line of what had actually occurred on the day of the attacks. Painstaking investigative work by our staff team led by John Farmer, Dana Hyde, John Azzarello, and Miles Kara demonstrated that important aspects of the account provided by NORAD brass and FAA officials during our earlier hearing were fiction, designed to put the response in a more positive light than was deserved. It was to be our most muscular fact hearing, demonstrating the lack of training to deal with the attack, the abysmal communications between the FAA and NORAD on 9/11, and the willingness of high-ranking officials to misrepresent the facts rather than own up to what had actually occurred in the fog of war.

Back in our May hearing, I had asked whether there were tape recordings made of NORAD's communications with the FAA, particularly on 9/11. Generals Larry Arnold and Craig McKinley responded that they had no knowledge of recordings. As a result of our staff's legwork and the issuance of a commission subpoena, we had now tracked down and reviewed scores of real-time recorded conversations between and among FAA and NORAD personnel on 9/11.

For our last hearing, we had the top of the military food chain, starting with General Richard Myers, chairman of the Joint Chiefs of Staff, as well as the top commanders of NORAD, both past and present. Again, I was chosen to be the lead questioner.

I wanted to know how much information had been shared with our top military commander about the potential for a spectacular attack to be directed to our homeland. Had he seen the August 6 PDB? Had he been advised of the arrest of Moussaoui? General Myers could not recall whether or not he had seen such information. I asked whether if he had received such information he might have been stimulated to resuscitate a training scenario proposed and rejected in 2000 where a hijacked plane was presumed to fly into the Pentagon. Myers said he could not answer my hypothetical, pointing out that the Defense Department's role was "force protection." This struck me as somewhat odd, given the attack on the Pentagon itself. Indeed, during an earlier interview of Donald Rumsfeld, I learned the macabre fact that the central coffee shop in the Pentagon was called Ground Zero.

I turned my attention to the NORAD commanders, Generals Ralph Eberhardt and Larry Arnold. I revisited the earlier testimony by Arnold and McKinley, which suggested NORAD was in position to shoot down the last of the hijacked planes, United 93, when in fact NORAD was unaware of the fact that flight 93 had been hijacked until after the plane had crashed into a Pennsylvania field. Indeed, General Arnold acknowledged he had been wrong in his prior account and had since been educated by the commission's staff.

Our staff was able to show that NORAD had mistakenly tracked a "phantom" American flight 11 heading to Washington, when in fact that plane had struck the World Trade Center. Not only had NORAD failed to note that error in recounting the time line and in prior testimony, the air force had actually published a book titled *The Air War Over America*, which proclaimed its fighters were poised to shoot down flight 93 had it approached Washington. The beautifully illustrated book, published in 2003, contained numerous quotes attributed to air force personnel in the heat of battle, describing how "We contacted them [Selfridge, Michigan, Air National Guard Base] so they could head off 93 at the pass. The idea is to get in there, close in on him and convince him to turn . . . As United 93 was going out, we received the clearance to kill if need be. In fact, General Arnold's words almost verbatim were: 'We will take lives in the air to save lives on the ground.'" It got worse. "General [Robert] Marr was focused on United Flight 93, headed straight toward Washington. The North Dakota F-16s were loaded with missiles and hot guns and Marr was thinking about what these pilots might be expected to do. 'United Airlines 93 would not have hit Washington, DC,' Marr says emphatically. 'He would have been engaged and shot down before he got there.'" The fiction continued. "Arnold concurs: 'I had every intention of shooting down United 93 if it continued to progress toward Washington, DC, and any other aircraft coming toward it that day, whether we had authority or not.'"

To my mind, this slick piece of air force propaganda devalued the legitimate courage and determination of the many military officers who performed admirably on that day.

John Lehman and Bob Kerrey praised NORAD's leaders for improvising on 9/11 to compensate for the lack of training to deal with such an event. From Kerrey's point of view, NORAD had "taken a bullet" for the FAA, whose tardiness in notifying NORAD was shockingly exemplified by a tape recording we played as part of the staff presentation that led off the hearing:

> FAA HEADQUARTERS: They're pulling Jeff away to go talk about
> United 93.
> COMMAND CENTER: Do we want to think about scrambling aircraft?
> FAA HEADQUARTERS: Oh, God, I don't know.
> COMMAND CENTER: That's a decision somebody's going to have
> to make probably in the next 10 minutes.
> FAA HEADQUARTERS: You know, everybody just left the room.

Kerrey pointed to a September 17, 2001, briefing at the White House, suggesting that a cover story was hatched "that produced almost a necessity to deliver a story that's different than what actually happened on that day [September 11]." Generals Eberhardt and Arnold denied there was a deliberate effort to misstate the facts, but neither had attended the September 17 briefing. General Myers, who participated in the briefing, had already left the hearing room to attend to other business by the time Kerrey had his turn at questioning.

Certainly, the inconsistencies and inaccuracies of the official postattack account by the military have helped provide a field day for all manner of conspiracy theorists. Led by the staff who produced a memo on the FAA/NORAD postattack stories, the commission voted to refer the issue to the inspectors general of the Departments of Defense and Transportation, as a less aggressive alternative to referring the testimony to the Department of Justice for a perjury investigation.

Years later, the Department of Defense inspector general issued his report, clearing NORAD brass of intentionally misleading the commission. Instead, the "inaccurate information" provided to the 9/11 Commission was the result of "inadequate forensic capabilities to ensure accurate and timely reporting." Those inadequate forensic capabilities will cross you up every time—every time you're caught trying to turn chicken shit into chicken salad, that is.

We concluded our last hearing with testimony from a variety of FAA officials, who reconfirmed that while they were on heightened security alert during the summer of threat, they did not revise the criteria for passenger screening to intercept bladed weapons shorter than four inches, nor did they require any procedures to harden cockpit doors against intrusion. In hindsight, either of those measures might have thwarted or at least mitigated the devastation of 9/11.

Among the true heroes of 9/11 were the FAA air traffic controllers—supervisors and specialists who first took it upon themselves to order a national ground stop preventing further commercial aircraft from taking off, and then safely guiding some forty-five hundred aircraft aloft safely to the ground in the midst of chaos.

When my turn came, I focused on the failure to share intelligence, particularly with respect to the FBI's arrest of wannabe al Qaeda hijacker Zacarias Moussaoui. None of the FAA officials had received word of Moussaoui's arrest. I was struck by the simplicity of the observation by Ben Sliney, an FAA official whose actions on 9/11 drew deserved praise, *that no one had ever suggested that hijackers could fly the plane.*

> BEN-VENISTE: On August 27th, the FBI supervisor in Minneapolis, trying to get the attention of those in headquarters at FBI, said he was trying to make sure that Moussaoui, and I quote, "did not take control of a plane and fly it into the World Trade Center"—August 27th, 2001. Did anyone receive, in words or substance, that information?
>
> [MONTE] BELGER [FORMER ACTING DEPUTY DIRECTOR OF THE FAA]: No.
>
> BEN-VENISTE: If you had had such information, and going back to the question of the tool box available to you, and if individuals, as yet unnamed, according to the suspicion, highly educated, by the Minneapolis office of the FBI, had the intention to take over a commercial airliner, that at least one of them had received flight training and had sought flight training for commercial airliners, recognizing that suicide hijackings were in the tool box of the other team—is there not something that you could have done, either in terms of screening at the airports, ratcheting down what passengers could carry onto the

airplanes, advising pilots about keeping the door of the cockpit locked and secured, is there nothing that could have been
done had you received that information?

The response to this mother of all run-on sentences was both instructive and heartbreaking.

> BELGER: I think, if we had received information as specific as you
> just laid it out, there are some things that we would have looked
> at doing.
> BEN-VENISTE: Such as?
> BELGER: Well, I think you described several of them.

We were done. Our twelfth and final public hearing was over on
June 17, 2004. We had a month to produce our final report.

AS WE APPROACHED THE deadline for turning in our final report, I realized that we had not answered the question of how the August 6 PDB had
come to be written. In the midst of the most intensive sorting out of what
we had found and putting it on paper, I asked whether our staff had interviewed the CIA analysts who drafted the PDB. What I learned was an
unpleasant surprise. Although Phil Zelikow claimed the interviews had
been done, one of our staffers had overheard Zelikow's end of the interview. Not only had our internal rule requiring a minimum of two staffers
to conduct each interview been ignored, but Zelikow's interviews of the
analysts were reportedly laced with leading questions minimizing the
importance of the PDB. I was livid.

The fact inquiry had ceased. We were in the midst of reviewing and
editing the report; commissioners and staff alike were pulling brutally
long hours going over drafts and redrafts. Nevertheless, I demanded the
opportunity to interview the authors of the PDB myself. Zelikow objected, claiming the analysts were reluctant to be interviewed and feared
setting a precedent that would compromise their future independence. I
got substantial push back from my colleagues Fred Fielding, John Lehman, and Jim Thompson. At one point, sitting across the conference table
from me, Lehman derided my demand as "silly." I did not believe it was
silly to protect the integrity of our factual investigation and let John know
in a way not subject to misinterpretation that I would not back down on
this. Before making my demand, I had learned that the two analysts who

had prepared the PDB were at CIA headquarters in Langley, but that the officer who briefed Bush on August 6 was traveling abroad and was unavailable. Tom Kean did not want this confrontation to escalate further. He agreed to have the analysts brought to our office to be interviewed by me and Jim Thompson, together with staffer Barbara Grewe.

It was July 13, only days before our final report would go to the publisher, that we sat down to interview CIA analysts Barbara S. and Dwayne D. We interviewed each one separately; their accounts bore no inconsistencies. Both analysts were well seasoned, with many years at the CIA under their belts. Contrary to Zelikow's statement about their unwillingness to cooperate, they told us they were pleased to come in and talk to us. Both stated that none of their superiors had mentioned any request from the president as providing the genesis for the PDB. Rather, they had jumped at the chance to try to get the president thinking about the possibility that al Qaeda's anticipated spectacular attack might be directed at the homeland. They did their best to obtain current information from their FBI sources regarding al Qaeda operatives in the United States.

Indeed, a shorter version of the August 6 PDB was circulated the following day, to a slightly wider audience of senior officials in a Senior Executive Intelligence Brief. But the memo was scrubbed to remove references to the ongoing investigations deemed too sensitive for wide dissemination. What more persuasive refutation to the mischaracterization of the August 6 PDB as strictly "historical" could one imagine? I thanked Barbara and Dwayne for their prescient analysis and wished them well in their careers.

PREPARING THE FINAL REPORT was a massive undertaking that had been under way for months. The essential building blocks for the report were the individual staff team reports or monographs that had been prepared along the way. In addition to factual accuracy, the hallmark of this effort was to be an absence of editorial slant and a spare, reportorial style. There was never a chance of getting consensus, much less unanimity, on issues relating to apportioning relative responsibility for what went wrong. Our mantra was to stick to the facts.

Nevertheless, disagreements broke out over various portions of the text and the voluminous footnotes. We discussed, debated, and worked through the issues. The hellacious job of assimilating and editing the staff monographs into a cohesive and stylistically homogenous draft fell to the "front office" of Phil Zelikow, Chris Kojm, Dan Marcus, and Dan's deputy counsel, Steve Dunne. Zelikow and his longtime collaborator, Harvard professor Ernest May, provided organizational vision; Chris Kojm, a brilliant writer, proved himself an outstanding editor; Marcus and Dunne worked tirelessly to assure the facts were accurate. The staff continued to work around the clock, answering questions and proposing language. The commissioners spent days in our conference room going line by line through the various drafts of the report, hashing out differences and making final edits.

By the end of the sixth draft, I was done. Totally exhausted.

While my greatest concern was the accuracy of the material contained in the report, I spent considerable time with the recommendations, which were to be the capstone of our effort. While most of the recommendations followed directly from our factual investigation, some of them did not. Here I was to defer to the expertise of my colleagues, who had more extensive experience, particularly in regard to foreign policy matters.

The one recommendation I am sorry I did not pursue had to do with breaking the stranglehold of foreign oil over our foreign policy decisions. I considered advocating for recommendations for an all-out Manhattan-Project–type effort to develop alternative fuel sources to help run the great engine of our economy. Was it too obvious, too unrelated to our core mission, too late in the day to raise a "new" issue? If we were to diminish our national thirst for foreign oil, how much of the misery of our Middle East policy might be avoided? At the end of the day, I just let it go.

THE PUBLIC HAILED THE commission's final report with great enthusiasm. In keeping with Phil Zelikow's initial vision, we negotiated a deal with a private publisher, W. W. Norton, to publish the report as a paperback book. It was in stores within one week of delivery of the manuscript, at $10 per copy, a fraction of the cost the Government Printing Office had quoted us. An astonishing 1.5 million copies were sold. In addition, the commission made the report available for free on the Internet, while a government paperback edition followed, matching Norton's price.

Politically, the Democrats and Republicans fell over each other to embrace the final report and pledge support for enacting our recommendations. Legislation was immediately introduced and enacted and reenacted—as recently as the Implementing the 9/11 Commission Recommendation's Act of 2007. Of course, the difference between legislating change and actually implementing reform is that the latter requires presidential leadership. The Bush administration's tragic unpreparedness in dealing with Hurricane Katrina was a stark reminder of the huge gap between saying and doing.

Slowly, painfully slowly, the FBI has begun to step up to the challenges of the post-9/11 world and assume the role as the primary agency to protect against organized attacks by terrorists within the United States. The question of whether protecting the homeland against terrorist attack is a law enforcement or military matter is nuanced, inasmuch as the greatest threat has come from jihadists trained overseas in remote enclaves. In fighting a "war on terror," military action accompanied by occupying ground forces has proved to be largely counterproductive, inciting religious and nationalistic outrage, and fostering heightened recruitment by jihadist extremist organizations like al Qaeda. The situation was deliberately muddled by the injection of domestic politics into the mix. Its hallmark was an unrelenting campaign based on the politics of fear and conflating the war in Iraq with the efforts to combat the jihadist terrorists who attacked us on 9/11. "Be afraid, be very afraid" was the administration's mantra.

"We are fighting them over there so we won't have to fight them here." This oft-repeated refrain of Bush/Cheney never defined who "them" was. Of course, the implication is that our troops in Iraq are fighting and dying while battling al Qaeda terrorists, when in reality most of the carnage has resulted from the crossfire of competing religious and political factions left in the wake of the destruction of Saddam's regime.

International cooperation and shared intelligence are obviously critical. And the use of military force against terrorist training facilities in remote locations should continue to be an important arrow in our quiver. But at the end of the day, combating terrorist organizations that must raise and distribute funds and whose members must travel and communicate requires the same kind of fundamental police work used in detecting and combating organized crime, narcotics trafficking, and narcoterrorist syndicates.

Nature abhors a vacuum. Behind the scenes, following the disclosure of the failings of the CIA and FBI in detecting the 9/11 plots, the Pentagon, under the muscular leadership of practiced infighter Donald Rumsfeld and abetted by Vice President Cheney and his minions, sought to expand its power into the realm of domestic intelligence gathering. Programs such as Eagle Eyes, Talon, Total Information Awareness, and Counterintelligence Field Activity arose like mushrooms after a rain to establish and maintain databases of information on U.S. citizens.

In order to preserve the essence of our democratic society, the military must not spy on our citizens at home. We relearned this basic civics lesson in the mid 1970s, when the Senate Church Committee's investigation disclosed an outrageous history of spying on the leaders of the civil rights movement and antiwar protesters during the Vietnam War. Under the leadership of Frank Church, chairman of the Senate Select Committee to Study Governmental Operations with Respect to Intelligence Activities, an extensive history of misconduct and spying against U.S. citizens by the CIA, FBI, NSA, and Pentagon was exposed. Following up on leads provided by former army intelligence officer Christopher Pyle, it was disclosed that more than 100,000 files were opened by the military, tracking the activities of U.S. citizens who were members of groups such as the NAACP, the National Association for Women, the Urban League, and the Anti-Defamation League.

With contempt for the Geneva Conventions' protections afforded enemy combatants and disdain for constitutional strictures against warrantless wiretapping, George W. Bush's behavior reminded me of Richard Nixon's famously arrogant pronouncement, "It's not illegal if the president does it." On the other hand, I was tremendously heartened by the determination of military lawyers and judges who battled against superior officers who were willing to kowtow to the administration and disregard fundamental standards of justice and humanity that had for so long defined America. In equal measure, resilient FBI agents and lawyers at the Department of Justice rejected the temptation to abandon the rule of law in favor of expediency. The superb performance of Department of Justice Inspector General Glenn Fine put him at the top of my list of those to whom we owe a debt of gratitude. The resolute actions of these men and women steeped in the core values of our constitutional democracy provide good reason for optimism about our future.

I hoped that by demanding documents and testimony from the highest officials of our government and operating and reporting to the public in the most transparent manner possible, we would avoid the cottage industry of conspiracy theorists that followed the Warren Commission's investigation of the Kennedy assassination. I believe that the steps we took greatly diminished the number of potential conspiracy nuts, yet there exist in certain corners of the Internet and on the counterculture lecture circuit a number of ardent disbelievers in the narrative recited in the commission's final report. The most heinous of these theories, essentially a blood libel against Bush and Cheney, holds that the 9/11 attack was a put-up job by the president and his neocon cohorts to enhance his waning political standing and assure George Bush's reelection. Only slightly less outrageous is the suggestion that Bush deliberately ignored explicit warnings of the coming attack for base political advantage. Of course, there are many professional conspiracy theorists who eke out a living or satisfy other egocentric needs by deliberately promoting such falsehoods. But many innocent individuals have been swayed by such ideas. The deep suspicion engendered by Bush and Cheney leading the country to war with Iraq under false and ever-changing rationalizations, their seeming inaction in the face of the possibility that the anticipated "spectacular" attack by al Qaeda would come within the United States, their opposition to creating an independent commission to investigate 9/11, the attempts to stonewall the commission's demand for documents and witnesses, and their hidebound refusal ever to acknowledge mistakes—all this led observers to a choice between incompetence and venality. Unsurprisingly, some chose the latter.

Despite the overwhelming positive response to our report, the commission was not without its critics. I have no doubt that by issuing a unanimous final report we immeasurably enhanced the likelihood that our recommendations for change would be accepted. But by the same token, some legitimate critics saw the flip side of unanimity as a watering down of the opportunity to attribute accountability for the failures leading to 9/11. It is true that potential sharp edges, my own included, were sanded down in favor of finding consensus in an impartial and honest recitation of the facts. And, in order to further improve the odds of our bipartisan recommendations being adopted, each member of the commission pledged that we would put aside partisan impulses and not actively campaign for a presidential candidate in the 2004 election. Yet I admit that watching Bush and Cheney campaign on the basis of superior national security competence in the face of significant evidence to the contrary was more than a little disturbing. It became clear to me that the power of the injunction to "Support our troops" cannot be overestimated, no matter what miscalculations and misrepresentations put our young men and women in harm's way.

Philip Zelikow's connections to the Bush administration, particularly to Condoleezza Rice, led to continuing questions about the integrity of the commission's product. *New York Times* journalist Philip Shenon hyped the marketing of an otherwise interesting behind-the-scenes account of our work with a mistaken and unsubstantiated claim that our executive director had manipulated the commission's fact finding to favor the Bush administration. Despite my disagreements with Philip Zelikow, I pointed out that Shenon's own reporting in the book refuted his hypothesis. Indeed, one of the prime examples put forward—a dispute between staff members and Zelikow over language he reportedly inserted in a draft interim report that promoted the idea of an Iraq–al Qaeda connection—was resolved internally when staff members confronted Zelikow and backed him down, eliminating the offending language from the staff report. The issue never made it to the commissioner level, where it most assuredly would have been resolved against any slant unwarranted by the facts. The commission's conclusion in our final report that there was no credible evidence of an operational relationship between Saddam and bin Laden, much less any connection between Iraq and al Qaeda regarding the 9/11 plot, was a direct slap in the face of the Cheney/Bush propaganda machine.

Moreover, any suggestion that Zelikow could skew the final report was belied by the endless debates and negotiations over language the commissioners engaged in as we went through draft after draft. Of course, Zelikow's decision to accept an offer from newly appointed Secretary of State Condoleezza Rice to become her counselor in 2005 only reignited the criticism by those who sought to find our work tainted by evidence of favoritism. The truth was that as a key adviser to Rice, Philip played a largely positive role, decrying the harsh treatment of detainees and arguing in other areas against some of the more extreme and ill-considered policies of the Bush administration. After two years at the State Department, Zelikow tendered his resignation and returned to the University of Virginia's Miller Center.

Although the commission produced a comprehensive report, it would be foolish to suggest that additional evidence bearing on 9/11 will not emerge in the years to come. As the poet Bliss Carman wrote, "A fact merely marks the point we have agreed to let investigation cease." But under all the circumstances, I believe the commission did a very credible job, and that the nation was well served by our efforts. I look back on the 9/11 Commission as one of the most difficult and challenging assignments in a long career. At the end of the day, I can say that I tried my best to do the right thing.